The Vanishing Rouble

Barter Networks and Non-Monetary Transactions
in Post-Soviet Societies

A remarkable and unexpected product of the transition from central
planning to the market economy in former Soviet societies has been the
explosive growth of barter on an industrial scale – the exchange of all
kinds of goods from aero-engines to potatoes to mining equipment, and
the resort to payment in goods in settlement of debts.

PAUL SEABRIGHT is Senior Research Fellow of Churchill College,
Cambridge and a Research Fellow of the Centre for Economic Policy
Research, London. He has been economic adviser in Poland, Russia,
Ukraine and Uzbekistan.

The Vanishing Rouble

Barter Networks and Non-Monetary Transactions in Post-Soviet Societies

Edited by
PAUL SEABRIGHT

CAMBRIDGE
UNIVERSITY PRESS

PUBLISHED BY THE PRESS SYNDICATE OF THE UNIVERSITY OF CAMBRIDGE
The Pitt Building, Trumpington Street, Cambridge, United Kingdom

CAMBRIDGE UNIVERSITY PRESS
The Edinburgh Building, Cambridge CB2 2RU, UK   www.cup.cam.ac.uk
40 West 20th Street, New York, NY 10011-4211, USA   www.cup.org
10 Stamford Road, Oakleigh, Melbourne 3166, Australia
Ruiz de Alarcón 13, 28014 Madrid, Spain

First published 2000

Printed in the United Kingdom at the University Press, Cambridge

Typeface *Times*   System *3B2*

A catalogue record for this book is available from the British Library

Library of Congress Cataloguing-in-Publication Data

The vanishing rouble: barter networks and non-monetary transactions in post-Soviet
societies / edited by Paul Seabright.
        p.   cm.
    ISBN 0-521-79037-9 – ISBN 0-521-79542-7 (pbk.)
    1. Barter–Former Soviet republics 2. Informal sector (Economics)–Former Soviet
republics. 3. Former Soviet republics–Commerce. I. Seabright, Paul.

    HF3626.5.V34 2000
    330–dc21   00-036103

ISBN 0 521 79037 9 hardback
ISBN 0 521 79542 7 paperback

Contents

Figures

Tables

Boxes

Preface

The idea of building an interdisciplinary perspective on the barter phenomenon grew out of conversations in Cambridge with Caroline Humphrey and Alena Ledeneva. These two most stimulating of colleagues and friends joined me in organising a conference at the Møller Centre at Churchill College, supported financially and morally by the Centre for History and Economics at Kings College, to whose directors Emma Rothschild and Gareth Stedman-Jones we would like to acknowledge our gratitude. Amy Price was a magnificent organiser. Some of the chapters in this volume were first presented at that conference, which was also supported financially by the European Bank for Reconstruction and Development. We should like to thank Steven Fries, the EBRD's research director, for his support, and also Simon Commander who has done much to make the international financial institutions aware of barter as a serious problem for post-Soviet societies. I should also like to thank Chris Harrison of Cambridge University Press for his encouragement of the project, as well as Barbara Docherty for astonishingly efficient copy-editing. The following have been at various times a source of ideas and inspiration on this complex subject: Wendy Carlin, Jayasri Dutta, Rachel Kranton, Denis Monnerie, Herakles Polemarchakis and Mark Schaffer. Finally, I should like to thank the Institut d'Anàlisi Econòmica of the Universitat Autonoma de Barcelona and its Director Xavier Vives for providing me with a most pleasant and stimulating environment in which to complete editing the book.

Contributors

David G. Anderson is lecturer in Anthropology at the University of Aberdeen. He is the author of *Identity and Ecology in Arctic Siberia* (Oxford, 2000). His continuing research is on ecological and economic relationships in northern Canada and in Siberia.

Wendy Carlin is Reader in Economics at University College London and Editor of the journal *Economics of Transition*.

Simon Clarke is Professor of Sociology at the University of Warwick and Scientific Director of the Institute for Comparative Labour Policy Research in Moscow. He is currently engaged in research projects on 'the development of trade unions in Russia' and on 'innovation in post-Soviet industry'.

Simon Commander is currently an advisor at the European Bank for Reconstruction and Development (EBRD) and Visiting Senior Fellow at the London Business School. He was previously at the World Bank in Washington, DC. He holds degrees from the Universities of Cambridge and Oxford.

Jayasri Dutta is Professor of Economics at the University of Birmingham. She was at the University of Cambridge and a Fellow of Churchill College when her chapter was written. She has worked on econometrics and economic theory, and her current research interests include monetary economics and economic development.

Steven Fries is Director of Policy Studies at the European Bank for Reconstruction and Development (EBRD). His publications include articles on monetary and financial economics and the economics of transition in journals such as the *Journal of Institutional and Theoretical Economics, Review of Financial Studies, Journal of Banking and Finance, Economics of Transition* and *IMF Staff Papers* and in books and periodicals published by the EBRD, IMF and World Bank. He received a DPhil in Economics from the University of

Oxford and was previously an economist with the International Monetary Fund.

Bogdan Gorochowskij is affiliated to the Humboldt University, Berlin.

Sergei Guriev is Assistant Professor of Economics and Director of Outreach at the New Economic School, Moscow. He is also a Senior Economist at the Russian European Centre for Economic Policy, Research Affiliate at the Centre for Economic Policy Research and Research Fellow at the William Davidson Institute at the University of Michigan.

Caroline Humphrey is Professor of Asian Anthropology at the Department of Social Anthropology, University of Cambridge, and Fellow of King's College, Cambridge. Her recent works on Russia include: *Marx Went Away, But Karl Stayed Behind* (University of Michigan Press, 1998); *The End of Nomadism? Society, State and the Environment in Inner Asia* (with David Sneath) (Duke University Press, 1999); 'Traders, "Disorder" and Citizenship Regimes in Provincial Russia', in M. Burawoy and K. Verdery (eds.), *Uncertain Transition: Ethnographies of Change in the Postsocialist World* (Rowman & Littlefield, 1999); 'Dirty Business, "Normal Life", and the Dream of Law', in Alena Ledeneva and Marina Kurkchiya (eds.), *Economic Crime in Russia* (Kluwer Law International, 2000).

Barry W. Ickes is Professor of Economics at The Pennsylvania State University. He is also the Financial Director and Member of the International Advisory Board of the New Economic School in Moscow. He holds a PhD in Economics from the University of California, Berkeley (1984), and is currently the Chair of the Board of Directors of the National Council for Eurasian and East European Research and American Editor of the Journal *Economic Systems*. He is the author, with Clifford Gaddy, of *Russia's Virtual Economy* (Brookings Institution, forthcoming).

Daniel Kaufmann works at the World Bank and is a Visiting Scholar at the Harvard Institute of International Development. A Chilean national, he completed his BSc studies in Jerusalem and received his PhD in Economics from Harvard University. In the early 1990s, he was the World Bank's Chief of Mission in Ukraine.

Alena V. Ledeneva is Lecturer in Russian Politics and Society at the School of Slavonic and East European Studies, University College London. She is the author of *Russia's Economy of Favours* (Cambridge University Press, 1998) and co-editor of *Bribery and Blat in Russia* (Macmillan, 2000) and *Economic Crime in Russia* (Kluwer Law International, 2000). Her particular research interest is the post-

Soviet Russian affairs – Russia in the global order, the Russian state and the rise of organised crime, the barter economy, social networks and patron–client relationships.

Dalia Marin is Professor of Economics at the University of Munich and Research Fellow at the Centre for Economic Policy Research. She works in the area of international trade, economics of transition and development, corporate finance and governance and growth empirics. She is Team Leader of the Research Group 'International Trade and Investment' in the Russian European Centre for Economic Policy (RECEP), Moscow, an economic policy think tank which advises the Russian government.

Christian Mummsen is currently an Economist in the European Department of the International Monetary Fund. At the time of writing his chapter, he was an economist in the Office of the Chief Economist at the European Bank for Reconstruction and Development (EBRD). He holds degrees from the University of Oxford and the London School of Economics.

Canice Prendergast is Professor of Economics at the Graduate School of Business at the University of Chicago. He is a labour economist, and much of his research has been on the compensation practices of firms and social influences on trade within firms. His recent research is on understanding why so much economic exchange is not carried out using money, even in highly monetised economies.

Mark Schaffer is Professor of Economics and Director of the Centre for Economic Reform and Transformation at Heriot-Watt University, Edinburgh, UK. His main field of research is economic reform in transition countries, and in particular enterprise restructuring and performance, financial markets and public finance and labour markets. He is also a Research Fellow of the William Davidson Institute at the University of Michigan, a Research Associate of the Centre for Economic Policy Research and a Research Fellow of the IZA Institute for the Study of Labour, Bonn.

Paul Seabright is Reader in Economics at the University of Cambridge, a Senior Research Fellow of Churchill College, Cambridge and a Research Fellow of the Centre for Economic Policy Research. From 2001, he will be Professor of Economics at the Université des Sciences Sociales de Toulouse.

Nikolai Ssorin-Chaikov has an undergraduate degree in history from Moscow State University and a PhD in Anthropology from Stanford University. He is currently a postdoctoral fellow at the Max Planck Institute for Social Anthropology. His research interests include (post)socialist economies and societies in Russia and Siberia, history of everyday life in the Soviet Union and Soviet/Russian indigenous policies. He is working on a book based on his PhD dissertation, which explores Soviet state symbols and institutions among Evenki of Sub-Arctic Siberia, and his other forthcoming publications include 'From Paupers to Professional Housewives: Soviet Welfare and Identity Construction among Siberian Evenki' and 'Evenki Shamanistic Practices in Soviet Present and Ethnographic Present Perfect'.

Lars Stole is Professor of Economics at the Graduate School of Business at the University of Chicago. He is an industrial organisation economist and has studied many aspects of price discrimination and nonlinear pricing. His recent research is on understanding why so much economic exchange is not carried out using money, even in highly monetised economies.

Introduction: barter networks and 'information islands'

PAUL SEABRIGHT

1 Money and barter

Due to a lack of pockets, wildebeest cannot carry cash or credit cards. Among animals, only marsupials have pockets, and then just to keep their young inside. And there are various difficulties, practical and theoretical, with an economic system based on inch-long blind and hairless kangaroos. (P. J. O'Rourke, *Eat the Rich*)

A reader of some of the remarkable stories of invention catalogued in this volume could be forgiven for thinking that baby kangaroos are among the very few items that have not at some point been employed as media of exchange in transition economies in recent years. Particularly in the countries of the former Soviet Union, an increasing proportion of economic transactions during the 1990s, especially those between large firms, have taken a complex non-monetary form. They have sometimes involved exchanges of goods for goods, more often circular chains of transfers of both physical and financial assets, sometimes the issue of bills of exchange (called *veksels* in Russian) that, whether denominated in money or not, frequently end up being redeemed in goods. What is notable about these transactions is not primarily their complexity – financial transactions in market economies (especially those involving derivatives) can be notoriously baroque – but rather two facts. First, they take place as part of the normal process of production and disposal of goods and services in the real economy. Secondly, they typically involve at least some party to a transaction accepting the delivery of goods they do not wish to own (or in specifications they would not choose) as part of the price of completing a transaction in which they have an overall interest. This second feature is the reason why it is convenient to refer to all of these types of non-monetary transactions as 'barter', even though many of them do not take the classic goods-for-goods form.

On the whole, transactions in mature market economies do not behave this way. It is precisely because of the complexity of *financial* transactions

1

that, aside from holdings by professional speculators, real goods and services tend to be owned by those who produce them or wish to consume them. They are transferred from one to the other against either money or credit payable in money.

This difference between the phenomena recorded in this volume and the characteristics of market economies is one of degree rather than kind, and it should not be exaggerated. Barter trade exists in market economies – in the international arena (see Marin and Schnitzer, 1995), in informal networks of individuals known to each other such as families and ethnic groups (Kranton, 1996), and in organised networks of traders using various coordinating mechanisms including coupon currencies and internet links. The International Reciprocal Trade Association[1] estimates that the annual dollar value of barter trade by North American trade companies and trade exchanges rose from $1 bn to over $9.1 bn during the two decades up to 1996. Though still a tiny proportion of US GDP, this represents an increase of over threefold in real terms, and the internet has certainly led to explosive growth since then, as any web search using the word 'barter' will reveal. Conversely, some of what is recorded in the statistics as barter trade for transition economies differs little from financial transactions in market economies. A bill of exchange issued by a firm and subsequently redeemed in money is no different from a junk bond, except that it may be passed from one to another of a firm's creditors through ad hoc bargaining rather than traded in a recognisable market.

Nevertheless, it is clear beyond reasonable doubt that barter in transition economies is different – in its scale, in its complexity and in the extent to which it affects (and probably distorts) the channels through which real goods and services circulate in the economy. This is a puzzle. In a command economy the distinction between barter and monetary exchange did not really exist, but it was widely expected that as restrictions on trade were lifted, patterns of transactions would increasingly come to resemble those in established market economies, even if the process might be slow. In Central and Eastern Europe outside the CIS the incidence of barter has indeed been falling, though the evidence presented by Carlin et al. in chapter 9 in this volume shows that it has not disappeared. But in the CIS barter has been on the increase, at least until very recently. Why? Does it matter? And what light does it cast on the way money functions in more normal conditions?

Standard accounts of the role of money in societies characterised by the division of labour stress its ability to avoid the dependence on the double coincidence of wants that plagues barter transactions. It is hard

---

[1] See < www.irta.net/barterstatistics.html >.

enough finding someone who wants to buy my product without restricting my search artificially to that subset of people whose products I in turn would like to obtain. The best terms I can find from among that restricted group may be less attractive than the terms I can obtain from someone else whose products do not interest me, but who can offer me something I can store, and exchange for other products later. What something might this be? We can call it a *medium of exchange*.

For a medium of exchange to be attractive it has to have a number of characteristics:

- It has to be reasonably easy *to store and to transport*. Water is a poor medium of exchange even in arid conditions where it has considerable value.
- It has to be sure *not to lose its value before I resell it* – through decay, vulnerability to theft, or simply through my own inability to tell the difference between good quality and bad. Bread is too perishable. Clothing, even valuable clothing, is too easy to steal. Diamonds, though highly valued, fantastically durable and easy to hide from thieves, have rarely been used as a medium of exchange because too much expertise is required to tell the difference between gemstones and fakes.
- It has to be *more widely acceptable* by other buyers than my own goods are. If it were not, then there would be no point in my accepting it either; I could just hold inventories of my own products until the time came to exchange them.

There has been a substantial literature examining in detail the implications of these features of media of exchange. The last point implies in particular that many possible commodities might serve as media of exchange provided there was a reasonable expectation on the part of citizens that other citizens would accept them (a point emphasised by Kiyotaki and Wright, 1989). Conversely, otherwise ideal media of exchange may fail to gain acceptance purely because citizens believe other citizens will not accept them. There is thus no guarantee that the media of exchange that emerge in a society will be efficient ones. To the extent that the state has some ability – through laws relating to legal tender, for example – to influence the expectations of citizens, its behaviour may significantly affect the character of the media that predominate.

The various threats to the value of media of exchange have also been widely explored. Banerjee and Maskin (1996) emphasise that the attraction of money has historically been that ordinary citizens could tell good from bad with a minimum of expertise. The reason for making money difficult and dangerous to counterfeit is not just to restrict supply (protect the state's monopoly) but also to sustain demand, by upholding citizens' confidence in the medium of exchange itself.

However, the state, although the guarantor of money's quality in one dimension, has in many circumstances proved also the greatest threat to its value. So-called 'fiat money' (consisting of intrinsically worthless notes and coins) is a socially valuable invention, because its value in circulation greatly exceeds the resource costs of producing it, thereby liberating real resources for more useful purposes than acting as a medium of exchange. But this fact itself makes money a tempting way of raising revenue without the politically unpopular necessity of announcing tax increases. Governments have often sought to use inflation to avoid explicit taxes and have paid an eventual price in high inflation. In chapter 1 in this volume, Dutta presents an account of the way in which *inflation* – which reduces money's attractiveness as a store of value – thereby also threatens its ability to function as a medium of exchange. This, then, has real costs to society.

In chapter 2 in this volume, Prendergast and Stole explore these costs in more detail. Without money, there will tend to be over-production of goods that can function as surrogate media of exchange (these will also tend to be goods of relatively low quality). In addition, trading networks will tend to be more restricted than otherwise, since simultaneous exchange may be harder to ensure in a barter than a money economy. When trades do not take place simultaneously, *money can substitute for trust* between the parties, and in the absence of money they are well advised to restrict their trades to those whom they know well.

In chapter 3 in this volume, Humphrey reviews the anthropological literature on barter, and considers especially the effect of *inadequate trust* on the relations between trading partners. Although barter has often been documented in a reasonably stable context in societies characterised by low levels of industrialisation, the kind of barter observed in transition economies today is perceived by its participants as neither normal nor desirable. Indeed, the trust demanded of participants (the need for which would be reduced by money), far from cementing social relations places new kinds of stress on them which Humphrey's chapter documents in some detail.

The social costs of barter may be clear, but the reasons why barter has become more rather than less prevalent in the CIS are much harder to assess with confidence. Transition economies have seen high rates of inflation in the early years after liberalisation of the command economy, and the CIS saw higher rates than in Central and Eastern Europe. However, inflation fell sharply in the CIS by the mid-1990s (by 1995 it was as low in Russia as in Poland), and yet barter has continued to grow significantly since then (see chapter 5 by Commander and Mummsen in this volume). Furthermore, other parts of the world – such as Latin America in the 1970s – have had long periods of hyperinflation without the appearance of barter on a comparable scale. These considerations suggest that, even if inflation was a factor in predisposing transition economies towards the use of non-monetary transactions, other factors have since become more important.

A number of surveys of barter (such as those discussed in Part II of this book) indicate that it is significantly associated with reported credit shortages on the part of bartering firms. Indeed, a strong credit squeeze has been associated with the stabilisation efforts of a number of transition countries, especially Russia and Ukraine. In other words, barter now seems to be linked to an unwillingness to offer money in transactions, not to an unwillingness to accept it. But since the only point of holding money is to be able to offer it subsequently in exchange, this does not explain how barter transactions might drive out monetary ones. Why does a shortage of credit not simply result in a fall in prices of goods, which would restore equilibrium in demand and supply?

Two important explanations suggest themselves. The first relies on the fact that *debt creates important externalities between creditors*. If a bank makes a loan to a firm that is already highly indebted, the effect of the loan may be as much to increase the chances of the firm's paying off its existing creditors as to undertake a profitable activity with its new resources. In these circumstances a bank has very little incentive to make new loans: it cannot readily collateralise the debt and appropriate the benefits of that loan for itself instead of seeing them appropriated by other creditors. Both financial activity and real production may therefore be stifled by a problem known as debt *overhang*.

If banks will not lend, who else might? Other firms might be induced to extend trade credit. However, if they extend trade credit for settlement in money, they face potentially the same problem as the banks – namely, the unenforceability of the loan contract in the face of claims by other existing creditors. But other firms can do something that banks are not allowed to do: they can *extend credit for repayment in kind*. Marin, Kaufmann and Gorochowskij argue in chapter 8 in this volume that this may be the most important explanation for barter. A barter deal is equivalent to a trade credit repayable (and therefore collateralised) in the very same goods that are produced by the borrowing firm. If the firm were required to repay in money, its other existing creditors would attempt to assert a claim. Requiring repayment in goods effectively shuts out the claims of the other creditors who are already in the queue. And the longer the queue, the more attractive an option barter becomes.

A second, and no less ingenious explanation is put forward by Prendergast and Stole in chapter 2 in this volume. If all firms were credit-constrained, and therefore all potential purchasers of my product were equally unwilling to offer me money, I might indeed simply lower my price until a buyer could be found. But Prendergast and Stole suggest that credit constraints may be distributed quite asymmetrically. Suppose that some potential buyers of my product could afford to pay the asking price in cash. By lowering the price to those who are credit-constrained I risk forgoing revenue from those who are not credit-constrained. So instead I may keep the cash price high, while arranging barter deals with those who have no cash to offer. In effect, the barter option allows me to engage in *price discrimination.* Not only may this explain why barter emerges in a situation of tight (though asymmetrically distributed) credit constraints. It also shows why prices may be less flexible than they would otherwise be – or, to put it another way, why the response of price inflation to monetary restraint may be particularly sluggish.

For the motive of price discrimination to be credible requires that there is an appreciable degree of *monopoly power* in the economy. There is a general consensus that conditions in the CIS are indeed highly conducive to the persistence of monopoly power. Furthermore both chapter 6 by Guriev and Ickes and 9 by Carlin *et al.* in this volume find a significant statistical association between the degree of market power and the likelihood that a firm will engage in barter (Kranton, 1996, also provides reasons for thinking that these two phenomena will be associated). Among other things monopoly power in the CIS has been held responsible for a large degree of 'disorganisation' (Blanchard and Kremer, 1997) in the process of reconfiguring production structure to meet the demands of the market economy. In particular, if production chains have previously been characterised by bilateral monopoly, then when one party to a transaction chooses to find a trading partner elsewhere the other will lose production opportunities for which there may be no ready substitute. In these circumstances trading networks can easily acquire the characteristics of defensive arrangements in which the fortunes of all the parties are interconnected: the disappearance of one part of the network threatens the economic viability of all.

Trading networks of this kind pose three particular threats to the efficiency of economic activity. One is that individual firms lose the incentive to produce efficiently since they know that other firms in the network have an incentive to support them if they perform poorly. The second, more subtle threat is to the division of labour: firms will prefer to trade with those in their network rather than seek better opportunities elsewhere. Prendergast and Stole in chapter 2, in particular, show how the insurance provided by its trading partners makes a firm less willing to deal with others who may produce better goods at lower cost, and thereby reduces the efficiency of production in the economy as a whole. A third threat comes through the diminished ability of firms to know about market opportunities if they continue to operate within restricted trading networks. There is a big puzzle about barter, which is that it implies firms are willing to hold goods in the marketing and disposal of which they have no comparative advantage. I produce shoes, and presumably know something about the market for shoes, and I trade with a firm that produces leather. My supplier knows something about the market for leather but much less about the market for shoes. Any arrangement which involves my using shoes as a medium of exchange to pay my supplier will result in the leather producer having to expend time, effort and investment resources in stocking, marketing and disposing of shoes. This is such a flagrant violation of the principle of comparative advantage – upon which all modern economic organisation is based – that it cries out for an explanation.

A very plausible explanation is simply that, in the conditions of economic chaos that have resulted from the transition process, particularly in the economies of the CIS, the degree of comparative advantage enjoyed by one firm over another in marketing and disposal may be extremely slight. A firm that has traditionally enjoyed monopoly power over its customers may have very little knowledge about potential markets elsewhere. As soon as economic liberalisation threatens the captive position of these markets the firm has no real idea where to turn. It may have enjoyed a geographical monopoly (within a region of Russia, say), but outside this region it may know no more about potential markets than any other firm chosen at random. Indeed, its supplier (who may be a firm located in a different region) might even know more about where to find customers for its final product than the firm does itself. We can think of the firm as inhabiting an 'information island' outside which its comparative advantage no longer exists. Trading networks may therefore represent its only points of contact outside the island – and barter a way to utilise the information these points of contact make possible. In an informationally transparent economy, it would make no sense for a leather producer to sell shoes. In an economy characterised by an informational fog, a leather producer in Minsk may know more about new opportunities for selling shoes there than a shoe producer in Moscow.

As barter becomes an economy-wide phenomenon it may even make the informational fog more dense. As Kranton (1996) suggests, the higher the proportion of traders who are locked into networks of reciprocal exchange, the higher the costs of searching for trading partners outside one's own network and therefore the greater the incentive to stay with the network rather than breaking away.

We can therefore see a way in which barter may become seriously entrenched in a society seriously disrupted by the circumstances of transition. 'Information islands' lower the private costs to firms of using barter transactions. Using barter makes firms highly dependent on their existing networks of trading partners and very reluctant to experiment with possibilities outside the network. It therefore ensures that new information does not become available which would increase the incentive of firms to avoid using barter. In these circumstances barter can be seen as a symptom of wider social dislocation of a kind that has undoubtedly characterised some transition economies (and markedly more so in the CIS than in Central and Eastern Europe). But, disturbingly, it may also reinforce that dislocation.

2 The structure of this book

This book brings together a large amount of material, both theoretical and empirical, that can help in the understanding of why barter transactions have emerged in transition economies, whether they matter and what light they cast on the role of money in more normal times. Contributors come from a range of disciplines including economics, sociology and social anthropology. Their collaboration is all the more important because of the fact that barter is a *network* phenomenon – it is frequently impossible to understand the reasons for a single barter transaction without understanding the network of transactions of which it forms a part (a point emphasised by Ledeneva and Seabright in chapter 4 in this volume). Theoretical economics has made valuable advances in recent years towards linking an account of the properties of networks to the behaviour of the individual participants in (or components of) those networks. It has particularly stressed the significance of network externalities, and the consequent fact that the structure of networks that emerges from the decentralised decisions of individuals may have properties that none of the participants would have wished. However, these theoretical advances have not been matched by empirical studies, where applied economics continues to rely on large-scale survey or census-based studies that take the individual, household or firm as the unit of analysis. Here the richer insights of smaller-scale studies such as those conducted by sociologists and anthropologists are particularly valuable, since they can show the character of network interactions in great detail. Naturally, the benefits of detail are purchased at the price of statistical representativeness, so it is precisely the interaction of large- and small-scale empirical studies that is particularly fruitful.

The volume is in three main parts following this introduction, and there is a concluding chapter. Part I contains the principally theoretical chapters by Dutta, Prendergast and Stole and Humphrey (chapters 1–3) that were described above. Chapters 1 and 2 contain a mathematical appendix for those who wish to follow the technical arguments closely, but the main text makes little if any formal demands.

Part II contains six chapters based on relatively large-scale survey material. Chapter 4 by Ledeneva and Seabright is an overview, drawing together material from a range of sources to describe the character of barter in transition economies. Chapter 5 by Commander and Mummsen tries to assess the particular nature of barter in Russia through an examination of the recent economic history of the country and the results of a survey of Russian firms. It contains the most detailed breakdown of any survey of the different kinds of non-monetary transaction. Chapter 8 by Marin, Kaufmann and Gorochowskij puts forward their explanation for barter based on its capacity to provide collateral for trade credit, and tests this against some rival explanations on the basis of a survey of barter deals in Ukraine. Chapter 6 by Guriev and Ickes also uses survey data, this time from Russia, and emphasises that the 'credit-squeeze' explanation for barter has to be interpreted with some care. Firms may have an interest in reporting themselves to be credit-constrained in order to strengthen their bargaining position with one another. Their ability to do so depends, of course, on their enjoying some degree of bargaining power – in reasonably competitive markets any firm feigning credit constraints to bargain with its trading partners would soon be replaced by another firm that did not. So it is not surprising that Guriev and Ickes find a statistical connection between firms' market power and their propensity to engage in barter – and their explanation of it in terms of mechanisms to enhance price discrimination echoes the suggestions made by Prendergast and Stole in chapter 2.

Chapter 7 by Simon Clarke evaluates from a range of survey data the extent to which non-monetary transactions have had an impact on the welfare of Russian citizens. There have been widespread press reports of payment in kind to workers, as a poor substitute for the payment of wages; it has also frequently been suggested that workers are able to offset the impact of falling real wages by bartering goods. Clarke finds that, for good or bad, the quantitative impact of these phenomena appears to be small compared to the large falls in real wages suffered by workers during the 1990s. Finally in part II, chapter 9 by Carlin, Fries, Schaffer and Seabright reports the results of a large-scale survey of firms in 20 transition countries. The survey was carried out by the World Bank and the European Bank for Reconstruction and Development (EBRD), and its large scale, plus its detailed information about the nature of the firms involved, offsets to some extent the fact that it does not differentiate between the types of non-monetary transaction undertaken but includes them all under a single heading of 'barter'. It finds significant inter-country differences in the character of barter; although it provides support for the view that barter in Russia and Ukraine is caused by market power and limited trading networks, and that barter has proved costly in terms of firms' longer-term willingness to restructure and improve performance, these findings are not replicated in other countries.

Part III contains four chapters based on detailed empirical studies in Russia by sociologists and social anthropologists. In chapter 10 Humphrey presents her own case material from Buriatica and Moscow *oblast* (region). She describes how barter is actually carried out: face-to-face encounters, bilateral exchanges, barter chains, reaching agreements on prices, finding new partners, solutions to the problems of delay, the barter of wages, governmental participation in barter and the crucial relation between barter and taxation. In chapter 11 Ledeneva explores the murky character of barter in the underground economy, showing how complex barter transactions may be carried out purely in order to avoid the eyes of the tax authorities. Her work emphasises the caution with which we must draw conclusions based on official surveys: an important part of the barter phenomenon is sitting in the shadows. Chapter 12 by Anderson describes the important role of barter in a far-flung region of Siberia, and reports a series of fascinating innovations, including the issue of surrogate currencies by regional and local authorities, to facilitate barter exchanges and cope with the inefficiencies they generate. Chapter 13 by Ssorin-Chaikov describes in detail one particular series of transactions through which a particular barter item passes – in this case the skin of a bear. The significance of the item, and the nature of the exchange between the parties, differs a great deal according to the context of the transaction and the status of the participants. Ssorin-Chaikov shows how the point of the transaction may not always be understood as an exchange of commodities but often represents also a kind of bargain over status.

What emerges most strikingly from the detailed accounts in part II is the remarkable ingenuity that participants bring to the process of barter exchange. Barter involves a continual *reinvention of the processes of social interaction.* There is much to admire in this, as well as cause for regret that barter absorbs so much ingenuity that would be better devoted to the transformation of outmoded and inefficient production methods.

Transition economies are embarked on a process that will at some point bring them much closer then they are today to the mixed industrial societies of the market economies. Barter is not unknown in these societies but it has a very different character, and the kind of non-monetary transaction that has been documented in Russia is unlikely to be well adapted to the needs of that transition. It may for all that be quite strongly entrenched, and in the conclusion Commander and Seabright discuss the various approaches that governments might take to the problems barter poses. They stress the need to see barter as symptomatic of wider social dislocation. They warn that, however well founded the fears about its adverse impact on society, simply seeking to ban it or make it more difficult to undertake will be entirely counter-productive. Barter is often a rational response of participants to very difficult economic and social conditions, and it is the conditions rather than the response to them that represent the challenge for public policy. The material in this volume provides some sense of the scale of that challenge.

References

Banerjee, A. and E. Maskin (1996). 'A Walrasian Theory of Money and Barter', *Quarterly Journal of Economics* 111(4), 955–1005.

Blanchard, O. and M. Kremer (1997). 'Disorganization', *Quarterly Journal of Economics*, 112(4), 1091–26.

Kiyotaki, N. and R. Wright (1989). 'On Money as a Medium of Exchange', *Journal of Political Economy*, 97, 927–54.

Kranton, R. (1996). 'Reciprocal Exchange: A Self-sustaining System', *American Economic Review*, 86(4), 830–51.

Marin, D. and M. Schnitzer (1995). 'Tying Trade Flows: A Theory of Countertrade', *American Economic Review*, 85(5), 1047–64.

Part I Theory

1 Some lasting thing: barter and the value of money

And thus came in the use of Money, some lasting thing that Men might keep without spoiling, and that by mutual consent Men would take in exchange for the truly useful, but perishable Supports of Life. (John Locke, *The Second Treatise on Government*, Section 47)

1 Introduction

Much of the work reported in this volume reflects interest in the growing phenomenon of trading in barter, often multilateral barter, in Russia in the 1990s. To monetary theorists, the timing is more than a little ironic. In the same decade, we have seen an explosion of theoretical research on the emergence of money as a medium of exchange.[1] Among other predictions, this theory suggests that a transition from barter to money is likely to be self-fulfilling, because a medium of exchange is all the more desirable if many others accept it; the process can be hastened by making money legal tender; its universal acceptability is then common knowledge among all participants in economic activity. Money is more efficient in exchange than barter, because it mediates possible failures of the double coincidence of wants; it follows, from this, that monetisation is an important component of the transition to a modern capitalist system. It is likely to happen of itself; the legalisation of money helps smooth the transition.

All of this makes perfect sense: it is unfortunate, then, that facts contradict such a reasonable theory. Russia, since 1989, has often been viewed as part of a great economic experiment of transition to modern capitalism. All the more vexing, then, that one part of the experiment has gone so wrong: with regard to the medium of exchange, we observe an

I am grateful to Elena Loukoianova for providing the facts, quantitative or otherwise.
[1] Ostroy and Starr (1974); Jones (1976) report early research on these issues; section 2 reports on more recent approaches.

15

apparent U-turn. In this chapter, I argue that the rise of barter in Russia, or similar societies, is relatively simple to understand if we think of money as a *store of value*, in addition to a medium of exchange. First, money can function as a medium of exchange only if it is a reasonable store of value; second, civil governments have an implicit agreement to guarantee the value of money. When governments, or their central banks, are in breach of promise, private individuals are well-advised not to keep to their part of the agreement, and accept otherwise worthless notes and coin in exchange for their produce. Enforcing the legal status of money is likely to hurt, rather than help, in such situations. The functioning of money as a medium of exchange is often traced to Walras, Wicksell, or even Hume. The principle underlying money as a store of value derives from Locke, quoted in the epigraph to this chapter. In the specific context of Russia, money has become an unsafe store of value, even as the need to store it has diminished. In response, private individuals prefer to do business in 'the perishable supports of life'. Indeed, the natural question is the reverse: in the circumstances why does the private sector agree to hold money at all?

Locke deduces the origins of money from its nature, and it may be useful to review the argument: it is actually far more transparent in our world than in his. There are three universal characteristics of money: it is *portable*, with low carrying costs; not immediately *perishable*; and not truly *useful* – i.e. it has little or no intrinsic worth. The first is important if money is to be used as a medium of exchange, the second if it is to be a store of value. The third is not strictly necessary for its functioning in either role. It does, however, allow monetary transactions to be efficient. Seed used as money is neither eaten nor planted, which is surely undesirable. Gold or silver or pieces of paper have little use otherwise, and can be used for the purpose of storage at negligible cost to society. Efficiency requires that money should be intrinsically useless but, paradoxically, be universally acceptable. This is why it needs to be part of a perpetual social contract. To be sure, consensus can make such a thing acceptable for the moment. To function as money, it must be acceptable, and valuable, in the near future, and commonly believed to be so. This argument applied again and again to each such future implies that money must be valued in perpetuity, as futures cumulate without end. The knowledge that it will not be acceptable to some generation to come leads to the logical certainty that it is worthless today.[2]

How, then, does the present consensus of money enforce itself in the future? If we have already agreed to allow a government to rule, in

---

[2] This is of course the 'Hahn problem' (Hahn, 1965).

exchange for which it will enforce our rights to private property, it is natural to extend its reponsibilities to that of maintaining the value of money. One of the important ways by which governments maintain the acceptability of money is by taking it in settlement of dues from private individuals. The European Central Bank (ECB) will not change our euros into beef, wine, or washing machines; fortunately, the treasuries of Germany or France will accept them in settlement of income taxes, highway tolls, or speeding penalties. If these governments were not very good at collecting their dues, and were to abandon the tax collection altogether, their promises about the value of the euro would not be worth quite as much. In Locke's world, we would have to deduce the impact of political instability or government failures on money; lesser political philosophers among us might accept payment in the king's coin even in the midst of a civil war. In today's world, there is a far more direct link between inefficient government and the value of money. Governments, or monetary authorities, possess the right to issue fiat money, and can print it at will to finance their expenditures if taxes are difficult to collect. Of course, this results in inflation, which erodes the value of money, and with it the government's command over real resources. If money continually loses its worth, private individuals are likely to turn to other stores of value, and index and even conduct their trades in it. If, as in the Russia of 1994, inflation were running at 311 per cent, a rouble would be worth half as much in six month's time. If I had meat to sell, to a distiller who makes vodka, it stands to reason that I would take his produce, as vodka will not depreciate by nearly as much as that. If, at the same time, the distiller has a much lower output today than normally (being one of many who have experienced an output shock of −21per cent), he has little reason to save from his income, and is thus happier to accept goods he can consume in exchange for his produce. The fact that his life expectancy has fallen to 58 years can only strengthen his resolve to cut back on savings and accept 'the perishable supports of life'.

Once barter begins to supplant money as a trading institution, inflation is likely to rise further. First, because the reduced demand for money lowers its price. Second, and perhaps more importantly in this environment, barter transactions are difficult to tax, or even account for. Falling tax revenues, and yet further increases in money supply to pay the government's obligations, makes demonetisation self-fulfilling. The likely cost of barter is in terms of seed, or shoes, or vodka neither consumed nor invested because they are held for the settlement of dues. At the same time, enforcing the legal acceptability of money is likely to be counterproductive, as the private cost of unreliable legal tender may add up to more than the social costs of barter.

2 Barter vs. money: the theory

I shall start by summarising what we understand about money and barter as competing forms of trade. As the theoretical research on the foundations of money as a medium of exchange is large and still growing, I will restrict attention to those aspects which are relevant to demonetisation and the rise of barter. Even then, as we see, virtually every insight has been discovered at least twice: I have made no attempt to be comprehensive. Most often, these theories are intended to explain the *emergence of money as a medium of exchange*, rather than being intended as realistic descriptions of prevalent institutions of trade. They do, nevertheless, have implications for the existence, and desirability, of barter. In developing these implications, I denote 'barter' to mean the trade of goods for goods, which includes the possibility of what is often called 'commodity money': the use of a single, or small number of designated goods for the purpose of exchange.

Why is fiat money – intrinsically worthless pieces of paper or coin, whose value fluctuates partly at the whim of governments and central banks – accepted in exchange for goods in every modern society? The first answer to this appeals to an underlying consensus. I accept money in exchange for my services because I can then exchange it for goods which I find useful: I take money because the grocer does. In other words, any one of us finds money acceptable because all others do. How does such an agreement come to pass, and is it always and everywhere desirable?

In answering this question, a theory must contemplate counterfactuals, of alternatives to money both historical and imagined. At a minimum, we should be able to imagine that human societies have the alternative of trading goods for other goods which is barter, or goods for promises to pay in the future (credit).

We begin by imagining a society populated by different kinds of people, who certainly differ in what they produce, and possibly in what they prefer to consume. A typical individual does not produce all the goods she would like to consume, and so must trade with others. An understanding of how they meet and trade may shed light on what they trade. So, suppose that there are three goods – meat, vodka and potatoes – produced by butchers, brewers and farmers, respectively. Individuals may also differ in the goods they like to consume: among this population, there are some vegetarians, and teetotallers. Meat-eaters prefer meat to potatoes.

Townsend (1980) considers a society where individuals live in different places. They meet when they travel, but may never meet again; indeed, they cannot make binding promises, so goods cannot be traded against promises. Suppose that most butchers are teetotal. This puts meat-eating brewers at a disadvantage; carrying their produce, they are likely to run across brewers who have vodka, but which they are unwilling to exchange for meat. This is, of course, the lack of 'double coincidence of wants', in Jevons' celebrated phrase. If barter were the accepted method of trade, many meat-eating brewers would trade and consume potatoes, being uncertain of whether they could trade their produce for meat. Money mediates more efficient trade in such situations, because they can buy meat for money which they have previously acquired by selling vodka to farmers. Nothing, so far, dictates what form this money takes. Indeed, we would expect that potatoes, being universally consumed, may emerge as commodity money. While this outcome is perfectly feasible, it may lead to inefficiently high levels of production (and/or too little consumption) of potatoes; the introduction of fiat money, as a legally enforceable medium of exchange, may be desirable (Engineer and Bernhardt, 1991). The assumption that no promises are binding is too stringent; we may reasonably expect to see some trades made against promises – between neighbours, say – and others in barter. Money, when introduced, replaces barter, and eventually coexists with credit as a trading mechanism (Bernhardt, 1990).

The form of money, or the medium of exchange, is examined more carefully in Kiyotaki and Wright (1989)[3] in contexts where individuals search for trading opportunities. The cost of transactions is measured by the delays induced by search, and these delays are the outcome of individual decisions and the institutions of trade. One of the important findings of this research is that agreement on a medium of exchange does not entail its efficiency in that role.

Suppose we know that potatoes are universally accepted in exchange for meat or vodka. Then, every individual would accept potatoes, possibly in anticipation of further exchange. Now, this could also be true of vodka, or of meat. If the costs of storage, or degree of perishability, are different, it may be that one (say, vodka) is the most efficient medium of exchange, and that this is yet inferior to fiat money. No one individual finds it in their interest to refuse a good which all others accept in trade; the choice of trading institutions may thus suffer from coordination failure, because the value of participating in such an institution depends on others' choices, irrespective of the social efficiency.

Are there forces, so far unexplored, which drive societies towards the choice of intrinsically worthless objects as media of exchange? One sort of

---

[3] See also Jones (1976); Diamond (1984); Oh (1989); Kiyotaki and Wright (1993) among others.

force derives from Gresham's law, that 'Bad money drives out good'. Williamson and Wright (1994) and Banerjee and Maskin (1996) evaluate the implications. Imagine that meat perishes fast, and is not a viable medium of exchange. Vodka and potatoes could both function as commodity money. Potatoes are of uniform quality, whereas vodka can be good or bad. Bad vodka, which looks the same as good vodka, is worth very little to a consumer. A teetotaller cannot tell good vodka from bad at the time of exchange. Suppose, now, that vodka is the current medium of exchange and a teetotal butcher is about to accept it in exchange for meat. He does not know whether this is good or bad, but is prepared to accept it in anticipation of, and at the rate appropriate to, further exchange. He can, however, deduce that a distiller who has both qualities of vodka in store is likely to give him the lower quality, keeping good vodka for her own consumption, or for trade with a discerning customer. As a result, he will accept it only at the price for low-quality vodka, and the brewer will give him only the low-quality brew. We have, then, a situation where bad vodka can function as a medium of exchange; while good vodka is bought, sold and consumed by informed traders, who trade it at its appropriate premium. This society can sustain quite another outcome, where potatoes are a medium of exchange, because they are of uniform quality. The former is a better choice of money, as the good which is used as a medium of exchange has little or no intrinsic worth.[4]

Suppose, now, that bad vodka is the chosen medium of exchange and, further, that it can be produced at negligible cost. Private producers are likely to produce it in very large quantities is indeed, until its price equals its marginal cost. If this marginal cost is small, private monies are likely to be produced in excessive quantities, driving the price level – the price of goods in money terms – to very high levels. Individuals must incur the cost of carrying these very large quantities of money for each purchase. The inefficiency of commodity money takes a slightly different form, that of excessive price levels (Shi, 1995; Trejos and Wright, 1995).

It is desirable, then, to have a more explicit social contract: that money should be intrinsically worthless, that it should be legal tender, but that its quantity should be restricted. In present contexts, the last is better understood as controls on the rate of growth of money rather than its quantity. Fiat money has negligible carrying costs; there are opportunity costs of holding it, which depend on inflation rather than the price level.

---

[4] Notice that this argument starts from a premise similar to Akerlof (1970) but reaches quite a different conclusion. Asymmetric information may help rather than hurt in choosing a medium of exchange, because efficiency is declining in its worth.

Suppose fiat money exists, and its quantity can be increased or decreased by the government. An increase in the quantity of money will increase the price level, and reduce the rate of return on money. If individual participants accept money for goods, the private sector as a whole must hold money over time. If the value of money declines rapidly, no individual will want to hold it over any length of time. Ideally, then, the value of money should keep pace with other assets that individuals could hold: this is often called the 'Chicago Rule' that the nominal interest rate should be zero (i.e. that the rate of price deflation equals the real interest rate).

Hayashi and Matsui (1996) evaluate this prescription in a society where fiat money functions as a medium of exchange. Individuals have the option of trading in barter if they wish. They find that the Chicago Rule is necessary for efficiency: money functions as both medium of exchange and store of value if inflation rates are low, and close to efficient. As inflation rates increase, money is no longer a good store of value, and more and more trades are made in barter. Eventually, if the growth rate of money is excessive, money no longer functions even as a medium of exchange. In the appendix (p. 28), I develop a particularly simple model which explores the switch from monetary trade to barter as inflation rates increase. This simplicity is achieved at the cost of economising on the specification of 'who trades what when and with whom'. I can only urge the interested reader to consult Hayashi and Matsui (1996), which spells out most of the relevant details.[5]

3 The facts

Table 1.1 summarises some of the macroeconomic facts of Russia in the period which saw the rise of barter. It is not a pretty story. This is clearly a society in a state of upheaval, as much political as economic. While miseries undoubtedly add up, some of them may cause others. Some of these facts are reasonably assumed exogenous to the monetary or trading system, but are nevertheless important in explaining its dysfunctions. Among these is the dramatic rise in adult (male) mortality, and the decline in output and productivity as part of a chaotic transition of the economic and the political system, reported in lines 1–5. It would be miraculous if tax, and other revenues of government, did not fall just as sharply at the same time. No such miracle occurred: from line 10 and

---

[5] They assume joint symmetry of preferences and technology to solve the model; unfortunately, this rules out the relative price effects of inflation which are an important component of the case in hand.

Table 1.1 *The facts: Russia 1992–1997*

Year	1992	1993	1994	1995	1996	1997
Life Expectancy						
1 Men	62	59	58	58	59.8	60.8
2 Women	72	71	72	72.5	72.5	72.9
Growth rates, real annual per cent						
3 GDP	−14.5	−8.7	−12.7	−4.1	−3.5	0.8
4 Industrial output	−18.0	−14.1	−20.9	−3.3	−4.0	1.9
5 Wages	−34.0	6.1	−8.6	−26.4	13.5	4.5
6 Consumption	..	−5.5	−9.2	−5.5	−5.6	2.0
7 Investment	..	−25.8	−26.0	−7.5	−18.5	−5.0
8 Govt. Consn.	.	−7.2	−2.7	1.2	−1.5	−2.0
Government budget as per cent of GDP						
9 Expenditure	37.2	40.7	45.9	37.0	40.1	40.7
10 Revenue	33.1	36.5	36.0	31.3	31.8	33.3
Broad money						
11 Growth	642.6	416.1	166.4	125.8	30.6	28
12 As of GDP	37.4	21.4	16.0	13.9	13.1	14.2
Inflation rates, annual						
13 CPI	1526	875	311	198	48	15
14 PPI	1768	942	337	237	51	20
Nominal interest rates, annual						
15 Treasury Bill	–	121	172	162	86	26
16 Central Bank	60	144	178	186	110	32

Sources: Goskomstat Yearbook 1998; Russian Economic Trends 1998.

line 3, the decline in real government revenues are about 30 per cent over this five-year period. Faced with declining income, a government can attempt to reduce its spending, or raise funds by seigniorage – i.e. printing money and issuing nominal liabilities. The facts leave little doubt about which of these happened in Russia: real government consumption fell by relatively little, amounting to a little over 12 per cent, as reported in line 8, leaving a large deficit to be covered. The quantity of money in the economy increased substantially, by factors of six or four in the early years. The stage was set for runaway inflation; for the clear perception that money is an unreliable store of value and that other, government-backed, nominal assets are scarcely better, as their interest payments fall far short of actual inflation.

Broadly speaking, this is a scenario where rational individuals should refuse to accept money in exchange for goods. A public sector employee has little option other than to be paid their wages in legal tender. Producers of meat and shoes and sealing-wax do have the option of barter, and are likely to exercise it. There are some details here which are particularly relevant to the advent of barter. First, the rates of inflation far exceeded the rate of growth of money supply. Second, the rate of inflation of the producers' price index (PPI), is always and everywhere larger than that of the consumers' price index (CPI). The fable which follows offers an explanation. It is specialised, and simplified, to imagine how transitions from money to barter may happen.

4 A fable

Imagine a world where the population produces, and consumes, two kinds of goods, meat and vodka. Butchers produce meat and sell this to finance their vodka consumption; brewers produce vodka and similarly sell some of their produce to buy meat. They are similar because both need time to produce: a typical butcher can produce meat every month, but would like to eat and drink every week. Similarly for brewers, who are a little luckier. Vodka, too, takes time to produce but unlike meat it does not rot and can be put away for future consumption. There are costs to storing vodka, including seepage. A litre's worth put away this week may yield less than a litre next week, but there is certain to be some left. Imagine too, that it is a nomadic world where promises are worth nothing: a distiller who sells a litre of vodka in exchange for a promise of a pound of meat next week may never see or hear from his trading partner again.

In this world, we claim, some amount of trading will take place. Suppose I am a butcher with 40 pounds of fresh meat to dispose of right now; I know, too, that the next time I will have a cow to slaughter is still four weeks away. Other butchers will sell meat in the intervening weeks. I should decide how much meat to consume this week (let's say 10 lb), and exchange the rest for vodka. Suppose I obtain 30 litres, because the price ratio is 1 : 1; I can store this in my cellar, and trade vodka for meat the next three weeks, until I have fresh meat again to sell. This, of course, is barter, where a storable good, vodka, is effectively used as a *store of value* and hence the *medium of exchange*. It is acceptable in trade because it is a good: other butchers drink it, much as I do.

We notice, then, that vodka is bought for consumption and for storage. This means that our society will not consume all the vodka it produces; put another way, the price of vodka will be relatively high in order to discourage its consumption. If vodka depreciates by 25 per cent per year, and 1,000 litres are used for storage purposes every week, this represents a net loss to society of 250 litres per year.

Suppose, now, that a butcher, called M, has the idea of introducing currency, or fiat money into this society. This money consists of a number of little pieces of paper, which is to function as a medium of exchange. Butchers and brewers alike can sell their goods for money, store this without cost and use their money to buy goods in times of need. Society will benefit, she says, because there will be more vodka to drink and just as much meat to eat. Any fears that this money may not be acceptable are misplaced. To prove this, M stands ready to sell her own produce in exchange for money at the going rate. So far, so good, and all butchers agree that this would be an excellent thing. What of brewers?

There is a little problem here. True, there will be more vodka to go around. But this will surely lower the price of vodka and brewers, whose real income depends on the purchasing power of vodka, will stand to lose from this. A long period of negotiations follows. M eventually convinces the chief distiller, V, that both groups can benefit. Remember, she says, that vodka depreciates by 25 per cent a year. Money will hold its value, so you, and your constituency, stand to gain this higher yield on your savings. After many calculations, V agrees on the social contract, that brewers will permit and cooperate in the use of money *provided* money holds its value, and yields a rate of return significantly larger than vodka. The moral of the fable is that fiat money, as an institution, may not be universally preferred. To achieve this, it must be a reliable store of value. Much as governments serve by social consensus if they are not too malignant, money mediates trade provided it is not too unreliable. Moreover, and this is the rest of the story, it is significantly easier to be rid of unreliable money than it is to remove malignant governments.

M, for all her faults, keeps her word on the value of money. Unfortunately, she is less good at looking over her shoulder, and is over-thrown by her erstwhile deputy, B. He, too, is a butcher, but one who feels no obligation to keep to that ancient social contract. Indeed, he discovers, that he has acquired the monopoly rights to print these little pieces of paper, and can actually buy vodka as well as meat with them. And so he does ... as he prints more and more money, inflation ensues, and money keeps losing its value. Brewers are the first to see the unfair-ness of this. At first, when the rate of inflation is still under 33 per cent,[6]

---

[6] This follows from the fact that purchasing power depreciates according to $\frac{\text{infl}}{1 + \text{infl}}$ and $\frac{0.33}{1.33} \simeq 0.25$.

they still accept money and store it rather than vodka, and ruminate in brewers' meetings in underground cellars that their great-grandfathers were much better off, even though they worked no harder and produced no more. Once inflation exceeds 33 per cent, butcher and distiller agree that B's money is just about worth the paper it is printed on, and that it is better to store their savings in vodka. As the word spreads, more and more brewers insist on being paid in meat, and butchers are happy to exchange their perishable goods in exchange for a durable. During this process of transition to a barter economy, the value of money must fall faster than the rate at which B prints it, because it is accepted in fewer and fewer transactions every time. At the same time, the price of vodka must rise *relative* to that of meat: in other words, the prices of storable goods inflate faster than those of perishables, and this exceeds the rate of growth of money supply. The loss of confidence in money fuels hyperinflation, because money becomes the proverbial hot potato which keeps changing hands faster and faster. In the end, this society will be back to where it started; unless, of course, B realises, like every other monopolist, that his gains are maximised by restricting his output, and that printing money faster than 33 per cent will leave his coffers empty.

It is reasonable to assume that intermediate or production goods are more storable than many consumption goods, and that their relative inflation rates are reflected in that of the two price indices. If so, the analysis suggests first, that barter in and of itself is not a bad thing, at least for individuals in a dysfunctional economy. It reflects a rational and desirable response by the private sector to extreme policy failures.

5 Further issues

The appendix sets out a formal model exploring these issues. The important elements are as before: political failures led, on the one hand, to declining income and even life expectancy. On the other, and more directly, the failure of government machinery contributed to the ability to raise adequate revenues, by taxation or sales of public output. The government was either unable or unwilling to reduce its expenditures to the same extent. The latter led to rampant growth in money supply, the former to reduced demand for real balances. Together, these provide more than adequate reasons for extremely high inflation rates, which were quick to follow. Once prices started to rise, and the purchasing power of money to fall with it, private individuals, including firms, found money – more specifically, roubles – a continually worsening store of value. As some moved to other ways of settling their trades, acceptability of the rouble plummeted and its velocity increased. In response, inflation rates began to outpace even the substantial rates of money growth. An important element of this story has the price of durables increasing faster than non-durables; this is likely to be reflected in the differential inflation rates of producers' and consumers' price indices.

There are several elements which I have omitted, which may well contribute to explaining exact details of the events.

Dollarisation

When the local currency becomes unreliable, private individuals may look to trade in some more reliable foreign currency, such as dollars or deutschmarks. This undoubtedly happened, and contributed in much the same way as barter to the acceleration of inflation. There is then a natural question of why all trades were not made in dollars rather than barter. One may be in more flagrant violation of the law than the other: a public sector employer may pay employees partly in claims to goods. More importantly, the supply of dollars or deutsche marks in circulation is likely to vary across regions. I would expect the extent of trading in foreign currency to be high in Moscow and St Petersburg, and barter to be more prevalent in Siberia or more remote areas. This may be thought of as a partial liquidity crisis.

Tax evasion

Inflation is one form of taxation; it is inefficient in its effects, but may be the only feasible instrument available to a state which is fast losing control of its administrative machinery. It is self-limiting, and barter is one of the mechanisms by which the effects of inflation are contained. Firms or individuals who trade in goods rather than money may lose less value by it. In effect, they insure themselves against the 'inflation tax'. At the same time, barter trades are more easily hidden from tax authorities; they are also more difficult to tax as governments find it costlier to attach the contents of my cellar than the contents of my bank account. On the one hand, the reliability of governments maintains the value of money; on the other, the functioning of the monetary system greases the wheels of governments. We observe, then, a failure of one reinforcing the failure of the other.

Barter networks and credit

The failure of money may encourage barter. It may also encourage transactions in promises, or credit. Groups of individuals or firms who accept each other's goods in settlement of dues form a chain, or network.

Once such a network is formed, it is feasible to accept payments in goods spread over time: heating fuel supplied in January can be repaid in steel rivets produced in September. One imagines that a major part of the cost of transactions is the formation of such networks in the first place; once part of a network, it is possible to make credible promises to pay back debt. Indeed, default is made particularly costly by the threat of losing the connections of the network. Hyperinflation increases the benefits of forming such networks; once the setup costs are sunk, these networks may continue, possibly as informal credit groups, even when inflation falls to more normal levels.

Unsustainable policies

What next, one may ask? Clearly, if governments were run by rational economic agents, they would be able to see that runaway inflation actually raises less, rather than more, revenues, and limit themselves to drawing their 'monopoly rents' from seigniorage. As we note, the rate of money growth slowed to 28 per cent in 1997, and to a yet lower 15 per cent in 1998. Inflation rates fell, indeed were lower than money growth rates. This last suggests an underlying 'remonetisation', and it would be of interest to verify whether the microeconomic evidence supports this view. There is a somewhat different aspect of this of interest to economists. We can deduce that the situation of 1991–6 could not persist. Undoubtedly, Russians knew this; and many economic decisions are likely to be affected in response to such temporary policy failures. Among others, decisions to produce, or sell, are likely to be postponed until the crisis is over – which, of course, deepens the nature of crisis.

Money and value

In building an economic hypothesis, I have stressed that money cannot function as a medium of exchange unless it is a reasonable store of value. The view that money is a store of value has been the basis of different theories of money, starting with Samuelson (1958).[7] It is one thing to say that efficiency requires that money yield the same return as other assets (the 'Chicago Rule'). It is quite another, one may say, to claim that this is true in reality. We have seen virtually no instances of major deflation in the post-war world, which would be necessary if money were to compete

---

[7] This can be extended to explain a precautionary motive for holding money in the presence of uncertainty, as in Bewley (1980); Dutta and Polemarchakis (1990); Dutta and Kapur (1998); among others.

with bonds or equity. The natural deduction is that money does not function as a reasonable store of value, and is held by rational individuals only because they are forced to, because it is legal tender and because they are obliged to pay for some transactions in currency.[8] The deduction is entirely correct as a matter of logic; its prediction – that individuals, or firms, hold no more money than they need for transactions – would appear to be false,[9] suggesting that some households or sectors hold part of their savings in cash. Clearly, this demand is likely to be particularly sensitive to inflation, even if barter were unavailable.

Appendix: a formal model

Imagine an economy spread over infinite, discrete time, with $t = 0, 1, 2, \ldots$. There are two goods x and y which are consumed every period. Individuals produce and consume these goods. A typical individual can produce one of these goods, costlessly, and consumes both. We assume that individuals are infinitely lived and have the same preferences, written as the utility function

$$(1 - \beta) \sum_{t=0}^{\infty} \beta^t U(x_t, y_t)$$

where the period utility, or felicity function is

$$U(x, y) = \frac{1}{2} \ln x + \frac{1}{2} \ln y;$$

and β their common subjective discount factor, $0 \leq \beta < 1$. Individuals would like to consume both goods every period and discount future consumption at the rate β.

Individuals differ in what they produce, and when they produce it. Some produce good x, and others produce y. Production occurs every other period. Some producers, of each type, get output in even periods, starting with period 0, and others produce in odd periods, starting with period 1. There are thus four types of individuals: types X_0, X_1 produce good x, and types Y_0, Y_1 produce good y, in even and odd periods, respectively. Production is costless, and capacity levels constant over time. Assume, for simplicity, that the aggregate output level of each

---

[8] This forms the starting point of the 'cash-in advance' hypothesis, (for example, Lucas and Stokey, 1987).

[9] For example, Dutta and Weale (1997), where we show that the household sector holds five or six times more cash than can be reasonably explained by the transactions motive.

type is Z. Thus, aggregate output in *each* period is Z units of x and Z units of y.[10]

Good x is perishable. Good y can be stored, but depreciates by the factor δ. If S_{yt} amount of y is stored, this yields $(1 - \delta)S_t$ units of y next period. I assume that it is impossible to borrow or lend.[11] I assume further, that goods markets are competitive at each t: each producer observes current price levels, knows the rate of return on alternative forms of saving and chooses how much to sell and what to consume. Demand equals supply in every market, which determines the relative price, q_t of y relative to x. Indeed, this price must be as follows. All individuals have the same preferences, and spend equal amounts on x and y every period. Aggregating over individual demands, we have $q_t y_t^d = x_t^d$. Good x is perishable, and aggregate supply is $x_t^s = Z$. Good y may be stored. If S_{yt} is the total amount of y stored in period t, its aggregate supply is $Z + (1 - \delta)S_{y,t-1}$; total demand is $y_t^d + S_{yt}$. Its relative price satisfies

$$q_t = \frac{Z}{Z + (1 - \delta)S_{y,t-1} - S_{yt}}. \tag{A.1}$$

The total amount stored is, of course, a consequence of individual decisions and the nature of trading institutions.

A.1 Barter trades

Suppose, first, that there is no such thing as money in this society. However, it is known that good y is storable, and individuals who wish to save store the appropriate amount of y. When, and how much, will an individual save?

Consider first an individual who has just produced. She will not be able to produce anything next period, and must save in order to finance her consumption next period. An individual in an unproductive phase could also save, to augment her income next period. This is never desirable, as future income is greater than current holdings, and individuals prefer to

---

[10] Many of these assumptions are immaterial, but simplify the presentation. The model is similar to that of Grossman and Weiss (1983) and Scheinkman and Weiss (1986), who assume that all consumption goods are perishable. If individuals themselves are finitely lived, the economy can be studied much as in Samuelson (1958).

[11] This is often deduced from more primitive considerations, such as individuals perpetually travelling in different directions on a turnpike, and so unable to make binding commitments to meet again (for example, Townsend, 1980). See also Kiyotaki and Wright (1989); Engineer and Bernhardt (1991).
This assumption has an unpleasant implication: individuals of type 1 have zero consumption in period 0. From this point on, the statements are exact for $t \geq 1$.

discount future consumption – i.e. $\beta(1 - \delta) < 1$. As a result, individuals will save only every other period, and choose savings levels to smooth consumption. The optimal consumption savings decisions are as follows. An individual will save every other period, and this savings is equal to proportion $\beta/(1 + \beta)$ of her income: call this σ, the individual (and aggregate) savings rate. She will spend equal amounts on each good, as before. With x as the numeraire, aggregate savings in period t are

$$S_t = \frac{\beta}{1 + \beta} Z(1 + q_t) \equiv \sigma Z(1 + q_t).$$

All savings are stored in y; thus, $S_{yt} = S_t/q_t$. Along with (A.1), we can deduce the dynamic behaviour of the relative price of storables over time. This price will converge to a stationary value, which is

$$\bar{q}_B = \frac{1 + \sigma\delta}{1 - \sigma\delta}.$$

This price is obviously greater than 1, and increasing in both β and δ. As we see next, the fact that $\bar{q}_B$ exceeds 1 is entirely owing to its transactions demand. Savings are increasing in β, and this raises q_t. It is increasing in δ, the rate of depreciation because of a supply effect, as the supply of durable goods decreases with the depreciation rate.

Finally, the stationary utility levels of X, and Y producers are

$$V_{BX} = \ln Z - \frac{1}{2} \ln q_B + \sigma \ln(1 - \delta)$$

and

$$V_{BY} = \ln Z + \frac{1}{2} \ln q_B + \sigma \ln(1 - \delta).$$

A.2 Money and prices

Suppose now that money is introduced for the purpose of trade. Money consists of pieces of paper issued (only) by a designated authority. The number of pieces of paper, or quantity of money, is M_t. These amounts are decided by the monetary authority.[12] The nominal price level is P_t (the money price of good x), determined as follows. Suppose M_t is the quantity of money, and μ_t the degree of monetisation – i.e. the proportion of trades carried out in money; in this world, sellers who have accepted money in exchange for their produce hold it till the next period.

---

[12] I assume that goods bought with newly minted money are part of government consumption.

Total money holdings are $\mu_t P_t S_t$, which must equal the stock of money:

$$P_t = \frac{M_t}{\mu_t S_t}. \tag{A.2}$$

Savings are, as earlier:

$$S_t = \sigma Z(1 + q_t). \tag{A.3}$$

Relative prices q_t respond to μ_t, as non-monetary savings represent demand for y, and $S_{yt} = (1 - \mu_t)S_t/q_t$ This modifies the price equation (A.1), to

$$q_t = \frac{Z}{Z + \sigma(1 - \delta)(1 - \mu_{t-1})\dfrac{1 + q_{t-1}}{q_{t-1}} - \sigma(1 - \mu_{t-1})\dfrac{1 + q_t}{q_t}}. \tag{A.4}$$

These three equations entirely determine the evolution of real variables – the relative price, savings and consumption, as well as the inflation rate, in response to changes in the monetary environment, M_t, μ_t.

A.3 The value of money

The degree of monetisation cannot be entirely exogenous: private producers accept money provided it is better than the alternative. Specifically, the yield of money is $P_{t+1}/P_t = 1/1 + \pi_{t+1}$, with π_t the inflation rate. If this is greater than the yield from storage – i.e. $\pi_{t+1} < \delta/1 - \delta = \bar{\pi}(\delta)$ – sellers would accept money rather than goods in exchange for their produce. This is true for all if it is for one; hence,

$$\mu_t = 1 \quad \text{whenever} \quad \pi_{t+1} < \bar{\pi}(\delta).$$

By a similar argument,

$$\mu_t = 0 \quad \text{whenever} \quad \pi_{t+1} > \bar{\pi}(\delta).$$

We notice, then, that barter and money can coexist in the long run if, and only if. $\pi_t = \bar{\pi}(\delta)$.

This puts a precise meaning to the phrase 'money must hold its value': to be acceptable in exchange, the *rate of inflation should not exceed the depreciation rate of physical storage*. Thus, the introduction of money can work only if monetary authorities can make a credible promise to hold inflation down to less than $\bar{\pi}(\delta)$. How, we may ask, can they do this, as many of the factors affecting inflation are beyond their control? We note, from (A.2), that

$$1 + \pi_t = \frac{M_t}{M_{t-1}} \frac{\mu_{t-1} S_{t-1}}{\mu_t S_t}.$$

As it happens, acceptance of money has a positive feedback effect which allows for self-fulfilling monetisation. Solving (A.2), (A.3) and (A.4), we obtain

$$\mu_t \geq \mu_{t-1} \Rightarrow \mu_t S_t \geq \mu_{t-1} S_{t-1} \Rightarrow \pi_t < \frac{M_t - M_{t-1}}{M_t}.$$

Once the acceptance of money starts to increase (i.e. if the degree of monetisation increases over time), the rate of inflation cannot exceed the rate of growth of money supply. This is entirely within the control of the monetary authorities. If they hold the rate of growth of money supply at or below $\bar{\pi}(\delta)$, money becomes acceptable to all, and a gradual transition to 100 per cent monetisation can occur. It is important that the growth rate be kept sufficiently low at all times: individuals with rational expectations will agree to hold money at time t only if they believe that

$$\pi_{t+k} \leq \bar{\pi}(\delta)$$

at every future instance $k \geq 0$. An inflation rate exceeding this at $t + 10$, say, will make money unacceptable at $t + 9$, because individuals prefer to store in goods which yield more. As a result, μ_{t+9} is very small (nearly zero), and P_{t+9} very large (nearly infinite), which means, of course, that inflation rates are high and that money is not accepted in $t + 8$, and so on. Monetisation unravels by the backward iteration of inflationary expectations.

A.4 Agreeable money

Money is acceptable if the inflation rate is kept at or below $\bar{\pi}(\delta)$. That is not to say that this is an agreeable rule for every individual or group of individuals. We recall that monetisation reduces q, the price of storables. From (A.4), $q_t = 1 < q_B$ whenever $\mu_t = \mu_{t-1} = 1$. The stationary utilities of individuals in a monetary economy are

$$V_{XM}(\pi) = \ln Z - \sigma \ln(1 + \pi);$$

$$V_{YM}(\pi) = \ln Z - \sigma \ln(1 + \pi);$$

as $\ln q_m = 0$. We note that $V_{YB} > V_{YM}(\bar{\pi}(\delta)) = V_{XM}(\bar{\pi}(\delta)) > V_{XB}$: producers of durables suffer income losses with the introduction of money. To achieve a social consensus on money, promised inflation rates must be yet lower than $\bar{\pi}$, possibly even negative. Specifically, this says that demonetisation may not be Pareto-inferior to monetary outcomes, as it is likely to change relative prices and thus incomes.[13]

---

[13] This is similar to the finding of Diamond (1965) that the 'golden Rule' of zero inflation is not always Pareto-superior to the equilibrium of a non-monetary economy. In this framework, the Golden Rule is universally desirable if individuals are sufficiently patient – i.e. β is close to 1.

A.5 Barter and demonetisation

From our previous arguments, it should be clear that the reverse transition – from money back to barter – is likely to occur if actual or expected inflation exceeds $\bar{\pi}(\delta)$. Certainly, this is likely if the rate of growth of money supply exceeds $\bar{\pi}(\delta)$. However, demonetisation may start far below that. Recall, from (A.2), that

$$1 + \pi_{t+1} = \frac{M_{t+1}}{M_t} \frac{\mu_t S_t}{\mu_{t+1} S_{t+1}}.$$

We saw earlier that a 'virtuous circle' of monetisation may start from the fact that inflation rates decline with monetisation. For exactly that reason, it can start a vicious circle of demonetisation. Specifically,

$$\mu_{t+1} < \mu_t \Rightarrow \pi_{t+1} > \frac{M_{t+1} - M_t}{M_t};$$

once individuals start accepting goods rather than money in trade, the rate of inflation will exceed the growth rate of money. In such a circumstance, a high but acceptable growth rate of money, close to $\bar{\pi}(\delta)$, no longer suffices to prevent demonetisation.

Finally, as we have noted before, demonetisation may respond to expectations of future inflation. Again, from (A.2), this may be expectations about rising money growth, or about the declining real balances. In the model, π_{t+1} declines with savings. From (A.3), $S_t = \sigma(1 + q_t)Z$. If individuals expect a decline in real incomes, or in savings propensities owing to, say, greater mortality, they are likely to expect greater inflation even if money growth rates are not expected to rise.

References

Akerlof, G. (1970). 'The Market for Lemons: Quality Uncertainty and the Market Mechanism', *Quarterly Journal of Economics*, 84, 488–500

Banerjee, A. and E. Maskin (1996). 'A Walrasian Theory of Money and Barter', *Quarterly Journal of Economics*, 11, 955–1005

Bernhardt, D. (1990). 'Money and Loans', *Review of Economic Studies*, 56, 89–100

Bewley, T. (1980). 'On the Optimum Quantity of Money', in J. Kareken and N. Wallace, (eds.) *Models of Monetary Economies*, Minneapolis, Federal Bank of Minneapolis, 169–210

Diamond, P.A. (1965). 'National Debt in a Neoclassical Growth Model', *American Economic Review*, 55, 1126–50

(1984). 'Money in Search Equilibrium', *Econometrica*, 52, 1–20

34   **Jayasri Dutta**

Dutta, J. and S. Kapur (1998). 'Liquidity Preference and Financial Intermediation', *Review of Economic Studies*, 65, 551–72

Dutta, J. and H. Polemarchakis (1990). 'Asset Markets and Equilibrium Processes', *Review of Economic Studies*, 57, 229–54

Dutta, J. and M. Weale (1997). 'Consumption and the Means of Payment: An Empirical Analysis for the United Kingdom', *National Institute for Economic and Social Research, Discussion Paper*, 97–23, forthcoming in *Economica*

Engineer, M. and D. Bernhardt (1991). 'Money, Barter, and the Optimality of Legal Restrictions', *Journal of Political Economy*, 99(4), 743–70

Grossman, S. and L. Weiss (1983). 'A Transactions-based Model of the Monetary Transmission Mechanism', *American Economic Review*, 73, 871–80

Hahn, F.H. (1965). 'On Some Problems of Proving the Existence of a Monetary Equilibrium', in F. Hahn and F.P.R. Brechling (eds.) *The Theory of Interest Rates*, London, Macmillan.

Hayashi, F. and A. Matsui (1996). 'A Model of Fiat Money and Barter', *Journal of Economic Theory*, 68, 111–32

Jones, R.A. (1976). 'The Origin and Development of Media of Exchange', *Journal of Political Economy*, 84, 757–76

Kiyotaki, N. and R. Wright (1989). 'On Money as a Medium of Exchange' *Journal of Political Economy*, 97, 927–54

(1993). 'A Search-theoretic Approach to Monetary Economics', *American Economic Review*, 83, 63–77

Lucas, R.E. and N. Stokey (1987). 'Money and Interest in a Cash-in Advance Economy', *Econometrica*, 55, 491–513

Oh, S. (1989). 'A Theory of a Generally Acceptable Medium of Exchange and Barter', *Journal of Monetary Economics*, 23, 101–19

Ostroy, J. and R. Starr (1974). 'Money and the Decentralization of Exchange', *Econometrica*, 42, 1093-1113

Ritter, J. (1995) 'On the Transition from Barter to Fiat Money', *American Economic Review*, 85, 134–49

Samuelson, P. (1958). 'An exact Consumption-loan model of Interest with or without the Social Contrivance of Money', *Journal of Political Economy*, 66, 467-82

Scheinkman, J. and L. Weiss (1986). 'Borrowing Constraints and Aggregate Economic Activity, *Econometrica*, 54, 23–45

Shi, S. (1995). 'Money and Prices: A Model of Search and Bargaining', *Journal of Economic Theory*, 67, 467–96

Townsend, R. (1980). 'Models of Money with Spatially Separated Agents', in J. Kareken and N. Wallace (eds.) *Models of Monetary Economies*, Minneapolis, Federal Reserve Bank of Minneapolis

Trejos, A. and R. Wright (1995). 'Search, Bargaining, Money, and Prices', *Journal of Political Economy*, 103, 118–41

Williamson, S. and R. Wright (1994) 'Barter and Monetary exchange under Private Information', *American Economic Review*, 84, 104–23

2 Barter relationships

CANICE PRENDERGAST AND LARS STOLE

1 Introduction

Economists interested in barter and non-monetary exchange often talk at cross-purposes to anthropologists and sociologists. Central to the anthropological literature is the notion of 'delayed reciprocity', where barter deals 'require delays in payment and several exchanges before the transactors are satisfied' (Humphrey, chapter 3 in this volume). This observation has been a central theme in the anthropology of exchange since Mauss (1990[1954]) and Malinowski (1961), and an important component of this research has focused on the realisation that such exchange requires institutions that persuade people to reciprocate favours. However, traditional monetary economics has largely dealt with cases in which such enforcement issues are absent, either by assuming simultaneous barter or enforceable long-term borrowing and lending contracts. Missing from this literature is the importance of implicit arrangements which are based on trust.[1] The purpose of this chapter is to redress this somewhat, relying on a large, recent literature on self-enforcing contracts, which often examines trade where money is absent. We argue that useful insights on barter can be obtained by using an economic analysis of repeated exchange with little or no money or external enforcement mechanisms, but where trust plays a central role.

This chapter is not meant to provide a holistic view of non-monetary social exchange in general, which involves an array of moral, religious, cultural and economic aspects. Instead, its objective is to address some aspects of repeated exchange which operate in the wild economic

We are grateful to Paul Seabright and an anonymous referee for helpful comments. Financial support from the National Science Foundation is gratefully acknowledged. Any errors are our own.
[1] For example, Lemon (1998) cites economists as 'believing barter to be the extreme case in which no trust is present in the system'.

environment of Russia.[2] It considers the operation of agents (firms or individuals) in an 'economy of favours' (Ledeneva, 1998a), each of whose objective in exchange is to maximise their own economic return subject to whatever social, institutional, or implicit constraints that they and their trading partners face. Given the breakdown of social commitments and moral obligations which characterise the descriptions of Russian exchange in this volume, we believe that the tools of economics can provide a useful framework for understanding some phenomena.[3]

Throughout the chapter, we borrow liberally from recent advances in the economic literature on repeated-game theory which studies environments in which there is little external enforcement of contracts, but where the individuals themselves must design informal institutions to manage trade.[4] With some notable exceptions such as Kranton (1996, 1998), there have been few attempts to understand barter arrangements from this perspective – a perspective which recognises the delay and trust which is inherent in barter exchange. We have also tried to minimize as much as possible the technical difficulties of the chapter. For those interested in a more technical treatment of some of these issues, see our companion papers (Prendergast and Stole, 1998a, 1998b, 1998c). In cases where some technical details are required, they are largely relegated to an appendix (p. 65) to render the chapter more readable.

A number of themes run throughout this chapter. The first theme which we emphasise is the costs of barter relative to a monetised economy. This is a central concern of classical monetary theory which emphasises reductions in trade which arise because there is an absence of a *static* double coincidence of wants.[5] Money, because of its commonly accepted value, provides for this double coincidence. We leave such inefficiencies

---

[2] As described in this volume, the environment of exchange is characterised by 'pride in acquiring' rather than giving (Humphrey, chapter 3 in this volume), replete with opportunities for 'cheating, defaulting and illegalities' and where there are 'no longer pregiven social commitments' (Anderson, chapter 12 in this volume). These aspects will be features of the economic model we offer below.

[3] Having said that, neither author is an expert on Russia, and we may ignore an aspect of Russian culture or institutions which will render an observation of less relevance or importance than it might be. Despite this, we believe that the theoretical apparatus offered here should help at least to frame some of the discussion of demonetisation, despite its absence of a 'thick description' of barter in Russia.

[4] For those interested in learning more about this literature, we recommend Fudenberg and Tirole (1991). For early work on self-enforcing contracts, see Telser (1980); Klein and Leffler (1981).

[5] To take a trivial example, if you only have broccoli to trade for my coffee, and I don't like broccoli and can't easily trade it on to someone else, the trade is unlikely to be consummated.

largely in the background and instead emphasise a series of more subtle and less studied issues. First, we begin with the most basic model of reciprocated exchange in section 2, where two individuals would like to trade with each other over time, but do not have money to facilitate exchange. The individuals are symmetric in that they value each other's good equally and with similar frequency, though (importantly) their demands are not simultaneous. In this simple setting, we illustrate the ability of the individuals to reciprocate trade when the penalty for failing to do so is the dissolution of the relationship, a common enforcement mechanism in many societies (see Sahlins, 1972, on this).[6] In our simple benchmark model with similar traders, the ability to trade depends on the importance of the relationship – namely, the frequency of interaction and the patience of the individuals, where traders compare the benefits of reneging on the relationship with the lost surplus that would ensue if they did.

The purpose of section 2 is simply to illustrate how the modern tools of economics can aid in our analysis of the decisions taken by agents and the resulting levels of trade.[7] The simple economic model we present, while useful in developing an understanding of the importance of future inter-actions, is limited in that there are many dimensions on which the model fails to capture important aspects of observed exchange. Recognising these limitations, we proceed through the remaining sections of the chapter by introducing variations into our framework to explore these additional issues.

In section 3 we adapt our model of repeated exchange to deal with the fact that one agent may need the good of this trading partner more than vice versa, or one agent may be more 'powerful' than the other. In this section, we demonstrate a second theme: such asymmetries can cause additional barter inefficiencies through different outcomes than those which would occur in an exchange environment mediated with money. For example, when individuals find it difficult to enforce trade through reciprocal exchange, production of 'unwanted' goods is typically higher than those which are in greater demand, in sharp contrast to the outcome

---

[6] In this sense, we differ little from Firth's (1939, p. 421) observation on the Maori that 'the main emphasis of the fulfillment of obligation lie ... [in] the desire to continue useful economic relations'.

[7] By 'modern' we mean the economic tools which have been developed in the past 25 years to deal with incomplete information and strategic interaction. These tools are complementary and distinct to the well developed methodology of neoclassical economics which has largely assumed full information and ignored strategic interaction. We make this distinction precise because it is our experience that most non-economists narrowly define economics as the application of the neoclassical paradigm.

of a monetised economy. The reason for this is that these unwanted goods serve, in part, the role of currency and one may find 'liquidity' value in them as a means of exchange. We also relate the resulting outcomes to discussions of pricing in chapters 10–13 of this volume, where we show how the terms of trade offered to those with 'unwanted' goods depend on the trading relationship. Specifically, the price paid for valued goods (in terms of 'unwanted' goods) gets worse as relationships become less important.

Another recurring theme of the chapters in this volume is the importance of networks for facilitating trade. Section 4 analyses a simple network to illustrate some issues which appear relevant to the Russian experience. Foremost among these issues is an understanding of the distributional implications of barter exchange in Russia, a third theme of the chapter. It seems clear from the work presented by Lemon (1998), and chapters 10–12 in this volume by Humphrey, Ledeneva and Anderson, respectively, that transacting through personal contracts does not lead to a level playing field. One can think of established network links as a scarce economic resource which takes time to develop, and whose presence tilts economic power towards the linked trading partners. In particular, established firms, often those from the Soviet era, appear to be in a particularly good position owing to both the volume of trade that they are involved in and the central position that they hold in production networks. These are the 'good old' contacts described by Ledeneva in chapter 11 in this volume. By contrast, some firms and individuals appear to have been left behind in this world of contacts, not least the Roma described by Lemon (1998). An additional implication of this, modelled in section 4, is the demand which this generates for middlemen, who appear to play a central role in many of the network discussions in this volume. However, these middlemen typically take advantage of their position in the networks and extract some of the surplus from the trade based on whatever they can contribute to the exchange. This section also points to an additional distributional implication of the barter economy – namely, that there are likely some individuals who have benefited from the demonetisation of the country, largely because it increases the value of their advantaged position in networks, which in a monetised economy would be of lesser importance.

A fourth theme which we address is how individuals choose to construct their networks. Many sociologists take a rather structuralist approach to networks (see Burt, 1992, for example), where networks are simply assigned, even though it frequently appears to be the case that individuals explicitly and strategically create networks. In Section 5 we consider an additional aspect of networks in that when money is absent, it induces individuals to have concentrated networks, rather than relying on many producers who may be able to produce at lower cost. An implication is that individuals will sometimes forgo the benefits of comparative advantage in order to keep a relationship going. The reason for such a policy of 'putting all your eggs in one basket' is that it tends to increase incentives for trustworthy dealings compared to situations where one's partner is of little importance. A related implication of this contribution is that in barter settings it may be difficult to break into a trading network, even in cases where a producer has something of value to another.

In section 6, we consider how barter markets can interact with cash markets. Specifically, we consider a world characterised by liquidity shocks, where individuals simply may not have enough money to buy their preferred goods. We are particularly interested in the effect of barter and liquidity shocks on prices. We assume that liquidity shocks are not common across all people in the economy: instead, they differentially affect people with low valuations more than those with high valuations. For example, people with low income are less likely to purchase certain goods at any given prices, even without a liquidity shock, and so it is these people who are most affected by such a shock. Using this assumption, we show three main effects of a liquidity shock on prices. First, if the liquidity shock is large enough, prices will fall below those which arise without a liquidity shock. This supports our usual notion that demands for money are tempered in a setting where there is little money. However, our second finding is that, again if the liquidity shocks are large enough, the reduction in prices caused by liquidity shocks is muted when sellers can also barter their goods. In other words, the opportunity to barter stops prices from falling as much as they would otherwise. As a result, the barter market constrains price reductions from a liquidity shock. Third, for less severe liquidity shocks, we show that prices will be above those without a liquidity shock, a result which arises either with or without the opportunity to barter. But the price movements induced by liquidity shocks are nonetheless more muted in the presence of barter. In other words, barter has the effect of reducing cash-price flexibility in response to shocks, as the barter markets provide an effective alternative to the cash market and become relatively more attractive when liquidity dries up. We conclude in section 7 with a brief discussion.

2 A simple model of reciprocal barter

We begin by considering the simplest possible setting of repeated exchange, where two symmetric individuals with equal bargaining power interact to supply goods to each other. To do so, we set up a stylised 'repeated game', in which two individuals trade with each other, but where the only way to reward a trade partner is by offering a good in the future; there is no money to satisfy a static double coincidence of wants. Periodically, each party demands goods from the other, and the other must make a voluntary choice whether to provide those goods. The individuals interact repeatedly so that one partner can use the threat of terminating the relationship as a way of persuading the other partner to supply goods to them. As a result, agents weigh the personal gain from continuing the relationship and supplying goods to the other at some immediate cost against violating the implicit duty to supply which would end the relationship. In this setting, not surprisingly, the importance of the future relationship to the individuals plays a critical role, with trade being easier to enforce when the relationship has dense or highly valuable future trading opportunities than when trade is sporadic or of low value.

The formal model we offer requires some notation but is logically straightforward. In keeping with the specifics of much of Russian barter, we assume an absence of a double coincidence of wants; instead there is some delay between exchanges so that the individuals must reciprocate goods and favours to each other over time. Consider two individuals who interact over time, potentially providing goods to one another other whenever called upon to do so. Each party to the relationship has a good which their partner may demand in any period of time. To be specific, we assume that when a good is demanded by individual A and q units are supplied by individual B, a value of q accrues to agent A at a cost of $c(q) = \frac{1}{2}q_i^2$ which is borne by individual B; the reverse is true when the demand is made by individual B. We can then define $v(q) \equiv q - c(q)$ as the joint *surplus* created from the trade of the good. Importantly, agents cannot satisfy their own needs. We consider the arrival of demands (which we sometimes refer to as projects) to be a random process with a project for person i arriving during a short period of time, Δ, with probability $\lambda\Delta$ – i.e. projects arrive according to a Poisson process. This seemingly complicated dynamic process is in fact extremely simple to deal with, as we will see below. With this description of the availability of productive projects, we can think of a higher λ as corresponding to more frequent trading opportunities. Indeed, simple statistical calculations verify that $1/\lambda$ represents the average time between opportunities. Another attraction of thinking about projects arriving randomly over time according to our λ distribution is that that a double *static* coincidence of wants occurs with insignificant probability; as a result, reciprocal exchange over time is the only possible avenue for trade.

Visually, the trading network can be illustrated as in figure 2.1.

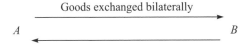

A   Goods exchanged bilaterally   B

Figure 2.1 Bilateral exchange

Recall that $1/\lambda$ represents the average time between trading opportunities. The time between trades is relevant as people are impatient: Everything else being equal, consumption today is better than consumption next year, and production today is more costly than production next year. We model this impatience by assuming that individuals have a subjective discount rate which can be thought of as an internal rate of interest; we denote this rate with the notation r. Mathematically, it will be the case that the ratio of the interaction rate to the value of that time, λ/r, will be the critical determinant for whether or not cooperative trade is sustainable. This ratio is a measure of the relative frequency of trade. A higher ratio implies that the expected present value gains from ongoing trade is higher, and hence we will see that cooperation through dynamic reciprocity is easier to sustain. Lower values of this ratio indicate that the relationship is more transient with only sporadic interaction.

To see the role of this ratio more precisely, consider trade in this environment where there is potentially reciprocated exchange. Here, the agents enforce reciprocal trades through the threat of dissolution of the partnership.[8] We initially consider symmetric solutions to this problem, where each agent receives the same quantity of q from the other.[9] Then if one agent requires q, the other agent is willing to provide it only if

$$V(q) \geq c(q), \tag{2.1}$$

where $V(q) \equiv \lambda/r[v(q)]$ represents the expected return of the indefinitely recurring relationship to a trader. Therefore, $V(q)$ is the value of the relationship. Note the importance of the λ/r term: a higher ratio directly implies a higher value to the relationship.

The requirement for cooperation in the incentive equation above forms the foundation for this chapter, so it deserves some elaboration. The person who is called upon to produce has a choice: either produce the good, which costs $c(q)$ or renege, in which case no costs are incurred. All other things being equal, the person would prefer not to incur this cost. However, if she fails to produce, she has reneged on the relationship and loses the future value of that relationship, which is $V(q)$, as the relationship is dissolved.

---

[8] 'We know what happens when a trade partner is disinclined to reciprocate – the sanction everywhere is dissolution of the partnership' (Sahlins, 1972, p. 312).
[9] This is the outcome that arises when maximising the sum of the two individuals' utilities.

Therefore only if $V(q) - c(q) \geq 0$ will she actually carry out her obligations.

The next step in solving this problem is in understanding how much trade individuals will be willing to fulfil. If each party could pay for the goods in a commonly accepted currency, the quantity traded would be $q^{eff} = 1$ – this is the 'efficient' level of trade which maximises the relationship's value, $V(q)$. However, our agents do not have money and must rely on the reciprocal exchange of favours. They choose the maximum level of q (up to the efficient level of 1) that the provider of the good is willing to offer. The trades can be characterised by two regions. For large enough λ/r, the incentive constraint (2.1) does not bind at the efficient level of trade, $q^{eff} = 1$, so they will produce efficiently. In other words, if agents interact frequently, or the surplus is large enough, trade is efficient and the absence of money is overcome by the existence of repeated exchange. In more colloquial terms, *trust can substitute for cash*. For lower rates of interaction, both quantities are below the efficient level, as the value of the relationship does not make producing higher output worthwhile. Note that the quantities of both goods continuously increase in λ/r so that as the relationship becomes more important, quantities rise to the surplus-maximising levels.

Example 1 For an illustrative case consider the setting in figure 2.2. The curve in the top graph gives the (maximal) flow value from the relationship $rV(q)$ as a function of the frequency of interaction (normalised by the cost of time) λ/r. This is the total surplus generated for each party. The curve in the bottom graph measures the provided quantity as a function of λ/r.

Figure 2.2 illustrates the importance of λ/r for trade, with quantities traded increasing in the frequency of interaction, up to the point of efficient trade, beyond which there is no reason to increase trade further. This section demonstrates the importance of repeated interaction in effecting barter exchange. If money were freely available, there would be no reason for repeated exchange. With money absent, the threat of dissolution acts to constrain cheating, and so it is important that the agents value the relationship in order to act honestly.[10] This section therefore illustrates one cost to

---

[10] In one sense, this section is little more than a formal illustration of the schema of reciprocity offered by Sahlins (1972). He characterises different types of reciprocity based on the distance of a trade partner from the individual. At the top of this hierarchy is generalised reciprocity, where high levels of trade are possible with members of one's own kinship groups. At the other extreme is the negative reciprocity offered to strangers, where an individual will happily harm the person he is trading with. This model describes distances in terms of λ/r.

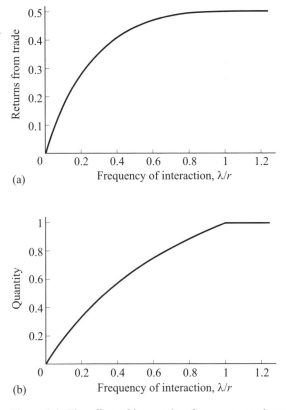

Figure 2.2 The effect of interaction frequency on dynamic reciprocity

barter exchange in repeated settings – namely, that individuals are sometimes focused on short-term gains so much that they renege on their reciprocal obligations. (Or, to phrase it another way, as individuals value
relationships less and less, smaller quantities of trade can be supported.)
There is much evidence to suggest that such inefficiencies arise. First, many
of the contributors to this volume cite the 'wild' nature of the Russian
economy where incentives to default prevail, while Ledeneva (chapter 11
in this volume) also emphasises the critical importance of 'good old'
personal contacts for ensuring that trade actually happens.

3 Inefficient, delayed rewards and the liquidity value of trade

This section deals with cases where one agent's goods are of higher value
that those provided by the other. Put simply, how does reciprocity operate

in situations where one agent demands more from the other than vice versa? So far, we have offered one reason why economic relationships without money can be inefficient: trade is not frequent enough (or, alternatively stated, individuals are not sufficiently patient). However, there are other problems which can arise when money is absent, many of which related to inherent asymmetries between the two parties. (Remember that in the previous section, we assumed that the two parties valued each other's goods equally.) A recurring theme on barter in this volume is that many of the goods traded are not so desirable to one of the parties, and may take time and involve other costs to offload. Equally there are cases where one party needs things frequently from the other, while the reciprocal demands from the other party are much more intermittent. There is furthermore considerable evidence from these chapters that the terms of trade depend on what currency is bartered, which this section also addresses.

When individuals value each other's contributions differently, two additional insights arise. First, agents trade with one another not simply for the consumption value of trade but also to provide 'liquidity', serving a role as a *quid pro quo* for the exchange.[11] The role of commodities as a form of money gives rise to qualitatively different outcomes than those which arise in a monetised economy. Second, pricing depends on both the goods traded and on the importance of the relationship, where low-value goods and goods in sporadic relationships may receive poorer terms of trade relative to high-quality goods.

Asymmetric values in trading relationships

In order for such liquidity provision to play a role, we first consider asymmetries between the agents, where one agent values a unit of consumption of the other's good more than vice versa. To this end, we extend our basic model of section 2 by assuming that one individual, person A, values a unit of the other agent's good at αq, where $\alpha > 1$. We call this high-valuation *consumer* the α-agent. The other individual, B, continues to have unit marginal utility for consumption. Note that higher optimal production, $\bar{q} = \alpha > 1$, is called for when serving the α-agent, relative to the other agent for whom optimal production remains at 1. These are the outcomes of a monetised economy. However, to induce the other person to offer higher quantities of the α-good in a barter setting, the agent must offer something in return. In the absence of money, this becomes the

---

[11] See Calvert (1989), who applies a similar game-theoretic approach to log-rolling by politicians.

other good, so that production decisions will be partly determined by the desire to satisfy the other agent's demands at the higher level of production. In this sense, production decisions will be partly determined by a wish to create a dynamic double coincidence of wants, as there is no static coincidence of wants.[12] The lower-quality good has a 'liquidity' or *quid pro quo* value in a barter exchange which accounts for why it is over-traded relative to the allocation in a monetary economy.

Our interest here is in identifying the quantities of goods which the individuals are willing to trade. In order to render the chapter more readable, we relegate much of the technical detail to the appendix (p. 65), where a more formal proof of the propositions is offered. In words, the quantities traded have the following characteristics. First, if the agents do not interact frequently, trade is below its efficient level, and trade of the low-value good *exceeds* that of the superior good. Ironically, the worse is the low-value good relative to the superior, the greater is its relative production. For intermediate rates of interaction, trade in the low-value good is below that of the superior good, but *higher* than the efficient level which would arise if money were available. Finally, if the individuals interact frequently enough, there is no difference between the outcomes with barter and with money.[13]

A visual characterisation of the solution is given in figure 2.3, where $\bar{q}$ is the production of the superior α-good and $\underline{q}$ is the production of the lower-valued good. In this example, we set $\alpha = 1.2$.

Remember that if money was freely available, the outcomes would be $\bar{q} = \alpha$ and $\underline{q} = 1$ regardless of the rate of interaction, λ/r. Such efficient levels emerge under dynamic reciprocity only if the rate of interaction is high enough; again, if the relationship is sufficiently important, trust can substitute for cash. More generally, though, from figure 2.3 one can see that there are three separate regions. The one that seems of most relevance to

---

[12] Throughout this section, we simply maximise the sum of utilities. An interpretation of this is that each agent is *ex ante* identical, where nature determines which agent is the α-agent. Decisions on the equilibrium are taken before the draw from nature, so all agents agree on the objective function.

[13] In this chapter, we implicitly assume that α is not too large so that the asymmetries are not too great for sufficiently patient traders to overcome; to be precise, we require that $\alpha < \sqrt{2}$. If $\sqrt{2} < \alpha$, the agent who produces the α-good will be unwilling to produce at efficient levels, even when $r = 0$. In other words, his costs of production exceed the (instantaneous) value of the other good. If this is the case, then as r tends to zero, the level of the low-value good produced will be higher than 1, as it is the only means of rewarding the agent. In this sense, over-supply of goods can occur for liquidity reasons, in the absence of anything to do with the repeated interaction that underlies the chapter. These are akin to the classical inefficiencies that are discussed in the static literature on barter. These issues are discussed in detail in Prendergast and Stole (1998b).

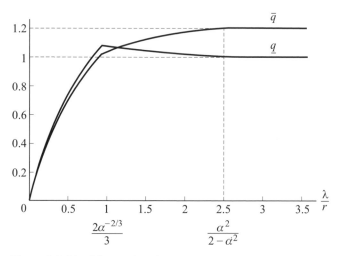

Figure 2.3 Liquidity and trade

the examples cited for Russia concern those where interaction is infrequent (λ/r low). This is the part where both lines are upward-sloping. For example, Humphrey (chapter 3 in this volume) cites the 'short horizons' of many barter participants. Note that when interaction is infrequent, production of the worse good $\underline{q}$ is higher than production of the better good and liquidity concerns reverse our normal intuition on the supply of goods, where goods with higher marginal valuations have higher production.[14]

We can easily rephrase these results in terms of pricing behaviour: in relationships where interaction in infrequent, those with poor barter goods get bad prices. In order to consume something that they like, those with poor barter goods generally pay a dear price, sometimes having to produce large quantities to get anything in return. This appears to correspond to a recurring theme in many of the chapters in this volume. For example, Anderson (chapter 12 in this volume) describes the 'exploitative side' of these trades, with barter prices being 'more expensive than purchasing goods at wholesale prices'. It is easy to translate our results into relevant prices: the price is the quantity of one good which must be

---

[14] It is worth briefly noting the two other regions of trade here, though it is not our primary focus. First, note that trade in the less desirable good declines in λ/r after some point. The reason for this is that in this region, as λ/r increases, the value of the relationship rises for all agents, thus reducing the need to over-supply the less useful asset. Thus increased patience reduces some trades. Finally, for large enough λ/r, the efficient allocation (i.e. the outcome of a monetised economy) occurs.

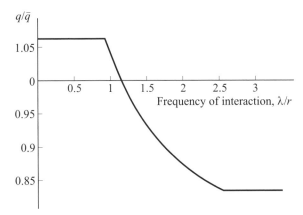

Figure 2.4 Pricing in relationships

offered to get a unit of the other. Not surprisingly, as the difference between the two goods' qualities increases, more of the low-valued good must be offered to get a unit of the better good; in effect, the price of the better good rises. From this perspective, it is hardly surprising that the prices denominated in petrol would be better than those denominated in electric energy which 'is not an easy currency' and 'produces big discounts' (Ledeneva, chapter 4 in this volume). In essence, prices reflect the quality of the bartered goods.

Another implication of this simple model is that it shows how pricing varies by the importance of the relationship. Figure 2.4 plots the price of the α-good denominated in terms of the other good as λ/r changes. This represents the amount of the less desirable good which must be offered to get a unit of the better good. It is immediately seen that the relationship is (weakly) downward-sloping, so that the cost of getting the better good falls as the relationship becomes more important. Also note that in relationships which are more important, the terms of trade get closer to the efficient level, with traded quantities similar to those which would emerge in a world with money.[15] When the relationship is unimportant, the price of getting the preferred good is highest and most out of line with the efficient price level. Thus pricing depends on relationships, as in Humphrey (1992, p. 123).

These observations illustrate how non-monetary exchange operates in a different fashion to monetary exchange. For instance, it is one of the most basic premises of economics that goods which have higher marginal surplus will have higher production than those which are less valuable.

[15] With money the ratio of production of the unwanted good to the other is $\frac{1}{1.2}$.

But this basic premise is violated here where there is more production of the less useful good. In addition, we have pointed out the poor terms of trade which arise when agents have goods which have poor liquidity: those who pay in petrol generally do better than those paying in bricks.

Asymmetric bargaining power

So far, we have considered only those cases where bargaining power worked such that the sum of individual utilities was maximised. Yet many of the papers in this chapters focus on the advantaged position of some agents relative to others, manifesting itself in terms of asymmetric bargaining power. A central theme of recent contributions to economics concerns inefficiencies that can be generated by bargaining distortions. Two cases are generally considered: those in which everyone knows the other's valuations and those where valuations are unknown. In this section, we consider the simplest case, where two agents trade with known valuations but where there is asymmetric bargaining power. In two related papers, we develop the effects of barter upon bargaining distortions in environments of incomplete information.[16]

When money is freely available, such asymmetric bargaining power worries economists little, as higher bargaining power results in a weak agent simply paying more money, with no change in the efficiency of the allocation. There is only a pure distributional effect, about which we have little to say. However, this is not so in the case of barter; here asymmetric bargaining power directly affects the efficiency of the allocation – judged relative to a monetary economy – as greater bargaining power is now manifested in terms of inefficient distortion of goods. For example, a farmer in Russia with little bargaining power may be required to hand over excessively large quantities of food to a powerful buyer, who offers little in return. In a monetary economy in which both parties had ample monetary assets, such bargaining power may result in large cash transfers, but not in inefficient allocations of goods. Such distortions in production are the standard efficiency losses of economics.[17]

In order to isolate the effect of bargaining power *per se*, consider a case where agents interact so often that the incentive constraints are irrelevant (in the context of the formal model, assume that interaction is very high)

---

[16] Prendergast and Stole (1998a, 1998c).

[17] It is worth emphasising that when we claim that asymmetric bargaining power in barter settings can generate inefficient allocations we are measuring the inefficiency relative to the monetary outcome. A barter allocation is still efficient in a money-less world, but the introduction of money could raise everyone's level of consumption without anyone being harmed by allowing an efficient reallocation of consumption across individuals.

and their demands are assumed to be symmetric, as in section 2. Suppose instead of simply assuming that the agents split the surplus, they bargain over the allocation. Following work by Rubinstein (1982), a simple way of parameterising bargaining power relates to the patience of the individuals involved. In this case, those with weak bargaining power cannot wait to consume the good, while those with stronger bargaining power are content to sit out some time before consuming. Although trades in these models occur immediately, the terms of trade benefit the more patient bargainer. Suppose initially that each party is equally patient. Then the bargaining outcome offers $q = 1$, the same outcome as with money. (Remember that we are restricting attention to the case where the agents have symmetric demands and interact frequently, so that we do not have to worry about the problems of the previous subsection.) This merely replicates our earlier results. However, the presence of asymmetric bargaining power will generate differences between the two allocations. As an example, consider the case where agent A has all the bargaining power, allowing her to make a take-it-or-leave-it offer to her trading partner. Then the barter allocation has B's consumption given by $q_B < 1$ and agent A's consumption given by $q_A > 1$.[18] In other words, asymmetric bargaining power *per se* causes problems, with the party with more bargaining power getting quantities which are too high while his less patient partner consumes too little relative to a monetised economy.

4 Networks and distributional effects of barter

Perhaps the dominant theme of the chapters in this volume has been the importance of contacts and networks in current economic exchange in Russia, and some of the more fascinating contributions illustrate the quite incredible sophistication of the networks which sometimes develop to satisfy a 'double coincidence of wants'. Ledeneva's (1998b) contribution here (chapter 11) is particularly apposite. The importance of this institution of exchange should not be under-estimated in understanding how barter affects modern Russia. First, as Anderson (chapter 12 in this volume) nicely puts it: 'the logic behind market economies is that commodities, such as money, are intended to bind together many diverse communities of exchange. The series of Russian financial crises ... ([has]) disqualified the [new] rouble from the role of an instrument of social integration'. Or to put it another way, one person's money is as good as another's,[19] so money facilitates exchange between individuals

---

[18] More precisely, $q_B = 2^{-1/3}$ and $q_A = 2^{1/3}$.

[19] Though Lemon (1998) would surely disagree with this statement in the context of the Roma.

with little in common. By contrast, one person's social contacts are clearly not the equal of another's.

This transition from an economy based on money to one based on contacts surely has important effects on distribution and social integration. In terms of the simple model above, individuals differ in terms of their trading intensities (i.e. λ/r), where those with less frequent interactions become excluded from trades which would otherwise occur with money. There can be little doubt from Lemon's (1998) contribution that this has adversely affected the Roma, who are often seen as untrustworthy by Russians. Equally, Humphrey (chapter 10 in this volume) notes that farmers are restricted to simultaneous barter arrangements, as they lack the relationships to ensure delayed reciprocity. Yet such exclusion is not restricted solely to particular ethnic or occupational groups. Instead, it is clear that individuals seek out trade partners with good pedigrees, or at least pedigrees where there is evidence of dense trade. As Anderson notes (chapter 12), there is a difficulty in building 'networks of alliance in a space where there are no longer pregiven social commitments.' Ledeneva (chapter 11) emphasises the importance of 'good, old' contacts, while Humphrey (chapter 10) notes the importance of networks that are often 'quite simply based on Soviet-era links', where firms 'prefer to work with solid government-supported firms'. Clarke (chapter 7) notes that two classes of contacts become important: those who 'had their roots in old administrative structures' and 'those outside the law'.

These observations seem to point to the importance of established trade partners, those with links to many other firms, which may be necessary to provide the ultimate 'cash' of the barter arrangement. Those with few links to other networks become poor trading partners, at least in the absence of middlemen. It is our sense that this is of critical importance for the Russian economy, and perhaps the political future. One implication of such barter networks is that they exclude individuals on the periphery (the Roma being the extreme social example of this) and also give a huge advantage to those who are already in established networks. It is not hard to see potential implications for restructuring and government in Russia. Particularly, because of demonetisation, older established firms, often those which are the 'dinosaurs' of Humphrey's (1998) analysis in chapter 10, are increasingly becoming central to economic exchange, despite the extinct nature of the outputs that they produce. Since these firms often have strong contacts to local government, it is also not hard to imagine a link to political entrenchment.

The importance of networks for facilitating trade has numerous implications. First, as described above, it can exclude peripheral individuals from exchange. A second implication, which we briefly model here, concerns the importance of middlemen to economic exchange. As Clarke (chapter 7) notes, 'to find new customers and suppliers, enterprises had to turn to intermediaries, ... individuals who had their own contacts and sources of finance'. To illustrate this, we consider a simple network which requires a middleman to facilitate exchange. However, an additional purpose of this is to note that the middleman does not come for free; positions in networks generate rents which reduce the value of trade to the parties who are involved in production. Indeed, we will show below that middlemen may actually benefit from the demonetisation process: they are needed only when times are sufficiently bad, and so (in some cases) may disappear when times get better.

This section also deals with the fact that not all trade consists of reciprocal barter. There is some liquidity in the system, though the trading individuals cannot be assured of having enough. To model this and the need for middlemen, we begin by extending the model of liquidity trade in section 3 by assuming that another individual can provide liquidity: as noted above, parties A and B may not interact enough to get to the same outcome as the monetised economy. This is where middlemen play a role. They can in effect partially monetise the barter transaction by providing transfers between the parties with some regularity. We model this simply here by assuming that there is another party, C. This party fills a need between A and B in the following way. We assume that A has a project with C where he can transfer a good to C. For simplicity we ignore the productive value of the trades with C by assuming that transfers from A to C are welfare-neutral, where a transfer of goods costing x to A has value x to C. In turn, C can transfer something to B, where a transfer of goods costing x to C has value x to B. Thus C plays no role other than to shuffle resources from A, the consumer of the superior good, to B the consumer of the low-value good.[20] Thus, when A wants something, B will provide it and gets (possibly) two things in return: goods from A and and a transfer from C. These occur some time in the future. (Without the middleman, B can obtain only goods from A.) The role of party C, who acts like a bank, is that it can transfer resources to B when available and required. To retain symmetry in the model, we also assume that C receives each of his projects (the project from A being one, the project to B being the other) with frequency $\mu\lambda$, where a higher

---

[20] In effect, the welfare-neutrality of C's transfer are as if the parties transact cash. But this is for simplicity. A perhaps more natural assumption would be to make the trades between C and the other parties inefficient rather than just neutral. In that case, the choice over using the middleman would depend on whether the liquidity creation by the middleman outweighed the costs of the inefficient trades.

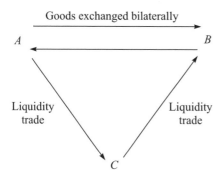

Figure 2.5 The network with a middleman

value of μ is akin to increasing the liquidity available to party C. As with the liquidity model of Section 3, agent A prefers the good provided by B (with marginal utility $\alpha > 1$) relatively more than B likes A's good (which has marginal utility of 1).

Visually, our network is given in figure 2.5.

Of course, the agent providing liquidity will not do so for free; A must pay him. Since it facilitates trade, C will demand a share of the increase in trade by threatening to abscond whenever he is required to give something to B. A must provide C with a credible promise of future returns to prevent this behaviour. Thus, when A has an opportunity to transfer value to C via some project, she will do so to the extent required. As with the previous sections, we assume that the parties maximise the sum of their utilities, subject to the relevant incentive constraints of the type described in section 2.[21] The main difference in the formal model is now that party C must be induced to hand over a transfer to B when he is called upon to do so.[22]

As in the previous sections, we do not provide exhaustive details of our theoretical results. Instead, we simply provide an example to illustrate the

---

[21] Some readers may be uncomfortable with this and would prefer a more explicit bargaining structure. An obvious alternative would be to use Nash bargaining. Nash bargaining is equivalent to maximising the product of the agent's utilities, subject to the relevant incentive constraints. However, as we show in other work (Prendergast and Stole, 1998c), this involves additional complications when monetary and non-monetary allocations are compared, as it changes the nature of the bargaining game. This adds additional complications which we do not discuss here: see our earlier work for details.

[22] Suppose that as part of an equilibrium allocation, agent C is required to give a transfer of t units of his good to B. Let V_C be the present value of the utility of agent C from the trading relationship with A and B. Then it must be the case that $V_C - t \geq 0$ for the agent to be willing to make the transfers when required to do so. Figure 2.6 takes account of these additional incentives.

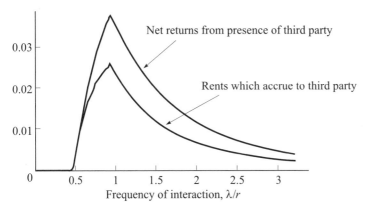

Figure 2.6 The effect of the middleman on surplus and rents

main implications of allowing middlemen. The outcome of the provision of liquidity by the middleman is provided in figure 2.6, where we assume that $\alpha = 1.5$ and party C has money with frequency 15λ, so $\mu = 15$. In figure 2.6 we provide two effects of the middleman. The top curve describes the increase in surplus to all three parties from the existence of the middleman. Since this is positive for levels of interaction above $\lambda = 0.5$, middlemen can improve overall surplus which explains why the agents use them. However, the bottom curve in figure 2.6 plots the middleman's profits. In other words, how much of the net gain accrues to the middleman?

As can be seen clearly, C gets some of the surplus that he creates, illustrating important distributional consequences of their role: middlemen do not come for free and sometimes can be very expensive. There are three regions worth remarking upon. In the first region, for sufficiently low interactions, there is no value to an intermediary such as C. The cost of transferring value through C is too high relative to the benefit of improved exchange between A and B, since A and B are unable to trade at even moderate levels. In the middle region of interaction, the use of C is a complement to A and B's interaction: the more they interact, the more value there is to transferring returns from A to B via C, as such transfers allow for more efficient (and asymmetric) exchanges. For sufficiently high levels of interaction, however, A and B can replicate the role of C in an autarkic trading network, so additional increases in interaction levels are a substitute for C's services. The reason for this fall is that parties A and B interact enough to execute their own trades and they need the middleman less as the interaction becomes more frequent. But then the interests of the middlemen towards demonetisation differ from those of the other parties, unlike the middle region. In particular, the two parties trading goods would prefer a sufficiently high level of interaction (or other monetary substitute) so that they can fulfil their trades themselves. By contrast, the middleman would be harmed in this case, as his role would become redundant.[23] In the context of Russia, this relates to the possibility that the 'dinosaurs' which Humphrey (chapter 10 in this volume) places in the centre of her networks may be harmed by the remonetisation of Russia, as their services are no longer necessary and the outputs they produce are of little value in a monetised economy.

The purpose of this example is not simply to show that there is a demand for middlemen when barter arrangements predominate. Instead, its main purpose is to show that there are important distributional consequences from that derived demand. In the examples given above, it also points to the fact that there could be a group of agents who benefit from the demonetisation process, as it implies that these individuals occupy a more central role in the required networks to facilitate trade. Since many of these central individuals in networks are also closely linked to local government, it raises the interesting question of the incentives of local government to aid any remonetisation process.

5 Choosing friends

So far, we have discussed two implications of network structure – (1) that peripheral groups can be excluded and (2) that there is a demand for middlemen who can extract rents for their services. In this section, we consider an additional issue of network choice – namely, how to choose a network, and how barter affects the diversity of agent with which one can trade.

Economics offers one simple rule for choosing trade partners: comparative advantage. In particular, one obvious advantage of markets is that it allows consumers and producers to profit from comparative advantage. This simple observation is the linchpin of many theories arguing in favour of free trade. One can phrase this in more familiar terms: that individuals should seek very diverse networks because they may find that the best provider of a given service varies across goods. The purpose of this section is to illustrate that with social exchange there exists a countervailing effect which argues for restricting the ability of agents to trade with each other.

Individuals often spend considerable time investing in relationships, and must explicitly choose which relationships to cultivate. As illustrated

---

[23] Of course, such middlemen may also have productive roles in monetised economies just as banks frequently add value.

above, trust is central to economic efficiency in a barter environment and may imply a different rule, namely, to 'put all your eggs in one basket' rather than hold a diverse set of networks. The reason for this is that although it may be inefficient (in the usual economic sense) to rely too much on a small number of personal contacts, trust is more likely to operate when trade is dense than when trade is spread across many trading partners. As a result, it can make sense to select a small number of partners and trade intensively with them, even though they may not be the least-cost providers of some goods that one may want. Thus the need for trust can make trading relations so tight that standard economic efficiency considerations are overturned.

In particular, we address the role of restricted trading networks in social relations, and argue that such restrictions are an integral component of social exchange.[24] We show that the decision on whether to restrict trades boils down to a simple trade-off between comparative advantage and contract enforcement considerations. If the comparative advantage is sufficiently small (i.e. no person is any better at producing a good than another), there is a role for restricted networks. Furthermore, as interactions become less frequent, denser networks become more likely. In other words, when agents interact less frequently, denser networks become more important. To put this in more familiar terms, the trend towards short termism in Russia that Humphrey (chapter 3 in this volume) emphasises makes efficient restricting of networks more likely.

We extend the basic model of section 4 to allow for (1) comparative advantage and (2) more agents, so that there is the possibility of choosing tighter or looser networks. We assume that there are four agents who can produce any of four goods. All trade must be enforced through reciprocity. We model comparative advantage by assuming that although each agent may produce any good at a cost of $c(q) = \frac{1}{2}q^2$, for three of the four goods the resulting consumption value to the other traders is q but for one good the resulting value to the other traders is αq, where $\alpha > 1$. Moreover, each agent has a comparative advantage in producing a

---

[24] Restrictions on the ability to trade take many forms. First, social sanctions can serve to restrict the willingness of agents to trade with one another. For instance, it is rarely socially approved for individuals to engage in extra-marital affairs, an obvious restriction on trade in sex. In many countries, such trade is illegal. Second, there are a plethora of historical and anthropological examples where clans were willing to trade only with one another, and would have little to do with 'outsiders'. In some primitive societies, individuals are assigned a trade partner who has an obligation to help him and to whom he will reciprocate. Such obligations do not operate for other individuals and attempts to steal a trade partner were often dealt with harshly. For instance, among the Sio of North East New Guinea it was considered an offence worthy of homicide to attempt to lure away one's trade partner (Harding, 1967).

unique one of these four goods. Thus the model extends that in section 4 by allowing agents to be talented at producing different goods. For notational convenience, let agent i produce good i with greater value, where $i = 1, \ldots, 4$. For simplicity, we assume that the agent does not demand the good in which he has a comparative advantage, but demands other goods with a common rate λ. As before, we also assume that each agent must obtain these other goods from other producers; the agents cannot produce to satisfy their own demands.

The standard economic model of comparative advantage in a monetary economy would say that each individual produces one good – the one that he is most efficient at producing. Thus, there would be specialisation, a characteristic of a monetised economy. In such an economy, if an agent demands good j, he will trade with agent j for α-units of the goods (as this is the efficient level, where marginal benefits equal costs), with surplus created of $\frac{1}{2}\alpha^2$.

Suppose, instead, that agents trade in a barter environment. In this case, networks will matter. We take a simple approach to understanding network structure by assuming that in order to trade with someone, an initial investment must be made at the start of any relationship. In other words, at the beginning of the game, a decision must be made by the agents whether to form a link with the other agents. If the link is not formed then, it cannot be generated later. To keep matters simple, all agents can see the network structure and the initial cost of forming a link is small enough to be ignored. Our main point in this section is to show that even when forming a link is (essentially) free, the agents may decide not to do so. Instead, they commit to put 'all their eggs in one basket' to facilitate trust.

What this setup is meant to reflect is that once alliances are formed, it is hard to find other trading partners. (An extreme example of this is marriage, where bigamy is illegal and extra-marital affairs frowned upon.) Our model simply assumes that once a network is formed, it is impossible to break into another; realistically, this is too extreme as individuals can spend time building up such links. Our objective is simply to show that restrictions on letting people easily move between networks may make economic sense in a world of barter.

What matters then for working out how much trade occurs is the punishments meted out to those who deviate: the greater the punishments, the more likely is an individual to produce as required. This in turn depends on who observes the behaviour of the individuals. If all agents observe any deviation from cooperative trade and are willing to punish the deviator by refusing to trade with the him in the future, then there is no value to restricting the trading network to obtain the socially optimal allocation of goods. (This would require everyone to cut off an agent from trade, even if that agent has reneged on only one of his obligations.) This statement is no longer true when there is limited observability of trades, or where agents are unwilling to punish transgressions which occur between other trading partners. We consider the case where only the agents involved in the trades can observe the behaviour of the parties (and the level of trade between them), so that the maximum punishment that can be imposed on the agents is that the bilateral relationship breaks down. More formally, we consider a class of equilibria where trade between any two agents is independent of relations between any other links.

In this setting, we consider two natural networks. First, we address the case where all agents trade according to comparative advantage. In other words, if any agent requires good i, the good is produced by person i. Thus, all links are formed. We then compare this to an institution where each agent is assigned a unique trading partner where they trade all their desired goods with that agent. This has the disadvantage that it reduces the value of comparative advantage in the economy, but will be shown to increase the threat attached to cheating.

As with the previous sections, we relegate the technical details to the Appendix, where the formal model is analysed. Nonetheless, it is intuitive that the tension in choosing networks is between the advantages of wide networks (taking advantage of comparative advantage) and their costs (when a trading partner is not very reliant on one, the temptation to renege is greater). The main result from the appendix is easily explained. First, for low enough levels of comparative advantage (i.e. if α is below some critical value α^*), the socially optimal network will consist of two distinct bilateral trading networks, even though these trading relationships fail to capitalise on some of the comparative production advantages which are present. This critical value of α always exceeds one if efficient levels of trade cannot be obtained without trading partners. Restricting networks increases welfare, thus overturning standard economic logic regarding the advantages of free trade. Furthermore, the desirability of such restricted trade increases as interactions become less common (or as the agent discounts the future more). In other words, there is little need to restrict trades among agents who interact extremely frequently, but as interactions become more frequent some constraints are needed.

The implications of this section are illustrated in figure 2.7.

Here we illustrate situations in which it is efficient to restrict networks in terms of frequency of interaction (λ/r) and the importance of comparative advantage (α). Below the curve drawn, it is efficient for individuals to trade with only one trading partner. They will forgo the benefits

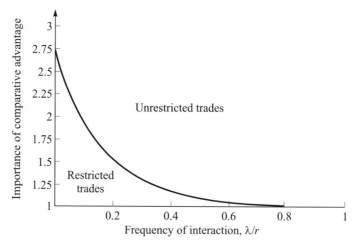

Figure 2.7 Optimal regions for restricted networks

of comparative advantage (i.e. trading with all three individuals), but can support more trade with their single trade partner when they are more reliant on one another. Above the line, agents should form more diverse links. Note that the line is downward-sloped, which implies that as interactions become more frequent it is less likely that the individuals need to restrict their networks.

The formal model above is simply meant to emphasise the importance of dense trade for reciprocity to operate. As a result, individuals may dedicate a large fraction of their trades to a single agent, even though that agent may not be the most effective provider of that good. At a more informal level, it also points to a difficulty which smaller firms may have in the network process. Although these new smaller firms may be more efficient providers of goods in the usual cost sense, trade partners may be hard to find as they see the importance of their existing networks, which though sometimes inefficient, are at least trustworthy.

6 Liquidity shocks and prices

So far, we have largely looked at barter arrangements as if there were not a money market also operating in tandem. This section, based on Prendergast and Stole (1999), begins to address what we feel is an important but unexplored topic in the context of barter societies – namely, the interaction between many currencies which simultaneously circulate, as occurs in Russia. It remains very unclear how these currencies interact with one another; their effects are hardly neutral on each other but exactly how the existence of roubles affects the use of pasta or social contacts remains unclear. Central to current trading in Russia is the absence of liquidity that drives much of barter trade. Our interest in this section specifically is in understanding the response of prices to a liquidity shock. To describe the issue, consider the following trivial example. Suppose that before the August 1998 shock everyone in Russia had £2 but that after the shock, liquidity dried up so that everyone has £1. An immediate question that arises is why prices do not adjust such that the real quantity of money is unchanged. In other words, why aren't prices simply cut in two?

Our answer to this relies on two building blocks.[25] First, we assume that prices may not be set competitively.[26] To model non-competitive setting of prices, we consider the standard monopoly setting where there is uncertainty about the valuation of a buyer for the seller's good. We assume that when a seller is offering his good to a buyer, the buyer values a single unit of the good at v, where v is uniformly distributed between 0 and 1. Only the buyer knows how much he values the good. Assume further for simplicity that the quantity supplied is discrete, equal to either 0 or 1, and that the cost of the good is zero. As a result, of these assumptions, it is always efficient (but not necessarily most profitable) to supply the good. If there are no other constraints or opportunities, it is simple to show that the monopoly seller would choose his price

[25] As in the other sections of the chapter, we do not provide much technical detail but instead offer an example which illustrates some of the relevant effects. This example is based on Prendergast and Stole (1999). The reader is referred there for more details.

[26] There is a considerable amount of discussion of current pricing arrangements in Russia. For example, in chapter 10 in this volume Humphrey notes the prevalence of exploiting opportunities by mispricing, where fixed prices are 'replaced by agonised bargaining', while Ledeneva in chapter 11 devotes considerable time to understanding the negotiations that operate in barter networks. One view of such pricing arrangements has been emphasised above – namely, that the prices that are charged are merely a manifestation of the fact that barter goods are not a general claim on goods in the way that, say, pounds would be, and so sellers demand more in cases where these goods are hard to sell on. For instance, this surely is the primary reason why prices denominated in bricks would exceed those in petrol. It may also explain why Commander and Mumssen (chapter 5 in this volume) find lower prices denominated in *veksels* than for straight barter deals. Yet there remains the suspicion that some of the pricing decisions that are being described also reflect the absence of competition that often characterises networks where there are a small number of traders. This would seem closer to the descriptions of many of the authors in this volume than simply the observation that efficient barter prices are being offered at all points in time, and raises the issue of how liquidity shocks, of the type that occurred in August 1998, affected the evolution of prices. In this section, we consider how liquidity shocks affect the exercise of monopoly power in a situation where barter exchange is also possible.

to be $\frac{1}{2}$. In such a case, only half the population (those with valuations above $\frac{1}{2}$) would buy, but profits would be greater than at any other price.

The additional assumption we make, however, is that there are liquidity shocks, where the buyer may be liquidity-constrained with not enough money to pay for the good. To fix this idea, we assume that he has m units of currency with which he can buy the good. Then his 'effective willingness to pay' will be the minimum of his valuation v and his money stock m. This represents a simple way to analyze the effects of liquidity.[27] However, importantly, not everyone is affected equally by the liquidity shock. Specifically, we assume that those who have low valuations are also likely to have little money. Put in loose terms, poor people are less likely to buy and are also those who are most affected by shocks to liquidity. Those in wealthier initial positions are more likely buyers both because of their wealth and because they are more likely to have money even after the liquidity shock, perhaps because of their better positions in trading networks, as described in Section 4.

One natural way to model this is through a correlation between valuations and money holdings. We use a particularly simple form of correlation, where we assume that $m = a + bv$, $a < 0$ and $b > 1$.[28] In other words, a 1-unit increase in valuations increases money stocks by b. What this means can be most easily seen from figure 2.8, where we have taken a simple example in which $b = 1.25$ and $a = -0.25$.

The solid line represents the effective willingness to pay. For those who have high valuations (above z in figure 2.8), the underlying valuation of the buyer is less than his money holdings. In other words, liquidity constraints are not important for that person, as he has enough money to pay for the good. However, this is not true for all individuals who value the good at less than z. In that case, the agents do not have enough money to pay their valuation: instead all that they can pay is their money holdings, m.[29]

Start by imagining that there are no opportunities for barter: this is not meant to reflect current reality in Russia, but is simply a counterfactual against which we will consider a world with barter. What we are most interested in is how prices are affected by the liquidity shock. Now remember from figure 2.8 that those who have valuations below z are

---

[27] Some readers may be uncomfortable with defining inherent valuations independently of money holdings. The simplest way to think of this is that m refers to a distinct composite good, where the marginal value of the seller's good (relative to the composite) is v.

[28] Of course, such a formulation has the unattractive aspect that money holdings can be negative for low valuations. This is only to simplify notation. Instead, one should think of money holdings as given by $\max\{0, a + bv\}$ and nothing in our results would be altered.

[29] In the absence of a correlation between m and v, there is no opportunity for strategic segmentation of markets of the type studied here.

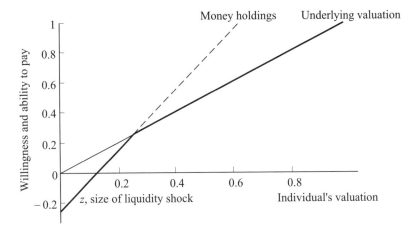

Figure 2.8 The effect of liquidity shocks on willingness to pay

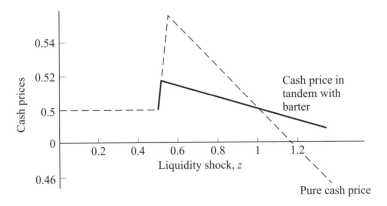

Figure 2.9 Prices

liquidity-constrained. Therefore, as z gets bigger, the environment becomes more liquidity constrained.[30] The dotted line in figure 2.9 gives optimal prices which arise as a function of the liquidity shock.

It is simplest to begin at the two extremes: (a) where z is low (less than $\frac{1}{2}$), so few are liquidity-constrained, and (b) where z exceeds 1, so everyone is liquidity-constrained. First, when few are liquidity constrained, the price charged is $\frac{1}{2}$, unchanged from the case where there is no liquidity shock. This arises simply because the only people affected by the shock

---

[30] This is equivalent to decreasing a with the technology above.

are those who would not have bought anyway: hence the optimal price is unchanged. When the liquidity shock is large, specifically when $z > 1$, everyone is affected by the shock. In this case, prices fall below their level when there is no liquidity shock. This reflects the imagined direct effect of an absence of liquidity on prices: if people don't have any money, you should not demand as much as when they do.

However, the intermediate regions are also of interest, as they illustrate how liquidity shocks cause sellers to increase prices over some range and then to reduce them. This arises for the following reason. Consider a liquidity shock which causes some marginal buyers (those around $\frac{1}{2}$) to be liquidity-constrained. One possibility is to reduce the price to pick these up: but this reduces the revenues on those with higher valuations who would have bought anyway. An alternative is to ignore these customers and choose a price at which only those who have high valuations (and money holdings) will buy. For intermediate ranges of liquidity shocks, the latter effect always dominates, so the optimal pricing strategy is to increase the price as customers initially become liquidity-constrained in the relevant demand region. In short, the liquidity shock decimates the demand of the moderate purchasers, so it now is more profitable for the seller to focus attention on the cash market's high-end purchasers.

But firms have another option which we have so far ignored: they can barter their goods through the kind of networks described at length in this volume. Rather than fully model the repeated barter environment as we have done in the previous sections, we instead simply consider a 'reduced-form' structure of barter where we note that there is some cost to trading through barter rather than directly selling for cash. This could be the cost which must be paid to a middleman, as in section 4, or the inefficient production which arises when goods are not equally valued by both parties, as on p. 46. Specifically, we assume that there is a 'tax' on barter which reflects this: where a unit of the buyer's 'commodity cash' (i.e. the goods which the buyer transfers to the seller in exchange for satisfying the buyer's demands) has value x to the seller (in terms of the composite), but which costs tx to the buyer to generate. We assume that $t > 1$, reflecting the standard inefficiencies of barter.

How does the opportunity for barter affect the cash market? Clearly, it now gives sellers the opportunity to sell their goods not only for cash but also they can offer their goods for barter also. This provides them with an additional outlet for their goods which increases their profitability, but importantly also gives buyers an alternative option, where they can barter instead of buying for cash. The solid line in figure 2.9 plots optimal money prices when barter is also an option. In this figure, we assume that $t = 1.5$.[31] Our primary focus is on the difference between the hatched line and the solid line: in other words, how does the existence of barter exchange affect money pricing? Again, consider the extremes. When the liquidity constraints are not important, there is no difference in the price charged, for the reason that the barter market is never used.[32] At the other extreme, where $z > 1$, when liquidity constraints are extreme, prices when barter is an option are still lower than when there is no liquidity problem. However, they are higher than when only the cash market operates. In other words, the existence of the barter market limits the incentive to reduce prices with liquidity shocks. In this region, both currencies circulate simultaneously, where those with high enough valuations (and money) use the cash market while those who do not will use the barter market.

Why is it that prices are higher when barter is an option? The reason is that the benefits to a price reduction in a world without barter are that customers who would not otherwise buy the product now will purchase it at the lower price. When barter is present, a price reduction (holding the barter terms fixed) will serve only to convert bartering buyers into cash buyers. While this is profitable to the seller, conversion is not as profitable as new sales. Hence, the presence of barter limits the incentive to reduce prices when liquidity shocks hit the system. Thus multiple currencies interact in non-trivial ways.[33]

For intermediate liquidity shocks (for z between 0.5 and 1), prices are lower when barter is an option. In this region, firms realise that if prices are too high, customers can substitute into barter. The firm then faces a trade-off when it increases money prices that it must simultaneously also make barter deals less attractive to the consumer. In this intermediate region, the costs of doing so are enough to constrain price increases, and so the firm does not target only the higher-valuation consumers in the way that it would if barter were not available.

---

[31] The more general importance of this assumption is that for the example we have computed it is the case that $t \geq b$. We have not yet analysed the case where this condition does not hold.

[32] One might imagine that those buyers without money would be offered the opportunity to barter in this region. However, this is not the case because there is the temptation that those who would otherwise pay with cash will now switch to barter. The cost of this transition is enough to cause the firm to offer no barter swaps.

[33] It should be noted that we have ignored one possibility here, which is where there is no cash market and instead the only form of exchange which occurs is where all goods are bartered. This will occur if the liquidity shock is so great that the firms decide that it is simply not worth selling on the cash market. We have ignored this here by extending the plot only to $z = 1.4$ (figure 2.9), and at this point the firms still use both forms of exchange.

7 Conclusion

Why write this chapter, which offers an economic model of the type of delayed reciprocity more commonly studied by anthropologists? If theoretical economics has anything to add to understanding non-monetary exchange, it must be through the insights that arise from the models (formal and otherwise) that it offers. Obviously, it is hardly valuable to convert anthropological ethnographies and descriptions into mathematical models simply for its own sake. Despite the fact we provide little in the way of the 'thick description' that is often advocated by anthropologists such as Geertz (1973), it is our belief that much can be learned from simple models of the type offered here. We believe that the role of such models is twofold.

First, economics typically deduces the behaviour of individuals from a small number of principles, such as profit and utility maximisation subject to the relevant social and institutional constraints. The behavioural assumptions under which our agents operate are one-dimensional (personal gain) and cast individuals as calculating the angles when choosing whether to cooperate with another or not. These principles do not explain the entire motivation of individuals when they make decisions; they are not meant to. Instead, they offer a parsimonious structure to understand how well simple specifications of preferences can explain observed phenomena. In this chapter, our premise is that individuals engage in trade to maximise economic gain, with the threat of dissolution acting to constrain cheating. Using this simple structure, we have offered what we feel are plausible outcomes which are consistent with the evidence cited in this volume so that it may be that a theory based on simple, broadly defined notions of rational choice can generate predictions which mirror the evidence provided by sociologists and anthropologists studying Russia. At a minimum, the models offered here should serve to clarify the way in which many economists think of barter in a repeated setting.

Second, economists use models for predictive purposes, an activity to which anthropologists are less inclined. By positing responses by individuals to various stimuli, we have provided predictions about the response of trade in Russia to its various stages of demonetisation. These predictions could be right or wrong, but at least they can conceivably be tested by looking at the response of trade, prices and networks to the economic environment. First, in section 2 we characterised the decline in trade which has occurred through demonetisation, with the greatest responses occurring in relations where trade was previously sporadic. A natural implication of this is that any subsequent remonetisation is likely to most directly affect those with weakest links to others. Second, we have pointed to the use of commodities as currencies, where we predict 'excess' trading in goods that is not highly valued compared to trade in a monetised economy. This arises as such goods must be used as commodities, and we would predict that the production of such goods may actually fall after a remonetisation process, unlike trade in more desirable goods. A related point is our prediction that the prices obtained for such less desirable goods is likely to be especially bad in sporadic relationships. Third, we have argued that there are distributional consequences from the demonetisation of Russia, and that not everyone may have lost out. In particular, the 'dinosaurs' of Humphrey's analysis chapter 10 in this volume occupy a central position in many networks, which they can use to their benefit. At the very least, we would argue that these firms have probably suffered less from the demonetisation than firms on the periphery. Fourth, we have pointed to changes in optimal network structures, where we believe that there is now increased pressure to find trading partners through which much trade travels rather than use looser, more diverse networks. Furthermore, such problems are most severe for those who do not have strong existing networks. Finally, we have illustrated how liquidity shocks affect prices in non-monotonic ways and also how the existence of barter exchange limits price changes with liquidity shocks. While these predictions obviously await more specific empirical testing, many of the contributions in this volume at least appear to support them.

Appendix: proofs of results

The liquidity value of trade: section 3

First, under what conditions will the agents be willing to supply the (first-best) efficient levels of output? The relevant incentive constraint is that of the agent required to produce $\bar{q} = \alpha$ good while enjoying consumption of $\underline{q} = 1$. He will be willing to provide quantity α iff

$$\frac{\lambda}{r}\left(1 - \frac{\alpha^2}{2}\right) \geq \frac{\alpha^2}{2},$$

or $\lambda/r(2 - \alpha^2) \geq \alpha^2$. This equation is nothing more than the analogue of the incentive constraint in section 2. Note that this condition can be satisfied only if $\alpha < \sqrt{2}$. Assume that this is the case for the moment; we will return to the situation where it is violated below. Then if $\lambda/r < \alpha^2/2 - \alpha^2$, the agent who values his good least will be unwilling to provide the efficient quantity for the other agent. The equilibrium to this problem is that the α-agent (i.e. the agent which has high value of consuming) will 'over-produce' in order to provide the other agent with a *quid pro quo* for him with production of the high-valued α good. Thus production has both a consumption value and a liquidity value. Let q be the production level of the low-value good and let $\bar{q}$ refer to the production of the better good.

Proposition 1 Assume that $\alpha < \sqrt{2}$. If $\lambda/r(2 - \alpha^2) \geq \alpha^2$, the first-best level of trade arises. For all other values of λ/r and α, (i) trade in $\bar{q}$ is increasing in λ/r, (ii) there exists a critical value of λ/r, such that trade in the low-value good, q, is increasing up to that critical level, and is decreasing in λ/r above that critical level. Finally, there exists a range of λ/r such that the low-value good is over-supplied in equilibrium.

Trading partners: section 5

First consider the case where agent i produces good i for all agents when it is demanded. Since there is limited observability of trades, the cost of cheating the demander is that no trade will occur in future with that agent. Let $\bar{q}$ be the quantity traded in this equilibrium. Then the incentive compatibility constraint is that

$$\frac{\lambda}{r} \left(\alpha\bar{q} - c(\bar{q}) \right) \geq c(\bar{q}).$$

The efficient level of $\bar{q}$ is α, so if $\lambda/r \geq 1$, this level of output can be attained. If this is the case, there is never any need to restrict trade to assigned trading partners. However, if $\lambda/r < 1$, the threat of dissolution of the bilateral relationship will not be sufficient to yield efficiency. As a result, straightforward manipulations yield a level of $\bar{q}$ for each good given by

$$\bar{q} = 2\alpha \, \frac{\lambda}{\lambda + r},$$

with total utility for each agent (across all three trades) given by

$$U^{ca} = 6\alpha^2 \left(\frac{\lambda}{\lambda + r} \right)^2.$$

In other words, there is not sufficient 'trust' to induce efficient production.

Suppose now that the societal norm is that an agent is required to get all his required goods from a single agent, where each agent is assigned to a single trading partner. Then as each agent demands three goods, this implies that each person will be provided with only one 'high-quality' good, as distinct from three in the previous case. This provides the obvious cost of requiring concentration of trades.

Consider the set of enforceable trades with this trading norm. Notice that the efficient level of trade here is where agent i produces a quantity α of good i and a quantity 1 of the other two goods demanded by his partner. More generally, let $\bar{q}$ refer to the traded quantity of the 'high-quality' good and let $\underline{q}$ be the traded quantity for the other goods. Then the incentive compatibility constraints for the agent are

$$\frac{\lambda}{r}\left[\alpha\bar{q} + 2\underline{q} - c(\bar{q}) - 2c(\underline{q})\right] \geq c(\bar{q}),$$

if the agent is required to produce the good he has a comparative advantage in, and

$$\frac{\lambda}{r}\left[\alpha\bar{q} + 2\underline{q} - c(\bar{q}) - 2c(\underline{q})\right] \geq c(\underline{q}),$$

to produce the other goods.

First, for high enough $\frac{\lambda}{r}$, the agents will supply the required level of each goods. Straightforward calculations show that this is the case if $\lambda/r \geq \alpha^2/2 + \alpha^2$. This yields utility of $\lambda/r(\alpha^2/2 + 1)$. Next, there is a region of the parameter space where the agent is willing to supply a quantity of $\underline{q} = 1$ but not a quantity of $\bar{q} = \alpha$. This implies that the agent will provide the efficient level of the goods in which he does not hold a comparative advantage but will provide some quantity strictly between 1 and α of the goods he produces best. The quantity level chosen on this good is determined by the $\bar{q}$ at which the incentive-compatibility constraint binds, which is given by

$$\bar{q} = \frac{lv + \sqrt{(lv)^2 + 2l(1+l)}}{1+l},$$

where $l = \lambda/r$. This region occurs for values of λ/r between $\alpha^2/2 + \alpha^2$ and $1/2\alpha + 1$. Finally, for $\lambda/r < 1/2\alpha + 1$, the agent is unwilling to supply output of 1 so all constraints bind, yielding quantities traded of $\bar{q} = \underline{q} = 2\lambda(\alpha + 2)/r(1 + 3l)$.

A simple way of understanding these components of the problem can be seen from figure 2A.1.

Here we have plotted the quantity levels as a function of the parameter values. Note that for $\lambda/r \geq 1$, efficient trade levels occur with comparative advantage. For lower parameter values, trade governed by comparative advantage falls but for some region remains constant with

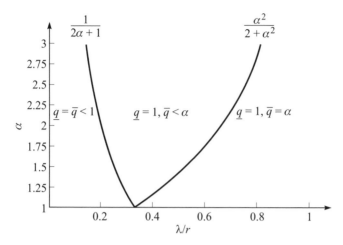

Figure 2A.1 Constrained regions for restricted pay

trading partners, owing to the extra sanctions associated with cheating. Next as λ/r falls further, the agents refuse to produce α but are willing to produce unit output, the optimal level for the goods in which the agent does not hold a comparative advantage. Finally, for $\lambda/r < 1/2\alpha + 1$, the agent is not even willing to trade unit output on any good.

Determining the optimal trading relation then simply becomes a comparison of the utilities on the two regions. Allowing trade with all agents has the advantage that the agents are producing the goods at which they have the greatest ability. However, this has the problem that the costs of deviating are possibly smaller than with a trading partner, as the maximum punishment is exclusion from trade in a single (albeit more desirable) good. This effect can be seen from the fact that without the trading partners, the agent is willing to supply the good at the efficient level if $\lambda/r \geq 1$, while with the greater costs of deviating from a trading partner the agent is willing to supply if $\lambda/r \leq \alpha^2/2 + \alpha^2 < 1$. This simply illustrates the advantage of requiring trades to be concentrated. Proposition 2 identifies the main results regarding trading partners.

Proposition 2 There exists a critical value of α given by a function $\alpha^*(\lambda/r)$ such that for all $\alpha < \alpha^*(\lambda/r)$ restricting trades to a single partner increases welfare, and for all $\alpha > \alpha^*(\lambda/r)$ allocating trades according to comparative advantage maximises welfare. Furthermore, for all $\lambda/r < 1$, $\alpha^*(\lambda/r)$ is strictly greater than 1 and is declining in λ/r.

References

Anderson, D.G. (1999). 'Surrogate Currencies and the 'Wild Market' in Central Siberia', chapter 12 in this volume

Burt, R. (1982). *Toward a Structural Theory of Action: Network Models of Social Structure, Perception, and Action*, New York, Academic Press

Calvert, R. (1989). 'Reciprocity among Self-interested Actors: Uncertainty, Asymmetry, and Distribution', in P. Ordeshook (ed.) *Models of Strategic choice in Politics*, Ann Arbor, Michigan, University of Michigan Press, 269–93

Clarke, S. (1998). 'Household Survival in a Non-monetary Economy', paper presented at the conference on 'Barter in Post-Socialist Societies', Cambridge University Press, December, chapter 7 in this volume

Firth, R. (1939). *Primitive Polynesian Economy*, London, G. Routledge & Sons

Fudenberg, D. and J. Tirole (1991). *Game Theory*, Cambridge, MA, MIT Press

Geertz, C. (1973). *The Interpretation of Cultures*, New York, Basic Books

Harding, T.G. (1967). *Voyagers of the Vitiaz Strait: A study of a New Guinea Trade System*, Seattle, University of Washington Press

Humphrey, C. (1992). 'Fair Dealing, Just Rewards: The Ethics of Barter in North-East Nepal', in C. Humphrey and S. Hugh-Jones (eds.), *Barter, Exchange and Value: An Anthropological Approach*, Cambridge, Cambridge University Press

(1999). 'How is Barter Done? The Social Relations of Barter in Provincial Russia', chapter 10 in this volume

Klein, B. and K. Leffler (1981), 'The Role of Market Forces in Assuring Contractual Performance', *Journal of Political Economy* 89(4), 615–41

Kranton, R. (1996). 'Reciprocal Exchange: A Self-sustaining System', *American Economic Review*, 86(4), 830–51

(1998), 'Expanding Markets, Specialization, and Reciprocal Exchange', University of Maryland, mimeo

Ledeneva, A. (1998). *Russia's Economy of Favours: Blat, Networking and Informal Exchange*, Cambridge, Cambridge University Press

(1999). 'Shadow Barter: Economic Necessity or Economic Crime?', chapter 11 in this volume

Lemon, A. (1998). 'Signs of Mistrust: Gypsies, Barter, Money and Exclusion', paper presented at the conference on 'Barter in Post-Socialist societies', Cambridge University, December

Malinowski, B. (1961). *Argonauts of the Western Pacific*, New York, E.P. Dutton

Mauss, M. (1990) (first published, 1954). *The Gift (Essai sur le Don)*, London, Routledge

Prendergast, C. and L. Stole (1998a). 'Barter, Liquidity, and Market Segmentation', University of Chicago, mimeo

(1998b). 'Monetizing Social Exchange', University of Chicago, mimeo

(1998c). 'Restricting the Means of Exchange Within Organizations', *European Economic Review*, 43, 1007–19

(1999). 'Notes on Liquidity and Price Discrimination', University of Chicago, mimeo

Rubinstein, A. (1982). 'Perfect Equilibrium in a Bargaining Model', *Econometrica*, 50(1), 97–109

Sahlins, M. (1972). *Stone Age Economics*, 1st edn., New York, Aldine de Gruyter

Telser, L. (1980). 'A Theory of Self-enforcing Agreements', *Journal of Business*, 53, 27–44

3 An anthropological view of barter in Russia

CAROLINE HUMPHREY

1 Introduction

If economists have tended to be preoccupied by the problems posed by barter for the efficient allocation of resources, anthropologists are concerned with socio–cultural practices and concepts. The question for them is whether 'barter' constitutes anything specific from this point of view, or is merely a collection of diverse activities in different social contexts. There is a definite overlap between the conventional understandings of the two disciplines, however. The received wisdom in anthropology has been that if barter has any specific characteristic, it is that it is 'purely economic'. Anthropologists have tended to conceive the adjective 'economic' in the narrowest terms (individual choices in relation to scarce resources), thus excluding the whole body of the new institutional economics. For a time, this approach meant that for anthropologists barter was not very interesting. 'Barter' had very few social implications, being merely a matter of sporadic, one-off swaps between people motivated by economic self-interest. Socially, it was peripheral and 'negative' (characterised by haggling and cheating) in comparison to the 'positive' features of long-term reciprocity and even altruism attributed to the kinds of exchange embedded in internal kinship and political relations (Sahlins, 1972). This view of barter has recently come under scrutiny, as I describe later. In brief, studies of a range of non-industrial societies have shown that fundamental social relations and important political and cultural values are revealed in activities describable as 'barter'. But do these observations apply only to small-scale, non-industrial societies? Is barter only 'social' when it is archaic?

This book, on barter in contemporary Russia, a vast, complex and industrial economy, enables us for the first time to try to answer these questions – 'for the first time' because never before have we been able to observe directly an entire modern economy that to a large extent operates

71

through barter. This chapter argues that barter in post-communist Russia creates specific social relations and in general is just as influenced by its political–cultural context as barter in 'traditional' kinds of society. This can be seen through looking at two features of barter revealed by the Russian case. The first is that barter is not limited to transient, bilateral swaps, but often consists of complex *debt chains* over long distances and sometimes lasting over years. While susceptible to dynamic changes in any given case, these chains can be seen to present certain types, or shapes, which traders constantly re-constitute from the people they know ('partners') and, as I shall show, barter comes to create relations that are social as well as economic. Secondly, barter cannot be fully understood simply as a matter of particular deals (whether between individuals or between firms), because there are larger institutional, societal and political forces which have interests in keeping the *system* of barter going in a situation where the alternative is re-monetisation of the economy.

The contemporary Russian political economy is dominated by the 'oligarchs' of privatisation and governmental fiefdoms, but it also relies on personalised, informal networks formed in Soviet times that are hidden from public view and yet spread out widely in the rest of the economy. Thus, while it need not be postulated that the immediate aims of transactors in Russian barter chains have anything other than a practical, economic purpose, it cannot be said that they operate on a blank or level playing-field. The hidden social resources and constraints do not determine what eventuates, however. The actual deals, the volatile, yet constantly reiterated 'surfaces' of barter as it takes place, are creating new socio–economic relations with their own vocabulary and customary 'ways of acting'. The task is to understand how these emergent relations in turn skew transaction decisions, despite the fact that the participants may see their activities as simply rational choices in the given circumstances. It will be suggested here that barter in Russia is producing distinct kinds of social relations that contrast with the more trusting relations associated with barter in traditional societies. Understanding what these Russian relations consist in may provide some clue as to how the barter economy may develop in the future, even if the economy is largely re-monetised.

2 Anthropology and barter

Anthropologists had theorised a contrast, even an opposition (Gregory, 1982), between 'gift' and 'commodity' exchange, in which barter was seen as a simple form of the latter. Gift was concerned with social reciprocity

(Mauss, 1954 [1925]) – that is, with the strengthening and increase of social relationships – and in this type of exchange the transfer of goods was more a symbolic token of a relationship than an end in itself. This could be seen particularly clearly when what people exchanged was 'the same' goods – say, pigs given in return for pigs. 'Gift exchange' occurred in societies dominated, even entirely mapped out, by kinship relations. In Lévi-Strauss (1969 [1949]) the Maussian theory of the gift was reformulated to propose a grand explanation of systems of marriage in Asia, ranging from elaborate cycles of transfers of women and goods linking many social groups ('generalised exchange') to narrow, bilateral exchanges of women which were held to result from the breakdown of the long cycles ('restricted exchange').

Barter, on the other hand, was held to have no such social rationale. It was defined by the interest of transactors in the goods themselves and therefore always involved the exchange of different items. The assumption was that bartered goods were consumed rather than traded on, and therefore the transaction implied no further links and indeed might never be repeated. In the influential writings of Sahlins (1972) barter was discussed separately from trade and trade networks, and thus was seen as a simple bilateral type of transaction. 'Stone-age' trade, on the other hand, was understood to be motivated by 'social' considerations, evidenced by the artificial construction of needs for the goods of other peoples,[1] relative lack of interest in the costs of production, set exchange ratios, long-term partnerships, and so forth. Sahlins' curious disjunction between trade and the ignoble activity of barter was perhaps an artefact of the English language and the historical connotations of the term 'barter' going back to Adam Smith (1776, 1, p. 17).

New studies of barter in a range of non-industrial societies in the 1980s undercut this notion of radical contrasts in principle between barter and trade and gift (Humphrey and Hugh-Jones, 1992). It was shown that barter in real (especially agricultural) contexts is first likely to be delayed (i.e. to operate on a credit basis) and second to be repeated with the same partners. Barter therefore demands a high degree of trust, and therefore tends to be conducted with kin or within other existing reliable relations. It was further discovered – for example, in highland Nepal in the late 1970s – that barter may create trust (Humphrey, 1985). Transactors would seek to obtain new goods by extending links outwards, establishing partnerships with hitherto unknown people and sacralising them as

---

[1] It was found that people who could perfectly well make some object did not do so but preferred to trade for it with another group, which suggested that trade was really a means of making a relationship with the other group (see Gell 1992, p. 148).

ritual friends (*mith*) in order to create a lasting and reliable relationship. This in its turn had subsequent social implications, since the children of *mith* partners were forbidden to marry, as if the two had become kin.[2]

More generally, it became clear that relatively stable systems of barter between functionally differentiated groups have operated over long time periods – for example, in the Andes, Himalayas or inland Amazonia. The rates of exchange and even the goods might change, but the relationships, at the level of exchanging partners, villages or ethnic groups, remained more or less constant. Barter thus served to link any given group with a number of others through series of dyadic exchanges. In a radically innovative paper Gell (1992, pp. 142–3) argued that these exchanges, rather than 'ceremonial gift', could be socially foundational. Opposing Lévi-Strauss who saw marriage exchange as the primordial transactional form from which all others might be conceived as deriving 'after the Fall' as it were, Gell argued that the really primordial transactional modes are swapping (barter) and sharing (provisioning motivated by moral obligations). In Melanesia, Gell wrote, ceremonial exchange is a 'later' hybrid of these two, derived in particular from the ideational template and the material resources of barter trade. Gell is suggesting (1992, p. 146) that it is the *social context*, not the bargaining character of the relationship that differentiates ceremonial exchange from barter trade.

As for inter-group trade itself, ethnography from several regions suggests that it is the social content of exchange partnerships that limits their spread - and that this social colouring is an artefact of economic rationality in the given context. In highland Nepal, not only were certain potential transactors excluded from trading partnerships (being seen as competitors, producers of like goods), but the necessary trust could not be easily created at a distance without modern means of communication. Furthermore, the setting up a ritual friendship at the margin of one's operations was a costly business. In an earlier paper on Nepal (Humphrey 1985), I deduced from this that barter trade on credit implies pockets of exchange, but a general lack of flexibility, in the economy as a whole – i.e. economic non-integration or disintegration. The same general observation about barter has been made for contemporary Russia by Makarov and Kleiner (1996, p. 22).

---

[2] In Highland Nepal, certain ethnic groups use barter deliberately, rather than money. In part this is because they wish to maintain a distance from the Nepali state and its taxation and in part to preserve trade (necessarily by barter) with kin and long-term partners living in Tibet. If they had been trading primarily with a money medium the need for long-term partners (*mith*) would be less, since the function of the latter is to produce a regular solution to the 'coincidence of wants' problem, which is far greater with barter.

The spread of the barter mode of transaction at the expense of the money one leads in the end to the disintegration of the economy into weakly interacting chains that are unstable in themselves. In the absence or weakness of a unifying link between the various divisions of the economy like money, the economy loses elasticity and productive resources lose their mobility.

A new insight into the social relations that may prevail in barter came with studies of its political (broadly understood) context, and this also has direct relevance for the situation in Russia. Although barter in principle implies that the transactors are equivalent *economic* agents who balance their desires in the deal, the actors can be very unequal in the wider political–economic context (Hugh-Jones 1992).[3] In both contemporary Russia and most non-industrial societies there are no external sanctions for reliable behaviour on the part of the powerful agents. In such a situation, I suggest, relations of dominance/dependence may take the place of trust in ensuring that payments are made.[4] As Strathern (1992, pp. 175, 188) points out, in highland New Guinea both 'the gift' and barter involve a prior coercion and the ability of one side to extract items from the other. The general message of both Gell and Strathern is that barter and ceremonial gift exchange in non-industrial societies may be more like one another than had previously been imagined, and they agree that it is not a matter of harmonious reciprocity in either case. But Strathern argues against Gell's idea that transactors are totting up amounts quantitatively. Rather, exchange, even barter she implies, involves comparing the *powers* of either side, exteriorising one's internal capacities in the form of material objects:

There are recognised strategies for keeping back items to produce at the right moment, for claiming to have wiped oneself clean, for what it will take to persuade someone - or get away with extortion ... Uncertainty is reinforced at every stage. Far from exchange relations providing some secure integrative framework, they problematise interactions by challenging persons to decompose themselves, to make internal capacities external (Strathern 1992, p. 188).

This being said, it does appear that there are historical and regional differences in the degree of rancour, as opposed to concord, manifest in exchange relations. In some cases, such as highland Nepal in the 1970s,

---

[3] In gift exchange and barter, no social equality is implied in the agreement to transact, only the formal equivalence of each partner as an agent about to act (Strathern, 1992, p. 188).
[4] Trust could coexist with inequalities of power in certain circumstances. The weaker partner might trust the stronger to act correctly in an open market situation – e.g. an individual would trust a bank not to fiddle her account statement if she knew that the bank would lose customers by acting dishonestly. This condition does not however, apply, in Russia at the present time.

barter can be seen as a system or equilibrium characterised by the actors themselves in a positive light (new partners are brought in as 'friends' to be welcomed and treated as quasi-kin), but in others regions, such as lowland New Guinea, barter takes place in a constantly reproduced situation, or equilibrum, of largely negative relations, uncertainty and coercion. The signs are reversed, as it were.[5]

What we can perhaps deduce from this is that barter promotes the creation of carefully husbanded mutual trust when the transactors are independent people (or groups) with more or less the same clout; but when the social context is one of inequality and aggression, coercion dominates over trust; coerced exchange does not remedy this situation but exacerbates it. This distinction between the prevalence of coercion and trust is far more relevant to the Russian case than the earlier contrast between 'commodity' and 'ceremonial gift' exchange. All the evidence suggests that barter in Russia takes place amid increasing inequality and in an atmosphere of widespread social anomie and suspicion of unknown people. Nevertheless, it is important that in practice, although coercion or trust may generally prevail in a given region, any actual economy in all its diversity is likely to combine both strategies. Barter in Russia seems to produce a particular, limited kind of social integration, limited both in the sense that barter chains are discrete and in the fact that relations between partners do not escape the fraught environment around them.

3 Some anthropological observations on barter in Russia

During 1992–99 there was a more or less constant increase in barter, rising to over 50 per cent of declared industrial sales in July 1998.[6] In some areas of the country, taking into account all sectors, including agriculture, small business and entrepreneurial trade, barter was between 80 per cent and 90 per cent of all transactions in summer 1998.[7] The

---

[5] Strathern in fact means to distinguish between two kinds of coercion. First, there is the formal fact of having to elicit wealth from someone in 'gift exchange', where the initial solicitory gift carries an obligation to make a major return gift. In this formal sense, 'gift exchange' is always extractive. Second, there is the separate matter of whether relations between partners are hostile or not, prevaricate, cheat, and so on. In the latter case, the coercion is extra pressure laid on by a dominating partner in antagonistic circumstances. (Marilyn Strathern, personal communication.)

[6] *Russian Economic Barometer*, based on a survey of 500 industrial firms, quoted in Roaf (1999). The volume of industrial barter went down slightly from July 1998 to January 1999.

[7] According to businessmen from a wide variety of firms in the Buriat Republic, summer 1998.

prevalence of barter is increased by the fact that some local governments take payments in products (though tax in kind was made illegal according to Federal law in 1998) as do major energy, gas, and transport companies.[8] Vast disparities in scale are encompassed by the term 'barter', from large transactions between the central government, provincial governments and the army,[9] to tiny swaps between householders. Furthermore, the situation is disparate in the various regions and volatile. So overall explanations are not easy. In this chapter I confine my discussion to two topics: (1) the social character of the barter chains and (2) the socio–political factors that help reproduce them and influence the way they work.

Widespread as it may be, barter in Russia does not consist of an undifferentiated network of transactions, but of several types with their own characteristics. Besides the simple one-off swap, there are three types of more complex arrangement designed to get over various practical problems brought about by barter (notably the non-coincidence of wants).[10] (1) _Lineal barter chains_ consists of a series of discrete swaps, where the chain aspect consists of the strategy whereby a given product transfers through intermediaries to the consumer. The motivating question here is something of the kind, 'How do I as a remote farmer get hold of batteries?' (2) _Star-shaped chains_ have a trader at the centre who makes a series of deals between himself and a number of other firms in order to convert the product he starts with into the good he wants (usually money). The question for the trader has the form, 'I've got railway sleepers, how do I turn them into money?' (3) _Circular chains_ occur when a given transactor creates a debt with another (by handing over some item or service) and makes sure the debt is handed on from firm to firm until it returns to him in the form of the good he wants. The question here might

---

[8] In April 1999 only 15 per cent of payments to Unified Energy Systems (EES) in Russsia were made in money, though this increased to 28 per cent in June. This information was provided in the context of a promise by the Russian government to the World Bank that it would eliminate barter by 2001 (_RFL Newsline_ 26 July 1999).

[9] In September 1998 it was reported that the central government was devising a system in which _oblasts_ and republics with developed agricultural sectors would supply food to army units stationed on their territory in order to pay off debts owed by the regional administrations to the central government (_Nezavisimaya Gazeta_, 11 September 1998).

[10] The three types are a simplification of complex relations in respect of timing, onwards marketing, part-payment in money, the involvement of foreign currencies and banks, and so forth (see Kobushko and Ponomarev, 1989). I do not discuss here international counter-trade, within which the term 'barter' is used technically only for the simple form of immediate, bilateral goods-for-goods exchange. However, within Russia _barter_ is used in ordinary language for the whole range of transactions without money or mainly without money.

be, 'If the brick-factory will take my coats, who will take his bricks [repeated for further deals in the cycle] until I end up with a computer?' (See also chapter 10, where (1), (2) and (3) are illustrated.)

It is the first of these types, the lineal chain, that is most similar to barter trade in a non-industrial context like highland Nepal, for in this case the wants of each transactor are satisfied at each deal. (The other two types of chain found in Russia are not paralleled in the ethnographic literature, as far as I know.) The lineal chain is made up of a number of bilateral deals. Now in any circumstances it is in the interest of the first seller and particularly the final buyer to shorten the length of such chains, since this is how they avoid losing value to middlemen. In both Nepal and rural Russia, the buyers try to solve this problem by making personal journeys to acquire goods. But if we take a closer look at even such a simple solution, we immediately face the complexities of given socio–economic and cultural contexts. In Nepal, people are prepared to walk for days carrying heavy baskets slung from their foreheads to reach an exchange partner. In fact, these treks are regarded as pleasurable affairs, often taken in company at a leisured pace, with stops at friends en route, and anticipating a known destination with an enjoyable battle of wits at the end. In Russia it is quite different: the distances are too great for walking and the goods required often too bulky, people are aggravated that bus fares have shot up and they will not (or cannot) pay them. A lift must be scrounged, but even this favour must be repaid. In the end, transactors like farmers often resign themselves to staying at home,[11] paying over the odds in meat or corn to middlemen, with a great cloud of resentment at the unfairness hanging over the deal. At the other end of these chains, factories often do not sell directly to retail outlets but have recourse to middlemen because they have no knowledge or facilities for reaching customers. They too are irritated. 'Are we expected to produce goods *and sell them too*? How are we to do that?' they exclaim.[12] In other words, the particular character of bilateral deals is conditioned by the context of present Russia, and I now briefly mention some salient features of this.

First, the *social bases for extensive trust* are far weaker in Russia than in 'traditional' societies. Ramifying kin links, tight-knit village or ethnic communities, institutions of 'ritual friendship', etc. may be present in some areas but they are not general. Second, no one forgets about money in Russia just because it is no longer available for widespread

---

[11] As a result, bus services are cancelled and/or the fares go up even more.

[12] This kind of remark was made by a variety of producers, from factory managers in Moscow *oblast* to farmers in Buriatiia (Summer 1998).

use. Goods are always *evaluated at money prices* before they are exchanged and professional traders would always prefer to have money than any other good.[13] Third, the *range of goods both produced and desired* is incomparably greater, so barter has to 'cope' with everything from Chinese thermos flasks to industrial cellulose. Fourth, the Russian economy is more insecure and volatile. The accustomed Soviet-era flows of goods according to centrally derived plans have evaporated. Massive inflation, unprecedented imports, breakdowns of transport, lack of legally sanctioned security and sudden impoverishment all discourage investment and promote the pursuit of *immediate gains*; and this, in a society accustomed to future-oriented values (the five-year plans) creates an atmosphere of anger and incomprehension. So barter is conducted amid prevailing mistrust. Though possibly less so than monetary exchange,[14] it nevertheless involves perceiving other people's lack of resources, ignorance or inefficiency in order to make a profit, and it evokes constant fears of default or cheating or theft.

The social content of barter relationships can be seen as bulwarks constructed against these very fears. In this respect, despite the colossal difference in the scope of insecurity, Russian barter has something in common with the precarious trade between warring tribes described by anthropologists for old Melanesia.[15] Let us again take the case of lineal chains, for here in both Russia and Melanesia the 'trade partnership' is the key relationship. (I am excluding at this point ad hoc, one-off deals, which are common in Russia, or the barter markets known in the New Guinea context; we are now discussing repeated deals for goods in constant demand.) As Gell observes (1992, p. 159), in the trade partnership each side guarantees, as far as possible, the safety of the other in their mutual trading activities, and this is the necessary condition for the ongoing existence of commodity exchange. He continues:

Traders do not meet to exchange compliments, but to exchange commodities; the voluntaristic amoralism of a partnership 'against all the world' can only be sustained through the transactional schema of object-exchange, because, lacking 'personal' referents, the relationship can only be established with reference to

---

[13] This is so despite massive inflation during the 1990s, showing that people prefer the freedom of choice given by money, despite its insecure value (see the discussion in Makarov and Kleiner, 1996).

[14] It might be argued that monetary transactions have more potential for ruthlessness in the abstract than barter, since in the former case anything may be reduced to a price, while in the latter each side has to pay at least some attention to what the other partner really (substantially) wants.

[15] Unlike in Nepal, it seems that Melanesian inter-group trade does not involve affines (kin by marriage) or ritual friends.

things, which are all that the parties to it have in common. In exchange, objects are focalised, quantified, valued, and so on; and there is recognition of debt, credit and reciprocity. It is the transaction of these objects, now commodities, that sustains the partnership.

This is apt for the Russian case, even though barter here is a relatively new phenomenon for individuals:[16] traders talk of the difficulty of finding new partners, how they keep the same partners for years on end and explain how they take care of the safety of visiting partners. Transactors are named colloquially by the goods they produce and trade, the *neftaniki* (oil), *lesoviki* (wood products), *gazoviki* (gas), *energetiki* (electricity), *zheleznodorozhniki* (railway tariffs) and so forth.

Gell goes on to say about Melanesian trade (1992, p. 159):

> Because the partnership-relation is valued as an end in itself, the objects involved carry a symbolic charge stemming from this source: they are over-valued because their presence evokes a valued relationship and a privileged kind of social interaction. Where there could be enmity and danger, lo! there is this shell, the axe.

In Russia too, the goods derived from such partnerships are over-valued, but with a crucial difference from Melanesia. The over-valuation is a grudging and quantitative matter. 'I have to pay about 2 per cent for the acquaintanceship (*za znakomstva*)', one businessman put it.[17] We are led to conclude that the barter partnership in Russia is not so much valued as an end in itself, but as a necessary relational expedient for conducting business. Furthermore, all partnerships involve a sort of inevitable irritation most of the time. This is because, as compared with the Melanesian economy, the proportion and variety of goods traded is vastly greater and it is unlikely that your partner can supply precisely what you need. Each side wants to consume, mainly because trading onwards involves trouble and expense. Barter partnerships thus exist as consumption-oriented, yet suspended in an atmosphere of frustration, because everyone is conscious that if only they had money (especially dollars) they could defer the infinity of their desires without trouble. The important point, however, is that the instrumental character of the trade partnership, together with the 'voluntary amoralism' noted by Gell, does not make it any less 'social'. On the contrary, such partnerships are an increasingly prominent part of the social landscape.

[16] This is reflected in the foreign vocabulary used, notably the English terms *barter* and *partner*.

[17] In other words, he gives around 2 per cent extra value for goods exchanged with his regular partners as compared with 'market' prices. Market prices are discovered at any particular moment from phoning wholesale depots, scanning newspaper lists of prices, and so forth.

It is interesting therefore to think about these highly equivocal trade partnerships in relation to the social constitution of the wider economy, including workplace relations and household economies. In the workplace there is still the idea of the *kollektiv*, a matey egalitarianism just about surviving from the Soviet era, which largely precludes taking advantage of co-workers. Household economies are based firmly on kinship, and they imply sharing or the moral obligation to provision others in kin relations to oneself (see Gell, 1992, p. 152). It is significant that both the work *kollektiv* and the family can be used to form the membership of a trading firm, but they do not provide a basis for barter partnerships, at least among Russians. Indeed, trading and its hazards is said to be antithetical to the moral obligations of kinship.[18]

There are also gender implications of the culturally specific ideas about trade in Russia. Probably different ethnic groups vary in this regard (we still do not know enough about this), but from what I could observe among Russians and Buriats, barter trade is overwhelmingly done by men and is seen as 'male' in its requirements for calculation, aggression, travelling and trickery. The classic exchange partnership – let us say the trader who swaps Russian timber for Chinese foodstuffs, or the farm manager who deals his meat for spare parts – is one between men, and the middlemen dealers who service the large industrial firms are known even in the economics literature as 'the boys' (*malchiki*) (Makarov and Kleiner, 1996). In part this relates to the unwieldy practical nature of barter – all those goods must be transported, stored, or guarded – and the existing male domination of the professions of truck-driver, security guard, rail manager, and so forth. But more ideationally, the barter partnership is an opportunity for demonstrating individual bravery and hardness in what everyone assumes is the intrinsically jungle-like 'market'. The post-Soviet 'feminisation' of the gender notions of women, by contrast, encourages women to retreat to the domestic economy, and when they do engage in barter this is often seen as something forced on them by dire poverty and as an aspect of provisioning. It is true that barter, because it can be done in private, arouses less shame for women than public selling at a market-place (Hohnen, 1997). Nevertheless it does appear that the ideological contrast between 'amoral' trading and 'moral' provisioning is being mapped with reference to gender stereotypes, and the effect of this in turn is to influence the character of barter. For here social relations – wary 'male' interplay through the medium of objects – are coming into

---

[18] This has two aspects. On the one hand, people say they cannot afford, as it were, to risk valued kin relations in the cutthroat world of business. On the other, kin may make implicit demands (to be provisioned) that are incompatible with the *quid pro quo* of the trade partnership (see discussion in Humphrey, 1999).

being that are no longer mediated by the morality of social reproduction, whether of the workforce *kollektiv* or of the domestic household.

Circular chains, being based on the transfer of debt, might seem to call into being at least the positive value of trust. One might even imagine an extravagant analogy between circular barter among firms and the Lévi-Straussian 'generalised exchange' whereby women ('the supreme value') pass onwards between clans. The trust in either case would be a product of a system whereby any given actor must render payment to one group, while receiving from quite another group. The analogy, unfortunately, is largely false, although it is instructive. In 'generalised exchange' the system rests on society-wide acceptance of a marriage rule (matrilateral cross-cousin marriage) that sends one's own sisters outwards on one side and pulls in brides on the other. Such a socially acknowledged rule does not exist in circular barter. Circular barter chains come into being not as a result of an unfocused 'general' social agreement, but at the behest of a particular firm that tries by this means to exchange some object it want to dispose of for something else that it desires. As a result, the sanction for keeping the chain going is something that must be imposed by this firm rather than a commonly acknowledged rule.

In the abstract one might imagine that all firms' desire to be seen as reliable would ensure repayments (a situation in which an economic model of self-enforcing norms would be a possibility).[19] But the ethnography is clear: large firms are frequently kept going through political patronage even when they are bankrupt and do not pay up, and small firms operate in a situation of ignorance about one another's viability. If being seen to be reliable is a sanction, it is not a very strong one. In fact, default is common and chains break down.

Now it is true – and this is what is instructive – that Lévi-Strauss points out that 'generalised exchange' is also inherently unstable: women are always bunching up in some part of the cycle, lacking in other parts, inequalities are generated, and this leads to breakdown of the circular aspect of the system. Matters may even degenerate (in other words, a social evolution may take place, though Lévi-Strauss does not quite describe how) to disintegration of the system and its replacement by endogamy (marriage inside one's own group, as in India) or the relatively fail-safe custom of swapping wives (bilateral, restricted exchange). Now analogous problems exist for the barter cycle: a firm may hoard, rather than pay the debt by passing on goods, or the holder of a particularly desirable object may swap it advantageously outside the circle instead of

---

[19] See discussion in Dasgupta (1997) on the use of game theory in economic models, proving that no external agency is required to sustain cooperation within groups.

passing it on to the next in line at the arranged price. It is precisely these problems, in the Russian context, that require us to think again about what 'trust' might mean.

The bottom line of trust from an economic point of view reduces to being sure that the said goods exist, that they are in the declared quantity and quality and that payment of them will be made when promised. This kind of trust has no external moral referent outside the deal itself and the belief generated by partners in the truth of one another's statements. Written contracts in Russia often bear only passing resemblance to the actual agreement (being designed for tax office eyes). Perhaps one could almost see them as expressive documents, demonstrations of law-abidingness; and this would be more of a political statement than anything else, for contracts are hardly ever enforced by law. 'Trust', it is clear, rests somewhere else. What actually happens is that companies are structured so that a particular manager in the initiating firm is given charge of his own chain, and then he travels along it, visiting and persuading his counterparts, taking gifts, arranging dinners, inviting the secretary out for an evening, and so forth. The chain requires constant servicing. 'Trust' here reduces to something that is induced by blandishments and it has a highly oral, 'personalised' (yet at the same time, impersonal and object-focused) character.

When such chains threaten to break down, the task of ensuring payment shifts up from managers to directors, who call upon friends, using 'trust' in the common sense of the word. This can be based on a shared sense of social standing and common difficulties. As one Vice-Director of a large firm in Moscow *oblast* (region) said:

I have personal relations only with other directors. We in Russia have the deeply collective (*sugubo kollektivnaya*) idea of mutual gain (*vzaimovyruchka*). If I turn to a Vice-Director in another firm, he'll help me just because I am also a Vice-Director. For example, I'll ring Vice-Director Shokarev, who helps us with the technical supplies for transmission-belt production, and say, 'I have a difficulty, I can't pay right now, do me a prepayment, please help me, give me a prepayment for 5 or 10 thousand items and I'll promise to pay for them by the end of the month.' And because I address him as Vice-Director and I am also a Vice-Director, and he also has difficulties in his life, he agrees and I can write him a letter saying I have taken the 10,000 parts. If we did not have these personal relations, he would not have done that.

The relationships within a barter circle are unlikely to be even – that is, to be similar between each of the companies. This is because the firms differ in size and clout and in their need to make these particular arrangements at all. In barter, some firms will always experience a given agreement as what they call 'forced' – i.e. to sell their products they must accept goods they do not want but have to trade on in order to acquire what they need (see Humphrey, chapter 10 in this volume).[20] Although circular chains in principle could avoid this problem, in practice, because the volume of the trade is determined by the debt of the initiating company, firms down the line may have to accept either more or less goods than they need and then to have to 'waste time' making extra deals outside the chain to dispose of the extra goods or acquire the ones lacking.

We can see the elements of coercion even in the notion of 'forced' barter, and it becomes overt when, as often happens, the initiating 'firm' in a circular chain is the local government. An example of this kind of chain is given in Ledeneva and Seabright's chapter 4 (see box 4.3, p. 102), where the Kurgan provincial government, acquiring buses, is part of a chain taking in the Urengoi *Gaszprom* deposit, the Chelyabinsk metal complex and the Nizhnii Novgorod automobile plant, these being located hundreds of kilometres apart and in different administrative regions. It is not that the local government is always in a dominating position in such deals, more that the involvement of government raises the stakes and politicises the circle. Roaf (1999) points out that administrations themselves may be subjected to 'forced' barter by powerful companies that are unable to meet their tax obligations in money, or have made a deal with sympathetic or corrupt officials. The skewing, or non-commercial enforcement, of deals down the chains organised by governments occurs because certain companies are supported for political reasons. Often this is because they are large employers, but it can occur because their directors are 'friends' of the politicians in power. These are the hidden links, often going back to Soviet times, that I referred to earlier (relationships traceable back to supply links under the plan, or to service in the army together, or attendance at the same educational establishment). The effect of all this is that hierarchies develop in established barter chains (as in Lévi-Straussian 'generalised exchange'), allowing dominant enterprises to squeeze weaker ones through threat of exclusion from the chain (Roaf, 1999).

To sum up, unlike the seasonal rhythms and accustomed sociality of barter in Nepal, barter in Russia is an unstable construct. It is not on the whole based on pre-existing social relationships (even if actors sometimes have recourse to them), and probably that would have been an impossibility given the complex, industrialised nature of the economy. Rather, barter in Russia creates its own relations, notably the 'exchange

---

[20] Roaf (1999) quotes a Russian source reporting an average share of forced barter of 40 per cent of the total volume of barter deals, with the highest proportion occurring in the firms most heavily exposed to barter.

partnership', a relation which wavers between 'trust' (a concocted kind of trust) and more or less open coercion. In the final part of this chapter I look at the socio–political configurations that support the continued existence of barter, and examine how the nature of barter relations contributes to this continuation.

4 The social bases of the barter economy: the case of factory directors

Makarov and Kleiner argue (1996, p. 26) that it is not only the relative lack of circulating money that keeps barter alive in Russia, but barter's 'solid social base'. This consists of three social groups whose interconnected ongoing existence depends on the continuation of barter and who therefore are actively interested in its maintenance. The first is the *middlemen*, 'the boys' whose way of life rests on exploiting the sales problems of manufacturers and the purchasing problems of workers who are not paid in money. The second is the *directors of large failing production enterprises* who have recourse to bartering their goods at low prices rather than going bankrupt. The third is the *financiers*, the large holders of money, who make profits not only by extracting money from businesses that pay their workers in kind, but also from financing the first group, the entrepreneurs.

Makarov and Kleiner show that the decisions taken in these groups are, if one can put it this way, 'excessively economic' (in the caricature of economics of anthropological jargon). In a brief chapter it is impossible to examine this in any detail, but let us take for example, the directors of factories who do not pay their workers in money. This often happens not because they cannot pay, but because *they do not want to* (Makarov and Kleiner, 1996, pp. 27–8). Now in Russia, no less than in any other industrial country, the expectation is that if you work in a factory you are paid in money. These directors are undoubtably breaking a social norm, and the simple explanations – that the law allows this,[21] that trade unions are weak, or that the directors are greedy – cannot be the whole story. Greed, after all in such situations, is not an ungovernable instinct but a way of conducting a social relation. As Dasgupta points out (1998, p. 12):

You can entertain personal aspirations and have needs without being greedy or self-centred. It is entirely possible for someone to be concerned with their own self, while at the same time to abide by norms of behaviour pertaining to

[21] As of mid-1998, the law did not require that the payment of wages would be the first claim on the accounts of an enterprise, MBT home page < http://www/trud.org.index7-10.htm > .

production and exchange, even when the risks of violating the norms are negligible; ... Internalised social norms of behaviour work by making people feel good about abiding by them.

Evidently, the 'greed' of the Russian directors goes beyond such personal aspirations and it is relational because it exists to the direct detriment of the interests of workers. The outrage felt by workers can be seen from the extreme measures they are prepared to take in protest (hunger strikes, etc., see the ITAR–TASS report on 15 September 1998 that workers at a power station in Vladivostok had taken their managers hostage until back wages were paid in full). Makarov and Kleiner (1996, p. 28) explain what is happening by the breakdown of vertical ties within the enterprise and the corresponding solidification of horizontal ties between managers at similar levels of different firms. In effect, the directors have removed themselves from the *kollektiv*:

> The forces of attraction of directors amongst themselves are much stronger than those between directors and workers in the same enterprise. The 'artel' or paternalistic form of industrial production formed over decades is now giving way to a hidden or open opposition between directors and workers.

Makarov and Kleiner point out that the social hierarchy so generated is one of administration or control (*upravleniye*), in which the horizontal links are between directors or managers of firms that make goods in adjacent stages of the production process. These are precisely the people involved in barter partnerships.

There must be many reasons why the vertical relations within the *kollektiv* are beginning to break down (it should be emphasised that this is a tendency rather than universal). The matter is complex and requires further research, but one factor must be the directors' perception that the expectations of workers belong to a previous era and therefore can be disregarded: for example, workers' assumptions that they belong to the enterprise and should not be sacked, their expectation of costly social services from the firm, their lackadaisical working practices – in short, the general feeling among directors, whether justified or not, that workers are a weight to be borne.[22] I argue here, however, that the character and practices of barter partnerships also serve to separate directors from workers. It is the directors who do barter on behalf of the firm, and for this they require access to wide information and an externalised perspective that usually only they have. This, as Makarov and Kleiner point out (1996, p. 29), raises their status in the company and gives them the

---

[22] Directors often aspire (or claim they do) to the notion of an efficient market economy, governed by the rule of law, and unencumbered by socialist 'survivals'.

illusion that they are irreplaceable.[23] Also, because barter, to a far greater degree than money transactions, is conducted by face-to face deals on the base of oral promises, it works through exchange partnerships that do in fact make the directors non-substitutable by other people.

The directors hold in their hands the flows of goods, and these take on a life of their own (this happens because incoming goods often have to be traded on – such as the institute 'producing' engineers that turned in effect into a trading firm bartering clothes and other goods with China, see chapter 10 in this volume). The wealth generation through barter may be greater than that through production, and in the case of firms that reduce rather than add value by their production (see chapter 6 in this volume), barter may be the *only* generator of wealth. This wealth has quite different, even antithetical symbolic connotations from that generated by the 'honest toil' of rugged home production: here we are concerned with the results of daring deals. This way of thinking may expand downwards into internal relations, for the wages of the workers are transformed into elements of the barter calculus when paid in goods; rather than pay out money to employees you barter in food, clothes, etc. to pay them and thereby make a profit for the firm. Moreover, other economic strategies, such as investment, are discouraged by Russian conditions. The precarious income of many companies, often reduced to trying to sell incoming barter goods before being required to pay back, renders investment out of the question for them. Thus, the internalised norms of the directors may be given an honourable appearance ('surviving in the "wild market",' which also has symbolic connotations of masculine heroism) while constantly operating to the detriment of the employees. For all these reasons directors' interests separate out from those of their employees. From the social point of view, the important point to repeat is that a kind of relationship has come into being, the trade partnership, that is not only disjunct from the reproduction of household economies, as described earlier, but also from the reproduction of the *kollektiv*. The influence of such a type of relation spreads: workers too, being paid in products, have recourse to barter in their own economic surroundings.[24]

---

[23] Soviet enterprises always were hierarchical and in part the current social separation of directors may be due to the fact that the Soviet *nomenklatura* (register of accredited 'bosses' in production and administration) has maintained its place in many state and former state enterprises. Makaroff and Kleiner are, however, making the point that barter requires additional and more active networking by directors than under the previous system, when goods were distributed by order from state planning departments.

[24] Sometimes employees sell by the side of roads, or swap with workers in other factories, but the most usual method is to set up a relation with a trader who will sell the 'wages' for money at a market.

In sum, the label of 'greed' would by no means do justice to the complexity of the directors' thinking. The sense that they are living in a peculiar historical period, because they know from their own experience that the Soviet social system had a temporal existence, enables Russian economic actors to stand back from their practices even as they live them out: 'uncivilised' barter for them is often contrasted with the idealised future of an economy governed by the rule of law. Yet the logic of barter in the Russian context is to promote immediate consumption, whether of money or anything else.[25]

5 Conclusion

Anthropologists would not deny the importance of economic studies of barter showing how it functions to distribute products through an economy, or demonstrating, by comparison with money transactions, its disutilities. They would bring to the fore, however, something different: how barter in given socio–historical contexts creates certain social relationships, and anthropologists would try to understand the cultural and symbolic aspects of these in relation to other forms of social organisation. I have argued here that barter in Russia creates 'exchange partnerships' which, sliding between trust and coercion, engender a 'male' quasi-solidarity that has symbolic values of bravery and self-sufficiency in what is assumed to be the wild, harsh arena of 'capitalism'.

But for barter, there would surely be a wide overlap between anthropological analysis and that of micro institutional economics, for the types of relationships emerging in barter would be part of an economic analysis of the emergent features of communities and societies derived from 'millions of decisions made by individual human beings' (Dasgupta, 1998, p. 4) and such relationships might be seen as 'social capital' in the kind of economics that uses that idea. The general difference between the two disciplines is that anthropologists usually do not see individual decisions as giving rise to institutions, but rather interpret the latter as having their own 'social' existence, with their own rules, resources, constraints, and sanctions, etc. operating through common understandings. The case of barter in contemporary Russia, however, which has come into being in its present form only in the last few years, calls such anthropological assumptions into question, for barter here is 'emergent' and is not yet an 'institution' of the kind that is reproduced over generations

---

[25] Another reason for this tendency towards consumption, apart from the difficulties of trading (setting up new partnerships) and investment, is that it is difficult to save money, since bank accounts are sequestered for high and numerous taxes.

(indeed, it may disappear quite soon). In this respect, anthropological and economic analyses might look quite similar.

However, what the anthropologist would try to discover is specific features, such as notions of appropriate economic behaviour for men and women, the expressions of domination and submission, the leeways given, the unspoken assumptions (and disagreements) about values – in short, the whole conglomeration of what Hertzfeld (1997) has called 'cultural intimacy', that in a given social context makes barter relationships what they are. The point is that these assumptions do not pertain to economic activities alone, and anthropologists would be interested in the cross-overs and boundaries created by them in respect of other aspects of society, rather than restricting a research topic by some analytically created definition of 'the economic'. This is why I have tried to highlight (in a schematic way, it is true) the place of trade partnerships in a wider social and political landscape. Barter practices have been dynamically creating a new kind of relationship which seems to be acquiring a life of its own.

Nevertheless, the different contexts and motivations of barter, beyond the immediate transaction, indicate that these barter relationships, while having common features, are not 'all the same'. For example, there is a possibly superficial but nevertheless locally remarked upon ethnic difference in how trade partnerships work between Buriats and Chinese (stronger trust because 'we are both Eastern peoples') and between Buriats and Russians (see chapter 10). Or there are the ideological implications of the kind of barter people now call 'forced' when the coercing side is in fact the weaker in the wider economic picture. In the 1980s this type of barter, which in effect forces the side receiving goods it cannot itself use to engage in marketing on your behalf, was extolled by Russian economists and promoted by the Chinese leader Deng Xiaoping as a means of 'democratic' penetration by socialist and Third World countries into international markets dominated by capitalist conglomerates (Kobushko and Ponomarev, 1989, pp. 35–6). Even now in Russia, the fallout from this kind of ideological thinking may be a factor in the continued allowance given to weak economic actors (collective farms, destitute factories) to go on paying the government and the utilities in kind. The same tolerance is not extended to entrepreneurial firms.

If understanding the everyday practice of barter partnerships can inform us about a new kind of social relation in Russia, examining barter in the broader socio–political context, including strongly held and lasting ethnic, cultural, or ideological assumptions, may help with the analysis of the more economic issues of how long barter will go on and whether, when the economy is re-monetised, similar relations will be perpetuated.

References

Dasgupta, P. (1998). 'Modern Economics and its critics, 1', unpublished
Gell, A. (1992). 'Inter-tribal Commodity Barter and Reproductive gift-exchange in old Melanesia', in C. Humphrey, and S. Hugh-Jones (eds.), *Barter, Exchange and Value: an Anthropological Approach*, Cambridge, Cambridge University Press
Gregory, C.A. (1982). *Gifts and Commodities*, London, Academic Press
Hertzfeld, M. (1997). *Cultural Intimacy: Social Poetics in the Nation-State*, London, Routledge
Hohnen, P. (1997). *A Market Out of Place? Re-making Economic, Social and Symbolic Boundaries in Post-Communist Lithuania*, PhD thesis, University of Copenhagen
Hugh-Jones, S. (1992). 'Yesterday's Luxuries, tomorrow's Necessities: Business and Barter in Northwest Amazonia', in C. Humphrey and S. Hugh-Jones (eds.), *Barter, Exchange and Value: An Anthropological Approach*, Cambridge, Cambridge University Press
Humphrey, C. (1985). 'Barter and Economic Disintegration', *Man*, ns 20(1), 48–72
(1999). 'Traders, "Disorder" and Citizenship Regimes in Provincial Russia', in M. Burawoy and K. Verdery (eds.), *Uncertain Transition Ethnographies of Change in the Post-socialist World*, Lanham, Boulder and New York, Rowman & Littlefield
Humphrey, C. and S. Hugh-Jones (eds.) (1992). *Barter, Exchange and Value: An Anthropological Approach*, Cambridge, Cambridge University Press
Kobushko, T.V. and S.A. Ponomarev (1989). *Vstrechnaya torgovlya: proshloye ili budushchee?*, Moscow, Mezhdunarodnoyye Otnosheniya
Lévi-Strauss, C. (1969 [1949]). *The Elementary Structures of Kinship* (1949), trans. J. H. Bell, ed. R. Needham, Boston, Beacon Press
Makarov, V.L. and G.B. Kleiner (1996). *Barter v rossiiskoi ekonomike: osobennosti i tendentsiii perekhodnogo perioda*, Moscow, Tsentral'nyi ekonomikomatematicheskii institut RAN
Mauss, M. (1954 [1925]). *The Gift: Forms and Functions of Exchange in Archaic Societies*, London, Cohen & West
Roaf, J. (1999). 'Recent Economic Developments', *IMF Report on Russia*, Washington, DC, IMF, unpublished
Sahlins, M. (1972). *Stone Age Economics*, 1st edn., New York, Aldine de Gruyter
Smith, A. (1776). *An Inquiry into the Nature and Causes of the Wealth of Nations*, 1, Penguin: Harmondsworth, 1979 edn.
Strathern, M. (1992). 'Qualified Value: The Perspective of Gift Exchange', in C. Humphrey, and S. Hugh-Jones, *Barter, Exchange and Value: An Anthropological Approach*, Cambridge, Cambridge University Press

Part II Large-scale empirical studies

4 Barter in post-Soviet societies: what does it look like and why does it matter?

ALENA LEDENEVA AND PAUL SEABRIGHT

1 Introduction

What makes the director of a large Russian engineering factory trade machine tools for a mixed consignment of potatoes and consumer goods? And are such business practices an encouraging sign of entrepreneurial adaptation to the new market economy, or a sign that things have gone disturbingly wrong?

Events since the collapse of the Soviet Union at the beginning of the 1990s have brought many surprises, particularly to those who thought that the direction of economic change was predictable even if its speed and the accompanying discomfort were not. Though severe economic disruption, political instability and the re-emergence of nationalism were all widely foreseen, most observers concurred in expecting economic transactions to become more market-based: more transparent, more anonymous, less dependent upon traditional systems of mutual obligation. For example, large enterprises, vertically and horizontally integrated, uniting very diverse productive activities under the same administrative structure, were expected to break up and be replaced by combinations of activity that embodied more natural synergies, and engaged in monetary transactions in the market to a much greater extent than before.

One of the great surprises, noted by some journalists and well known to those who have visited firms in the CIS but so far given attention by comparatively few scholars of the economic transition, has been the existence of barter transactions on a very large scale. These are not just transactions between individuals trading household commodities or personal services with each other (a well known phenomenon under communism[1]). Enterprises are trading commodities with each other instead of

We are grateful to Caroline Humphrey and Federico Varese for helpful comments. Errors remain our own.
[1] Ledeneva (1998).

trading them for money, and they are doing so at all stages and all scales of production. No goods are too large or too sophisticated to be part of a barter deal (tanks, aero-engines, oil and gas refinery equipment have all featured in deals known to us[2]).

How do these transactions differ from ordinary market transactions? For these purposes we can take market transactions to involve the delivery of goods or services against money or other financial assets. The key characteristics of financial assets are that they have no value in consumption but can be easily stored and exchanged for other goods whose consumption is valued directly. The kinds of exchange to which we have referred may involve complex networks of transactions, at least some components of which differ from market transactions in one of two main ways:

- One kind of component of barter deals has involved what might be called *commodity currencies*: enterprises in the shoe-producing sector use shoes in payment for materials, for example, and a leather supplier accepts shoes in payment in order to be able to use them in turn to pay its supplier of animal hides (see box 4.1, p. 96). Here physical goods are accepted by those who do not wish to consume them directly; they function in a similar way to financial assets even though the cost and inconvenience of storing them may be very high.

- Another kind of component of barter deals involves barter in a more fundamental sense, which we might call *matching demands*. Here the commodities traded are those directly required by one party or the other rather than accepted solely as a medium of exchange (as when a firm demands payment for its engineering products in the form of food or consumer goods that can be used directly to pay its workforce – see box 4.1). One very common form of this transaction is the payment of wages in the form of the enterprise's own output. Makarov and Kleiner (1997) have compiled a list of items used as a payment to workers of big industrial firms in 1996 from press reports: foodstuffs (sausages, cucumbers, sugar, flour, meal tokens); dacha equipment (shovels, buckets, spades, motor-seesaws); household items (refrigerators, TV sets, bicycles, gas-guns); underwear and so on.[3] This kind of transaction requires what has traditionally been known as 'the double coincidence of wants': each party to the transaction must not only *demand what the other supplies* but *supply what the other demands*. The effort and resources devoted to searching for such

---

[2] Fieldwork by Seabright in Central Asia (1995), Ledeneva in Russia (1998).
[3] Makarov and Kleiner (1997), p. 26.

trading partners may be high, and there is a significant danger that one party or both will feel obliged to settle for goods it does not really want in preference to the risk of failing to trade at all. Indeed, employees often find themselves having to act as an unpaid sales force for their employers since their own willingness to consume the firm's output directly is limited.

Under either of these two forms the transactions may involve a simultaneous contract, in which case we can talk of 'intentional barter' since both the parties to the transaction intend to make an exchange of goods or services at the time the transaction is planned (or, strictly speaking, at the time the transaction is executed; sometimes there is an agreement – *dopsoglashenie* – additional to the main contract allowing the substitution of payment in goods for payment in money). Quite often, though, the barter transaction takes place in order to clear a prior debt, in which a previous supply of goods or services incurred a financial obligation which it is subsequently decided to settle in physical goods. In these circumstances the transactions are called offsets (*vzaimozachety*). They are clearly a distinct phenomenon since they may imply a degree of coercion, or at least the acceptance by the debt-holder that its value as a financial instrument is less than it was once hoped to be.

In reality, as we discuss below, many transactions between firms in post-Soviet societies are highly complex deals that involve both matching demands and the use of commodity currencies, as well as combinations of offsets and intentional barter, as part of a chain with many different links. They also involve a number of surrogate financial instruments such as promissory notes (*prostoi veksel*), bills of exchange (*perevodnoi veksel*) and interest-bearing notes. These differ from the complex financial instruments in market economies not so much in their intrinsic character as in the fact that there are no organised markets for them; instead they are typically exchanged in a bilateral, ad hoc and often fraudulent fashion[4] – the ultimate in junk bonds (see box 4.2, p. 97). In this overview chapter we seek to do three things. First, we summarise what is known about the extent, variety and character of the barter phenomenon, calling on a combination of published information, press reports, survey data and our own fieldwork. There have been a number of recent large-scale surveys (including those reported in this volume), and we do not attempt to summarise them here, but concentrate instead on more qualitative reports, mostly from earlier years. Our case study evidence is often particularly revealing of the kinds of barter transaction involved, even

---

[4] Gudkov (1998), p. 5.

Box 4.1   One commodity currency and many matched demands
(Seabright)

At a leather factory outside St Petersburg in 1993, the finance director pays
her supplier of animal hides by arranging a shipment of shoes. Why? Her
main client is a shoe manufacturer, whose only trustworthy means of payment is shoes. This means that shoes have become a parallel currency for
the entire sector, right back to the collective farms that raise the cattle. But
currency needs to be stored somewhere. So this year's investment budget
has been earmarked to build a new warehouse, all for storing shoes. It's
more expensive than opening a bank account, but at least the shoes hold
their value ...

Actually, not quite all the investment budget is for shoes. A small
amount has been set aside to make sausage skins. Why? The supplier of
hides is getting restive, for good hides can be sold for hard currency abroad.
But the supplier has his own problem, which is that to use the meat which
he also produces he needs good-quality sausage skins. So the finance
director in St. Petersburg has had an idea, which is to make her company
indispensable to him by producing the elusive skins. Leather manufacturers
may know nothing about making sausage skins, but these are extraordinary
times.

At a shoe factory in Tashkent in Central Asia in 1995, even more
complex deals are in the making. The finance director has tried in vain to
persuade his suppliers to take shoes in payment, so now he is setting up as a
supplier of general consumer goods. His senior management colleagues
spend their time scouring local markets and telephoning their friends in
other firms. Tomato paste, porcelain and pasta are particularly prized, for
not only can they be used to pay suppliers, but they come in handy to pay
the workforce as well.

I visit a plastics factory and try to talk to the director about his
restructuring plans. But he has other things on his mind. 'We've
found a reliable source of potatoes', he tells me, with evident pleasure.
'The workforce will be very glad; the arrears in their wages had been
building up. There's not much else to pay them with. Though to tell the
truth, we tend to turn a bit of a blind eye these days to pilfering from
the company stores.'

In Kiev in 1995 I meet an energetic young man who has set up a
dairy-processing plant on the land beside a coal-fired power station. The
collective farms in the region are all hopelessly in arrears for their
electricity, and besides useless *karbovanets* all they have is milk. The
power station is not interested, unless some means can be found to
process the milk. It doesn't sound very ecological, and it will doubtless
be redundant in five years' time, but in the meantime it is working so
well that plans are afoot to build a pasta factory and a brewery on the
same site.

Box 4.2   The normal use of bills of exchange (Ledeneva)

'For instance, our firm and *RAO Gazprom* sign an agreement that they pay
me with a *Gazprom* bill of exchange. But their chain is organised in such a
way that they do not even hand over this document to me. They take it
from one of their offices to another and that's it. I do not have any *veksel*,
they supply gas to Chelyabinsk, and I receive my inputs from Chelyabinsk.
They try to make their financial deals with Chelyabinsk look good or
something, but obviously, this is not a proper *veksel*.

'*Lukoil* pay me for the oil and gas equipment with a 2-year *veksel*. They
know I won't be able to keep it for 2 years. The discount would be
enormous, 80 per cent or so. So they give me an oral promise that if I
take it to their oil-processing firm in Perm', I will receive oil-products at
today's market price for the nominal sum of the *veksel*. So I choose barter,
take oil-products and trade them further. Still better than to cash that bill
of exchange at a bank. Sometimes the bills of exchange they pay with are
issued not by *Lukoil* but by some association or organisation. If the latter
go bankrupt, *Lukoil* won't have any responsibility for their promissory
notes. These promissory notes are coupled with a personal agreement
that *Lukoil* will buy them back in a year, or that in a Perm' *Lukoil* oil-
processing firm it will be accepted as a *Lukoil* one. Smaller and dependent
firms are forced to agree to these conditions in the face of such monopolistic pressure.'

---

if it lacks statistical representativeness. Secondly, we set out a number of
hypotheses about the causes of barter transactions, discussing what kind
of further information would be necessary to enable us to choose between
them on empirical grounds. Thirdly, we discuss their implications for
public policy: is barter no more than a symptom of economic dislocation,
a phenomenon that can be expected to disappear as economic conditions
improve? Or is it an independent cause for concern, a problem that
requires a policy response?

An important feature of barter is that it is a *network phenomenon*. It
frequently involves inter-related though non-simultaneous transactions
between multiple trading partners; the reasons for any given bilateral
deal can frequently not be understood without knowing the network of
transactions of which it forms a part. The network structure of the deals
arises as a natural response to the difficulty of matching demands, since it
may be easier to find a chain of partners whose demands are mutually
consistent than to find a single pair of trading partners. The double
coincidence of wants is more improbable than their indirect coincidence
– just as friends are rarer than friends of friends. This network character

therefore provides an urgent need for case study and ethnographic material to complement large-scale survey data. It also suggests that any analysis of the policy implications of barter needs to draw on the literature about network competition. Whether barter will diminish with macroeconomic stabilisation depends on the nature of the competition between barter networks, about which more analysis and more evidence are still needed.

2 The scale of barter

Development over time

Since the Russian crisis of August 1998 there have been numerous press reports of barter on a large scale in Russia, with figures of more than 50 per cent of GDP being commonly mentioned. It is sometimes asserted, and more often implied, that barter is a phenomenon of relatively recent origin. Official figures also imply that it is predominantly a phenomenon of 1995–8, and that the first references to it in the Western press were in 1995. The 1998 *EBRD Transition Report* reported data from the *Russian Economic Barometer* implying a steadily increasing incidence of barter from below 20 per cent of GDP in the first half of 1995 to nearly 50 per cent in the first half of 1998, a growth closely tracking the increase in inter-enterprise arrears. However, it seems at least possible that the official figures under-state the incidence in earlier years. The evidence for this comes from several sources:

- First, there are studies of or reports from particular regions or sectors: these have no claim to be statistically representative, but their message is consistent with barter's having become already a well established phenomenon in the early 1990s. Visits by Seabright to several firms from a variety of sectors in the region of St Petersburg in 1992–3 indicated a large incidence of barter in these firms, which respondents reported to be typical of other firms they knew. One study from that period claims that 40 per cent of export–import transactions occurred in barter, while within Russia, 58 per cent of coke supplies, 25 per cent of coal, 34 per cent of metal supplies and 35 per cent of machines and equipment were transacted in barter.[5] Woodruff (1999) reports that at the beginning of 1994 around half of all payments to electric power companies were already made in kind, and barter seems to have continued to rise from that point; in at least some regions barter accounted

---

[5] Nesterovich (1993).

for over 75 per cent of payments by the summer of 1994.[6] In 1995, in a few Russian regions, according to Buklevich (1998), the volume of barter transactions had reached 40 per cent of regional budgets.[7]. In their study of 17 big firms in machine-building, chemicals, electronics and the light and food industries of Moscow, Ekaterinburg and Ivanono,[8] Makarov and Kleiner (1996) found out that almost 70–80 per cent of inputs were acquired through barter transactions. These estimates are confirmed by the data of Kuznetsova and Butkevich (1996).[9] Other estimates of the scale of barter in 1995-6 range from 34 to 50 per cent of gross industrial output.[10] More recently, a study of small and medium-size firm (SMEs), producing non-consumables showed that 75 per cent of the sample firms had recourse to barter.[11] Fieldwork by Ledeneva reveals a great deal of 'shadow' (officially undeclared) barter transactions taking place in the SME production sector in 1998; none of this is reported in enterprise books or accounts.

• Secondly, given the nature of central planning there is every reason to expect barter to have played a significant role in the early phase of reform. Under central planning the distinction between barter and monetary transactions did not really exist, since apparently monetary transactions were no more than the accounting counterparts of flows of goods and services determined by the planners. Furthermore, conditions of pervasive shortage meant that enterprise managers needed to work energetically to match demands in exactly the same way as is required under pure barter. Without free markets financial assets were not demanded as media of exchange. Consequently, once price liberalisation and other features of the market economy were introduced, unless they could be expected to work effectively it would not be surprising to find enterprise managers continuing to work in the habitual fashion. On this view it would not be barter which was the novelty, but ordinary market transactions. It would be quite natural for barter to have been established on a large scale as early as 1992–3.

It is also of interest to know whether there has been a change in the kinds of transaction undertaken over time. This question is particularly difficult to answer since journalists and researchers have become

[6] Woodruff (1996), p. 4.
[7] Buklevich (1998).
[8] Makarov and Kleiner (1996), p. 5.
[9] Kuznetsova and Butkevich (1996).
[10] Glisin and Yakovlev (1996).
[11] Alimova and Dolgopyatova (1998).

progressively more interested in the phenomenon and have therefore tended to ask more detailed questions. Nevertheless, it is likely that the proportion of offsets has increased over time relative to intentional barter. It would also be likely (though we know of no direct evidence for this) that barter chains have grown in length and complexity as firms deploy their entrepreneurial talents to overcoming the formidable problem of the double coincidence of wants. The use of surrogate financial instruments has probably also grown over time.

Makarov and Kleiner (1996) also claim that barter in the early to mid-1990s took the form of two distinct waves. In the first wave (around 1992–3) it was a demand-side phenomenon, in that firms were unwilling to accept monetary payments but there was no shortage of firms able and willing to make them. In the second wave (1994–5), they claim, it became a supply-side phenomenon in that firms had insufficient working capital to make monetary payments. Though their study does not claim to be statistically representative, it covers a number of sectors and is one of the earliest detailed studies of the phenomenon in existence.

Geographical and sectoral variation

Difficulties in assessing the average incidence of barter are compounded when it comes to assessing its variation across countries, regions and economic sectors. The following conjectures are supported to varying degrees by official data and case study evidence:

- Barter is much more a phenomenon of the countries of the *former Soviet Union* (FSU) than of the formerly centrally planned economies of Eastern Europe, where it has not been reported on any significant scale. This might be for one of two reasons: because the Soviet Union was more economically integrated than the CMEA, or because the non-CIS countries decoupled from the rouble zone at the beginning of the transition and adopted independent macroeconomic policies. The experience of the Baltic States (which occupied an intermediate position, having separate currencies from an early stage but being highly integrated with the Soviet Union) suggests that both factors may have been important. Barter was significant in Latvia, for example, until the mid-1990s (unlike in Central and Eastern Europe), but had disappeared by 1998 (unlike in Russia),[12] though anecdotal evidence suggests it may be reappearing.

[12] Interviews by Seabright (September 1998); Roberts Kilis (personal communication).

- Barter has been widespread among the *non-Russian states in the CIS*, but may have involved less commodity currencies and more matched demands than barter in Russia. Interviews of several firms by Seabright in Ukraine and Uzbekistan in 1995 showed all of them to be engaged in matching demands. If correct, this may be due to the fact that the average large non-Russian firm transacts to a significant extent with Russian firms, whereas the average large Russian firm transacts primarily with other Russian firms (this follows from the relative size of the economies concerned). Cross-border trades involve currency risk and the risk of future trade restrictions in addition to all the other risks of transacting in a post-Soviet environment. These additional risks may be enough to make firms unwilling to accept goods in exchange unless they are ones for which they can see an immediate use. Accepting a commodity currency involves an additional degree of risk that the firms are unwilling to contemplate.
- There is some evidence that transactions with public utilities (electricity companies, for example) are more likely to involve barter than other transactions of equivalent size and complexity. Defence contracting firms are also predominantly likely to be involved in barter, since they have been particularly prone to non-payment by government. As regards the type of products involved, relatively simple, undifferentiated commodities (such as oil or timber) are more likely to be traded as part of a barter transaction than are complex differentiated products. And when the latter do appear in barter deals (e.g. aero-engines) they are more likely to do so with matching demands than as commodity currencies. The latter is entirely consistent with the view that the kinds of good that can function effectively as commodity currencies need not only to be physically durable but also of readily verifiable quality.[13]

3 Barter and networks

Box 4.3 illustrates a number of examples of the network characteristics of barter. A number of firms may be involved in a transaction, and this fact alters the economic implications in several respects:

- In ordinary bilateral transactions it can usually be presumed that the terms of the transaction depend only on the preferences of the two parties involved. In a network transaction a particular exchange in the chain may be undertaken because of the requirements of some

[13] A view formalised in Banerjee and Maskin (1996).

Box 4.3   Man is born free but everywhere is in chains (Ledeneva)

Case 1   Payment of local taxes
The deputy director of a Kurgan oil and gas equipment enterprise reports that his firm owes taxes to the local budget. Oil and gas equipment is supplied to Urengoi, one of the *Gazprom* deposits, which pays gas to the Chelyabinsk metal complex (*ChMK*). *ChMK* supplies metal to Nizhnii Novgorod automobile plant (*GAZ*), which supplies chassis for buses to the Kurgan bus plant (*KAZ*). The latter now has a debt to the former, but instead they agree that the product of *KAZ* – buses – is accepted by the city budget in payment of local tax from the Kurgan oil and gas equipment enterprise.

Case 2   Payment of telephone and electricity arrears
The Kurgan oil and gas equipment enterprise supplies its product to *Chernogorneft* (oil-deposit). Instead of paying for it directly, the latter makes a 'shift-a-debt' deal, by which another oil company, *Sidanko*, becomes a payee. *Sidanko* does not pay the Kurgan enterprise either; it supplies oil products to a company *E-Frass*, which, following the chain, supplies diesel fuel to an automobile plant in Nizhnii Novgorod (*GAZ*). *GAZ* pays with the cars which get accepted by *Kurganenergo* and the local telephone station as a payment for the Kurgan oil and gas equipment enterprise's debt.

Case 3   Mutual offset blocked by monopolists
'The Ministry of Finance has to pay for the military orders fulfilled by *KMZ* but doesn't pay. As a result, *KMZ* can't pay its debt to *Gazprom*. We are customers of *KMZ*; we owe *KMZ* for our inputs and would be happy to conduct a mutual offset because *Urengoi Gazprom*, one of the *Gazprom* branches, owes us 2 million. It's been already more than a year, and they won't pay it back even through a mutual offset. Yamburg Gazprom owes us more than 3 million, also for more than a year. *ZapSib Gazprom* owes us 1 million. This would make 6 million. But being monopolists, they simply don't take this into account and try to squeeze cash out of *KMZ* under the threat of its closure.'

Case 4   Barter for scarce supplies
'For producing oil and gas equipment I need metal from *KMZ*, which has a monopoly. The director of that plant can dictate his terms. He gives me a list of difficult items (*tonkoe mesto*), say payments for energy, for timber, for metal, or supplies of aluminum etc. – perhaps 20 of his problems. I decide which ones I can solve, choose three or four directions and start building up chains. It is understood between us, permanent partners, that we cannot change direction every time. They know the problems I solve: I can pay their electric energy expenses, I can pay for their gas or supply gas for their heating and technological needs, I can arrange aluminium supplies – these are my four directions. On top of this I pay their transport expenses, since it so happens that the railway owes me as a result of another barter chain.'

third party. This fact may be important for understanding both why transactions are structured in this way, and who benefits from them. To put it in economic terminology, barter transactions typically give rise to externalities.

• These externalities may not always be beneficial in wider social terms, but may simply reflect the fact that in barter transactions firms become individually more indispensable to others in the chain. This is because it is harder to find others that offer the precise combination of goods and transaction terms demanded by the trading partner. In effect, transacting in barter increases the differentiation of firms from each other and thereby diminishes the extent of competition between them; it is as though it created distinct islands of *local monopoly power*.

• The fact that transactions occur in chains means that the *financial* performance of any individual firm (and therefore its chance of escaping bankruptcy) depends less than under market transactions on the real productivity of the firm itself. It depends correspondingly more on the overall performance of the firms that are parties to the chain. A chain transaction is like an insurance contract: it protects individual firms against the shocks of their economic environment, but like all insurance contracts is subject to moral hazard – namely, a weakening of the incentive for each firm to improve its own productivity. Note that this may not reduce the overall incidence of bankruptcy: it simply links the probability of bankruptcy to the *profitability of the chain* rather than the profitability of the individual firm.

This is happening continuously. If there are no officially processed bankruptcies, it does not mean that we do not have bankrupt enterprises. There are thousands of them. They are the ones nobody works with or works at very high warranty. There is a certain degree of trust involved in a chain as every party comes in with a known interest and a known product. If they say that they will pay with oil-products, I trust they have them. But parties do not provide guarantees for one another. Rather, everybody pushes everybody else to a collective bankruptcy by increasing direct transaction costs (the longer the chain, the more costs it involves and more harmful it is) and indirect, hidden ones. (Ledeneva, interview with factory manager, 1998)

• Finally, an important consequence of the network phenomenon is the possibility of '*lock-in*'. This is something that has been extensively studied in the literature on the economics of network competition. It refers to the fact that, in the presence of network externalities, firms may systematically choose intrinsically inferior technologies or production processes because they happen to be part of more developed networks. The success of the IBM personal computer over

Apple and the QWERTY keyboard over intrinsically more efficient rivals are only two of the many examples that have been cited in the literature on technological adoption and diffusion. It may be that barter chains exemplify this phenomenon on a fragmentary but much more widespread scale. In other words, firms could be systematically choosing inferior production methods – or, more probably, continuing with inferior existing methods – in preference to making the effort to improve and upgrade their methods. Chain transactions sharpen the tension between the demands of everyday survival – stick by your friends, trust only those you know – and the requirements of adaptation to the market economy in the longer term: the need to find new markets, forge links with new suppliers, develop new products, adopt new processes.

To summarise, taking the network character of barter transactions seriously means that it will not be possible empirically to determine the causes of the phenomenon by examining the characteristics of individual firms and their immediate trading partners. The predicament of other firms in their chain may be at least as important a part of the explanation. It also means that the decisions of individual firms will influence the financial performance and survival prospects not merely of themselves but also of the other firms in their chain. This insures individual firms to some extent against the economic storms in their environment but also blunts their incentives to innovate and improve.

4 Causes of barter

There are a number of distinct, though not necessarily mutually exclusive hypotheses about the causes of barter. In no particular order, these represent barter as:

- a flight from money owing to hyperinflation
- a response to the high cost of working capital
- a lack of trust in the banking system
- a response to inter-enterprise debt arrears
- a means of evading taxes
- a means for firms to collude in over-valuing their output to soften budget constraints (the 'virtual economy' hypothesis)
- a means of increasing the enforceability of private contracts in the absence of a credible system of civil law
- a more general symptom of a breakdown of trust in those economic institutions that depend on collective confidence about the functioning of the market economy.

Table 4.1 *Consumer price inflation, 1991–1998, year-end*

Year	Russia	Ukraine	Belarus	Poland	Czech Rep.	Hungary
1991	161	161	161	60	52	32
1992	2,506	2,730	1,559	44	13	22
1993	840	10,155	1,996	38	18	21
1994	204	401	1,960	29	10	21
1995	129	182	244	22	8	28
1996	22	40	39	19	9	20
1997	11	10	63	13	10	18
1998	150	22	60	10	9	14

Source: EBRD Transition Report 1998.

Although in our view the available evidence does not allow us to decide confidently between these hypotheses,[14] a number of remarks can be made about their *prima facie* plausibility. First of all, if lock-in effects are important, then the reasons for which barter has become initially established are not necessarily the reasons why it subsequently continues; this caveat should be borne in mind in interpreting the evidence that follows. Secondly, different explanations may be appropriate for different regions and sectors; however, the striking contrast between the FSU and other formerly planned economies suggests there are likely to be at least some common features across regions and sectors. So what can we say about each of these hypotheses?

- *Hyperinflation*: On the face of it this provides a persuasive explanation for the difference between the FSU and other (European) formerly planned economies. Table 4.1 illustrates. Inflation peaked at over 1,000 per cent per annum in all the former Soviet Republics during the 1990s, and in none of the European countries except some members of the former Yugoslavia, for which war provides an obvious explanation. However, inflation has fallen significantly in the FSU since 1995. If barter were entirely a phenomenon of the post-1995 period (as on the official accounts) that would make inflation an unlikely explanation. However, the fact that barter has become entrenched when inflation was falling certainly means inflation cannot be the sole explanation.

- *The cost of working capital*: Inflation would not be a convincing reason for barter if it were compensated by nominal interest rates at least

---

[14] Other chapters in this volume attempt this more systematically.

equal to the rate of depreciation of money, and if these deposits could be used as means of payment. In fact, there has been a large spread between deposit and loan rates in a number of high-inflation countries, with deposit rates well below and loan rates well above the inflation rate. *This has been a continuous phenomenon since 1995.* It has also been much more characteristic of the CIS than of Central and Eastern Europe. Figure 4.1 illustrates by comparing Russia and Poland, and although Russia's inflation rate has been comparable only recently, even then its spread between deposit and lending rates has been substantially higher. A further telling illustration is provided by the observation that in 1995 Poland's average deposit rate was 18 per cent and its average loan rate 23 per cent. In 1996, with inflation at comparable levels, Ukraine's deposit rate was also 18 per cent – but its loan rate was 49 per cent! (In Russia the rates were 7 per cent and 35 per cent, respectively.) These conditions imply that holding money is unattractive (a reason to prefer holding goods). But they also mean that borrowing to finance working capital is unattractive (a reason for firms to persuade their suppliers to accept payment in goods). In effect, high interest rate spreads increase the transactions costs of holding money to such an extent that even physical goods, with their notoriously high transactions costs, become an attractive alternative.

- *Untrustworthy banks*: The failure of deposit rates to keep pace with inflation is compounded if banks cannot be trusted – either because they may go bankrupt, or because they are prone to error or fraud in

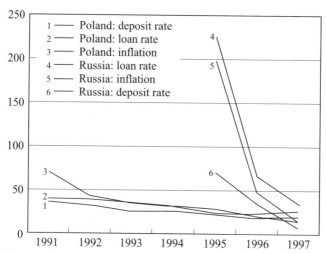

Figure 4.1 Interest rates and inflation in Russia and Poland, 1991–1997

Table 4.2 *Scale of lending in transition economies, 1993–1997*

Country	Ratio of credit to the private sector to GDP (per cent)					Country average
	1993	1994	1995	1996	1997	
Belarus		18	6	7	9	10
Bulgaria	4	4	21	37	13	16
Croatia	47	29	31	29	38	35
Czech Rep.	51	60	60	57	68	59
Estonia	11	14	15	18	26	17
Hungary	28	26	23			26
Kazakhstan	45	25	7	6		21
Latvia	17	16	8	7	11	12
Lithuania	14	18	15	11	10	14
Poland	12	12	13	15		13
Romania	–	–	–	–	–	–
Russia	12	12	8	7	8	9
Slovak Rep.	32	24	28	32		29
Slovenia	22	23	27	29	29	26
Ukraine	1	5	1	1	2	2
Annual average	23	20	19	20	21	21

Note: = not available.
Sources: IMF, International Financial Statistics; EBRD.

keeping account of transactions. The former is well documented, and there is a large amount of anecdotal evidence of the latter. Of course, this is no argument against making transactions in cash, but cash bears no interest, needs to be stored in a safe place and is awkward for high-value transactions.

- *Debt arrears*: We reported above that official accounts showed debt arrears in Russia increasing on a par with barter as officially measured, so this explanation would be compatible with official accounts. This would make offsets the main form of, and reason for, barter. In particular, it provides a ready explanation for why firms have recourse to barter even when the transactions costs are high: a heavily indebted firm may simply be unable to obtain cash because no bank will lend to it. Table 2 provides some corroborating evidence for this hypothesis since it illustrates the very low levels of bank lending to the private sector in the countries (such as Russia and Ukraine) where barter has been most extensively documented.

- *Tax evasion*: There are two reasons why barter might make tax evasion easier. First, it may be possible to cite lower than cash prices for both sides of the transaction in order to reduce liability to VAT and profits tax. The latter is no longer legal in Russia, as transactions prices are calculated not according to the report of the parties but according to 'average prices' published in the *Ekonomicheskaya Gazeta*. Secondly, the transaction itself may be easier to hide as it does not pass through an account. This has become particularly important in Russia since a decree of August 1996, which imposed draconian restrictions on legal persons in arrears to the budget or non-budgetary funds. When it appeared, *Kommersant Daily* commented that it would treat any tax debtor as a virtual bankrupt and would deprive managers of control over, or interest in, the profitability of their enterprises.[15] The decree also contradicts articles of the civil code. Under the decree, any enterprise or organisation which falls behind its payment to either budget or non-budgetary funds is required to open a special 'tax debtor's account' (*schet nedoimschika*) or designate an existing current account for this purpose. All funds from the organisation's other accounts – and this is what every organisation would try to avoid – must be channelled to the *schet nedoimschika*, as must all income (no cash may be withheld for minor expenses), with the exception of funds for wages, payment to the budget and non-budgetary funds and the financing of budgetary programmes. This includes all funds from accounts opened by all representative offices and other branches of the company which are not 'independent subjects' of tax legislation. This is intended to make it more difficult to evade taxes and to facilitate enforcement of regulations which allow the tax authorities considerable scope for dictating the order of payments made by a tax debtor. The availability of *schet nedoimschika* also implies that no loan can be given to this firm by a bank, even if a loan is meant to discharge the inherited stock of debt.
- *The virtual economy*: This explanation (due to Gaddy and Ickes, 1998) takes barter to be the means whereby enterprises that are either value-subtracting or just highly unprofitable at market prices can continue to operate. This amounts to an economy-wide version of a phenomenon well known in the banking sector – namely, the incentive for banks to pretend that non-performing loans are in fact sound, and to lend to enterprises the money with which to service their existing loans (this is a kind of Ponzi finance scheme, the banking equivalent of a chain

---

[15] *Kommersant Daily*, 28 August 1998, quoted in Tompson (1997), p. 1166.

letter). Two challenges to such a hypothesis are, first, that of explaining why barter has become widespread in the FSU but not in Eastern Europe (even though value-subtracting enterprises were as common in the latter as the former).[16] Secondly, it needs to be explained why all the parties have an incentive to collude in the deception (especially the producers of natural resources).

• *Contract enforcement*: Barter may be a means whereby fulfilment of contractual terms can be more easily assured in the absence of a credible system of civil law.[17] Enforcing a monetary debt may be more difficult, in part precisely because of the very feature which makes money attractive in normal times – namely, its anonymity. A promise to deliver a consigment of machine tools is easier to enforce; the counterparty can be shown the machine tools, and there will be fewer rival claimants to the debt. This explanation certainly helps to make sense of the greater predominance of barter in the CIS, since these countries did not have a civil code from pre-war times to which they could revert when communism collapsed, and there is over-whelming evidence that the credibility of contractual enforcement is much lower in the CIS than elsewhere.[18] One interesting question pro-voked by this analysis would be the question whether barter is com-plementary to or a substitute for the resort to organised crime as a contractual enforcement mechanism.[19] We know of no evidence on this.

• *Breakdown of trust*. It may be that the resort to barter is symptomatic not so much of lack of trust in certain specific institutions (the rouble, the banks) as of a general sense of insecurity about economic condi-tions which makes people reluctant to trust in holding their wealth in any form that is not directly consumable or capable of being traded at short notice. It is hard to know how to evaluate this suggestion, but it is worth observing that in previous periods of historical insecurity many assets (such as gold) have emerged as stores of wealth without this leading to widespread barter trade. A more promising suggestion is that, in spite of price liberalisation, many markets are characterised by prices that fail to clear markets and which therefore lead to persistent shortages. This would result in physical goods, when available at all, having a scarcity value that is not reflected in their market price and is therefore superior to their nominal monetary value. Note that this is

---

[16] Hare and Hughes (1991).
[17] Marin and Schnitzer (1995) apply this argument to international countertrade.
[18] Fingleton *et al.* (1996).
[19] See Varese (1994), pp. 224–58.

the opposite of the 'virtual economy' hypothesis since the latter argues that goods have a true or shadow value below their nominal monetary value. The breakdown of trust places the explanation for barter on the demand side, whereas the virtual economy hypothesis places it on the supply side.

To summarise, the majority of these explanations appeal to the low *demand* for monetary means of payment while two of them (debt arrears and the virtual economy) appeal to the low *supply* of monetary means of payment.

What are the implications of these various hypotheses for the effects of barter on the economy, and the prospects for the future?

5 Consequences of barter

The private costs of barter transactions to the firms undertaking them are fairly evident, though their magnitude is rather startling. As the examples in box 4.1 indicate, where parallel currencies are involved, substantial investment resources may be diverted into stocking, protecting, transporting and using the products that are bartered. More subtly, there may be a large diversion of management time,[20] effort and ingenuity into solving the problem of the 'double coincidence of wants'.[21] Anyone who doubts whether former command economies have adequate entrepreneurial talent to make the transition to capitalism cannot but marvel at the ingenuity and resourcefulness deployed in putting together barter deals. Sadly, so much entrepreneurship is used up in this process that there is little left for devising new products, finding new markets and improving production methods (see Carlin *et al.*, chapter 9 in this volume).

The fact that there are large private costs to barter does not in any sense imply that firms are foolish to undertake it. Indeed, all of the explanations we have discussed imply barter to be a privately rational response to a very distorted economic environment. The problem is the absence of attractive alternatives (such as a well functioning macroeconomy or banking system) which have something of the character of public goods. In addition, there are larger social costs – in particular, a distortion of the entry and exit decisions of firms, and their choice of goods to produce and methods to adopt. We have already indicated how

[20] Up to 80 per cent according to interviews with Ledeneva.
[21] These costs are sometimes borne by banks who charge for the service – around 1.5 per cent is typical (Ledeneva).

the network character of barter transactions leads to a moral hazard problem; likewise, the fact that the scarcity values of goods may diverge from their monetary prices creates distorted production incentives – as in the example in box 4.1 of the firm producing sausage skins purely because these are valuable in exchange. It would be premature to claim that these distortions are in any way comparable to the distortions of the planned economy, but at the very least they are making the passage away from the planned economy much more painful than it should have been (and has been in the countries of Central and Eastern Europe).

Finally, one of the hardest kinds of cost to evaluate is the cost of 'locking-in'. Certainly, if anything like the 'virtual economy' story is accurate, then the presence of barter becomes self-perpetuating since the parties to the transaction do not wish to question the inflated values on which the transactions are based. (This is very similar to the problem known in banking as 'gambling for resurrection', which is that banks become more reckless the worse the deterioration in their portfolios).[22] Other kinds of lock-in may be more subtle: firms do not experiment, they do not dare to risk switching supplier, so they never become aware of alternatives to their current ways of doing things. The presence of so much risk in their daily environment becomes a deterrent to seeking out risk for their own and society's profit.

What kinds of policy intervention seem appropriate under these various hypotheses? To the extent that the alternatives to barter have the character of public goods, the state has a reason to supply them much more reliably and plentifully than is happening now, at least in the CIS. What is harder to say is whether there is anything to be gained by making barter more difficult for firms, in the absence of attention to the conditions that make firms seek out barter in the first place. Certainly, the case for direct policy intervention to prevent barter is, to date at least, unproven, and the attendant risks are very high.

6 Conclusions

The barter chain has a certain similarity with *krugovaya poruka* (the circular guarantee) – a practice enforced by the Russian state for centuries. The state imposed a collective tax responsibility on the community, thus generating mutual debts within the community. Peasant communities were pressed by severe taxation, while being sustained from outside (by a strict passport regime and attachment to land) as well as from inside (by

---

[22] See Fries, Neven and Seabright (1998).

the community watch system). External tax pressures brought into being a complex web of mutual debt obligations, with rich families establishing their 'monopolistic' dues. However distant a modern industrial firm may seem from a peasant family, the pressure of taxes, dependence on 'neighbours' in their technological network for obligatory payments and inputs and an inability to 'disappear' as many small or shadow businesses do, makes *krugovaya poruka* a poignant metaphor for the predicament of many enterprises in the CIS today. Whether this predicament will be short-lived, or whether it is becoming ever more entrenched, is a serious and so far unanswered question.

References

Alimova, T. and T. Dolgopyatova (1996). 'Strategiya predpriyatiya na rynke resursov', *Ekonomika i Zhizn'*, 8

Banerjee, A. and E. Maskin (1996). 'A Walrasian Theory of Money and Barter', *Quarterly Journal of Economics*, 111(4), 955–1005

Buklevich, V. (1998). 'Denezhnye surrogaty ne spasayut byudzet', *Ekonomika i Zhizn'*, 34

Fingelton, J., E. Fox, D. Neven and P. Seabright (1996). *Competition Policy and the Transformation of Central Europe*, London, CEPR

Fries, S., D. Neven and P. Seabright (1998). 'The Performance of Banks in Transition Economies: A Success Story?', EBRD, mimeo

Gaddy, C. and B. Ickes (1998). 'Beyond a Bailout: Time to Face Reality About Russia's 'Virtual Economy',' Washington, DC, Brookings Institution, Pennsylvania State University, February, mimeo

Glisin, F. and A. Yakovlev (1996). 'Pyataya chast' nalichnogo oborota v promyshlennosti okazyvaetsya nelegal'noi', *Finansovye Izvestiya*, 69

Gudkov, F.A. (1998). *Veksel'. Defecty formy*, Moscow, Kontsern 'Bankovskii Delovoi Tsentr', 5

Hare, P. and G. Hughes (1991). 'Competitiveness and Industrial Restructuring in Czechoslovakia, Hungary and Poland', *European Economy*, special edition, 2

Kuznetsova, N. and Butkevich, V. (1996). 'Byudzet v pleny neplatezhei', *Ekonomika i Zhizn'*, 24

Ledeneva, A. (1998). *Russia's Economy of Favours: Blar Networking and Informal Exchange*, Cambridge, Cambridge University Press

Makarov, V.L. and G.B. Kleiner (1996) 'Barter in the Russian Economy: Characteristics in the Transition Period', *Working Paper*, WP96/006, Moscow, CEMI Russian Academy of Sciences (in Russian), 5

(1997). 'Barter in the Economy of Transition: Specifics and Tendencies', *Ekonomika i Matematicheskie Metody*, 33 (2), 26

Marin, D. and M. Schnitzer (1995). 'Tying Trade Flows: A Theory of Counter-trade', *American Economic Review*, 85(5), 1047–64

Nesterovich, V. (1993). 'Etot gonimyi spasitel'nyi barter', *Ekonomika i Zhizn'*, 14, April

Tompson, W. (1997). 'Old Habits Die Hard: Fiscal Imperatives, State Regulation and the Role of Russia's Banks', *Europe–Asia Studies*, 49(7), 1159–85

Varese, F. (1994). 'Is Sicily the Future of Russia?', *Archives Européenes de Sociologie*, 35(2), 224–58

Woodruff, D. (1999). *Money Unmade: Barter and the Fate of Russian Capitalism*, Ithaca, Cornell University Press

5 The growth of non-monetary transactions in Russia: causes and effects

SIMON COMMANDER AND CHRISTIAN MUMMSEN

1 Introduction

In Russia and the rest of former Soviet Union (FSU), recent years have seen possibly the largest departure from conventional monetary transacting since the end of the Second World War. The growth in non-monetary transactions such as barter has occurred alongside large-order accumulation of arrears in the economy. The arrears have not only been inter-firm but have also included government, utilities and workers. While the accumulation of arrears has occurred at various points throughout Russia's transition (most strikingly in 1992), since 1994 there has been a clear and continuous increase not only in the scale of non-payments but also in the use of non-monetary transactions. So the obvious questions that arise are: why, and how are these phenomena related?

While the available statistics are far from robust, recent time series estimates show large and steady increases in the share of barter in total industrial sales. *The Russian Economic Barometer* panel suggests that between the first quarter of 1995 and 1998 the share of barter in industrial sales jumped from under 20 to around 50 per cent.[1] However, what has loosely been termed barter has actually lumped together a variety of transaction types, including money surrogates. Evidence from other parts of the former Soviet Union – such as Belarus and Ukraine[2] also indicates large shares of barter, for both domestic and external trades. There is also evidence that use of clearing arrangements for barter and use of money surrogates has become particularly widespread in Russia, pointing to the relative scale and sophistication of the system of non-monetary transactions.

Our chapter attempts to sort out analytically and empirically the meaning, scale and implications of this large-order recourse to use of

---

[1] Aukutsionek (1998).
[2] Kaufmann and Marin (1998).

barter and money surrogates. Empirically, the results come from a 350-enterprise survey carried out in Russia in October–November 1998. The survey was implemented in 34 *oblasts* (regions) and was primarily targeted at industrial enterprises with the inclusion of some service sector firms.

The chapter is organised in six sections. Section 2 briefly provides the appropriate vocabulary, details the range of non-monetary instruments used in Russia and rapidly surveys the range of competing and complementary explanations for the growth in non-monetary transacting. Section 3 concentrates on the role of macroeconomic policy and highlights the importance of a credit squeeze in shaping the non-monetary economy. Section 4 turns to the micro foundations and provides an analytical framework for understanding why Russian firms may transact in these exotic ways. Section 5 reports the principal findings from the survey. Section 6 then considers the costs of barter and non-monetary transacting. Section 7 concludes by considering a range of policy options.

2 Non-monetary instruments: some definitions

In thinking clearly about non-monetary instruments, it is important to separate out the various transactional forms. Four major types appear to stand out:

1 *Barter*, where the transaction involves goods for goods.
2 *Money surrogates* – primarily commodity or financial *veksels*, which are promissory notes issued by enterprises, banks or government with specified maturities and discount rates. There have been two broad types of issuers; those who use *veksels* for managing liquidity and those who issue them in lieu of default. The discount rate adjusted for maturity reflects the position of the issuer.
3 *Offsets* or *zachety*, where the dominant transaction involves debt for goods. Offsets have commonly been used to clear obligations among groups of firms, between firms and tax authorities and between firms and utilities or government. Multilateral offsets were originally introduced in 1994 primarily in the form of Treasury obligations and tax offsets and were used to clear enterprise tax arrears and budget payment arrears through chains of mutually indebted enterprises. Such schemes have been modified over the years, but the underlying rationale has remained the same.
4 *Debt swaps*, *sales* and *roll-overs*.

Available evidence suggests that the weight of these transaction types has varied over time. For instance, the share of offsets and surrogate money in total non-monetary transactions has increased substantially.[3] In addition, the use of clearing-scheme-based trades has also proliferated. Estimates of the stock of outstanding *veksels* have necessarily been very imprecise, ranging as high as two-thirds of broad money or over 10 per cent of GDP.[4]

3 Macroeconomic policy and the dynamics of barter

The dramatic growth in barter and other non-monetary transactions since 1994 has occurred against a background of an attempt at macroeconomic stabilisation built around a sharp tightening of monetary policy, some fiscal correction and a fixed exchange rate. This section argues that – while being effective in largely squeezing inflation out of the system (annualised inflation fell to below 5 per cent in the first half of 1998) – the underlying, and primarily fiscal, sources of instability remained largely unaddressed. Further, the manner in which the deficit was financed over this period had significant implications for the real economy and ultimately for the integrity of the banking system. These factors were also important in sponsoring the shift into non-monetary transacting.

Fiscal policy

Fiscal policy was tightened significantly after 1994 with the primary deficit (the deficit excluding interest payments) actually moving into slight surplus by the first half of 1998. However, the consolidated deficit remained stubbornly in the range of 6–8 per cent of GDP. Explicit subsidies to the enterprise sector were whittled down to no more than 2 per cent of GDP. But this is a serious under-estimate. World Bank estimates of total subsidies to the firm sector over the period 1996–8 are in the range of 16 per cent of GDP between 1996 and 1998 with over half accounted for by implicit subsidies, including through tax arrears, offsets and inflated procurement prices.[5]

The manner in which fiscal tightening occurred also proved significant. Expenditure control was achieved primarily through sequestrations that were in turn linked to large accumulations of government arrears – over 5 per cent of GDP by early 1998. Non-payments on the part of government in turn led to the proliferation of tax and budget offsets, as well as the widespread acceptance of settlements in kind. By 1996–7 non-cash tax

[3] Tchaidze and Tsibouris (1998).
[4] For example, OECD (1997); Oxford Analytica (1998).
[5] World Bank (1999).

Table 5.1 *Russia: lending, treasury bill and deposit rates, 1995–1998*

Category	1995	1996	1997	1998
Deposit rate	71.0	44.4	16.8	17.1
Lending rate	147.4	91.4	32.0	41.8
Treasury bill yield	132.4	63.1	23.4	42.6
Inflation (cpi)	197.7	47.8	14.7	27.8

Sources: World Bank; EBRD.

payments accounted for around 40 per cent of federal revenues and over 50 per cent of provincial budgets[6] and declined further thereafter.

Finally, the source of deficit finance changed sharply over the period 1995–8. The growth of a treasury bill (GKO) market substituted domestic debt finance for money creation and was associated with a dramatic increase in the domestic debt. Between 1995 and mid-1998 the stock of outstanding Treasury bills jumped from 4 to 17 per cent of GDP. Further, while yields on GKOs fluctuated substantially, they remained persistently high in real terms throughout this period.

Monetary policy

Over the same period, there was also significant tightening in the monetary stance with a sharp deceleration in the growth of rouble broad money and in base money. Table 5.1 gives the evolution of both nominal deposit and lending rates as well as yields on Treasury bills. What is obvious is that interest rates and their spread remained high throughout – though declining after 1996. The spread notably widened again in the first half of 1998, averaging over 30 percentage points. The size of the spread obviously cannot be attributed to the magnitude of bad loans in the system alone, but reflected a widespread lack of confidence in the banking system. The fact that real lending rates were also high over this period clearly discouraged borrowing by viable firms, while Treasury bills provided a relatively attractive destination for liquid assets. In addition, despite the deceleration in inflation, the velocity of circulation of broad money barely declined and remained high.

Figure 5.1 suggests strongly that not only was there very limited lending by banks to the private sector throughout this period – by the first

---

[6] OECD (1997). An MBK estimate for a sample of 210 firms for first half of 1997 had over 55 per cent of federal tax obligations being made in kind.

☐ Commercial bank credit to private sector GDP, percent (left axis)
➜ Bank claims on the government relative to claims on to private sector,
    percent (right axis)

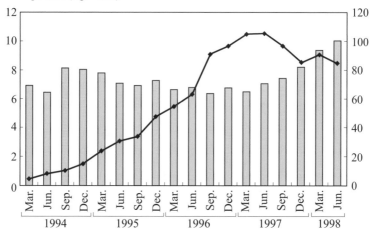

Figure 5.1 Commercial bank credit to private sector, March 1994–June 1998

half of 1998 such lending accounted for under 10 per cent of GDP – but
that the banks had strongly shifted their portfolios to financing the
government. As early as the first quarter of 1997 over 35 per cent of
commercial bank credit was to government, rising to over 45 per cent by
mid-1998. Further, while it is difficult to get any accurate sense of the type
and incidence of bank lending to firms, earlier evidence points not only to
a dominance of short-term, collateralised lending but also to significant
concentration in bank credit to firms.[7] In short, the bulk of firms had
little, if any, access to bank credit.

Trade credit and arrears

Prior experience – as well as accumulated evidence from Central Europe –
suggests that firms facing credit squeezes have commonly resorted to
increased use of trade credits. In a number of cases, this has also been
associated with an increase in overdue payables and hence in arrears. In
Russia, trade credit more than doubled as a share of GDP between 1995
and mid-1998 suggesting that most firms had greater recourse to trade
credit at a time when bank credit was dwindling.

[7] See, for example, Fan, Lee and Schaffer (1996).

The growth in trade credit could be interpreted as a necessary step in the evolution toward market institutions, particularly since the netting out of arrears in 1992 had subsequently led to a dramatic curtailment of trade credit in an environment with an already historically low level of trade credit. However, it is also clear that since 1994–5 there has been a strong, parallel expansion in arrears. Overdue payables climbed from under 40 to around 55 per cent of total payables between 1994 and early 1998. Furthermore, over time there was a clear departure from proximate balance between payables and receivables. In 1994 net arrears accounted for around 10 per cent of gross arrears and survey data showed that, once sector and other controls were applied, the primary determinant of payables default was default from customers (receivables): a chain effect.[8] By mid-1998 the ratio of net to gross arrears had shifted to over 40 per cent. This change could point to larger transfers – or redistributions – of liquidity across firms, compromising any simple, circular representation of arrears,[9] but this seems an unlikely explanation. Rather, this points to *net credit infusion*, an issue that we return to in more detail below.

To understand this shift, one can best start by looking at the change in the composition of arrears. Turning attention to the evolution of payables, there is a substantial decline over the same period in the share accounted for by suppliers. Arrears to the enlarged budget ballooned from around 29 billion roubles in 1995 to around 400 billion roubles by mid-1998: a real increase of over five fold. Further, the share of arrears to the budget and off-budget funds in total arrears doubled from around 20 to 40 per cent between 1994 and 1998, and this excludes arrears to important quasi-fiscal institutions such as the utilities. Indeed, by mid-1998 overdue payables were roughly four times larger than the stock of commercial bank credits to firms. Wage arrears remained roughly stable throughout. This suggests that the primary asymmetry at work may not have been the transfer of liquidity across firms, but the transfer of liquidity from the budget and other quasi-fiscal institutions to firms. This observation is crucial for understanding the growth of the non-monetary economy, as developed in section 4.

Money surrogates and arrears

As already indicated, the use of money surrogates – principally *veksels* – has been a major feature of the Russian economy. While the motives

[8] Alfandari and Schaffer (1996).
[9] See Calvo and Coricelli (1994).

behind recourse to money surrogates have varied and with it the degree to which such surrogates have been liquid, their issuance has had significant implications at a macroeconomic level. Although it is difficult to identify precisely the size of the innovation in the money supply associated with money surrogates, a simple exercise using a set of available data points starting in mid-1996 and continuing through to October 1998 indicates that *veksels* issued by credit institutions comprised roughly 7.5 per cent of broad money in July 1996, rising to around 12 per cent by mid-1998.[10]

The innovation in money surrogates and the growth in arrears had also large implications for credit in the system and for the velocity of money. Indeed, by mid-1996 the stock of overdue payables was roughly 50 per cent larger than broad money itself.[11] Using a narrow measure – GDP/rouble M2 – gives velocity of between 7 and 8 with a slight decline between mid-1996 and 1998, rising to over 9 in the aftermath of the August 1998 crisis. This high velocity can be attributed to a continuing preference among the population for non-rouble balances and a general lack of confidence in the banking system. But, using an extended measure of velocity – GDP/(M2 + overdue payables + *veksels*) – not only gives a far lower level (at July 1998, this measure of velocity was below 2) but also a steeper rate of decline.[12] Indeed, this expanded measure of money velocity gives a more accurate sense of the actual monetary and credit stance. Part of what happened was that private credit – including arrears – substituted bank credit.

4 Micro foundations of the non-monetary economy

This section examines the microeconomic foundations of non-monetary transactions in Russia. The root causes of Russia's non-cash economy are derived from incentives of the firm and the state. We first summarise tax-related arguments for barter, they provide a detailed analytical frame-work for credit-related causes of barter, and the critical role of the state in fuelling the non-monetary economy. We then discuss the network effects of barter which help spread the use of barter across the economy, and finally summarise how these various effects have led to the growth of the non-monetary economy in Russia.

---

[10] These estimates are from data provided by the Central Bank of Russia. They underestimate the total supply of *veksels*.

[11] Note that if net overdue payables are used, velocity shifts to 3.8 in December 1996 and 3.1 in June 1997, with net payables amounting to between 50–55 per cent of broad money.

[12] See also Clifton and Khan (1993); Coricelli (1998).

Tax and payment systems

There are a number of possible reasons for the use of barter that relate to the tax and payment system. Among these are several possible motives for a firm to use barter with other firms as a way to avoid or evade tax payments.

- *Barter prices and tax avoidance:* When firms exchange goods in a barter deal, they can agree on any nominal price without affecting the real exchange rate between the goods. The value of a bilateral barter deal can be 'inflated' or 'deflated' by increasing or decreasing the accounting prices of the goods exchanged relative to their cash market values. Inflated barter prices increase revenues and costs on the books of both firms, while their profits would not be affected as long as the relative price (the real exchange rate between the two goods) is not distorted. Hence, firms can use barter to artificially lengthen or shorten their profit and loss accounts and balance sheet. While this allows a great deal of flexibility in accounting, there is little evidence that clever manipulation of nominal prices in inter-firm barter deals has been successfully used for tax minimisation. Quite to the contrary, most firms believe that inter-firm barter actually increases their tax bill. This is corroborated by the observation that barter prices almost always exceed cash prices (see also table 5.5), with margins of up to 50 per cent. Equally, the cash value of *veksels* is often a fraction of their nominal value. As Russian taxation rules tend to tax not only value added and profits but implicitly also revenues, inter-firm barter at inflated nominal prices will tend to increase the tax bill of the firms involved. To decrease taxes, barter prices should be deflated or the real exchange rate of the goods should be distorted to reduce accounting profits of a profitable firm and increase the profits of an unprofitable firm.
- *Accounting rules:* The Russian corporate tax system has until recently worked on a cash basis. This diminished firms' incentive to enforce timely payment by customers, resulting in an accumulation of arrears. In turn, arrears tended to encourage settlement in kind through offsets. Taxation has recently been changed towards an accrual-based system, but firms still have an option to account on a cash basis. However, there is little empirical evidence that accounting rules have played an important role in causing barter.
- *Tax evasion and bank transfers:* Firms seeking to hide certain income streams from the tax authorities may want to avoid the banking system. As Russian banks often act as intermediaries for tax collection,

avoiding bank transfers means reducing both visibility of transactions and physical access to the companies' resources. More generally, bank transfers are often costly as they take very long and these delays are not compensated. As large cash payments are risky, barter can be a method of payment that is legal and safe, while avoiding explicit and implicit banking costs. However, barter carries high transaction costs in itself and it is thus unlikely to be an efficient payments mechanism.

• *Tax bargaining:* For large Russian firms, tax payments are often more a matter of discretion and bargaining power than rules. Bargaining occurs typically *ex post* as most firms are already in tax arrears and the key question is when to settle what part of those arrears. At end-1997, the government published a list of the worst offenders, including automotive producers Avtovaz and KamAZ, and threatened to close them down if they did not pay their huge tax debts. In the end, not a single one of the large tax debtors was closed and tax arrears were only partially settled. In such an environment, politically influential firms actually have an incentive to economise on cash and thus use non-cash methods of payments as this increases their individual bargaining power *vis-à-vis* the state. Given that regional and federal governments generally care about the survival of these firms, it is likely that the eventual partial settlement of the tax arrears will be less for firms that have little cash. However, it is unlikely that tax bargaining – although important – would over-ride the objective of firms to raise cash revenues.

Although these factors may have played a role in some individual cases, the empirical evidence on tax avoidance or evasion as a direct motivation for inter-firm barter is fairly weak. Furthermore, it is unlikely that tax motives could explain the rapid rise in non-monetary transactions between 1993 and 1998. There is, however, another far more important link between non-monetary transactions and taxation in Russia: tax payments in kind and tax offsets. This type of non-monetary transaction between companies and the state has been correlated with the rise in inter-firm barter and the rise in arrears as shown in figure 5.2. We will return to the issue in detail below.

Credit reallocation, creation and innovation

Spot barter as trade credit
Some barter deals are pure bilateral exchanges of inputs between firms. In addition, inputs are often traded through elaborate multi-party chains of barter (e.g. coal, steel, rail transport). Chains can be agreed *ex ante* or

occur *ex post* through offsets of arrears that have accumulated. While the exchange of inputs can occur on the spot, the use of barter chains and *ex post* debt offsets indicates that there usually is a time dimension.

A fundamental insight is that 'spot barter' (the exchange of goods that takes place at one point in time) can indirectly replicate inter-firm trade credit. The maturity of this implicit trade credit is equal to the difference of the 'subjective' marketing time of the goods exchanged. When firms sell their output in a barter deal, they often receive in return goods or services that are not immediately useful to them. It takes time and effort to sell the goods or money surrogates received in barter deals for cash or use them for settling payables or purchasing inputs.

As an example, suppose that a final goods producer engages in a spot barter deal with its supplier, exchanging the final good against inputs received from the supplier. Unless the supplier can turn the final good immediately into cash or use it immediately as its own input, the supplier has implicitly granted a trade credit to the final goods producer. The maturity of the implicit trade credit from such a spot barter deal equals the marketing time of the final good as perceived by the supplier. This 'subjective' marketing time could be: (a) the time it takes the supplier to sell the final good for cash; (b) the time it takes until the good can be used for wage or tax payments; or (c) the time it takes to arrange another barter deal to purchase inputs or offset the supplier's debts. Note that in cases (b) and (c), the trade credit is partly passed on by the supplier to its workers, the state, or its own suppliers, unless these parties have immediate use for the good.

In the case where the supplier's subjective marketing time equals that of the final goods producer, it can be shown that spot barter, trade credit and bank credit are equivalent ways to provide the final goods producer with working capital. The relative price used in the spot barter deal should reflect an implicit interest rate related to the good's marketing time and the time preference of the final goods producer and supplier. In reality, this equivalence may not hold strictly. The final goods producer would usually have a comparative advantage in selling its product relative to the supplier. Hence, the implicit trade credit granted by the supplier in a spot barter deal may be longer than the subjective marketing time of the final goods producer. Conversely, the two parties may barter precisely because the input supplier has identified new customers for the final good and may thus be able to sell the product more rapidly than the final goods producer.

Barter and credit risk: goods now vs. money later (or never)
Spot barter and trade credit are both instruments to shift working capital from an upstream to a downstream firm. However, there is one

fundamental difference: spot barter allows trade credit without the credit risk (or with credit risk reduced and shifted elsewhere). Russian firms selling to cash-constrained customers usually face a fundamental trade-off: 'goods now vs. cash later (or perhaps never).' By accepting goods now, the firm secures immediate control rights and avoids credit risk. The disadvantage is that barter incurs additional transactions costs.

When a supplier ships its products to a downstream firm, it can wait for payment and thereby grant a straightforward trade credit. This implies that the supplier assumes a certain level of credit risk which depends on the creditworthiness of the downstream firm. When the supplier instead accepts the output of the downstream firm as an immediate payment for its deliveries, then no credit risk in relation to the downstream firm is incurred. The supplier acquires immediate control rights over its claims. If there is a liquid cash market for the good and if marketing is risk-free, then credit risk is avoided altogether. Similarly, if the supplier knows that it can pass on the final good to the tax authorities or its own suppliers at a later stage, no credit risk is incurred. By avoiding credit risk, spot barter can be very attractive in the Russian context where ownership and creditor rights are weak.[13] Of course, in most cases, the marketing of a product is not risk-free and marketing risk would typically be higher for parties that did not produce the good themselves (for instance, because of informational asymmetries about the quality of the product). Hence, spot barter does incur a certain type of credit risk in practice. However, the point is that this type of credit risk may be lower than the risk incurred by waiting for cash.

The credit rationale for offsets, veksels *and tax offsets*
The mechanism of barter as a risk-free trade credit applies also to offsets. Offsets work as a type of *ex post* barter deal whereby an earlier delivery of goods on credit (which may over time have turned into arrears) is eventually settled in kind. The firm accepting goods to offset its receivables effectively does two things: it settles its claims immediately (thus avoiding a continuation of credit risk) and prolongs the trade credit by the maturity of the marketing time of the goods received.

---

[13] Note that this is a different argument from another one put forward as a reason for international barter transactions. When the goods are exchanged with a time lag, the supplier of the first good has a claim on a good in the future rather than on cash in the future. Under certain legal circumstances, this may be preferable in the international context as claims on goods may be easier to enforce. In the Russian context, however, this argument is not convincing as any claim is hard to enforce, be it on cash or on a good. By contrast, a spot barter deal avoids credit risk from the beginning, while still creating trade credit as described.

Veksels can also create inter-firm trade credit. The issuer of the *veksel* is the recipient of the trade credit and the holder of the *veksel* provides the trade credit. However, by selling it down before its maturity, the holder of a *veksel* can shift the trade credit provision to someone else. This leads to the emergence of a secondary market where *veksels* are traded against cash or goods at a discount reflecting the time to maturity and the creditworthiness of the issuer. An important feature of both *veksels* and offsets is that they facilitate multi-party chains of non-monetary forms of payment.

The credit rationale of barter and offsets extends also to tax payments. When the state receives tax payments in kind, it usually takes time until these goods can be put to use, either for direct consumption by budgetary institutions or for on-sale to other entities. In the case of ex post settlement of tax arrears in kind, a similar principle applies: the state settles an implicit credit, securing control rights but with a delay equal to the time it takes to make use of the good received.[14]

Reallocation vs. creation of credit
Some non-monetary transactions create trade credit between firms, but do not create net credit for the enterprise sector as a whole. These include: (a) inter-firm trade credits and arrears; (b) spot barter between firms of goods with differing subjective marketing periods; (c) time-lagged barter or offsets between firms; and (d) commodity *veksels*. Such transactions simply reallocate credit between enterprises. This reallocation, if undertaken voluntarily by firms, can smooth inefficiencies in the credit system. Firms with relatively good access to bank credit can shift credit to enterprises with more restricted access to bank credit. Firms with excess liquidity can shift credit to enterprises that are short on cash. This reallocation of credit allows firms to circumvent high interest rates charged by banks and may alleviate information asymmetries between banks and enterprises concerning the creditworthiness of some borrowers.

However, efficiency enhancement has probably not been the prime motive behind the rise in non-monetary transactions in Russia. In the case where barter is *ex post* (in the form of offsets) or where barter is forced upon a supplier, efficiency is rarely the main consideration. As discussed in section 3, the rapid growth of barter from 1993 to 1998

---

[14] In the case of tradable tax offsets issued by the state (in return for purchases of equipment or utility services), the credit creation flows the other way around: as a firm holding a tax offset paper may not be able to use it immediately for on-sale or for offset of its own debts, it effectively grants a credit to the seller of the tax offset. The tax offset effectively functions as a *veksel* issued by the state with a maturity depending on the time of the next tax payment of the holder of the tax offset.

was closely associated with the rise of trade credit and arrears. With GKO yields rising and bank credit to enterprises becoming more scarce, enterprises increasingly relied on their suppliers for trade credit to cover their working capital needs. The lack of bank credit thus translated into growing inter-enterprise credit, as well as inter-enterprise arrears. Given the lack of creditor rights, barter and offsets became prime instruments for the creation and settlement of trade credit between firms.

Hence, the growth of the non-monetary economy in Russia had less to do with reallocation of credit within the enterprise sector, and more to do with a reaction to a credit squeeze on the enterprise sector as a whole. The liquidity-constrained downstream firm employed barter to acquire trade credit from its supplier. However, if the supplier was itself liquidity-constrained, it had to pass the buck further upstream by paying its own suppliers in kind. Given that most manufacturing firms faced similar credit constraints, it is unlikely that the rise of barter can be associated with inter-firm trade credit alone. Given the general credit crunch in Russia, upstream firms were neither willing nor able to support the general rise in trade credit and quasi-trade credit. The gradual rise in non-monetary transactions was fuelled by another party: the state.

Fuelling the non-monetary economy: the role of the state

The Russian barter story crucially hinges on the observation that there has been a continuous infusion of net credit into the enterprise system. Apart from bank credit and bank *veksels*, transactions that create credit for the enterprise system as a whole rather than only for an individual enterprise include the following: (a) tax arrears and deferrals, (b) tax payments in kind and tax offsets, (c) wage arrears, (d) wage payments in kind, (e) arrears to utilities and (f) utility payments in kind.[15] In-kind payments constitute credit whenever the good is not immediately useful for the recipient – i.e. it cannot immediately be sold for cash, used as an input, bartered against an input or offset against payables.

Late and in-kind payments to the state, the utilities and workers have played a central role in the emergence of the non-cash economy. Figure 5.2 illustrates the growth of in-kind and late payments to tax authorities from 1994 to 1998 which coincided with the rise in industrial barter. Although reliable data are not available, anecdotal evidence suggests that tax offsets were even more widespread at the regional level. Figure 5.3 shows the rapid rise in overdue payables of enterprises, including

---

[15] Points (e) and (f) assume that state-owned utilities have access to implicit state credit (or bank credit).

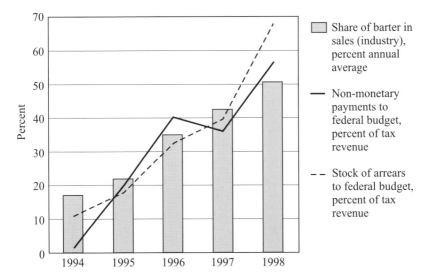

Figure 5.2 Late and in-kind tax payments and industrial barter, 1994–1998

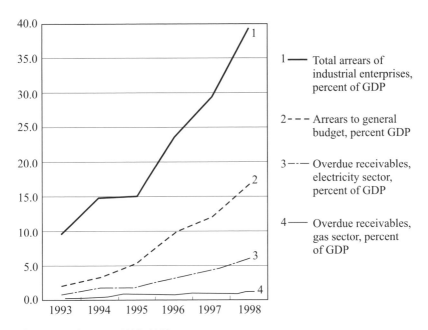

Figure 5.3 Arrears, 1993–1998

payables to the general budget. Payments arrears to the state utilities also increased over time. According to an estimate in mid-1998, only around 10 per cent of gas and electricity bills were settled in cash, while offsets accounted for about half of payments to these utilities.

Late or in-kind tax and utility payments can stimulate inter-firm barter in a variety of ways. When the state or state utilities accepts goods in lieu of monetary payments, these goods will have to be passed on to other enterprises in return for services received. The state thus becomes a central cornerstone in the barter chain.

A more indirect link between late or in-kind payments of tax and utility bills and inter-firm barter arises from the fact that such 'soft' forms of payment are effectively an implicit subsidy to loss-making activities. Arrears are often free of interest. Moreover, goods delivered in lieu of tax and utility payments tend to be accounted for at often highly over-valued prices, although they should really be *discounted* given that the state does not have an immediate budgetary use for most goods delivered. The worse a firm does, the more it benefits from such implicit forms of support from the state. Hence, unprofitable firms are allowed to produce high volumes, while their low levels of cash generation affect their suppliers which are forced to accept late and in-kind payments of their deliveries.[16]

The link between inter-firm barter and in-kind tax payments is reinforced by the frequent use of 'tax offsets' in public procurement. Tax offsets are promissory notes issued by the state to pay for goods and services procured. Tax offset notes can be used by the holder to settle tax bills. Article 410 of the Civil Code allows debts (including tax debts) to be traded. The recipient firm (such as a military enterprise, construction company or utility) can thus either use these offsets to reduce its own tax bill, or sell it to another party. As tax offsets are frequently sold to another party, usually not against cash but against other goods, services or offsets, the result will be an expansion of the non-monetary system. As such, the state creates and injects quasi-money into the enterprise system, fostering the expansion of non-cash transactions.

The state's reluctance to enforce timely cash payments for tax and utility, combined with an ineffective bankruptcy system, is thus the most crucial element in the growth and persistence of non-monetary forms of payments in Russia. There are several underlying reasons for the state's leniency (or weakness):

- The *social consequences of mass lay-offs* in large loss-making enterprises are often deemed unacceptable, given the absence of an effective

---

[16] In the short run, taking production patterns as given, tax payments in kind are of course a net injection of credit into the enterprise system, thus freeing up cash for other uses.

social safety net outside the firm. Regional governments in particular have become the biggest subsidisers of large loss-making enterprises with high local importance. Given the close links between governments and managers of key enterprises, enterprise decisions have often some political dimension, including an interest in maintaining employment and production levels. Indirect state support in the form of late or in-kind tax or utility payments is implicitly 'traded' against maintaining employment, social services and production.

- Close relationships between state officials and company managers also open up opportunities for *corruption*, with barter as a practical way to hide such practices. Creative pricing of goods sold to the state, in particular, can be used for bilateral gain to the detriment of the budget.
- The pressure to *raise tax revenues* is also a possible motive for accepting payments in kind. With many tax debtors unable to pay, the state may accept payments in kind in order to get some revenues on the books, thus avoiding a further accumulation of arrears. The state's illiquidity itself led to an increasing use of tax offsets to pay for public procurement and thus indirectly to further growth of the non-monetary economy.
- The over-valuation of barter goods often reflects a reluctance of regional politicians and enterprise managers to accept the *decreased economic viability and importance* of certain large enterprises. As Gaddy and Ickes (1998a) argue, there is an element of make-belief associated with the 'virtual economy' created by barter. As inter-firm barter deals – just as in-kind tax payments – are accounted for at inflated prices (see survey evidence in table 5.5), enterprises tend to lengthen balance sheets, inflating both revenues and costs. While this can lower perceived profitability, it increases perceived revenues and thus exaggerates the importance of the enterprise. Hence, when a firm faces a negative demand shock and should in response reduce production volumes and/or price in response to, it may instead choose to maintain output and revert to barter to also maintain price (and thus revenue). This type of non-profit behaviour is of particular importance in large industrial enterprises that are closely linked to regional governments.

Networks and market thickness

Once a critical number of firms is engaged in barter other firms, even those that are not at all cash-constrained, can be drawn into the system. Non-monetary transacting can reinforce inter-firm relationships. The Russian manufacturing sector operates with large-scale enterprises with strong vertical links and widespread incidence of dual monopoly. In this environment, it is often necessary for a supplier to grant trade credits via barter to its only customer in order to survive if the customer is short of cash as a result of high exposure to non-monetary transactions.

The enterprise survey shows that almost half of barter is arranged through intermediaries. This indicates a certain degree of 'thickness' of the non-monetary market. Certain goods may be traded much more heavily in barter chains, partly arranged by intermediaries, than on cash markets. Defecting from the non-cash market may thus be associated with marketing costs that exceed those in economies with liquid cash markets. This could explain why companies – even liquid and profitable ones – may rationally pursue some degree of non-monetary transacting. For the economy as a whole this equilibrium may be quite costly (see section 6). Although market thickness is not one of the root causes of barter, it helps explain why the non-cash economy has persisted. Moreover, it implies that barter encompasses both viable and non-viable firms, making policy options more difficult (see section 7).

Pulling the pieces together

Bringing together the key aspects of the previous sections, the Russian barter story can be summarised as follows. The macroeconomic dynamics, described in section 3, led to rising interest rates and a squeeze of bank credit to enterprises. In this environment, enterprises reacted by reallocating credit and innovating in quasi-monetary instruments. The resulting general equilibrium of barter and arrears is graphically represented in figure 5.4.[17]

As firms became increasingly illiquid, they accumulated arrears (in the figure, passing on receivables R) and began paying their suppliers (F_1, F_2), workers (L_1, L_2, L_3) and the tax authorities in kind (with final good Y_3) rather than in cash. This in-kind settlement implies an indirect trade credit granted by the recipient as most goods do not have an immediate cash value. For the recipient, it was increasingly rational to accept payments in kind rather than waiting for cash payments in the future, given that payments discipline and creditworthiness were declining and creditor rights were weak. The growing illiquidity of firms, coupled with an ineffective bankruptcy system, thus led to the relentless growth of barter and

---

[17] Figure 5.4 assumes that there is a chain of firms in an upstream to downstream relationship. Good Y_3 is the final good which serves as barter payment for inputs, taxes, utilities and wages. Suppliers, workers, utilities and the state also provide credit by getting compensated in receivables.

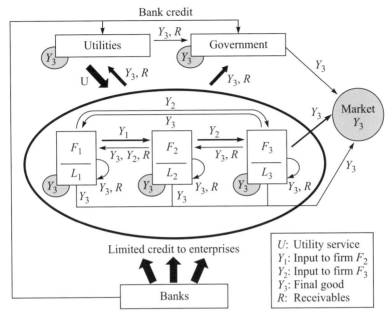

Figure 5.4 Barter and arrears flows

arrears. At the same time, firms started innovating in quasi-money such as *veksels* and debt swaps, while intermediaries increasingly coordinated the non-cash economy, thickening the non-cash market and thus making barter a way of life for both good and bad firms.

However, the system would not have expanded as much without the most crucial element in the story: the state. While phasing out direct subsidies to enterprises, the state increasingly injected 'soft' credits into the ailing industrial sector by allowing firms to pay their taxes late and in kind (at overvalued prices). This was also done indirectly via the utilities, which accepted late and in-kind payment of bills. This injection of 'soft' credit was partly due to concerns about employment, but also a result of corruption, fraud and tax evasion, further undermining the state's fiscal position and thus further fuelling the rise in interest rates and the crunch of bank credit to enterprises.

The consequence was an economy where accounting prices had little to do with cash values. Inflated barter prices exaggerated the revenues of manufacturing enterprises, while distorting business decisions and fostering corruption. Falling transparency on the enterprise level further eroded access to outside finance. Over time, a thick non-monetary economy helped to lock enterprises into networks, inhibiting restructuring.

Table 5.2 *Survey: summary statistics, 1997–1998*

Sample size/no. of enterprises	350
Mean employment, 1997 (no.)	1,630
Mean employment, 1998 (no.)	1,477
Mean capacity utilisation, 1997 (Jan.–Jun.) (per cent)	59.5
Mean capacity utilisation, 1998 (Jan.–Jun.) (per cent)	57.7
Mean capacity utilisation, Oct.–Nov. 1998 (per cent)	55.7
Ownership in 1998 (unweighted share of sample)	
State and municipal (per cent)	11.7
Limited liability (per cent)	6.3
Joint stock (per cent)	79.8
Individual and other (per cent)	2.2

These efficiency losses of the barter economy are discussed in more detail in section 6.

5 Survey results

Sampling and basic characteristics

The survey was carried out over a four-week period between mid-October and mid-November 1998 in 34 *oblasts* (regions) of Russia. An initial sampling frame of nearly 1,050 firms was used. From this frame and by telephone interview, it was found that 64 per cent of these firms had some current exposure to barter. Final sampling was restricted to firms with such exposure and the questionnaire was then applied to a total of 350 firms. The survey is thus primarily informative about variation in the weight and distribution of non-monetary transactions in a sample of firms with some positive exposure to barter and other transactions. Although this does not allow comparison of firms with and without barter, it is instructive to note the fact that nearly two-thirds of firms contacted had some involvement in non-monetary transacting.

Table 5.2 provides some basic descriptive statistics. The great bulk of firms in the survey were industrial; only 11 per cent were service sector firms. Firms were quite evenly distributed over industrial branches. Roughly 80 per cent of the sample were either privatised or private firms; a minority had remained in state hands. The mean employment size was large – significantly in excess of 1,000 employees. Mean capacity

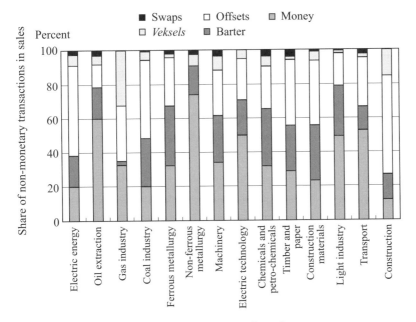

Figure 5.5 Incidence of non-monetary transactions, by sector

utilisation was quite low, at around 55 per cent and declining over the reference period, 1997 and 1998.

Summary of findings

Figure 5.5 demonstrates unequivocally that firms in our sample have a substantial exposure to non-monetary transacting. Indeed, the mean value for the share of non-monetary to total sales was greater than 0.6. Further, the majority of firms had exposure to at least three out of the four non-monetary transacting forms and nearly 90 per cent had exposure to both barter and offsets. These two instruments emerged as dominant although a significant number of firms also used *veksels*. Clearly, as suggested in section 4, a thick market in non-monetary transactions has emerged with the bulk of firms operating across a range of instruments and parties. This suggests again a high degree of coordination as well as the importance of complex deals.

There is not much variation in the share of non-money to total sales across sectors and ownership forms. Use of barter and offsets was not only widespread but together commonly accounted for over half of total sales. It was only in a clear minority of branches that the ratio of money

Table 5.3 *Share of responses where reason is given as 'very important'*

Reason	Barter	Offsets	*Veksels*
Liquidity of partner	74	73	66
Lack of alternative partners	18	20	18
Claim on old debts	48	50	42
Liquidity at own firm	72	73	68
Maintain output	49	51	43
Better prices on non-money deals	9	8	9
Decrease transaction costs	8	10	8
Better from tax standpoint	13	17	14
Allow money to be used to better effect	28	30	29
Facilitate sales	30	26	24
Help capture new markets	17	14	11
Recommended by local or federal authorities	5	8	7

to total sales exceeded 0.5. Exposure scaled by ownership further indicates relatively limited heterogeneity, although it appears that being in the state sector was generally associated with a higher money share in sales. The widespread exposure to offsets underlines the importance of complex – multilateral – deals and transactions.

Turning to motivation, Table 5.3 indicates – in decreasing importance – that own or partner liquidity has been unambiguously the dominant reason. This corroborates the analytical framework laid out in sections 3 and 4. However, other motives for using the various non-monetary instruments, such as maintaining output, collection of outstanding debts and accelerating sales, stand out. Most striking is the apparent absence of any strong tax motive for use of any of these instruments.

Figure 5.6 breaks down the types of transactions by their partners. What is obvious is the very high shares of respondents using barter and offsets to transact with utilities and, to a lesser extent, budgetary organisations. In the former case, nearly two-thirds of respondents used barter and offsets. This result is effectively replicated when breaking down the incidence of non-monetary transactions by type of cost (see figure 5.7). Again, what is most striking is that for the major utilities – electricity, heating, gas and water – barter and offsets covered 70–75 per cent of the total cost of these components. Further, although the monetary share of federal tax payments averaged over 60 per cent, in the case of local taxes and off-budget funds, offsets and barter accounted for 60–70 per cent of the value of payments. In other words, not only have the quasi-fiscal and fiscal institutions allowed late payments but they have

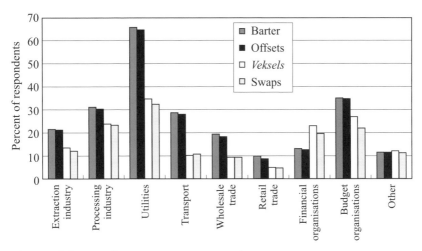

Figure 5.6 Partners in non-monetary transactions

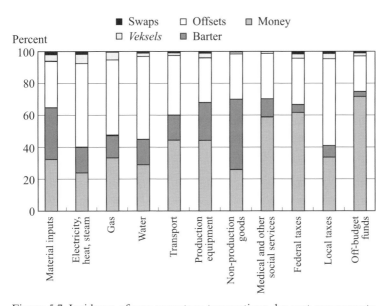

Figure 5.7 Incidence of non-monetary transactions, by cost components

also sanctioned very substantial shares of total payments by firms in kind or through offsets. These numbers are clearly consistent with the analytical framework laid out above.

Given this analytical framework, the relationship between access to credit, arrears and exposure to non-monetary transacting is clearly crucial. In what follows we summarise detailed results contained in a parallel paper, which contains a fuller empirical analysis.[18] Table 5.4 reports some key results. There, the non-monetary share in three cost components – material inputs, utility (namely, electricity, gas and water) and budget cost at federal and local levels and payments to off-budget funds, respectively – is related to access to credit, arrears in payables and – to capture any scale effects – by the average share of non-money in revenue of other firms in the same region, as well as a set of controls. The estimation for each of these cost categories is by instrumental variables with predicted values for access to credit and overdue payables being plugged in.[19] In the case of the input cost regression (column (1)) we found little evidence for endogeneity in the credit and payables variables and estimation was hence by ordinary least squares (OLS). The results of the estimations indicate that arrears are negative and insignificant in the regressions of non-money in utility and budget costs, but are positive and significant in the input cost regression. At the same time, lack of bank credit is positive and significant in the utilities and budget equations but insignificant in the input cost equation. The scale variable is significant in the input cost regression which points to the role of thick markets in inter-enterprise transactions. The scale effect is even stronger in the budget cost regression which can be attributed to the way in which barter and offset chains tend to originate with the budget. The control variables indicate that employment size is always positive and significant. State ownership is negatively associated with the use of non-money while the economic sector controls show strong variation.

To conclude this section, our more detailed empirical work suggests that lack of access to credit and firm illiquidity are unambiguously associated with both higher arrears and exposure to non-money. The link from credit constraints to arrears is particularly tight. Lack of access to bank credit tends to be linked to higher arrears in payables, even when controlling for arrears in receivables. Arrears thus tend to substitute bank credit, with a particularly important role for budget arrears. Moreover, there is clear evidence of a feedback from arrears to problems with bank credit, suggesting that arrears and illiquidity feed on each other and, in turn, lead to additional movement away from conventional monetary transacting. Further, the survey shows that non-monetary deals with utilities and the budget have emerged, alongside arrears, primarily as substitutes for lack of bank financing, while inter-enterprise non-monetary

[18] See Commander, Dolinskaya and Mummsen (2000).
[19] For complete description of the procedure, see Commander, Dolinskaya and Mummsen (2000).

transactions have largely evolved as a mechanism for dealing with the arrears problem itself. Fiscal and quasi-fiscal institutions have been central to the growth of multilateral non-monetary deals in the Russian economy.

6 The costs of barter

A firm's individual incentive to barter is not necessarily inconsistent with profit maximisation. Credit innovation and thin cash markets can be good reasons for a firm to engage in barter. Moreover, when faced with a large aggregate demand shock, barter may have helped some potentially viable firms to survive that would otherwise have perished in the absence of an efficient banking sector. For the economy as a whole, however, the proliferation of non-monetary transactions has on balance been immensely costly.[20]

Transaction costs

There is strong evidence that barter imposes net costs on participants. Our enterprise survey shows that arranging barter deals takes longer than cash sales (see Table 5.5). Furthermore, barter chains and circles imply the need for intermediaries. The survey shows that half of enterprises believe that barter is unprofitable for both parties involved, which indicates some degree of transactions costs. These costs are partly associated with arbitrage by intermediaries. It should be noted, however, that a sizeable minority of firms believes that non-monetary transactions are profitable for both parties involved, pointing possibly to tax and credit motives.

Fiscal and social costs

Perhaps the most pernicious effect of Russia's non-monetary economy has been the negative impact on the state's finances. The barter system has been kept running by a constant injection of 'soft' credit to the enterprise system via delayed or in-kind payments of taxes, utility charges and wages. This contributed to Russia's persistent fiscal problems, which were at the heart of the August 1998 crisis. A vicious circle arose with budget deficits pushing up interest rates, driving bank credit away from enterprises and towards GKOs, leading to even less bank credit to

---

[20] It should be noted, however, that it is difficult to move away from the current suboptimal equilibrium. This is discussed in section 7.

Table 5.4 *Credit, arrears and non-money*[a]

	Non-money in input cost (OLS estimation) (1)	Non-money in utility cost (OLS estimation) (2)	Non-money in budget cost (OLS estimation) (3)
Difficulty with bank credit	1.55	74.33*** (IV)	68.03**** (IV)
Overdue payables	2.03*****	−0.91 (IV)	−2.18 (IV)
Non-money in region	0.47***	−0.19	0.86*****
Log employment	2.82****	9.31*****	4.05****
Russian market	0.13*	0.14	0.02
State-owned	−12.12****	−21.65*****	−9.85*
Moscow	−8.62	−23.57**	−11.16
Industrial regions	0.21	−2.48	−0.27
Electric energy sector	11.55***	27.08***	28.42****
Oil-extraction sector	−2.09	−34.38****	−13.27*
Gas sector	−5.89	−15.86**	−5.98
Coal sector	6.23	12.21	26.22****
Ferrous metallurgy sector	8.26	−23.40****	−8.58
Non-ferrous metallurgy sector	−30.23*****	−12.46	−2.83
Chemicals and petro-chemicals sector	1.38	−16.20***	−11.81****
Forestry, timber and paper sector	2.60	2.92	5.71
Construction and construction materials	11.72***	8.06	9.65*
Light industry sector	−7.69	−13.62*	6.79
Transport sector	−7.97	−1.24	14.92*
Constant	1.39	−28.84	−78.55*****
Hausman Test[b]	0.57 (0.57)	1.48 (0.23)	2.56 (0.08)
N	331	175	265
R^2	0.24	0.33	0.34

Notes: [a] Huber–White heteroscedasticity correlated standard errors.
[b] Hausman Test: F-statistic, p-value in parentheses.
* Significant at 20 per cent, ** significant at 15 per cent,
*** significant at 10 per cent, **** significant at 5 per cent,
***** significant at 1 per cent.
IV: Instrumented by profitability (97), loss-making (97), overdue receivables.

enterprises and thus to more non-monetary transactions. Crucially, the indirect subsidies distributed via the barter system have incurred dead-weight losses for the state, compared with direct subsidies, they have also greatly obscured not only fiscal but also social policy.

The social costs of the non-cash economy relate primarily to wage arrears and payments in kind. Hence, the 'gain' of keeping the production wheels rolling and employees at work has been partly offset by late and in-kind wage payments. Moreover, the fiscal pressures resulting from the non-cash economy have severely undermined the state's ability to finance a social safety net. This implies that structural change has become even more unattractive politically and socially, providing a continued rationale for the non-cash economy.

Slow restructuring and weakened competition

The non-monetary economy has weakened product market competition, slowed down enterprise restructuring and inhibited innovation in products and processes. The larger and more complex the non-monetary market, the more difficult it becomes for an individual firm to break out of it. The enterprise survey shows that 40–45 per cent of barter deals were arranged via intermediaries. In an environment with a thick non-cash market, many firms can choose between a large and organised non-monetary demand for their products and a small, and perhaps remote, cash market. Attempts to defect by pressuring their key customers to pay in cash may sideline a company and make it more difficult to purchase vital inputs.

Barter deals can create artificial demand. When an automobile producer uses cars to pay its workers, its suppliers and the tax authorities, they may then choose to on-sell these products, but – given marketing costs – will have a significant incentive to use these cars themselves. This tends to create 'virtual' markets for goods that may otherwise be uncompetitive. The effect is likely to slow down product innovation and lead to a persistence of inefficient production lines.

Lastly, competition in the product market will be weakened. Many firms rely on a few key customers in barter deals. Dual monopolies abound and firms are often 'locked into' chains of barter with few significant outside options. This tends to segment markets and weaken competition among enterprises. This is particularly damaging in Russia, where competition is already very weak in many markets, partly because of high transport costs and a low share of international trade in GDP, and partly because Russian industry operates at a fairly high scale, with strong vertical links and dependencies.

Table 5.5 *Costs of non-monetary transactions*

(a) Price distortions

Per cent of respondents using respective deals	As compared to cash prices, non-monetary prices are:				
	Much higher	A bit higher	Same	A bit lower	Much lower
Barter	25	28	38	7	2
Offsets	24	26	43	5	2
Veksels	16	25	50	6	2
Debt sales, swaps, roll-overs	22	26	44	6	2

(b) Time costs

Per cent of respondents using respective deals	As compared to money, non-monetary deals take:				
	Much more time	A bit more time	Same time	A bit less time	Much less time
Barter	69	17	10	2	2
Offsets	73	16	8	2	1
Veksels	56	23	17	1	3
Debt sales, swaps, roll-overs	71	17	7	2	2

Reduced flexibility and transparency at the firm level

The non-monetary economy can have a detrimental impact on the economic health and stability of industrial enterprises. In money-based economies, holding cash is vital for enterprises. If they are hit by a temporary negative demand or credit shock, they can use existing cash reserves to keep the enterprise running without major disruption. In Russia, the non-monetary system implies that firms hold very little cash at any point in time. This makes them more vulnerable to temporary fluctuations in supply and demand, especially given the scarcity of bank credit. Hence, although barter can create additional credit, it reduces flexibility. Reduced flexibility could potentially lead to the collapse of profitable, but temporarily cash-strapped, enterprises.

Perhaps even more damaging has been the effect of barter on firm transparency and access to outside finance. As noted earlier, barter prices tend to be highly distorted in nominal terms. Both revenues and costs are over-stated in the accounts (see table 5.5), implying a downward distortion on operating profitability (profit/revenues). Box 5.1 shows that this can have highly confusing implications for analysing a firm's activities. It is shown that firms may appear to be selling exports at a loss, 'just to raise cash', while in truth it may just reflect exaggerated barter prices for domestically procured inputs.

The result of the price distortions emanating from the non-monetary economy is that it becomes difficult for outsiders to judge whether a company is profitable or not or what is an appropriate business strategy to pursue. Banks will be faced with greater information problems, leading to even lower willingness to lend. Furthermore, governments will be unable to distinguish good from bad firms, certainly complicating any industrial strategy that requires discrimination over types of firm. The price distortions arising from non-monetary transacting thus lock the Russian enterprise system into a bad – no restructuring – equilibrium.

Box 5.1   Price distortions and firm profitability

Every year, firm F produces 20 units of good Y and requires 10 units of good N as inputs. It sells 10 units of Y for export for cash and barters the other 10 units against the 10 units of input N from domestic supplier S. The world price for both N and Y is p. The barter deal thus reflects the world market relative price. However, barter allows the two firms to inflate their prices, for example by 50 per cent as in case 2 below. Apart from inputs from S, firm F incurs marginal costs of $(1/10)$ c.

Case 1 nominal barter price is p		Case 2 nominal barter price is $1.5p$
Total revenues: $20p$		Total revenues: $25p$
Cash revenues: $10p$		Cash revenues: $10p$
Total costs: $2c + 10p$		Total costs: $2c + 15p$
Cash costs: $2c$		Cash costs: $2c$
Profit (cash = book) : $10p - 2c$	$=$	Profit (cash = book) : $10p - 2c$
Gross margin: $(10p - 2c)/20p$	$>$	Gross margin: $(10p - 2c)/25p$
Export margin: $(5p - c)/10p$	$>$	Export margin: $(2.5p - c)/10p$
Domestic margin: $(5p - c)/10p$	$<$	Domestic margin: $(7.5p - c)/15p$

The inflation of domestic barter prices raises domestic costs and revenues relative to export revenues. This exaggerates the margin on domestic sales and distorts downwards the margin on export sales and on overall sales. If the enterprise just breaks even (i.e. $c = 5p$), then exports appear to be loss-making and domestic sales profitable when barter prices are inflated.

7 Barter or money? Some uncomfortable policy choices

The proliferation of non-monetary transactions in Russia can best be understood in terms of financing innovations in the face of shocks to bank credit and to explicit budgetary support. Part of this response can be construed as substituting indirect credit from the state and workers for bank credit. Yet these responses have come with considerable costs, as section 6 has demonstrated. These costs should be viewed dynamically, not least because the thicker and more coordinated the market in non-monetary transactions, the more difficult it becomes to re-substitute bank for non-bank credit, while also placing additional barriers on the ability of banks and government to screen firms because of the noisy signals sent by barter. In this light, clearly the key challenge is not just the desirability of moving away from non-conventional trading and payments indiscipline, but also the mechanics.

Constraints

The first constraint is that not only do most Russian firms currently lack access to bank credit but that the banking system has all but collapsed. Even before August 1998, the banks were unable to play a conventional role of intermediators. Lack of confidence in the currency and in banks themselves has led to a continuing reluctance on the part of households to hold rouble deposits. This has – among other things – reduced the effective base for seigniorage and the inflation tax. Thus, even supposing a willingness and ability on the part of banks to provide credit to creditworthy firms, the supply of loanable funds would be directly and adversely affected by the lack of demand for bank deposits on the part of households.

The second, crucial constraint relates to the question of creditworthiness. The aggregate credit shock described in section 3 led to firms relying heavily on non-monetary transactions and was ultimately sanctioned by both quasi-fiscal and fiscal institutions participating and effectively granting net credit to the system. Chains of transactions have proliferated, alongside progressively more complex instruments. A thick market in non-monetary deals has emerged. One consequence has been unambiguously higher levels of output and employment. Another consequence has been the growing inability to sort firms in terms of underlying viability, given the noise imparted by non-monetary transactions and arrears. We now consider, in the light of these constraints, a number of stylised policy options.

A 'tough' approach

Put simply, such an approach would require rapid closing down of the sources of 'soft' finance and their associated transacting instruments, consistent with the goals of stabilisation and structural reform. Top of the agenda would necessarily be eliminating credit creation by quasi-fiscal and budget institutions alongside intolerance for use of money surrogates and in-kind settlements.

However, this type of approach would tend to close down legitimate trade credit without addressing the underlying banking sector failure. It would also probably pull down both good and bad firms. This latter effect results not just from information failures but from chain effects and the thickness of the market in non-monetary deals. Put differently, assuming that a sharp credit crunch embracing non-bank credit can be enforced – itself a big assumption – the likelihood of a domino effect is high. Furthermore, in the absence of bank lending to enterprises, a one-step move to hard budget constraints would not even necessarily raise social welfare. The output and employment contraction could be expected to be large. This obviously raises important political economy considerations, particularly given the revealed preference for employment stability among Russian policy-makers. Indeed, such an approach is likely to be incredible, particularly in the absence of a credible threat of bankruptcy and a workable system of benefits and adequate level of fallbacks for job losers.

A 'soft' approach

This type of approach would probably involve explicit relaxation in the monetary stance and a commitment to inject net liquidity into the system. The underlying argument is that firms are credit-constrained and that increased liquidity would effectively substitute private credit and non-monetary instruments. To the extent that substitution of private credit and non-monetary transactions by bank credit and money dominated, this could be associated with an immediate jump in the price level consistent with the new money supply target but not necessarily with any inflationary persistence. However, these assumptions are not warranted.

First, there is currently little intermediation by a banking system that has all but collapsed. The demand for bank deposits is low. Second, even assuming a pure substitution effect through an injection of liquidity, the new level of money supply could only be consistent with an enlarged fiscal deficit, at a time when the basic financing instruments for that deficit have been effectively reduced to money creation. Putting these factors together suggests that the inflationary consequences would be substantial and immediate. An increase in the money supply would likely be associated with a *fall* in money demand and thus a rise in inflation.

Third, the premise of a significant substitution effect on impact is itself questionable. This is because the costs to the individual firm of 'defecting' from non-monetary transacting is likely to be a function of the scale of that market. The thicker and more coordinated that market, the higher the costs of defecting. Interestingly, this basic ambiguity also emerges from the firm survey discussed above. When asked what the effect of a hypothetical imposition of timely, cash payments by utilities would be on the incidence of non-monetary transactions, roughly comparable shares – 40 per cent – of respondents believed that this would either increase or decrease use. Further, when asked what would be the effect of an increase in the money supply, just over half of the respondents thought that it would reduce non-monetary transacting, but as much as 20 per cent thought it would actually increase the scale of non-monetary transacting.

In short, given the constraints outlined in section 7, the trade-off between inflation, employment and output is likely to be highly sensitive to the demand for money and to institutional weaknesses.

A comprehensive approach

Several elements of such an approach can be identified. The first involves restricting the scope for non-monetary transactions and progressively reducing the thickness of that market. The objectives should include lowering the costs of 'defection' to money for agents. Implementation would require not only winding down acceptance of in-kind and late payments by budget and quasi-fiscal institutions but also in shifting tax monitoring and collection away from the banking system. Aside from providing direct incentives for firms to transact in money, this will be critical in rebuilding the banking sector's ability and credibility in intermediation. The biggest challenge, of course, is precisely the latter. Given the scale of bank failure and the low efficiency of Russian banking technology, intermediation can probably be accelerated only by permitting entry of foreign banks alongside providing access to branch structures. Foreign entry is, however, likely to be difficult politically.

Yet to break the regime of 'soft' budget constraints will require direct attention to the principal sources of credit to the firm sector, as well as measures to increase the willingness of incumbents to accept restructuring and job losses. With respect to the first, the governance of the large energy firms, particularly *Gazprom*, is central. The clear objective must be to shift management's incentives toward profit-maximisation and tax compliance. One approach would be initially to reassert greater effective federal control over such firms, followed by establishment of adequate control oversight, leading ultimately to new leasing and management arrangements.[21] In exchange for allowing participation in a supervisory board, foreigners might be induced to provide required investment in these firms. At the same time, such participation could help ensure that such firms are no longer used as the sources of 'soft' finance for the failing parts of the economy.

However, even if the supply of 'soft' credit can be affected by changes in governance, experience also suggests that no credible enforcement of hard budgets, including tightening the bankruptcy constraint, will occur without providing an explicit system of fallbacks for losers – and, as importantly, by relaxing the constraints on entry of new firms and their cross-over into the formal sector. For the former, this will involve establishment of a functioning system of benefits with adequate targeting of them. For the latter, there will have to be non-trivial changes to the tax code, as well as systematic elimination of other barriers to entry.

Lastly, where political economy considerations are paramount and outside opportunities limited, there will be a case for explicit subsidies to declining firms or regions. These should generally take the form of time-bound financial support, ideally linked to social and environmental goals, rather than production. In such cases, it is altogether preferable that those subsidies be placed on-budget, rather than provided through the set of indirect channels that has given rise in recent years to the exotic transacting modes that this chapter has chronicled.

References

Aghion, P. and S. Commander (1999). 'Some Proposals for Improving Corporate Governance while reducing Barter and Fiscal Imbalances in Russia', London, EBRD and Cambridge, MA, Harvard University, mimeo

Alfandari, G. and M. Schaffer (1996). '"Arrears" in the Russian Enterprise Sector', in Commander, Fan and Schaffer (1996), 87–139

Aukutsionek, S. (1998) 'Industrial Barter in Russia', *Communist Economies and Economic Transformation*, 10(2), 179–88

Blanchard, O. and M. Kremer (1997). 'Disorganisation', *Quarterly Journal of Economics*, 112(4), 1091–26

Calvo, G. and F. Coricelli (1994). 'Credit Market Imperfections and Output Response in Previously Centrally Planned Economies', in G. Caprio *et al.* (eds.), *Building Sound Finance in Emerging Market Economies*, Washington, DC, IMF and World Bank.

---

[21] Such a proposal is contained in Aghion and Commander (1999).

Calvo, G. and M. Kumar (1994). 'Money Demand, Bank Credit and Economic Performance in Former Socialist Economies', *IMF Staff Papers*, 41(2), 314–49

Clifton, E. and M. Khan (1993). 'Interenterprise Arrears in Transforming Economies: The Case of Romania', *IMF Staff Papers*, 40(3), 680–96

Commander, S., Dolinskaya, I. and C. Mummsen (2000). 'Determinants of Barter in Russia: An Empirical Analysis', EBRD and IMF, mimeo

Commander, S., Fan, Q. and M. Schaffer (1996). *Enterprise Restructuring and Economic Policy in Russia*, Washington, DC, World Bank

Commander, S. and C. Mummsen (1998). 'Micro-foundations of Barter in Russia', EBRD, December, mimeo

Coricelli, F. (1998), *Macroeconomic Policies and the Development of Markets in Transition Economies*, Budapest, Central European University Press

EBRD (1997). *Transition Report 1997*, London, EBRD

(1998). *Transition Report 1998*, London, EBRD

Fan, Q., Lee, U. and M. Schaffer (1996). 'Firms, Banks and Credit in Russia', in Commander, Fan and Schaffer (1996), 140–65

Gaddy, C. and B. Ickes (1998a). 'To Restructure or Not to Restructure: Informal Activities and Enterprise Behavior in Transition', Washington, DC, Brookings Institution and College Park, Pennsylvania State University, February, mimeo

(1998). 'Beyond a Bailout: Time to Face Reality About Russia's "Virtual Economy"', Washington, DC, Brookings Institution and College Park, Pennsylvania State University, June, mimeo

Gorochowskij, B., Kaufmann, D. and D. Marin (1998). 'Barter in Transition Economies', Berlin, Munich and Washington, DC, University of Munich, September, mimeo

Kaufmann, D. and D. Marin (1998). 'Disorganisation, Financial Squeeze and Barter', Munich and Washington, DC, World Bank, July, mimeo; a revised version of this is chapter 8 in this volume

Ledeneva, A. (1998). *Russia's Economy of Favours: Blat, Networking and Informal Exchange*, Cambridge, Cambridge University Press

OECD (1997). *Economic Survey: Russian Federation*, Paris, OECD

Oxford Analytica (1998). 'East Europe Daily Brief: Russia – Non-Monetary Exchange', 26–27 August

Poser, J. (1998). 'Monetary Disruptions and the Emergence of Barter in FSU Economies', *Communist Economies and Economic Transformation*, 10(2), 157–77

Tchaidze, R. and G. Tsibouris (1998). 'Non-Cash Settlements of Expenditures in the Baltics, Russia and Other Former Soviet Republics', Washington, DC, International Monetary Fund

World Bank (1999). 'Non-Payments in Russia', Washington DC, World Bank, mimeo

6 Barter in Russia

SERGEI GURIEV AND BARRY W. ICKES

1 Introduction

One of the striking features of Russia's economic transition has been the enormous growth in the use of barter. What was a passing phase of transition in Central Europe has become an endemic feature of the Russian situation. The Russian economy has experienced redemonetisation (Ickes, Murrell and Ryterman, 1997): in 1992 barter accounted for some 5 per cent of enterprise transactions, but by 1997 this had increased to at least 47 per cent.[1] Estimates of barter turnover vary from 30 per cent to 80 per cent of inter-enterprise transactions (Aukutsionek, 1998; Commander and Mumssen, 1998). Barter is also used in paying taxes to local, regional and even federal governments. Even wages are occasionally paid in kind (Friebel and Guriev, 1999).

The emergence of barter as a stable institution of exchange is a challenge to modern economic theory. Introductory textbooks in economics point out that barter is inferior to monetary exchange in terms of transaction costs. This is why barter is so rare in modern economies. Russian reality, however, is diametrically opposed to the conventional wisdom. As we argue below, Russian enterprises prefer to use barter even when they have a choice to pay in cash. Why is the Russian economy demonetised? Is it good or bad? Is it possible to remonetise it – and if 'yes', how? Is Russia especially vulnerable to barter or can its demonetisation

We thank Dmitri Kvasov, Kostya Rybakov and Anton Suvorov for excellent research assistance, Paul Seabright and seminar participants at NES and RECEP for excellent comments on previous drafts. This work was done as part of the GET project of the New Economic School. The financial support of the Ford Foundation and the MacArthur Foundation are greatly appreciated.

[1] See (Aukutsionek, 1998; Hendley, Ickes and Ryterman, 1998) for time series evidence on barter. Hendley, Ickes and Ryterman (1998) points out that barter is prevalent across Russian regions, with Moscow being the relative exception.

disease spread over to other countries? Such are the questions we are going to address in this chapter.

2 Endogeneity

Popular discussions of barter in Russia typically assume that barter arises from factors outside the control of enterprise directors. Barter is often seen as the outcome of forces external to the enterprise, and over which it has little control. This is not a useful assumption, however. Barter is, in fact, a choice variable for enterprises; it is a strategy that an enterprise can employ to reduce the total costs of procuring inputs. To understand why enterprises may prefer to use barter it is necessary to understand the choices facing enterprises.

We begin with the premise that barter is a *choice* that enterprises make.[2] Whether an enterprise engages in barter or not depends on an evaluation of the costs and benefits of barter. While employing barter involves the usually noted transactions costs, it also affords the buyer the opportunity to pay an effectively lower price.[3] Many papers that analyse barter in Russia study this trade-off to understand why enterprises engage in barter. In this chapter, we want to take a further step and ask what actions enterprises will take if they find that barter is to their advantage.

If we suppose that the effective price of purchasing inputs is cheaper using barter, it follows that enterprises will prefer to pay with barter than with money. There must be some way for sellers to limit the use of barter. One method would be to limit barter to enterprises with which there are good relations.[4] Alternatively, it may be thought that barter will be used only by enterprises that cannot afford to pay with cash – that is, barter is the result of a liquidity constraint.[5] Notice, however, that if enterprises receive a discount for being in financial stringency, it will pay to *pretend* to suffer from financial stringency. In other words, enterprises will have an incentive to signal that they are liquidity-constrained.

The insight that enterprises may pretend to be liquidity-constrained has important implications for studying barter. Consider, for example,

---

[2] This premise is a recurrent theme of the chapters in this volume.
[3] This still begs the question of why the seller is willing to accept lower-priced goods. Presumably, the key reason is the ability to pass these off for payment in taxes. This begs the further question of why governments are willing to allow tax offsets. The prevalence of tax offsets, especially at the regional level, is an accepted fact. But the motivation is more complex. See Gaddy and Ickes (1998) for a discussion.
[4] See Gaddy and Ickes (1998).
[5] As argued in Woodruff (1999), where barter is a means of cutting the price to enterprises that cannot pay the nominal amount with money. See also Ericson and Ickes (2000).

one standard approach to understanding the causes of barter in Russia: enterprise surveys. A number of papers (such as Aukutsionek, 1998; Commander and Mummsen, 1998) use this approach and find that directors consider liquidity to be the major determinant of barter. Enterprise A's director says that his enterprise delivers output to enterprise B in exchange for goods rather than money because enterprise B does not have cash. Notice, however, that the response of the enterprise director may be biased. This is not to suggest that he is being dishonest, but it is quite possible that even if enterprise B had cash *he might have preferred to use it for other purposes*, given the knowledge that enterprise A would accept payment in kind. So enterprise B does not have any incentive (and probably has a disincentive) to show its cash and the lack of cash, if any, may be endogenous: the assumption by the director of enterprise A that cash is lacking is a large part of the reason why it is lacking.[6] Respondents to surveys may thus over-state the liquidity problems of their counterparts.

Notice that this bias is not due to dishonest reporting on the part of respondents. Rather it is due to the respondents' incorrect information about the liquidity situation of their partners. Moreover, this incomplete information is the result of the *strategic* decision of the partners: to be able to use barter it may be necessary to conceal the true financial state of the enterprise in order to qualify for non-cash settlement. Hence, not only is barter endogenous – a point recognised by much of the literature (though not necessarily the general public) – but the *apparent* liquidity position of the enterprise is as well.

An alternative approach

To cope with the potential for bias – owing to incomplete information possessed by sellers and the strategic use of financial information by buyers – we have taken an alternative approach to analysing the role of liquidity. We start with directors' estimates of how much of their enterprises' revenues took the form of cash and barter. We then match this data with information on the enterprise's financial accounts collected by *Goskomstat*. Because the latter data is not transaction-specific, we

---

[6] It is important to understand that microeconomic arguments rely very much upon the structure of monetary and barter prices, and that these prices arise in turn as outcomes of enterprises' decisions to involve in monetary and barter transactions. See Guriev, Pospelor and Shaposhrik (1998) for a general equilibrium model with money and barter where prices are endogenised and show that barter may partially crowd out money in equilibrium.

presume that it is less likely to be contaminated by the bias discussed above. We then use this matched data set to study barter in Russia, and to find out what characteristics of an enterprise make it use barter.[7]

The data
The data set we use was put together as part of a research project at the New Economic School on 'Non-Monetary Transactions in Russian Economy.' This data set was created by matching the surveys of managers of Russian industrial firms conducted in 1996–8 by Serguei Tsoukhlo of the Centre for Business Trends (Institute of Economies in Transition, Moscow) with a *Goskomstat* database of Russian enterprises (Federal Committee of Statistics of Russian Federation).This database includes compulsory statistical reports that all medium and large enterprises must submit to the Russian Federal Statistics Committee. There are over 16,000 enterprises in the database. Since the *Goskomstat* data were most complete for 1996 and 1997 we focused our empirical work on these two years.

Our data on the proportions of revenues in cash and non-cash form are taken from a survey of directors conducted in the autumn of 1996, 1997 and 1998 by the Centre for Business Trends at the Institute of Economies in Transition. The sample is fairly representative and includes large industrial enterprises in all industries.[8] The barter data are answers to the following (eight) questions: 'how much of your firm's inputs (outputs) were paid in roubles, in dollars, in kind and in promissory notes?'

The barter data included 600–700 enterprises for each year. After matching these with the *Goskomstat* data we ended up with 987 observations, made up of 475 enterprises (52 per cent) in 1996 and 512 enterprises in 1997. Among these, 264 enterprises appeared both in 1996 and 1997. Some information on the enterprises in the sample is given in table 6.1.

3 Empirical results

The prevalence of barter in Russia

The dramatic growth in barter in Russia has been widely noted (for example, by Commander and Mumssen, 1998; Hendley, Ickes and Ryterman, 1998). Our concern here is with its prevalence across

---

[7] This approach is also used in Commander and Mumssen (1998).
[8] Ferrous metallurgy, chemical and petrochemical industries are slightly over-represented. As for the regional variation, the Far East is under-represented while Western Siberia and the Volgo-Vyatka regions are over-represented.

Table 6.1 *Share of barter in sales, November 1998*

Industry	No. of enterprises in sample	Share of barter in sales, November 1998, weighted av. (std dev.)
Electricity	4	0.67 (0.12)
Fuel	6	0.21 (0.23)
Ferrous metals	32	0.50 (0.19)
Non-ferrous metals	6	0.26 (0.19)
Chemical and petro-chemical	44	0.46 (0.21)
Machinery	307	0.48 (0.23)
Pulp and forestry	75	0.47 (0.23)
Construction materials	71	0.51 (0.22)
Textile	164	0.43 (0.25)
Food	82	0.28 (0.21)
Other	15	0.17 (0.18)
Total	806	0.44 (0.24)

enterprise types and industries and other characteristics. As a measure of barter we use the share of barter in total sales. We also have data on the share of barter in payments for the enterprises' inputs. As one can imagine, the latter two statistics are very highly correlated. Table 6.1 shows the average share of barter in sales for various industries.

The share of barter differs across industries but the differences are not statistically significant.[9] One of the stereotypes regarding the Russian economy is that it is clearly split into 'real' and 'virtual' (or 'market' and 'non-market') economies.[10] The idea is that some enterprises use only money while others use only barter. However, the data are inconsistent with this picture of a sharply segmented economy, suggesting rather that Russian enterprises use a mixture of monetary and non-monetary means of payment. Some enterprises are indeed always paid in money, but the vast majority of enterprises are paid both in barter and in money. This is quite evident in figure 6.1, where we observe that the share of barter in sales is distributed rather uniformly over a broad range.

---

[9] With the exception of electricity where barter is significantly higher than in other industries.

[10] This 'dichotomy' conjecture has probably been inspired by stylised models (such as Gaddy and Ickes, 1998b, and Polterovitch, 1998). Yet, as is evident from Igor's Rules (see p. 155)), most enterprises attempt to have a foot in 'each market'.

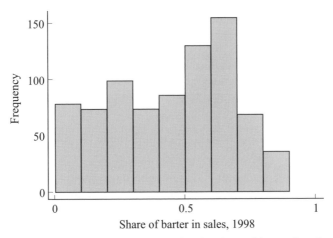

Figure 6.1 Distribution of enterprise, by share of barter in sales, 1998

The largest numbers of enterprises fall in a range of 50–70 per cent of barter. But the data indicate that shares of 10–20 per cent are as common as 70–80 per cent.

One implication of the broad variety of barter experience is that the choice of whether or not to use barter is an element of *strategy* for the enterprise. Because the effective price paid depends on the means of payment, enterprises try to pay with goods when they can, reserving the expenditure of money for those transactions where cash is essential. The resulting shares of barter across industries reflect the opportunities facing enterprises and market conditions.

This suggests that a central issue in understanding barter in Russia is the question of why the effective price of products paid for in goods is typically less than that of cash. That is, why under current Russian conditions, is there an effective discount for barter? There are two aspects to this. First, there may be factors such as the tax system which penalise the use of money.[11] If cash receipts are more heavily taxed, then parties to a transaction may split the surplus generated by barter. Second, sellers rarely offer cash discounts, primarily owing to legal restrictions. The same nominal value of receipts is received whether the payment is made in cash or coal. If it were possible for the buyer to sell the coal for the nominal price there would be no reason (aside from tax considerations) to use barter. Hence, the use of

[11] See Gaddy and Ickes (1998a) for a discussion of the cost of using cash in the Russian economy.

barter suggests that the market value for the goods used to pay in kind is below the nominal market price. Hence, the costs of barter are disproportionately borne by the seller. This is why sellers typically restrict barter transactions to close trading partners. We explore several of these explanations below.

Another important finding from our data is that there are economies of scale in barter transactions. Controlling for market concentration,[12] a 1 per cent increase in the enterprise's size (measured as sales revenue) results in a 0.025 per cent increase in the share of barter in sales. The explanation for this is straightforward. The barter market is so comprehensive in modern Russia that everything can be bought for payments in kind and therefore virtually every product can be used as a means of payment. But in order to join the barter network, an enterprise has to pay a fixed entry cost – most commonly to hire a 'barter broker'. It could also be that larger enterprises are more likely to be older, and involved in inherited barter chains. New, smaller enterprises cannot afford to join the barter network or cannot find a vacant niche in it. Hence the size–barter relationship.

A key empirical finding is that, in addition to the static economies of scale, there is also a dynamic economy of scale in barter: *ceteris paribus*, an enterprise that uses barter today is more likely to use barter tomorrow. This is a robust finding that stands up to the inclusion of all types of independent variables. Indeed, our empirical analysis suggests that barter today is by far the variable that best explains barter tomorrow. This could be owing to learning by doing, or simply to fixed costs associated with forming barter relationships: once formed, the marginal cost of maintaining barter is much lower.

Barter has become so common in the contemporary Russian economy that even exporters and foreign-owned enterprises have become involved in it. As table 6.2 shows, barter is employed by all types of enterprises: public or private, and whether it has domestic or foreign owners. Although the share of barter in sales appears to differ according to ownership type in table 6.2, these differences are not statistically significant. When we include enterprise size in a regression of barter share on ownership type, differences among the latter do not matter: all ownership types use barter to roughly the same extent. This may be owing to the fact that our classification of ownership types is very rough. We are not able, for example, to distinguish between insider-dominated and outsider-dominated private enterprises. Hence, the degree of outside ownership may matter in ways that we cannot capture given our

---

[12] We discuss the effects of concentration in section 4.

Table 6.2 *Barter shares and enterprise types*

Ownership	Share of barter in sales weighted av. (std dev.)
Federal	0.26 (0.22)
Regional	0.22 (0.17)
Municipal	0.21 (0.21)
Public organisations	0.45 (0.29)
Private	0.41 (0.23)
Mixed private and public (Russian only)	0.39 (0.23)
Mixed foreign and Russian	0.51 (0.10)
Total	0.37 (0.24)

ownership data.[13] It is important to note, however, that once barter becomes widespread we would expect any differences introduced by ownership type to diminish.[14]

We have also found that access to global markets has a little impact on barter. One would expect that an enterprise exporting one more rouble of its output abroad would sell one less rouble for barter. However, the enterprise would then have to pay cash for its own inputs, which is more costly. The data support this hypothesis: an increase of one rouble in exports leads to a decrease of roughly 20 kopecks in barter sales. One may suspect that these are the 'wrong' exports – i.e. exports to cash-constrained CIS countries – but the distinction between CIS and non-CIS exports turns out to be insignificant.

Explaining differential use of barter: Igor's Rules
What explains the variety of barter experiences across enterprises? Gaddy and Ickes (1998a) suggest that the behaviour of Russian

[13] Unfortunately, our data does not allow us to test for differences between inside and outside ownership. Using standard survey data, Ickes and Ryterman (1997) found that barter was greater in enterprises with more outside ownership. The presumed explanation is that barter is a method for concealing income from outside owners. It would also be interesting to see if there is a difference between *privatised* and *de novo* private enterprises, but our data set does not allow us to distinguish between these. Notice that such a test would have to also control for the likelihood that *de novo* firms are more likely to be found in consumer goods industries, which are likely to deal more in cash. See p. 164–7.

[14] This would follow as long as enterprises of different types interacted with each other. If enterprises of similar ownership only interacted with each other, the story might be different.

enterprise directors can be described by *Igor's Four Rules of Management Planning*:[15]

I_1 *Have some percentage of your sales to the federal government* – ideally, at about the level of your estimated federal taxes. You know you will not be paid for these sales, but you use it to offset taxes.

I_2 *Have the capability to provide municipal services so that you can offset local taxes* – an ideal method is to have a construction division that can fix schools, etc.

I_3 *Set up some barter operations for the rest of your inputs, especially fuels, electricity and so on* – It is best if you have some products that utilities need. Then they will pay you in *veksels* that you can redeem for the inputs.

I_4 *Export something to a paying, hard-currency market* – you need some cash for your operations, mainly for wages and for urgently needed non-wage inputs. Exports need not be of your major product.

Igor's Rules describe behavioural rules for an enterprise director. The degree to which they can be followed, however, will vary across enterprises. There are two important aspects to this. First, there are industry and enterprise characteristics that are critical. For example, enterprises will differ in their ability to follow I_1, because not all enterprises have federal orders. Similarly, the ability to supply municipal services is easiest for those with large construction crews. Even within the same industry the ability to follow the various rules will differ owing to particular characteristics of the good and the nature of production.

Consider the implication of I_3. Enterprises that follow this rule will employ barter to at least the extent of their purchases of material inputs. An enterprise that was in complete compliance with this rule would use barter for all non-wage inputs. Cash would be used only for paying wages (if the enterprise also followed I_1 and I_2). This suggests that the share of barter in total sales will depend on the nature of the production process itself.

The second factor is perhaps even more important. Even controlling for enterprise and industry characteristics, the ability to follow these rules will depend on the quality of relationships that enterprises have built up with officials. This is especially true with respect to I_1 and I_2. The ability to pay taxes using offsets is heavily dependent on the quality of relationships that an enterprise has built up with key officials.

---

[15] Igor had a final injunction – Whatever you do don't make a profit: the government will take it all in taxes. Of course what Igor really means is 'do not make a profit that can be observed'.

Tax evasion

One important factor contributing to the growth of barter in Russia is tax evasion.[16] Barter in some cases allows enterprises to avoid declaring some income. By avoiding money altogether, the transaction is not recorded in the banking system.[17] But a more important reason than tax reporting is tax collection. Barter allows the enterprises to avoid the first line of tax collection in Russia today: the banking system. Any enterprise that is in arrears to the government for unpaid taxes is by law subject to having its bank accounts blocked. All transactions that flow through the banking system are available for collection by the State Tax Service for enterprises that are delinquent on their tax obligations. This provides a direct incentive for enterprises with tax arrears to avoid using the banking system, as the effective tax rate on revenue is 100 per cent.[18]

Enterprises can use various approaches to circumvent blocked accounts. They can hold multiple accounts, open new ones and close old ones at a rapid rate, and generally try to stay one step ahead of the tax inspectors. Offshore accounts is another alternative. Using cash – that is, banknotes – is a third. But clearly, another way to avoid using the banks is to avoid money altogether – i.e. barter or *veksels*.

Legally, barter transactions are taxable. And many, though far from all, barter transactions are recorded for the tax authorities, the statistics agencies and others to see. Enterprises thus incur a tax liability on sales for which they are paid in barter goods. But the burden then falls on the tax collection end. Since no money is deposited on the enterprise's bank accounts, the convenient and automatic mechanism of direct deduction does not work. The enterprise never received cash from the sale and thus has no cash with which to pay taxes.[19]

Evidence on the role of tax evasion as a motivation for barter is mixed. Some studies (for example, Hendley, Ickes and Ryterman, 1998) find survey evidence in favour of the tax evasion hypothesis while others do

---

[16] See, for example, Yakovlev (1999).

[17] A more preferred method is to use off-shore payments to hide transactions from the tax authorities, but this is hard for enterprises to accomplish if they are not engaged in international trade.

[18] This is discussed at length in Hendley, Ickes and Ryterman (1998).

[19] If it were the case that barter constituted only a relatively small percentage of enterprise sales, with the rest in monetary form, then the tax authorities might realistically expect the enterprise to be able to pay enough in cash from its other sales to cover the taxes incurred on the barter transaction. But when barter and other related non-monetary payments constitute as much as 90 per cent of all sales for some enterprises, enterprises simply do not have the cash and will not pay. The same goes for other obligations of the enterprise – to suppliers of material inputs, utilities, etc.

not (Commander and Mummsen, 1998).[20] But in most cases these studies focus the question too narrowly. They typically ask whether enterprises use barter to evade taxes. A more appropriate question would ask whether enterprises use barter to reduce the *effective* tax burden. Enterprises often use barter not to *evade* taxes but in order to *pay taxes.*[21]

Consider, for example, an enterprise that is in position to follow Igor's Rule I_2. The enterprise could pay its tax liability in money, but this would require selling its output for cash. Alternatively, the enterprise can negotiate with the government to supply some service as an offset for taxes. If the enterprise has resources that are not fully utilised the latter alternative is likely to reduce the effective tax burden. This would not be the case if the enterprise faced a perfectly elastic effective demand for its output. In that case, it could use the resources to produce and sell the output to obtain the cash with which to pay taxes. But most Russian enterprises face a highly inelastic demand curve with respect to cash sales: to increase cash sales requires a steep discount on the price. In that case negotiating an offset with the government is often the preferred option.

Notice that once the government is willing to engage in tax offsets the options open to enterprises expand. Now the enterprise can potentially use the receipts from barter transactions to pay taxes. This reduces the cost to the seller of accepting goods rather than cash. This is especially true when the non-cash receipts take the form of *veksels* from the natural monopolies, such as *Gazprom* or *UES*.

The essential point is that once the government is willing to engage in tax offsets enterprises face two effective tax rates, depending on whether taxes are paid in money or goods. This, in turn, alters the return to barter sales.

Liquidity hypothesis

Many authors, most notably Commander and Mummsen (1998), argue that the proliferation of barter is owing to a lack of liquidity. The question of cause is difficult to explore. Because of the network aspects of barter there is an important element of hysteresis involved: a factor that initially pushes enterprises into barter may not be the main factor that causes it to persist. It could be that initially some enterprises were

[20] Commander and Mummsen (1998) also point out that tax rates did not increase dramatically in 1995, which makes it hard to understand how tax evasion could account for the rapid growth of barter since then.
[21] This point was first noted in Gaddy and Ickes (1998a). Commander and Mummsen (1998) refer to this as 'tax bargaining'.

Table 6.3 *Liquid assets as a function of the level of barter (standard errors in parentheses)*

Share of barter in payments for inputs (per cent)	Average liquid assetts/(annual sales)
0–10	0.028 (0.02)
10–20	0.024 (0.02)
20–30	0.037 (0.03)
30–40	0.014 (0.01)
40–50	0.004 (0.003)
50–60	0.024 (0.03)
60–70	0.047 (0.09)
70–80	0.200 (0.54)
80–90	0.006 (0.005)

pushed into barter by a lack of liquidity but then the widespread use of barter results in enterprises using it regardless of their financial position.[22]

As we have noted, most surveys find that liquidity problems are the leading explanation for barter in Russia (Commander and Mummsen, 1998). This is a rather robust finding, but it suffers from the problem that sellers may not know the true liquidity situation of the buyer. Buyers may claim lack of liquidity in order to pay with goods. Hence, the standard empirical analysis of this question suffers from a potential source of bias owing to the fact that perceived liquidity is an endogenous variable.

The approach we take to test the liquidity hypothesis does not suffer from the same problem as previous approaches. This is because we obtain data on the financial position of the enterprise directly,[23] rather than from reports of sellers. Of course, we do face the general problem that enterprises may wish to under-report their true financial position, but that would make lack of liquidity appear to have a larger effect on barter.

Formally, the liquidity hypothesis states that enterprises engage in barter owing to a lack of liquidity. Therefore they cannot maintain transactions balances at a sufficient level to pay for their inputs with money. Some portion of their transactions must be paid for with alternative

---

[22] Commander and Mummsen (1998) also argue that the factors that initially cause barter may not be the same as those that cause it to persist.

[23] That is, from *Goskomstat*, as described in section 3.

Table 6.4 *Barter and liquidity, 1996 (standard errors in parentheses)*

Liquid assets/sales	−0.02	(0.12)
Log sales	0.014	(0.011)
Export/sales	−0.18**	(0.07)
Constant	0.13	(0.23)
No. of obs.	350	
R^2	0.16	

Note: ** Significant at 5 per cent

means.[24] However, the risk of a reporting bias on average means it would be misleading to look at the average liquidity position of firms in table 6.3. What matters is whether the *variation* in liquidity explains *variation* in barter across firms.[25] Table 6.3 shows that there is no significant direct correlation between barter and availability of liquid assets. Of course, this comparison does not control for other (potential) determinants of barter. Consider then equation (6.1), where B_i is the share of barter in sales for enterprise i, L_i is a measure of the enterprise's financial position, and X_i is a vector of enterprise characteristics such as size, share of exports in sales, labour productivity, regional and industry dummies, etc:

$$B_i = \alpha_0 + \alpha_1 L_i + \alpha_2 X_i \qquad (6.1)$$

The financial position is measured as stock of liquid assets divided by annual sales.[26] Our results suggest that there is no relationship between the financial position of the enterprise and the likelihood of barter. This is evident in table 6.4 which reports the results for a typical estimate of (6.1). Using export shares and size as control variables, we can reject the hypothesis that barter can be explained by the current liquidity problems of enterprises.[27]

[24] There is also the related assumption that the lack of liquidity cannot be resolved through borrowing from financial markets. Some enterprises do manage to borrow from suppliers by delaying payment – arrears – a phenomenon that is often associated, but is clearly different from, barter.

[25] Ideally, we could also check whether change in liquidity over time leads to more or less barter in the same firm. Unfortunately, we still do not have good data on firms' balance sheets for 1997.

[26] One might argue that enterprises have an incentive to under-report their actual financial positions. But it is hard to see why the frequency of under-reporting would be correlated with the prevalence of barter.

[27] The regression also included industry dummies for 11 categories. Data on liquid assets for enterprises in 1997 are still very incomplete, hence the regression covers only 1996 data.

These results indicate that the only variable that has explanatory power for the decision to barter is the share of export sales. Presumably this reflects the fact that exporters have lower costs of acquiring cash than non-exporters, so their optimal choice between barter and cash is different.[28]

It appears that enterprises which have a choice to pay either in cash or in kind, prefer to keep the cash and pay in kind.[29] This is consistent with the hypothesis that the transaction cost structure in the contemporary Russian economy is upside down: monetary transactions are more costly than barter. One can offer numerous explanations for the high costs of monetary transactions in Russia (Guriev, Pospelor and Shaposhnik, 1998): high taxes, insecure property rights, imperfect credit markets, rent-seeking by banks and other intermediaries.

4 Barter as a means of price discrimination

We believe that a discussion of barter in Russia is incomplete without taking into account at least one more aspect of the problem – namely the role of *market power*. The anecdotal evidence suggests that the natural monopolies – *Gazprom* (the natural gas monopoly), *RAO UES* (the electricity monopoly) and *MPS* (the railways) – known as the 'three fat boys' (*tri tolstyaka*) – are heavily engaged in barter transactions. *Gazprom* and *RAO UES* frequently complain that they collect only about 10 per cent of their revenues in cash. The rest is paid in *veksels*, coal, metal, machinery and even jet fighters. It is often argued that the natural monopolies continue to supply for barter because political pressure is exerted on them to do so.[30] However, as we argue below, there may also be an economic rationale behind barter sales in concentrated industries. The natural monopolies can use barter to price-discriminate among customers, collecting cash from rich ones and payments in kind from poor ones.[31]

The model we have in mind is rather simple.[32] The model considers N sellers selling a unit of good to a continuum of buyers who can use the

---

[28] This also explains why the devaluation of the rouble after August 1998 has led to some reduction in barter intensity. The rouble value of export earnings has increased further, moving the optimal barter–cash choice for exporters and increasing the relative size of export industries in the Russian economy.

[29] This is an application of Gresham's law. Barter drives out monetary transactions, to some extent.

[30] For example, in Gaddy and Ickes (1998b).

[31] Woodruff (1999) makes a similar argument. The key issue, of course, is how to identify who can actually afford to pay more.

[32] See Guriev and Kvasov (1999) for a rigorous formulation of the model, and for proofs.

good to produce certain output. The value of buyers' output is their private information. In the model of Ellingsen (1998) buyers are liquidity-constrained. In our model they are not. Each seller chooses how much to sell for cash or for the buyer's output. In the equilibrium, buyers who produce output with a value greater than the cash price of the input will choose to pay in cash, while those who produce output of lower value will choose to give up their output.

Barter is inefficient: with positive probability there is no double coincidence of wants and the seller (recipient of barter goods) throws the payment in kind away. Nonetheless, since barter allows them to sell to customers who would not otherwise buy the sellers' good, sellers sometimes prefer to sell for payments in kind. The other inefficiency comes from the fact that barter allows even value-subtracting buyers to keep producing since they are pooled with more efficient ones in the barter market.

Certainly, such price discrimination can exist only in a world of imperfect competition where the cash price is above the sellers' marginal cost. Otherwise the sellers are not interested in selling to customers who cannot afford to buy at the cash price.

Figure 6.2 presents the structure of equilibria as a function of a number of sellers. First, there can be barter equilibria in which buyers who produce high-value output buy for cash at the price p^b while all others trade in their output for the input. This equilibrium can exist only when the average value of payments in kind is higher than sellers' marginal

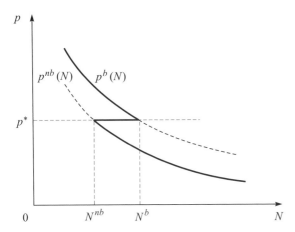

Figure 6.2 Oligopoly price, p, as function of number of sellers, N

cost. It turns out that this condition holds only when the industry is sufficiently concentrated.

The other equilibrium is a 'no-barter' equilibrium which is identical to a conventional Cournot equilibrium. It exists when the industry is sufficiently competitive. If the Cournot price p^{nb} is sufficiently low then sellers infer that the buyers who do not want to buy at this price produce poor-quality output. There is no point in selling to such customers.

It turns out that these two equilibria coexist at certain intermediate levels of concentration. Moreover, at these concentration levels there exists another (unstable) equilibrium. In the latter equilibrium, average quality of payments in kind is exactly equal to marginal costs and sellers are indifferent whether to sell for barter or not sell at all.

The structure of equilibria is rather intuitive.[33] First, both in the barter and the no-barter equilibrium, cash prices go down if number of sellers increases. Second, for a given number of sellers, the cash price in barter equilibrium is greater than price in no-barter equilibrium. This is also intuitive. In the barter equilibrium, sellers have more incentives to charge higher prices because the marginal buyers who would leave the market in case of the no-barter equilibrium now simply switch to barter and are therefore contributing to the profits from barter sales. Third, in barter equilibrium the cash price should be above some level p^* otherwise the average quality of payments in kind is below marginal cost and barter is not profitable. Similarly, in no-barter equilibrium, price should be below p^*.

The intuition for multiplicity of equilibria is as follows. Whenever one seller chooses to sell more for cash, it increases the supply in the cash market and therefore the cash price of the good goes down. The additional cash sales are purchased by buyers who were initially the most efficient ones among those buying for barter. With these buyers leaving the barter economy, the average quality of payments in kind goes down. Thus other sellers will have incentives to sell more for cash and less for barter. This externality is somewhat similar to aggregate demand externality in new Keynesian macroeconomics.

The share of barter in sales as a function of number of sellers N is shown in figure 6.3. If the industry is highly concentrated $N < N^{nb}$, there can only be a barter equilibrium and share of barter in sales is positive though declining with N. If the market is very competitive, there is no barter at all. Thus, at some $N \in (N^{nb}, N^b)$ there must be an abrupt jump from barter to no-barter equilibrium.

---

[33] See Guriev and Kvasov (1999) for a rigorous proof.

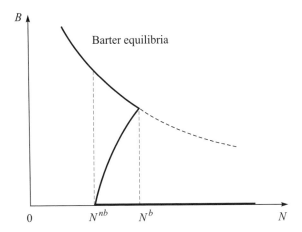

Figure 6.3 Share of barter in sales as a function of number of sellers in the industry

Empirical analysis of the price discrimination model

The model implies the following empirical predictions. First, the greater the degree of market concentration $1/N$, the greater the level of barter in sales, $b = R/(R + Q)$. Second, if the market is sufficiently competitive $(1/N < 1/N^b)$ then barter disappears altogether. Third, there should be a structural break in the range $1/N \in [1/N^b, 1/N^{nb}]$ where a small decrease in concentration results in an abrupt fall of the share of barter down to zero.

The data

We employ the data set described above, augmented with information about market structure. The concentration ratios CR4 (share of the four largest enterprises in total sales of the industry) were calculated for 5-digit *OKONH* industries (more than 300 industries) using the *Goskomstat* database.[34] In our sample, not all industries are present so that we have on average four enterprises per industry, with up to 30 enterprises in some industries. An alternative approach would be to calculate CR4s for 4-digit industries. However we believe that such concentration ratios are less informative. In Russia's *OKONH*

[34] We thank David Brown and Annette Brown for providing us with the concentration ratios they have calculated. The CR4s they have obtained coincide with ones that Federal Antimonopoly Committee has included in its annual report.

classification many 4-digit industries include 5-digit industries that use each other's outputs as inputs in their production and therefore do not compete with each other.

Empirical results

The main regression we run is an OLS regression of the share of barter in sales (y) on the concentration ratio in the enterprise's industry ($CR4$) and a proxy for size ls (logarithm of sales). We have included the proxy for size in our regression because there should evidently be economies of scale in using barter. In terms of our model, the greater the size of the enterprise the fewer the transaction costs of barter $(1 - \alpha)$ are.

Since our model applies to inter-enterprise transactions we need to control for sales to foreign and retail customers. The former is easy to measure: we shall use the export share in sales ex.[35] It is less clear how to control for retail sales. To proxy for sales to consumers we have used a dummy variable (CGI) that is associated with sales in the industry. We set $CGI = 1$ for consumer good industries and $CGI = 0$ otherwise. In our sample, 28 per cent enterprises are in consumer good industries. Unfortunately, CGI is a very crude estimate of enterprise exposure to the consumer market and is, in fact, industry-specific rather than enterprise-specific. Moreover, even producers of consumer goods are not necessarily selling directly to consumers or even to retail trade. Hence, one should be careful with interpretation of regressions with CGI. Nevertheless, we include CGI in the regression because it can help us control for an alternative explanation of the positive correlation between concentration and barter.[36]

This alternative explanation is related to the so-called 'distance to market'. The idea is that in consumer good industries there are many small enterprises, and all enterprises receive cash from individual consumers (or retail trade). In the intermediate good industries, the minimum efficient scale is high, there are fewer enterprises and they supply to other enterprises (or wholesale trade) who are willing to pay in kind. Thus, if we assume that the farther upstream an enterprise is the less cash is paid, there should be a positive correlation between distance from the market and barter. Since there is also a positive correlation between distance and concentration, barter and concentration should be correlated.

---

[35] We have also tried the share of non-CIS exports in sales and obtained similar results.

[36] We have not included any other industry dummies in the regressions. The main idea of our theory is that all industries are alike and the only thing that matters is market structure.

Table 6.5 *Summary statistics*

Variable	Mean	Std dev.	Min	Max
y	0.39	0.25	0	0.83
ls	17.13	1.76	9.10	22.27
$CR4$	0.38	0.26	0.04	1
ex	0.07	0.16	0	0.97
CG	0.28	0.45	0	1

To control for any year-specific effects, we include a dummy variable, *year*97 which equals 0 if the observation belongs to 1996 survey and 1 if it is from the 1997 survey.

The summary statistics for the key variables are shown in table 6.5. The correlation matrix is shown below.

The signs of pairwise correlations are intuitive. There is more barter in larger enterprises and in concentrated industries who sell less to foreign customers and consumers. There is more barter in 1997 than in 1996 (see Guriev and Ickes, 1999, for analysis of dynamic economies of scale in barter). Consumer good industries are less concentrated.

The results of the basic OLS regression are shown in Table 6.6. In most specifications, the share of barter depends positively and significantly on concentration. When we include *CGI* in the regression, both the magnitude and the significance level of this relationship tends to fall. Therefore, the 'distance-to-market' explanation of the correlation between barter and concentration is also consistent with the data.

We also test for the presence of a structural break based in terms of concentration. We introduced a dummy variable, *D*, that takes the value of 1 if $CR4 < 0.15$ and 0 otherwise. We have tried a few cutoff points including different cutoff points for 1996 and 1997. We have chosen the

	y	ls	$CR4$	ex	CGI	*year*97
y	1					
ls	0.14***	1				
$CR4$	0.11***	0.25***	1			
ex	−0.02	0.28***	0.20***	1		
CGI	−0.18***	−0.16***	−0.28***	−0.20***	1	
*year*97	0.10***	0.00	0.02	−0.07	0.02	1

Table 6.6 *Effects of concentration on barter*

y					
CR4	0.07** (0.03)	0.08** (0.03)	0.04 (0.03)	0.06** (0.03)	0.05* (0.03)
ls	0.017*** (0.007)	0.020*** (0.005)		0.018*** (0.005)	
CGI			−0.11*** (0.04)	−0.10*** (0.02)	−0.10*** (0.02)
ex		−0.11** (0.05)	−0.15*** (0.05)	−0.10** (0.05)	
year97	0.05*** (0.02)	0.05*** (0.02)	0.05*** (0.02)	0.05*** (0.02)	0.05*** (0.02)
const	0.05 (0.08)	0.02 (0.08)	0.08 (0.08)	0.38*** (0.02)	0.38*** (0.02)
N	987	987	987	987	987
R^2	0.03	0.04	0.06	0.05	0.05

Note: * Significant at 10 per cent, ** significant at 5 per cent, *** significant at 1 per cent.

cutoff 0.15 as the best fit in terms of significance of coefficients. In our sample, 26 per cent observations have $CR4 < 0.15$. The results of the regressions with the structural break are presented in Table 6.7.

The results are fully consistent with our model. If concentration is greater than the cutoff level, the coefficient on $CR496$ is positive and significant but small (0.12). If concentration is below the cutoff level, the coefficient on concentration is positive, significant and much greater. Indeed, it is equal to $0.12 + 0.99 = 1.11$. In terms of figure 6.3, the coefficient 0.12 is the slope of barter equilibria curve (mapped into $(1/N, y)$ coordinates) while 1.11 represents the abrupt jump from barter equilibria curve down to the no-barter equilibria curve. Above the cutoff, there is a unique barter equilibrium where barter increases with concentration. Below the cutoff, there are stable equilibria. Since at very low concentration levels, the barter equilibrium disappears, there

Table 6.7 *Barter, concentration and structural breaks*

y					
CR4	0.12*** (0.04)	0.13*** (0.04)	0.14*** (0.04)	0.14*** (0.04)	0.13*** (0.04)
D*CR4	0.99*** (0.22)	0.67*** (0.22)	0.95*** (0.22)	0.67*** (0.22)	0.93*** (0.22)
ls	0.019*** (0.005)	0.018*** (0.005)		0.020*** (0.005)	
CGI	−0.11*** (0.02)		−0.11*** (0.02)		−0.11*** (0.02)
ex	−0.16*** (0.05)		−0.11*** (0.05)	−0.11*** (0.05)	
year97	0.04*** (0.02)	0.05*** (0.02)	0.05*** (0.02)	0.04*** (0.02)	0.05*** (0.02)
const	0.02 (0.08)	0.00 (0.08)	0.33*** (0.02)	−0.03 (0.08)	0.33*** (0.02)
N	987	987	987	987	987
R^2	0.08	0.04	0.07	0.05	0.06

Note: * Significant at 10 per cent, ** significant at 5 per cent, *** significant at 1 per cent.

Table 6.8 *Probit estimates*

	b	b	b_1	b_1	b_2	b_2
CR4	0.52*** (0.20)	0.38* (0.20)	0.57*** (0.17)	0.36** (0.18)	0.34** (0.14)	0.10 (0.15)
CGI		−0.24*** (0.11)		−0.37*** (0.10)		−0.47*** (0.08)
const	1.11*** (0.08	1.23*** (0.10)	0.89*** (0.07)	1.08*** (0.09)	0.50*** (0.06)	0.73*** (0.08)
N	1267	1267	1267	12671267	1267	

Note: * Significant at 10 per cent, ** significant at 5 per cent, *** significant at 1 per cent.

must be a discontinuous change from the barter equilibrium curve to the equilibrium without barter. We interpret the fact that the coefficient on concentration below the cutoff is very large as evidence of such a discontinuity.

Another way to test the prediction that barter disappears with an increase in competition is to estimate a probit model. We have generated a binary variable b_0 that takes the value of 1 whenever $b > 0$ and zero if $b = 0$. In our sample, only 12 per cent enterprises have zero barter, thus the mean of b_0 is 90 per cent. The results are reported in table 6.8. The probability that an enterprise is involved in barter increases with concentration.

It is also of interest to check whether concentration has any impact on the probability of having a very low barter share. Indeed, occasional barter deals occur in OECD economies as well. We have looked at two cutoff points, 0.1 and 0.2. In our sample, 13 per cent enterprises have a share of barter in sales below 10 per cent and 27 per cent of the enterprises have a barter share below 0.2. We have introduced two binary variables, b_1 and b_2. The binary variable b_1 is 1 whenever $b > 0.1$ and 0 otherwise. Similarly, $b_2 = 1$ when $b > 0.2$ and $b_2 = 0$ otherwise. The results of probit estimates with cutoff levels are also shown in table 6.8. The probability of having very low barter decreases with concentration as well as the probability of having no barter at all.

We have, once again, included *CGI* in the regression. The purpose is to check whether exposure to the consumer market deters barter which, in turn, results in a positive relationship between concentration and the probability of being involved in barter. Again, it turns out that enterprises in consumer good industries are less likely to use barter. However, the coefficient on concentration remains positive (though becoming smaller and less significant) even if we control for *CGI*. We have also tried to check effect of exports but found no significant relationship.

Multiple equilibria and path-dependence

Our discussion of the liquidity hypothesis raised an important question about the notion of causality in analysing barter: the initial cause of the phenomenon may not be the critical variable explaining its current existence. It may be that a liquidity squeeze was the key factor that caused enterprises to switch to barter, but our evidence indicates that financial stringency is not the key factor explaining its current use. The cause – a liquidity squeeze – may be the shock that pushes the economy into a new, barter equilibrium. Once the economy is in that equilibrium the absence of the initial cause may be irrelevant for barter's persistence.

Our results concerning the relationship between barter and concentration – barter is more likely with higher market concentration – raises a similar issue. If barter is explained by a high concentration of market power, why is it observed in Russia and virtually non-existent in other economies? One answer to this question would be that in Russia markets are more concentrated than in other economies. This claim is well accepted by the general public and policy-makers but it is not supported by data (see Brown and Brown, 1994; Brown, Ickes and Ryterman, 1994). Our model may offer another explanation. As we have seen, for some levels of concentration there may be two stable equilibria: one with barter and one without barter.

Therefore we may have path-dependence or the so-called 'hysteresis effect'. In 1995, a liquidity shock threw the economy into a high barter state. Since that time, price flexibility should have restored the equilibrium level of the real money stock. However the real money supply is now two–three times as low as it used to be. In Polterovitch's (1998) terms, Russian economy is in the 'institutional trap of barter'.

The multiple-equilibria argument is rather common in modern literature on transition and development. It is basically the essence of so-called 'post-Washington Consensus' that is gradually replacing the Washington Consensus on economic transition. The post-Washington Consensus states that institutions matter a great deal for transition and may fail to emerge spontaneously. Government should intervene to promote good institutions, otherwise the economy will find itself in a low-level equilibrium. However, what our model suggests is not simply a re-statement that Russia may be in a low-level equilibrium. We have shown that at some level of competitiveness the barter equilibrium disappears and industry jumps to the no-barter equilibrium. This argument suggests non-trivial policy implications. In order to reduce barter, government policy should promote competition. Moreover, even if competition policy may have had little effect on barter so far, this does not mean that the government should necessarily give up. Our model (and the empirical analysis) suggests that barter may fall dramatically when a certain threshold level of competition is achieved.

5 Networks

One of the most interesting aspects of barter in Russia is its multilateral nature.[37] Most barter is not bilateral. Rather, enterprises are typically embedded in a network (Ledeneva and Seabright, 1998). As an incisive report from a leading Russian economics research institute, the Institute for the Economy in Transition (IET), noted:

The barter chain itself turned out to be a special kind of consumer of the output. But its needs differed from the needs of liquid demand. The barter chains frequently reminded one of the 'production for production's sake' of the [Soviet] planned economy, when a quasi-cooperation gave rise to closed autonomous systems that served only themselves. In a number of enterprises which we surveyed, the share of output necessary simply to support the viability of the chain itself was as high as 30 percent.

The IET went on to conclude that the growth of barter, especially multilateral barter, had not only quantitative but also qualitative features: 'In several of the enterprises we studied in the past two years [1995–6], we saw a growth in production not of liquid output [output that could be sold for cash] but of output that enjoyed demand in the barter schemes.' The task of finding products that would be acceptable to the power companies became paramount. It compelled many enterprises to shift the structure of their output not towards the real market, but in the attempt to satisfy directly or indirectly the rather specific needs of the natural monopolies. This created the conditions for the exact opposite of market restructuring – an adjustment away from the market.

As barter spread outside of traditional multilateral chains and began to be employed with non-traditional customers, the quality of the goods exchanged deteriorated. Enterprises face two prices for their product: a barter price and a cash price. Given the bias in Russian law against cash discounts, enterprises choose instead to provide lower-quality goods in exchange for barter, while reserving better quality products for cash sales.

One result of the proliferation in barter was a curious investment 'boom' among the least likely candidates. One economics weekly wrote:

[37] This point was first emphasised in Ickes, Murrell and Ryterman (1997); Hendley. Ickes and Ryterman (1998).

'One can observe a paradoxical pattern: the worse the enterprise's economic condition ..., the higher its level of investment 'activity.'' The solution to this apparent riddle, they explained, was that these weak enterprises, surviving through the system of barter and offsets, ended up receiving huge amounts of some of the most popular barterable goods – construction materials of various kinds – which they then had to put to use by building something or other. As a result, around 60 per cent of capital investment is construction of new residential and production buildings. But they are never finished: 'Under conditions of the traditional Russian practice of construction delays, [these investment projects] have a zero or even negative economic effect.' In terms of economic efficiency, the only consolation is that a substantial portion of the construction materials delivered to the construction sites do end up in socially useful projects, albeit through illegal channels, since they are pilfered by workers and used to build garages or dachas for themselves or their friends and neighbours.

An important implication of the *network character* of barter is that a history of relationships is important to support these transactions. Because restructuring often involves changes in suppliers and customers, barter may weaken incentives to restructure (Ickes, Murrell and Ryterman, 1997). Barter may thus be a force 'conserving' relationships among enterprises. Aukutsionek (1998) also finds that old links play a significant role in barter relationships. The emergence of specialised intermediaries and the survival of Soviet industrial links could add up to a 'lock-in' effect, which helps perpetuate barter.[38] The empirical evidence is consistent with this hypothesis.

6 Implications of barter

Barter is clearly chosen by enterprises to reduce the cost of making transactions. Nonetheless, the widespread use of barter has implications for the economy. This is especially true if barter is used as a means of evading budget constraints, as in the 'virtual economy' argument.

The model in Gaddy and Ickes (1998a) implies that some managers will choose to invest their effort and capital in restructuring while others will invest in relationship capital. The latter pays off in better network capital and therefore lower costs of barter. The choice between the two types of investments depends on the nature of the enterprise's initial conditions. Since managerial effort (time) is scarce, the model implies that we should observe a negative correlation between restructuring and barter. This

---

[38] This is studied, among others, by Kaufmann and Marin (1998).

would be an important implication of barter: it enables enterprises to delay restructuring.

The hypothesis that we wish to test is that enterprise directors, such as Igor, invest in relational capital or restructuring, and that barter is used as a strategy to avoid restructuring. At any point in time, the enterprise has an inherited level of relational capital. Given that, there is some optimal level of barter for the enterprise. If the director now chooses to invest in relational capital the optimal level of barter should increase.[39] But greater investment in relational capital means less investment in restructuring. So restructuring should be associated with a decrease in barter. Hence, the empirical prediction is that restructuring is inversely related to the change in barter.[40] We offer some empirical evidence on this relationship.[41] As a proxy for restructuring we take the change in labour productivity in the firm in 1997 relative to 1996. We then regress this proxy on the change in the level of barter from 1996 to 1997. Our basic equation is:

$$llp97_i = \alpha_0 + \alpha_1 llp96_i + \alpha_2(b97_i - b96_i). \tag{6.2}$$

We also estimate the equation with size and the ratio of gross profits to sales as regressors.[42] As is evident in table 6.9 the results are robust to the inclusion of these variables.

Our base specification for (6.2) is given in column (1) of table 6.9. It is interesting, however, to check whether it is the *level*, rather than the *change in the level*, of barter that is critical. We test this in the remaining columns of table 6.2. The estimates indicate that levels of barter are not statistically significant when introduced separately, and that it is the difference that matters.[43] This presumably follows from the fact that we are measuring productivity in 1997 relative to 1996. Our results

---

[39] In terms of the model in Gaddy and Ickes (1998a) the cash constraint of the enterprise would bind at a lower level of cash sales if the amount of relational capital increases.

[40] A more ideal test, perhaps, would regress the change in labour productivity on the change in barter from an earlier period, say 1992. Enterprises that invested in relational capital would have a large increase in barter since then, compared with other enterprises. Lacking data for this earlier period, we estimated (6.2).

[41] Note that we are not testing whether increased barter *causes* less restructuring. Rather we are analysing whether increased barter and less restructuring are associated.

[42] We measure size by the log of sales. This presents a problem because if barter is useful in inflating revenues our measure of productivity will be over-stated. But notice that the direction of this bias goes against our maintained hypothesis, making it harder to reject the null. A similar problem may be present with respect to profits. We also estimated the equation with profits replaced by costs. This did not change any results, as in our data set the correlation between (the log of) sales and (the log of) costs is very high (0.989).

[43] Thus when we enter $b96$ and $b97$ separately, the coefficients take the opposite sign and are statistically significant.

Table 6.9 *Restructuring and barter (standard errors in parentheses)*[a]

	(1)	(2)	(3)	(4)	(5)
$llp96_i$	0.78*** (0.05)	0.88*** (0.04)	0.80*** (0.06)	0.78*** (0.06)	0.78*** (0.06)
$b97_i - b96_i$	−0.42** (0.17)				
$b97_i$		−0.12 (0.12)		−0.33 (0.23)	−0.52** (0.20)
$b96_i$			−0.15 (0.16)	0.32 (0.21)	0.35* (0.19)
$profit96_i$	0.83*** (0.13)	0.38*** (0.09)	0.54*** (0.11)		0.84*** (0.13)
$size96_i$	0.09*** (0.03)	0.08*** (0.02)	0.08** (0.03)		0.09*** (0.03)
$const$	0.91** (0.41)	0.06 (0.33)	0.86 (0.45)	0.79* (0.47)	1.03** (0.42)
N	150	344	261	150	150
R^2	0.83	0.80	0.72	0.77	0.83

Note: * Significant at 10 per cent, ** significant at 5 per cent, *** significant at 1 per cent.

suggest that it is precisely those enterprises where barter has increased over this period which have had the poorest economic performance measured by labour productivity.

We have also tried to control for industry and regional effects by introducing appropriate dummies into our regression. Some of the industry and regional dummies were significant but there was no change in the coefficient on the change in barter, and the R^2 increased by only a negligible amount. Hence, the effect of a change in the level of barter on the change in labour productivity appears to be robust.

The results of the analysis are consistent with the argument that barter is associated with a lack of restructuring. In our sample, labour productivity falls by 7 per cent per annum. The variation from this trend is negatively correlated with change in barter level. On average, an increase of share of barter by 1 per cent decreases productivity by 0.3 per cent.

In a general equilibrium model of the virtual economy Ericson and Ickes (2000) show that a 'virtual economy trap' may exist, where enterprises refuse to restructure. This arises when restructured enterprises do not achieve sufficient improvements in efficiency to overcome the cheaper price of energy that results from using barter. As a result of government incentives that induce *Gazprom* to subsidize energy to certain customers, there is just too large a surplus generated by barter to be overcome by restructuring, at least within the bounds placed on the restructuring parameters. Notice that this type of argument is implicit in analyses that presume that barter is used as a means to price discriminate among users.[44]

---

[44] For example, Guriev and Kvasov (1999); Woodruff (1999).

To avoid having to pay the higher price the customer may refuse to signal the ability to pay a higher price.[45] This is accomplished by refusing to restructure.

There would seem to be many other equilibria also. But the result, that firms gaining from barter would refuse to restructure, seems robust. Only if the government removes its incentives for barter, and/or *Gazprom* loses the ability to discriminate among users would the incentives to restructure become dominant for firms in barter networks. This then poses a substantial barrier to the successful transformation of the Russian economy.

7 Conclusion

Barter has important implications on the *transparency* of the economy. The proliferation of barter in Russia has increased the difficulties for outsiders to monitor enterprise behaviour. This weakens corporate governance by making it easier for managers to hide income from the shareholders of the enterprise. It also weakens the process of tax collection, and thus contributes to the fiscal crisis of the Russian state. By making transactions less transparent it weakens the role of the budget constraint in governing enterprise behaviour. Indeed, it may be argued that this is an important motivation for participants to use barter. In this way, barter has had an insidious effect on one of the key goals of market reform: to harden budget constraints and create a focus on the bottom line.

What is clear is that demonetisation of the Russian economy involves an increase in *idiosyncratic* exchange. The terms of transactions depend more on who the parties are than on the items exchanged. That is why networks are so important to the institution of barter. This is another tendency that is opposite to a central goal of market reform: to increase the scope of 'arm's length transactions.' Barter at one level appears to be a survival mechanism used by enterprises to avoid the costs of restructuring. Once it has become widespread, however, it also becomes a strategy used by enterprises to improve their financial (interpreted broadly) position. This is why the barter equilibrium may be so difficult to break out of. Once the economy settles into a barter equilibrium it cannot be broken simply by shutting down the loss-makers.

Our empirical results are consistent with both aspects of barter: as a survival strategy and a strategy to reduce the payment for inputs. The inverse relationship between barter and restructuring points to the role of

[45] This is another example of our argument about the endogeneity of barter.

survival.[46] But the widespread nature of barter is also supported by our inability to find a relationship between barter and liquidity. Moreover, our results on market power and barter demonstrate how barter can become an instrument used to increase profits from transactions. The fact that multiple mechanisms are at work in generating barter suggests that there are no simple means of extricating the economy from this predicament.

References

Aukutsionek, S. (1998). 'Industrial Barter in Russia', *Communist Economies and Economic Transformation*, 10(2), 179–88

Brown, A. and J.D. Brown (1998). 'The Evolution of Market Structure in Russia: Implications for Competition', Stockholm School of Economics, mimeo

Brown, A., B.W. Ickes, and R. Ryterman (1994). 'The Myth of Monopoly: A New View of Industrial Structure in Russia', *Discussion Paper*, World Bank

Commander, S. and C. Mumssen (1998). 'Understanding Barter in Russia', *EBRD Working Paper*, 37

Ellingsen, T. (1998). 'Payments in Kind', *Working Paper*, 244, Stockholm School of Economics

Ericson, R.E. and B.W. Ickes. (1999). 'A Model of Russia's "Virtual Economy"', June, mimeo

Friebel, G. and S. Guriev (1999). 'Why Russian Workers do not Move: Attachment of Workers through Payments in Kind', RECEP, mimeo

Gaddy, C. and B.W. Ickes (1998a). 'To Restructure or not to Restructure: Informal Activities and Enterprise Behavior in Transition', *Working Paper*, 134, Ann Arbor, William Davidson Institute

(1998b). 'Russia's Virtual Economy', *Foreign Affairs*, 77(5), 53–67

Guriev, S. and D. Kvasov (1999). 'Barter in Russia: The Role of Market Power', The New Economic School, June, mimeo

Guriev, S. and B.W. Ickes (1999). 'Barter in Russian Enterprises: Myths Versus Empirical Evidence', *Russian Economic Trends*, 2, 6–13

Guriev, S., I. Pospelov and D. Shaposhnik (1998). 'A General Equilibrium Model of Russia's Virtual Economy: Transaction Costs and Alternative Means of Payments', New Economic School, mimeo

Hendley, K., B.W. Ickes and R. Ryterman (1998). 'Remonetizing the Russian Economy', in H. G. Broadman, (ed.), *Russian Enterprise Reform: Policies to Further the Transition*, Washington, DC, World Bank, November

Ickes, B.W., P. Murrell and R. Ryterman. (1997). 'End of the Tunnel? The Effects of Financial Stabilization in Russia', *Post-Soviet Affairs (formerly Soviet Economy)*, 13(2)

---

[46] See also Gaddy and Ickes (1998a) and several of the chapters in this volume.

Kaufman, D. D. and D. Marin. (1998). 'Disorganization, Financial Squeeze and Barter', Working Paper, 165, William Davidson Institute; revised version of this is chapter 8

Ledeneva, A. and P. Seabright (1998). 'Barter in Post-Soviet Societies: What Does it Look Like and Why Does it Matter?', paper presented at the conference 'Barter in Post-Socialist Societies', Cambridge University, December, chapter 4 in this volume

Polterovitch, V. (1998) 'Institutional Traps and Economic Reforms', *Working Paper*, Moscow, The New Economic School

Woodruff, D. (1999) *Money Unmade: Barter and the Fate of Russian Capitalism*, Ithaca, Cornell University Press

Yakovlev, A. (1999). 'Black Cash Tax Evasion in Russia: Its Form, Incentives and Consequences at Firm Level,' Higher School of Economics, mimeo

7   The household in a non-monetary market economy

SIMON CLARKE

1 Introduction

The Russian economy is 'non-monetary' in the sense that the bulk of inter-enterprise and even governmental transactions are not conducted in monetary form but through barter chains and the use of various kinds of non-monetary instruments. However, retail trade and the provision of consumer services are almost entirely monetary: it is not possible for households to issue bills of exchange to buy their groceries or to settle their utilities bills, nor is it generally possible to acquire goods in shops or retail markets for anything other than cash.[1] While enterprises and government bodies have adapted quite comfortably to life without money, households with falling money incomes have a steadily declining capacity to meet even their most basic needs directly through the market.

Households are the primary victims of demonetisation, but they are not necessarily passive victims. Household responses to demonetisation have important implications for the reproduction of the non-monetary market economy. If households respond in the normal way to falling money incomes – by drawing on their savings, falling into debt and reducing their money spending – then demonetisation will translate, perhaps with a lag as savings are run down, into an old-fashioned Keynesian deflationary spiral.[2] On the other hand, if employers arrange

---

[1]   As David Anderson's chapter 12 in this volume shows, in some regions there are quite well developed local surrogate currencies which are used in retail trade. It is common for various kinds of tokens issued by employers or benefit offices in payment of wages or benefits to have limited circulation in local retail trade, but they almost always trade at a considerable discount.

[2]   This presumes that falling money incomes are, at least to some extent, a result of demonetisation and not just of the 'transitional depression'. There is now a large literature on demonetisation, but little engagement between the contending views (Ickes and Ryterman, 1992, 1993; Rostowski, 1993; Fan and Schaffer, 1994, Delyagin, 1997; Denisova, 1997; Klepach 1997; Makarov and Kleiner, 1997; Shmelev, 1997; Aukutsionek,

to pay wages and benefits in kind or with non-monetary tokens (or quasi-monies) which can be used to purchase means of subsistence, households will be integrated into the non-monetary economy and will be able to sustain their demand for goods and services despite their falling money incomes. To the extent that these practices develop, the deflationary consequences of demonetisation are averted. Finally, however, households may withdraw from the corporate economy by engaging in production for subsistence or exchange with friends and neighbours. To the extent that this happens, living standards will be maintained, but there will be a diversion of demand from the corporate economy to the household economy.

In this chapter I will look at the ways in which households have adapted to the non-monetary market economy. In section 2 I will briefly review the development of Russia's barter economy. I will then examine the scale and character of the demonetisation of household budgets (section 3) before looking at the responses of employers and households to demonetisation (sections 4–8). Since most discussion of these issues is conducted without any reference to the evidence, I will concentrate on a presentation and assessment of the available data. I will focus particularly on urban households since the situation in rural districts, where living standards are much lower and opportunities for self-sufficiency much higher, is very different. Section 9 is a brief discussion of conclusions.

In the discussion I will refer principally to four sources of data. First, *Goskomstat's Household Budget Survey*, which has been derided in the past but has been conducted on a more rigorous basis since 1997. Second, the data from the Russian Longitudinal Monitoring Surveys (RLMS), conducted since 1994 by a group at the Institute of Sociology of the Russian Academy of Sciences, sponsored by the University of North Carolina at Chapel Hill. Third, data from a large household survey conducted by the Institute for Comparative Labour Relations Research

1998a, 1998b, 1998c; Clarke, 1998; Gaddy and Ickes, 1998a, 1998b, 1998c; Hendley, Ickes and Ryterman, 1998; Makarov, 1998; Poser, 1998; Yakovlev, 1998; Woodruff, 1999a). In general, western commentators such as Gaddy and Ickes have focused on demonetisation as a potentially inflationary means by which enterprise directors have avoided the imposition of 'hard' budget constraints, while Russian commentators such as Delyagin, Makarov, Klepach and Shmelev have seen demonetisation as a deflationary response to a liquidity squeeze imposed by inappropriate western-sponsored monetary and financial policies. The former diagnosis implies more rigorous deflationary policies to restore the value of money, the latter implies reflationary policies to stimulate the recovery of the real economy. The response to the crisis of August 1998, in which controlled monetary expansion was associated with remonetisation and the non-inflationary growth of the real economy, strongly supports the latter interpretation.

(ISITO) in four Russian cities (Samara, Kemerovo, Lyubertsy and Syktyvkar) in April 1998. Fourth, data from the bi-monthly surveys of the All-Russian survey organisation, VTsIOM. As we will see, the data from these various sources is in most respects remarkably consistent.

2 The rise of the barter economy

Russia's barter economy bears the marks of its origin in the Soviet economic system. The Soviet economy was a non-monetary system in which economic relationships between enterprises were administratively regulated, with money playing only an accounting role. This 'accounting money' was quite different from the cash which was used to pay wages with which workers could buy their essential means of subsistence, whose issue was strictly controlled in the attempt to maintain macroeconomic balance. This system was gradually falling apart through the 1980s with money and market relations beginning to play a role, but even in 1991 market relations and monetary transactions were of only marginal importance. When the disintegration of the Soviet Union and the radical reform policies of 1991-2 led to the collapse of the old administrative structures there were almost no commercial and financial institutions in place which could mediate market and monetary transactions.

From the beginning of 1992 enterprises were suddenly free to trade with whomever they wanted. However, their working capital was destroyed by inflation in the first months of 1992, as were both the savings of the population and the purchasing power of wages. In principle enterprises and consumers were free to buy, but in practice they had no money with which to buy. The government was at first not willing to provide money because it believed that expanding the money supply would only fuel the enormous inflation that its liberalisation policies had provoked. The result was that enterprises could continue production only by maintaining relations with traditional suppliers who were willing to provide raw materials without payment, or by arranging barter deals with new suppliers and customers.

In the absence of money, the first stage in the growth of a market economy saw a rapid increase in inter-enterprise debt and in barter trade, which reproduced familiar forms of behaviour and created at least a caricature of familiar institutions. Barter had played an important role in informal inter-enterprise transactions throughout the Soviet period, while offsets had been the normal way of settling accounts between enterprises which delivered goods to customers not against payment but against the plan. To find new customers and suppliers, as many had to do following the break-up of the Soviet Union, enterprises had to turn to intermediaries to arrange barter or export deals: individuals and organisations who had their own contacts and sources of finance. Some of these individuals and organisations had their roots in old administrative and political structures, particularly those such as the *Komsomol* and the KGB which had their own inter-Republican networks. Some had built up their positions as intermediaries working outside the law in the Soviet period. But the lack of development of appropriate market institutions and the absence of the effective enforcement of the laws of property and contract meant that even those with a legitimate background had to rely on the threat of violence to enforce contracts and protect their goods. As a result, deregulation of the market in 1992 did not lead to a free market but to the criminalisation and monopolisation of economic relationships as those who controlled the emerging financial and commercial intermediaries quite literally took the law into their own hands, using their own 'security services' to enforce contracts. The criminalisation of the economy was reinforced by the tax system and the form of privatisation which gave enterprise directors and the new financial and commercial structures a common interest in concealing profits and illegally diverting them into the 'shadow economy'.

The expansion of credit from mid-1992 led to some decline in inter-enterprise debt and barter relations and saw the beginnings of market relationships. However, from the end of 1993 the government increasingly followed the advice of the IMF and applied the restrictive financial and monetary policies which are used in monetised market economies to combat inflation. But in Russia these policies did not have the consequences intended, because Russia was *not yet a monetised economy*: although the administrative-command system had been destroyed, old relationships and old ways of doing things persisted so that money had not yet become established as the yardstick for economic decision-making. The government's policies drove down inflation but they also further intensified the criminalisation, monopolisation and demonetisation of the economy and the concentration of financial resources in the hands of financial and commercial structures which operated outside the law. High interest rates meant that enterprises were forced back into increasingly complex barter arrangements and fell ever more deeply into debt to their suppliers, partner banks and commercial intermediaries, which could then use this dependence as a lever to exert control over the enterprise and strengthen monopoly structures.

The situation was further exacerbated by the tax regime, which provided a very strong incentive for economic actors to leave the monetary economy, since the tax authorities had first claim on their liquid funds.

This intensified a vicious circle in which the punitive tax regime induced enterprises to engage in non-monetary forms of exchange, reducing the tax take of the government. The government then had little choice but to validate the expansion of credit achieved by the creation of non-monetary instruments by sanctioning arrears in tax and utility payments and defaulted on its own payment obligations, including its obligations to pay its suppliers and employees and to pay statutory social and welfare benefits. Government services and suppliers then did not have the money to meet their own bills, further tightening the noose of non-payment.

The government's policies not only led to the demonetisation of the economy and the subordination of enterprises to criminal structures, but also made the state itself increasingly dependent on those same structures. Because enterprises did not have the money to pay taxes, the government had to borrow increasing amounts of money at very high rates of interest from the commercial banks, denying access to bank credit to enterprises which might have used that credit to pay taxes. The irony is that much of the credit which the banks extended to the government had in fact been created by the banks on the basis of the government's own deposits, either tax revenues collected by the banks on the government's behalf, or government remissions paid through the banks. Most of the rest of the money in the commercial banks was money which had been illegally extracted from state and 'privatised' enterprises through commercial and financial structures – and, increasingly, the profits gained from speculation against the currency and speculation in government debt. Meanwhile, most of the population kept its dwindling savings in cash or in low-interest deposits in the state savings bank, unless induced to hand their money over to various pyramid frauds.

Once the government had closed the circle, the demonetisation of the Russian economy was no longer simply a matter of the prevalence of non-monetary instruments and barter transactions in place of the trade and bank credit on which enterprises rely in a monetised market economy, it became a whole economic system in which the lack of liquidity 'locked' the key actors into a network of mutual interdependence. This system may ultimately have served nobody's interests but it was stable because their interdependence meant that none of the central actors had the immediate interest, or even the ability, to break out of it.

3 The demonetisation of the household budget

We have already noted that the Russian economy, like the Soviet system from which it emerged, is not entirely non-monetary. Enterprises and organisations may not be severely constrained in their economic activities by the size of their money holdings, but this has never been true of households. Although many items of consumption in the Soviet system were heavily subsidised, workers were paid in cash, pensioners drew their pensions in cash and households were required to pay in cash for their purchases of food and clothing, they had to pay in cash to travel on the bus or the train, they often had to find cash to pay for medical treatment and they were required to settle their bills for housing, municipal services, energy and telephone in cash. Demonetisation of the economy has therefore had a much more substantial impact on the household economy than it has on the corporate sector. But the household is not just a passive victim of demonetisation, it is a crucial link in the transactions chain. There are very narrow limits to the extent to which the government and public utilities can provide credit to sustain the production of goods and services that nobody has the money to buy. Ultimately these goods and services have to reach a point of final sale. Thus the Russian household has to be the principal source of final demand that supports the chain of monetary and non-monetary transactions.[3] Household cash purchases put money into the hands of retailers and service-providers who are then in a position to use their possession of cash to shop around for supplies, introducing an element of competition into final product markets which can eventually diffuse through the whole economy. If household money spending is expanding, then it has the potential to dissolve the whole system of non-monetary exchange. This is exactly what happened at the end of the Soviet period as households began to disburse their accumulated money balances and the Soviet system disintegrated as enterprises' acquisition of money freed them from central control.[4] However, if household money income is contracting then households do not have the money to translate into effective demand. If monetary contraction is not simply to foster a deflationary spiral, then enterprises and households have to find new ways of supplying what has become an ineffective demand. Before looking at household responses, we need to examine the extent of the demonetisation of the household budget.

---

[3] I will not discuss international trade here, although it has played an important indirect role in sustaining and redirecting the flow of cash even when it has been on a barter basis. This is because exports have largely been of primary and intermediate products which have no cash buyers in Russia, while imports have been dominated by final products destined for cash sale to domestic consumers.

[4] This tendency can be neutralised if the government is able to mop up the cash surpluses by sequestering enterprise cash balances from which wages are paid, as was the case in the Soviet system. This Soviet practice is reproduced today in the right of the tax authorities to sequester the bank balances of all those they deem to be in tax arrears.

4 Household monetary income and expenditure

The household sector has been dealt a double blow by the decline of the monetised economy. On the one hand, the flow of cash into the household budget has fallen sharply as about a quarter of all jobs have been lost since 1990, with unemployment rising to around 13 per cent and a large number of teenagers and those approaching or beyond pension age withdrawing from the labour force; many of those still employed are laid off or put on short-time; the value of wages, pensions and welfare benefits has lagged far behind the rate of inflation and wages and pensions have gone unpaid. On the other hand, the demands for cash payment have escalated as subsidies for consumption have been removed and services that were formerly provided free are now available only for a charge.

Survey data on household money income paints a remarkably consistent picture, with all the all-Russian sources for the period 1996–8 (*Household Budget Survey*, RLMS, VTsIOM) showing an average household money income per head in the late 1990s which is equivalent, when deflated by the consumer price index (CPI), to the level of that of the late 1960s, or half the level that it had reached at the end of the 'period of stagnation' in 1985 and just below the 1985 official subsistence minimum (in 1998 the minimum pension was less than one-third and the minimum wage was one-tenth of this figure). This is the most recent valid reference point for comparison, since the inflation of the Gorbachev period provided households with increasing money incomes, which peaked in 1990 at 50 per cent above the 1985 level, but these incomes were unrealisable because of shortages of goods at official prices.

It is often argued that the published data is seriously misleading because there is a large 'hidden economy' through which households receive substantial supplements to their officially declared monetary incomes, either through the payment of additional wages which are kept off the books in order to reduce taxation, or through unregistered secondary employment. However, the official data already includes a substantial estimate for 'unrecorded activity', amounting to an additional 27 per cent of GDP in 1997 (the methodology of this estimate, worked out in collaboration with the World Bank, is described in some detail in *Goskomstat*, 1998a, pp. 9–130). Whatever reservations one might have about the methodology, this is the best available and most consistent estimate of the scale of unrecorded activity, while the survey data on wages and social transfers received by households is very consistent with the corresponding macroeconomic income and expenditure estimates. There is thus no evidence that the survey data seriously distorts the real situation.

There is a serious distortion in the published national income data. Until 1997 *Goskomstat* included an additional estimate for unrecorded income in the National Income accounts that was simply lumped under the heading of 'property, entrepreneurial and other income', the total of which by 1995 exceeded the total of reported wage incomes. Since 1997 an estimate for 'hidden wages', amounting to an addition of 14 per cent in 1993, 21 per cent in 1994 and 30–32 per cent between 1995 and 1998 (*Goskomstat*, 1999c, p. 64), has been retrospectively separated out. However, these supplementary estimates are accounting fictions that have been introduced to balance the books, mainly to compensate on the income side for ludicrous estimates of the increase in household foreign currency holdings (amounting to between 15 per cent and 20 per cent of total household money income each year since 1994: *Goskomstat*, 1999c, p. 107; *Russian Economic Trends*, 1997.1, pp. 85–9), which in turn have been invented to cover for unrecorded capital flight in the balance of international payments (much of which may be an illusion arising from under-reporting of the cost of imports by importers seeking to reduce liability for import duties).

In 1998, *Goskomstat* estimated that 'hidden wages' amounted to a total of 319 billion roubles, against which the macroeconomic data purported to show a net increase of 19 billion roubles in savings deposits (although the data on savings deposits themselves shows a net increase of only 1.3 billion), 214 billion households' net purchases of foreign currency and 28 billion increase in rouble holdings of the population (*Goskomstat*, 1999c). In 1997, the addition for 'hidden wages' of 300 trillion roubles was substantially less than the even more absurd estimate of 410 trillion savings and increased foreign currency holdings. In 1996, *Goskomstat* estimated 'hidden wages' at 250 trillion roubles, with net foreign currency purchases of 252 trillion and 85 trillion increased savings and rouble holdings, while the budget survey for the fourth quarter of 1996 indicated net foreign currency purchases of 0.28 trillion roubles out of total net savings of 2 trillion roubles (Ministry of Labour and Social Development and *Goskomstat Rossii*, 1997).

These fictitious additions to household income radically alter the officially reported distribution of income by income sources, suggesting a booming entrepreneurial economy to compensate for the collapse of the traditional waged economy. On the old form of reporting, wages amounted to 38–40 per cent and social transfers to 13–15 per cent, with entrepreneurial and other income amounting to a massive 44–7 per cent of household money income. The revised method of reporting raises the wage share to 49–53 per cent of money income, but still leaves entrepreneurial income amounting to around a third of household money income. The *Household Budget Survey*, by contrast, showed in the last quarter of 1996 (the last time the survey collected income data) that wages comprised 70 per cent of household income (77 per cent for urban households), social transfers 16 per cent (15 per cent), private transfers 4 per cent (4 per cent), entrepreneurial income 5 per cent (1 per cent), property income 0.4 per cent (0.7 per cent) and income from sales of property 3 per cent (1 per cent).[5] This is far more plausible than are *Goskomstat*'s macroeconomic estimates and is consistent with all other data sources on income and expenditure (and on employment, which show very low levels of entrepreneurial activity). The 1996 RLMS and 1998 ISITO surveys found a much higher reliance on social transfers, at 33 per cent and 31 per cent of household money income respectively, with wages accounting for only 62 per cent of household money income in the ISITO survey. The latter survey found evidence of under-reporting of secondary earnings, a generous allowance for which would add 6 per cent to the reported household money incomes, but even then entrepreneurial incomes amount to only a very small share in the total (Clarke, 1999b).

The collapse of money incomes and the reduction of subsidies on food and public services has been reflected in a substantial shift in the composition of household money spending. According to the *Household Budget Survey*, spending on food has increased from 31.5 per cent of consumer spending in 1990 to reach 51.4 per cent in 1998, with a further 6.6 per cent of the household budget spent on alcohol and tobacco and eating outside the home. In 1998 the poorest 10 per cent of households spent 17 per cent of their household money income on bread alone, more than they spent on all non-food products. Spending on housing and communal services has increased from 3.1 per cent to 5.2 per cent of household money income. Meanwhile, spending on non-food items has slumped, with spending on shoes and clothing falling from 23.6 per cent to 13.0 per cent of the budget, and spending on jewellery and other goods falling from 3.8 per cent to 0.6 per cent. According to the RLMS data, by the end of 1998 one-third of households had had to borrow money, but only 8 per cent managed to save anything at all, half of those putting by less than 15 per cent of their income. According to the data on bank deposits, the amount of money held by the population on deposit in the savings and commercial banks increased year on year, amounting to about 3 per cent of their annual money income between 1992 and

---

[5] Questions about income were dropped because of a supposed discrepancy between income and expenditure data, although reported mean income was within 1 per cent of reported mean expenditure. The discrepancy was not with the budget survey income data but between the budget survey and the national income accounts.

1996, although the real value of those deposits was destroyed by inflation – first in 1992, when the real value of deposits at the end of 1993 amounted to only 4 per cent of their value three years earlier, and then in 1998, when the real value of bank deposits, many of which were frozen, was halved.[6]

5 The non-payment of wages and benefits

Much of the fall in household money incomes is a result of the sustained and ever-deepening recession of the Russian economy, with employment having fallen by around 25 per cent since 1990 and the real value of wages and pensions having fallen to less than half the 1985 level by 1998. Wage inequality also doubled over the period of transition, so that many households had seen an even greater fall in the real value of their wage incomes.[7] To what extent this recession is a result of the demonetisation of the Russian economy that has been precipitated by deflationary policies is (or should be) a matter of debate that I do not want to enter into here.

The non-payment of wages and benefits, on the other hand, can be considered to be a direct reflection of the demonetisation of the economy to the extent that they are not paid as a result of deficient cash flow rather than of underlying insolvency. The survey data suggests that the non-payment of wages has amounted to a huge loss of money income since non-payment became endemic from 1995. According to VTsIOM's polls, which are the most commonly cited source, by the end of 1996 fewer than one-third of people were being paid in full and on time in any one month, around 20 per cent were being paid in full with a delay and over one-third were being paid nothing at all. The situation improved through the middle of 1997, but still up to a quarter of people were being paid nothing and up to 10 per cent were being paid only in part, the mean amount

---

[6] The budget survey figures for 1996 and 1998 are close to those of the RLMS and ISITO surveys, except that the latter both indicate substantially higher spending on housing and communal services than does the budget survey, despite the fact that subsidies to housing and communal services still account for about 4 per cent of GDP. The international financial institutions (IFIs) have been pressing the government hard to cut this subsidy by 'cost recovery', the euphemism for increasing charges, partly in order to reduce the budget deficit. This may increase the cash take of the government from the depleted money incomes of the population, but withdrawing more money from the economy will only further foster the cycle of demonetisation and decline.

[7] The Gini coefficient for officially reported wages increased from 0.24 in 1964 (Redor, 1992, pp. 55-6), through 0.31 in 1991 to 0.45 in the second half of the 1990s (Clarke, 1999a, chapter 2). Since higher earnings are more likely to be under-reported this is probably an under-estimate of the scale of wage inequality.

received being just under half the pay due for the month in question. During 1998 the situation deteriorated rapidly once more, so that in May 1998 more than 40 per cent of respondents said that they had been paid nothing the previous month, more than 20 per cent of whom had not been paid for the previous three months and almost 15 per cent had been paid only in part.[8] The RLMS data paints a very similar picture: 21 per cent of those employed in September 1996 told RLMS that they had been paid nothing in the previous month and 55 per cent said that they were owed money by their primary employer. In the last quarter of 1998, 64 per cent told RLMS that they were owed money by their employer and 31 per cent had been paid nothing the previous month.[9]

This data on the scale of non-payment does not appear to be consistent with data on the accumulated wage debt of those in arrears. According to RLMS, in the last quarter of 1998 the amount owed to those in arrears was the equivalent of 4.1 times their normal monthly wage. In the ISITO survey in April and May 1998 the incidence of wage debt ranged from 23 per cent in Lyubertsy to 63 per cent in Kemerovo. The mean debt of those who were owed money was more uniform, ranging from 2.8 months pay in Lyubertsy to 4.9 months in Kemerovo. These figures are not very different from the *Goskomstat* data, based on reporting by enterprises, indicating that the average wage debt of those enterprises reporting arrears at the end of 1998 was the equivalent of 3.7 months wages at the current wage rate (although the *Goskomstat* data suggests that around half the employed population is owed wages, rather than the two-thirds suggested by RLMS).

The discrepancy between these two sets of data appears to be considerable. For example, VTsIOM reported that 51 per cent of respondents had been paid nothing at all in June 1998 and 13 per cent had been paid only in part, which would imply that well over half the wages were unpaid that month. This was also a peak month for the increase in wage arrears in the

---

[8] The *New Russia Barometer* survey, which is also conducted by VTsIOM, seems to suggest lower levels of non-payment of wages, finding in March and April 1998 that only 8 per cent of respondents were working without pay, 24 per cent were working and being paid wages with delays, 22 per cent were pensioners facing pension delays and 39 per cent were paid their wages or pensions regularly and on time. The survey also found that only one-sixth of unemployment benefit claimants were paid on time, while almost two-thirds never received payment (Rose, 1999, pp. 18–19).

[9] There is quite a large discrepancy between the individual and the household RLMS income data in this regard. In about a third of households, all of whose working members had reported that they had been paid nothing the previous month, the head of household reported that there had been income from wages. In about a tenth of the households in which individual members reported a wage, the head of household denied that there was any wage income.

Goskomstat data, but non-payment according to this source amounted at most to 5 per cent of the total wage bill in June. The two sets of data could be reconciled if wage arrears were being paid off almost as fast as they were accumulating, in which case those who were being paid should receive substantially more than their normal wage. However, over a third of those who told RLMS in the winter of 1998 that they had been paid something the previous month had received less than their normal wage and almost half received their normal wage, while only 20 per cent received significantly more than their normal wage and only 5 per cent received more than twice their normal wage, suggesting that there was not much repayment of wage arrears to balance the new arrears accruing. Overall the figures suggest a net non-payment of about a quarter of the monthly wage, yet the *Goskomstat* data suggests that wage arrears were being paid off quite rapidly during the last quarter of 1998. The reasons for the discrepancy are by no means clear, but the data on the stock of arrears is more plausible, and less ambiguous, than the data on the scale of non-payment.[10]

Although non-payment is a scandalous violation of the most basic rights of Russian workers, from a purely quantitative point of view the non-payment of wages has only a marginal significance. On the one hand, unpaid wages account for less than 5 per cent of net overdue enterprise debt. On the other hand, while those who are not paid their wages may suffer hard, and non-payment extends insecurity to all households, the non-payment of wages accounts directly for only a small proportion of the loss of household money income since 1992. Although the average of those enterprises reporting arrears was almost four months' wages and some workers had not been paid for years, the total accumulated arrears at their peak in September 1998, having built up steadily over the previous three years, amounted to a cumulative income loss of less than 3 per cent of GDP.[11] Between the end of 1995 and the end of

[10] Part of this discrepancy might be accounted for by an ambiguity in the question: respondents who have been paid, but more than a month in arrears, may say that they have not been paid their previous month's salary, which is what they are asked by VTsIOM. On the other hand, RLMS asks respondents if they have been paid anything at all the previous month and gets the same results. There is no apparent relation between the responses and the time of the month at which the question is asked.

[11] This data under-states the extent of non-payment since trade and services and small businesses, where non-payment is significant but less extensive, do not participate in the system of state reporting of wage debts. In the ISITO survey 20 per cent of employees of new private enterprises were owed money for wages, and the mean debt owed to those people was substantially more than that owed to employees of state and former state enterprises and organisations, at the equivalent of 5.6 months' wages, against 4 months for the latter.

1998 the arrears of those enterprises reporting arrears had increased from an average 1.4 to 3.7 months' pay, which equates to a loss of 10 per cent of monthly earnings over the previous three years for those suffering non-payment. In August 1998, one of the worst months, non-payment accounted for a one-off loss of about 5 per cent of that month's household money income. By comparison, the surge of inflation in the same month devalued household money incomes by more than a quarter, a loss which has persisted cumulatively since it has not been recovered by subsequent increases in money wages.

The pattern of non-payment of social benefits is similar to that of the non-payment of wages, since the primary reason for non-payment of benefits is the non-payment of payroll-related contributions to social insurance funds, the total owed by large and medium enterprises by May 1998 amounting to 196 billion roubles ($32 billion at the then-current exchange rate) (calculated from data in *Goskomstat*, 1998b). Pensions are by far the largest social transfer, accounting on average for 12 per cent of household money income. Although pension arrears mounted from 1995, they were largely paid off in the second half of 1997 and have since been kept in check. In company towns and the more remote regions where wages may have been unpaid for months on end, pensions provide virtually the only infusion of cash into the local economy. According to the RLMS data, in the autumn of 1996 a third of pensioners had not received their pension the previous month, while the figure had fallen to 15 per cent in the autumn of 1998. In the ISITO survey very few pensioners had substantial pension arrears in the spring of 1998. The situation with other benefits is rather different: according to RLMS two-thirds of those eligible for child benefits and half of the very small number eligible for unemployment benefit in October 1996 had not received them the previous month. In 1998, 80 per cent of those eligible for child benefit were in arrears and over a third of those eligible had not received their unemployment benefit.

Even if the non-payment of wages and benefits makes only a small contribution to the fall in average household money incomes, it can have an impact out of all proportion to its size since it can leave particular households with no money income at all, and so with no means of surviving in a monetary economy, compelling the households affected, and perhaps also their employers, to develop alternative means of securing their subsistence. Thus the wider significance of non-payment is not so much in its direct impact on the household budget as in its role in the reproduction of the demonetised economy.

6 Non-monetary forms of payment

Non-monetary forms of payment are ways in which employers can help employees to overcome the problems that arise when there is no money with which to pay wages. Like all of the features of the barter economy, these forms of payment build on familiar Soviet practices and institutions that developed in the shortage economy. In the Soviet period everybody had plenty of money, the problem was to turn the money into goods. The problem had become acute by the end of the Soviet period, when rising money incomes against fixed state prices meant it was almost impossible to buy anything worth having through the normal channels. In that context enterprises used a variety of methods to ensure that their employees' basic needs were provided for.

Employer-provided benefits

Soviet enterprises always provided a proportion of the workers' remuneration in kind through the provision of housing, cultural, sporting, social, medical and welfare facilities. Enterprises were compelled to privatise or divest a large part of these facilities to municipal authorities during the early stages of reform, which they did with alacrity since they constituted a huge financial burden. Almost three-quarters of all the enterprise housing and social assets were disposed of between 1993 and 1995, with a further 10 per cent being transferred over the following two years. Many of the remainder were simply written off because they were falling apart and nobody would take them on. Nevertheless, enterprises quite often retain a degree of financial responsibility and sometimes still provide subsidised access to these facilities for their employees (Healey, Leksin and Svetov 1998).

According to *Goskomstat's Household Budget Survey*, almost a third of households receive some subsidies or benefits either through their employer or some other social organisation. However, there is no evidence that the provision of such benefits is connected with the demonetisation of the household economy, for the better-off households and urban households are significantly more likely to enjoy them. There is a direct progression from the bottom to the top income decile, with those at the top receiving 10 times as much as those at the bottom and those in the towns getting almost three times as much as those in the country. Nevertheless, even among urban households these benefits account on average for only about 1 per cent of the total value of household spending (*Goskomstat*, 1999a).

Table 7.1 *Subsidies and benefits received by households, 1997–1998, Household Budget Survey, urban households*

	1997:1	1997:2	1997:3	1997:4	1998:1	1998:2	1998:3	1998:4
Percentage of households with at least one member enjoying this benefit								
Any benefit	32.8	34.1	36.5	38.4	36.3	35.6	36.3	37.3
Food	10.3	9.8	9.8	8.7	6.8	5.9	6.1	5.3
Transport	16.9	19.0	20.9	21.3	20.9	21.1	21.8	22.4
Housing	8.7	11.3	14.1	15.8	17.1	17.0	16.7	18.2
Holiday	0.9	2.0	1.8	0.5	0.4	1.5	1.3	0.5
Medical provision	1.2	1.0	1.4	1.4	1.3	1.1	0.8	0.8
Pre-school childcare	3.2	3.4	3.2	3.5	3.3	3.5	3.3	3.3
Subsidised provisions	0.1	0.1	0.1	0.1	0.1	0.0	0.1	0.1
Gifts	3.2	0.8	0.8	4.5	1.8	0.5	0.5	5.1
Other	2.8	2.5	3.2	3.6	3.2	3.2	2.8	3.3
Amount in roubles for each recipient								
Food	70.9	70.4	84.8	87.7	87.4	83.2	82.0	82.8
Transport	39.6	43.8	52.7	45.1	40.9	43.6	49.4	43.1
Housing	32.3	33.3	32.7	36.5	38.4	37.8	35.0	38.1
Holiday	338.5	414.6	424.4	505.0	362.1	414.9	511.0	457.2
Medical provision	107.0	58.6	65.9	76.2	52.2	78.1	68.2	87.4
Pre-school childcare	183.9	161.0	147.3	165.6	205.4	230.2	182.9	245.6
Subsidised provisions	35.5	49.8	40.0	135.9	22.5	36.8	52.3	83.8
Gifts	36.7	93.2	134.0	21.7	28.8	47.8	73.2	25.2
Other	55.9	67.1	43.4	38.4	29.2	34.2	31.4	28.2

Source: Goskomstat (1999a).

The incidence and scale of benefits reported to the *Household Budget Survey* are summarised in table 7.1. The most significant benefits are housing and transport subsidies, the provision of which appears to have been increasing. This may be a reaction to the increased cost of these facilities, expenditure on which as a percentage of household income peaked in 1996. Around 20 per cent received some form of transport subsidy, which usually takes the form of the free provision of works buses or travel passes for local transport. Subsidised vacations, medical expenses (in addition to routine health care) and childcare are the most valuable benefits, but are not widely available. Around 5 per cent of households appear to get a small gift at new year, but apart from this very few households seem to be provided with in-kind material support by their employers. Most significantly, from our point of view, the proportion of respondents receiving free or subsidised food in canteens has fallen steadily from 10 per cent at the beginning of 1997 to only 5 per cent by the end of 1998.[12]

The company store

As shortages grew during the 1980s it became increasingly common for enterprises to open shops on the premises to provide their employees with groceries and consumer durables at fixed state prices that could not be obtained outside. Many enterprises established their own supply networks to ensure that they were able to supply their employees with food. This might involve the enterprise buying or leasing a neighbouring collective farm with which they would often have had a relationship dating back to the days of shortages. This practice continued after price liberalisation, with such shops often selling the produce at below-market prices, although the *Household Budget Survey* data indicates that subsidised provision is largely a thing of the past.

When the financial crisis in 1992 left enterprises unable to pay wages, many of them allowed workers to buy goods from the factory shops on account, either by keeping a record of their purchases or by providing them with tokens that could be used in the company shop. It was not long before enterprises expanded the range of goods supplied and organised their barter transactions with an eye to supplying their own workers. Some enterprises even diversified by extending their retail outlets and opening them to outsiders. When enterprises ran into difficulties with supply or when workers complained at the limited choice available, the enterprise might make arrangements with local shops to accept their tokens, which they would later redeem for cash or in barter goods.

[12] The ISITO survey asked about the availability of various benefits at the respondent's place of work, rather than whether the respondent actually received such benefits, the results indicating that the availability of benefits is much higher than the take-up. The survey suggests that 45 per cent of workplaces in the four cities surveyed provide subsidies for vacations, 20 per cent for childcare, 16 per cent provide subsidised food and 20 per cent subsidised transport, while 23 per cent provide loans and 45 per cent provide financial assistance. The provision of these benefits is not connected with the incidence of non-payment but seems to be a normal feature of welfare provision that depends on the prosperity rather than the poverty of the enterprise. The provision of the various benefits is significantly correlated with each other, but the correlation coefficient with the incidence of non-payment is negative, though insignificant. There is a significant but very small (0.048) positive correlation between the provision of subsidised food and payment in kind. Although the provision of benefits is positively correlated with income in the *Household Budget Survey* data, the scale of provision is the lowest of all in Moscow city (*Goskomstat*, 1999a).

The extent to which this kind of local system of barter is established seems to depend primarily on the extent of the demonetisation of the local economy. During the 1980s workers welcomed the opportunity to buy goods that could not be obtained elsewhere, but once shortages came to an end the 'company store' and payment in tokens became increasingly unpopular with workers, who would regularly complain that they were over-charged for poor-quality goods. If employers are able regularly to acquire subsistence and consumer goods by barter, unless the local economy is almost entirely demonetised there is no reason why they should not put the goods on sale and pay money wages with the proceeds, and this has indeed become a common practice. Thus we would expect a system of local barter to develop only when demonetisation reaches a fairly high level so that enterprise tokens acquire quasi-monetary status. There is no data on the extent of the sale of goods to employees at the workplace, whether in cash or for tokens. However, the total retail sales reported by *Goskomstat* appear if anything to be somewhat greater than consumption figures for the same items reported by the budget survey, which would seem to indicate that the bulk of consumption is met through the system of retail trade.

Payment in kind

The purest form of demonetisation of the wage relation is payment in kind. It is quite normal in a market economy for a firm to offer its employees goods for their own consumption at a discount or as a supplement to the wage. Coalminers, in Russia as elsewhere, are entitled to a coal allowance and it is very common for agricultural workers to receive a part of their wage in kind. In the RLMS data the incidence of payment in kind in the countryside has been consistently around 13 per cent higher than in the towns, suggesting that something like that number of rural workers traditionally received part of their wages in kind. Many Soviet enterprises had informal norms which defined how much of the product it was legitimate for employees to steal. There is no data available on the extent of these traditional forms of payment in kind. When economic relations broke down in the summer of 1992 many enterprises gave workers the products of the enterprise or goods obtained through barter to sell on their own account, providing the enterprise with a sales outlet and the workers with a way of earning some money when the enterprise could not pay wages. The impression is that this practice became less prevalent as a professionalised system of retail trade developed and that payment in kind nowadays is primarily in the form of goods which the workers will consume themselves or exchange with friends and relatives. Enterprises will still sometimes offer a consignment of consumer durables acquired through barter to their employees which can be purchased on account, against wage arrears. Workers will often grudgingly accept such goods even at a substantial premium, on the grounds that a bird in the hand is worth two in the bush. Payment in kind tends to be supplementary to the non-payment of wages and is more often used as a means of paying off wage debt than of paying current wages.[13] Both payment in kind and the company store provide incentives for the growth of barter by providing the enterprise with a means to close the barter chain by offloading barter goods received in exchange for its own production onto its own employees.

The 1998 RLMS asked their respondents how much of the goods they had received from their enterprise in lieu of wages they had sold, and only one in 10 of those who had been paid in kind had sold any of the goods received, although the majority of those who did sell goods had sold all the goods they had been provided with. In the ISITO survey, the proportion selling goods received varied considerably, from 3 per cent of those receiving goods in lieu of wages in Syktyvkar and Kemerovo, where payment in kind is much more common, to 10–16 per cent in Lyubertsy and Samara.

It is not only employers who pay employees in kind. Since a large proportion of payments by enterprises to the Employment Fund, Pension Fund and Social Insurance Fund are made in non-monetary form, including in the form of barter goods, these organisations offer goods to claimants in lieu of payment of their benefit entitlements. There is no systematic data on the extent of this practice. However, anecdotal evidence suggests that most people simply leave their meagre arrears to accumulate in the rather forlorn hope that they will someday be paid. Local authorities have also organised chains for the clearance of household debts for housing and municipal services against entitlement to benefits and even, in the case of teachers and health workers, the wages of municipal employees, a common practice which is described in its most systematic form in Anderson's chapter 12 in this volume. Again, there are no data on the extent of such practices. Although ad hoc arrangements seem to be common, more systematic variants do not seem to be very widespread.

The RLMS data in table 7.2 suggest that payment of wages in kind has increased substantially since 1995. In the ISITO household survey, the

---

[13] In the survey data used in this chapter, responses about payment in kind are independent of responses about the non-payment of wages so that reported payment in kind is in addition to reported non-payment of money wages.

Table 7.2 *Incidence and scale of payment in kind, 1994–1998*

RLMS urban households	1994	1995	1996	1998	ISITO
Paid in kind, first job (per cent)	5	4	9	12	17
Paid in kind second job (per cent)	4	3	5	8	
As per cent of wage paid last month (*normal wage), first job	136	54	99	81(49)*	36*
As per cent of wage paid second job	36	62	81	53	

incidence of payment in kind ranged from 3 per cent of employees in Lyubertsy to 38 per cent in Kemerovo, where it seems that 13 per cent of the entire wage bill is paid in kind. When wages are paid in kind, the proportion of the wage paid in kind is substantial, amounting to one-third to one-half of the normal wage. A comparison of the incidence of payment in kind and the non-payment of wages indicates that these two phenomena have become increasingly closely related as their scale has increased. This indicates that payment in kind has developed as a way of paying off wage arrears to employees, rather than serving as a means of supplying employees with scarce goods, as had been the case in the past, or being a substitute for the payment of current money wages by cash-strapped employers. On the other hand, although in the RLMS data the amount paid in kind the previous month was significantly greater for those with wage arrears, in the ISITO data there is no significant difference in the proportion of monthly wages paid in kind between those with and those without arrears. Both the RLMS and the ISITO data imply that around 6 per cent of the monthly wage bill is covered by payment in kind (table 7.3). This is not far off our estimate for the peak scale of non-payment of wages and marks a significant contribution to the demonetisation of the economy.

7 Withdrawal from the market economy

Payment in kind provides relief for something like 15 per cent of those who have not been paid their wages. Those who have neither wage income nor payment in kind and who have exhausted their savings have little choice but to withdraw from the market economy and meet their needs by other means. One direct form of withdrawal from the market is to take goods and services without payment. This is an option that is available with regard to housing and utilities.

Table 7.3 *Incidence of payment in kind and wage debt, 1994–1998*

RLMS, urban households	1994	1995	1996	1998	ISITO
No wages owed and no pay in kind	62.6	62.3	44.2	38.0	57.6
Pay in kind but no wages owed	2.6	2.0	1.8	2.8	3.7
Pay in kind and wages owed	2.5	2.3	7.2	9.0	13.0
Wages owed but no pay in kind	32.2	33.5	46.7	50.2	25.7

According to the RLMS data in October 1998, 38 per cent of households owed back rent and utility payments, up from 30 per cent in 1996 and 22 per cent in 1995, the average debt having increased from 1.8 to 2.6 to 3.2 times the average monthly payment of those who did pay over that period. The other form of withdrawal from the market is the household's production of its own means of subsistence, primarily by growing its own food.

We have already seen that food accounts for a growing proportion of expenditure out of a declining household money income. Although a few employers are able to ensure that their employees receive food, whether by supplying provisions through the workplace or by paying wages in kind, many households struggle to find enough money to feed themselves properly. Two-thirds of RLMS respondents in the winter of 1998 said that they were very concerned that they might not be able to provide themselves with the bare essentials over the following year; 28 per cent of household heads in the ISITO survey said that they did not even have enough money to buy sufficient food for their families.

According to the official statistics, well over half of the total amount of food produced in Russia by value is produced on the garden plots of the population. In 1998, allowing for food imports (particularly of meat and milk products) the official statistics indicated that 90 per cent of potatoes, 80 per cent of fruit and vegetables, more than a third of meat, half the milk and milk products, half the wool and a third of the eggs consumed came from household plots (calculated from *Goskomstat*, 1999c, pp. 204, 220-3). These figures would seem to suggest that Russians have returned to the land with a vengeance, responding to the economic crisis by reverting to peasant self-sufficiency, and this is certainly an image that is fostered by the media. However, these figures are very misleading, primarily because *Goskomstat*'s category of domestic production (*khozyaistvo naseleniya*) combines household subsistence production with almost all smallholding agriculture. Thus the growth of domestic production reflects above all the partial dismantling of state and

collective farms and the growth of formally independent peasant production.

This is by no means to deny that the use of land by Russian families is
not widespread. According to the 1994 microcensus, 58.3 per cent of all
households had a plot of land. 22 per cent had a plot adjoining their
home, 16.9 per cent an allotment or a plot attached to a dacha, 9.5 per
cent a vegetable garden, 7.7 per cent a plot and vegetable garden adjoining their home and 2.2 per cent some other kind of combined plot of land
(*Goskomstat Rossi*, 1997). The issue is what people do with this land.
There is no doubt that the rural population grows and raises a large
part of its own food on the land, but Russia is a highly urbanised society.
What is the role of the dacha for the urban population?

Since 1997 the *Goskomstat Household Budget Survey* has investigated
in detail the extent of domestic production for home consumption. The
findings put the statistics on agricultural production in a very different
light. Although in the countryside 45 per cent of food by value was home
grown in 1997 and 40 per cent in 1998, overall only 18 per cent of food
was home-grown in 1997 and 16 per cent in 1998, because in the urban
areas the figures were far lower – 9 per cent of food by value was home
grown by urban families in 1997 and 8 per cent in 1998. These figures
include not only large cities, but also small towns. In Moscow and St
Petersburg, which together account for 12 per cent of the urban population of Russia, virtually nothing was home-grown.[14]

In the four cities covered by the ISITO survey, the proportion of food
that was home-grown varied considerably from one city to another (table
7.4). Most households grew either all or none of their potatoes or vegetables, with more variation in the home-growing of fruit, which was much
more common in Samara than in the other three cities. Across all four
cities just over a third of potatoes were home-grown, but only around 10
per cent of fruit and vegetables. Almost no meat or dairy produce was

[14] Ovcharova and Korchagina calculated on the basis of unpublished *Goskomstat* budget
survey data for 1996 that domestic production accounted for 43 per cent of total food
consumption by value: urban households grew 23 per cent of their own food by value and
rural households 75 per cent (Ovcharova, 1997). However, this estimate also seems to
derive from production data. A direct calculation from the published budget survey data
on consumption and expenditure (which gives money expenditure and the quantities
purchased and consumed for the main food groups) suggests that in the last quarter of
1996 across all households 24 per cent of food by value was home-grown, while in St
Petersburg 3 per cent and in Moscow 4 per cent was home-grown. This is still well above
the RLMS estimate that 14 per cent of food by value was home-grown in the last quarter
of 1996 (Mroz, Popkin, *et al.*, 1997). According to the 1998 RLMS data, urban
households grew 12 per cent and rural households 49 per cent of their food.

Table 7.4 *Percentage of potatoes, vegetables and fruit home-produced across all households, ISITO Household Survey, April–May 1998*

	Samara	Kemerovo	Lyubertsy	Syktyvkar	Total
Potatoes	23	65	17	50	38
Vegetables	9	12	5	7	9
Fruit	26	7	8	1	13

home-produced in any of the four cities. While those households with a dacha put a great deal of time and effort (and money, particularly for transport) into growing their food, and most of those with a dacha did grow food on it, the total saving on the household budget, even in the best of cases, was very small. This is not surprising because the consumption of potatoes, vegetables and fruit in total amounts to only around 20 per cent of the value of the food consumed by the average Russian household. This means that even in Kemerovo, where two-thirds of all potatoes were home-grown, the gross monetary saving from all home agricultural production was only just over 1 per cent of the average amount of money spent on food. When we take into account the amount of money that households said they spent on their dacha, which is almost certainly a substantial under-estimate, many households were out of pocket. It should not be surprising to find that in the ISITO survey data, and in the RLMS data for urban households, those who grow their own food do not spend any less money on food than those who meet all of their food needs in the market. Whatever other functions it may serve, the dacha does not represent a reversion to subsistence production (see Clarke, 1999b for more detailed analysis and discussion of these results).

Although domestic agricultural production does not provide a substitute for monetary expenditure on food for the urban population as a whole, maybe it does provide a solution for those households which have little or no money income. The household budget survey data immediately leads us to doubt this hypothesis, for the amount of home-produced food is a steadily increasing function of income (although it is a slightly diminishing proportion of total household spending): the wealthiest 10 per cent of the population grow six times as much per head as the poorest 10 per cent (*Goskomstat*, 1999a). This is confirmed by analysis of the ISITO, RLMS and microcensus data on the use of dachas and the domestic production of food, all of which show that the poorest families are, if anything, the least likely to use a dacha (Alasheev, Varshavskaya and Karelina, 1999; Clarke, 1999b; Yaroshenko, 1999). In the ISITO data, those who say that they do not have enough money even to buy food are *less* likely to grow their own potatoes. The existence and extent of administrative leave, wage delays and short-time working all have absolutely no impact on the probability of the household producing any of its own food in either the ISITO or the RLMS surveys. Thus there does not appear to be any support for the idea that domestic production is an alternative to earning money in order to buy basic consumption needs, nor that it is a response to a lack of household monetary income.

The depth of the Russian economic crisis and the demonetisation of the economy may provide a powerful incentive for households to grow their own food, but an incentive is not enough. It is obvious that the household must have land, but it must also have the monetary resources required to buy agricultural inputs and to travel to the dacha, and its members must have the physical capability and the free time to devote to agricultural production. Thus, the domestic production of food may be a response to the general crisis but it does not provide a means of survival for those households which are short of money. It would seem more plausible to argue that rather than being the last resort of those on the brink of starvation, domestic agricultural production provides an additional form of security for those who are already quite well placed to weather the storm.

8 Household exchange

Those who do not have enough money to provide for their own needs may be able to call on the support of others, or they may be able to meet their needs by engaging in forms of natural exchange. Two-thirds of all households in the ISITO survey reported their involvement in exchange relations, providing help to or receiving help from others, with about 25 per cent giving help but not receiving it, 20 per cent receiving help but not giving it and 20 per cent both giving and receiving help.[15]

Monetary transfers were only a small part of the exchange networks in which the ISITO respondents were embedded. While 25 per cent of

[15] The proportion involved in exchange relations is higher than appears in RLMS, which reported in 1998 that 17 per cent of households were donors, 17 per cent recipients and 6 per cent both gave and received, with a further 7 per cent having lent to others, but the RLMS question related only to the previous month. For an analysis of the rather unsatisfactory first phase RLMS data see Cox, Zereria and Jiminez (1995).

households had given money and 10 per cent made loans to others during the previous 12 months, 30 per cent said that they had given food and 20 per cent gave goods. The median value of the goods and money received amounted to 6 per cent of the recipient households' average money income, or an average of 3 per cent of money income across all households (as noted below, however, this probably under-states the value of food received from others). This is consistent with the budget survey data, the 1996 survey indicating that gross private cash transfers averaged 4 per cent of household money income, while the more recent data indicate that gross transfers of food amount to the equivalent of 2–3 per cent of money income across all households. The amounts which households report to RLMS that they receive from friends and relatives in cash and in kind are rather higher, amounting over all households to between 5 per cent and 9 per cent of the average household money income between 1992 and 1998, with no clear pattern over time, although there does seem to have been a sharp fall between 1996 and 1998. Not much can be read into these differences because the evaluation appears to be very sensitive to the form of the question.

Private transfers of goods and money between households are extensive and for many households on low incomes can comprise a substantial portion of the household's income. However, it seems that giving and receiving are elements in relations of reciprocal exchange rather than charitable donations from the more to the less fortunate, so that giving and receiving depend on the embeddedness of the household in social networks rather than having anything to do with household income or misfortune. Thus, in the ISITO data there is no significant relationship between the income of the household and the amount received in donations as a proportion of household income, richer households receiving substantially more than poorer households. Poorer households are more likely to be net recipients of help, but this is because richer households tend to give substantially more, even in relation to their income, particularly at the top of the income scale. Households with wage delays, administrative leave, payment in kind or short-time working do not receive any more assistance than households without these misfortunes.[16] Much the most powerful influence on the amount given

---

[16] Income is not significant in the 1998 RLMS data, but giving and receiving seems to be more systematic in the 1996 data, where smaller households, those with young children and those with lower income tend to be net recipients while households with pensioners and more working members tend to be net donors. Households with higher incomes tend both to give and to receive more. However, there is no significant relationship between giving and receiving and the non-payment of wages or payment in kind in any of the RLMS data.

and received is the embeddedness of the household, indicated by the number of network connections cited by household members. Richer households are even more likely than poorer ones to be involved in exchange networks. However, this may be partly because those who are inserted in exchange networks are much less likely to be poor in the first place: in the ISITO survey the density of social networks in which the individual is involved has a very powerful impact on the ability to get a job, to earn more money, to undertake secondary employment and so on.[17]

One of the most common forms of giving relates to the domestic production of food: most households which produce their own food give a significant proportion of their produce to others. In the ISITO survey over 60 per cent of households which produced their own food gave away an average of 30 per cent of the produce to others. However, the exchange of food is more complicated than this: one-quarter of the households with dachas also received some food from other people, while one in six households which do not work a dacha were nevertheless in a position to give food to others: overall at least 14 per cent of households both gave and received food in the previous year (table 7.5).

The key question with regard to the receipt of foodstuffs is whether such donations represent a charitable gesture towards those in hardship, or an element in a network of reciprocity in which the recipient is expected to provide something in exchange. Our own ethnographic research inclines us towards the latter interpretation, and this is strongly supported by the data. When we run a series of regressions with the percentage of each product received as the dependent variable, we find that there is no significant relationship between household money income and the receipt of food products, nor is there any tendency for lower-income households to receive more than those who are better-off, indicating that in general such donations are not a form of social support for lower-income households from their better-off friends and relatives, but primarily involve transfers between those who have a dacha and those who do not (table 7.6).[18] There is a negative relationship between

---

[17] Over all households net receipts should be nil. However, in both the ISITO and the RLMS data, households report giving substantially less than they report receiving. This is more likely to be accounted for by an under-valuation of gifts than an over-valuation of receipts.

[18] The dependent variable in table 7.6 is the average of the percentage of potatoes and of vegetables reported by the household head as being received from others, weighted in the ratio of one to two, which is the ratio of the value of consumption of these items reported for urban households by the *Household Budget Survey*. Income is not significant in any functional form. There is no significant difference in the likelihood of receiving food by

Table 7.5 *Methods of provisioning, ISITO Household Survey, April–May 1998*

Per cent of households	Samara	Kemerovo	Lyubertsy	Syktyvkar	Total
Have a dacha	50	67	33	57	52
Receive some food from others	16	19	12	18	16
Buy all of their food	34	14	55	25	31

the proportion of income spent on food and the receipt of food from others, but this is not sufficiently strong to be statistically significant (except in the case of high-cost meat) – such receipts would appear in general to be a bonus rather than a means of meeting essential subsistence needs. Thus, the acquisition of food is generally a by-product of involvement in reciprocal social relationships which provide other and more significant rewards.

Those most likely to receive foodstuffs are not those most in need but those best equipped to reciprocate: we find that households comprising a single person of working age are far more likely than any other household type to be a recipient of all kinds of produce. More generally, the young are far more likely and the old far less likely to be recipients of food, the reverse of the case with regard to dacha use. Neither single-parent households, nor pensioner households nor those with dependent children or invalids receive any more of their food from others than the average household. Those in temporary difficulties as a result of layoff, short-time or non-payment of wages are not likely to receive significantly more food than others. The fact that produce is often obtained in exchange for labour is indicated by the fact that those who said that they worked on somebody else's dacha received more than twice as much food as others. Finally, many of those who said that they gave food to others or received food from others did not include this in the

any income decile against any other. This is supported by similar findings in Valery Yakubovich's analysis of the data on exchange networks derived from this research (Yakubovich, 1999). Relatively few households receive the higher-value items (fruit, meat and dairy products) from others, but there is a significant negative relationship between household income per head and the proportion of meat and dairy produce received from others. However, the *Goskomstat Household Budget Survey* shows that in 1997 and 1998 the value of food received from others is a steadily increasing function of household prosperity, with the richest decile in 1998 receiving on average more than six times as much as the poorest, and they receive more even as a proportion of their much higher spending on food (*Goskomstat*, 1999a).

Table 7.6 *OLS regression, dependent variable: percentage of potatoes and vegetables received from others, Household Survey, April–May 1998a*

	Unstandardised coefficients	Std. err.	*t*	Sig.
(Constant)	34.914	6.773	5.155	0.000
Give money to others	−0.0124	1.063	−0.012	0.991
Have a car	−0.143	1.244	−0.115	0.909
Have a dacha	−13.456	1.146	−11.742	0.000
Household income per head (100Rs)	−0.710	0.942	−0.754	0.451
Have a child requiring care	2.909	1.554	1.871	0.061
Have an adult requiring care	1.341	1.812	0.740	0.459
There is a spouse	0.644	1.348	0.478	0.633
Number under 7	−1.538	1.655	−0.929	0.353
Number aged 7–16	−2.478	1.028	−2.410	0.016
Number of adults	−1.716	0.763	−2.248	0.025
Proportion of adults working	−2.829	1.768	−1.600	0.110
Proportion of adults pensioners	−5.340	2.481	−2.152	0.032
Household head under 25	10.376	2.482	4.180	0.000
Household head 40–59	−7.134	1.449	−4.923	0.000
Household head 60 and over	−5.464	2.478	−2.205	0.028
Number with a rural background	1.768	0.852	2.074	0.038
Days layoff per head	0.00594	0.035	0.169	0.866
Wage debt per head (100Rs)	0.372	0.262	1.423	0.155
Short-time working per head	−0.00257	0.022	−0.119	0.905
Proportion of income spent on food	−5.794	3.318	−1.746	0.081
Kemerovo	2.026	1.363	1.487	0.137
Syktyvkar	−0.792	1.429	−0.554	0.580
Lyubertsy	−3.489	1.578	−2.211	0.027

Note: a Adjusted R^2 0.159.

help that they said they gave or received about which they were asked elsewhere in the questionnaire, indicating that for most people giving and receiving the products of the dacha is not considered as help but as a normal aspect of reciprocity. Thus the receipt of food, like the receipt of money and other goods, appears to be a part of a wider network of reciprocal interaction between households, sometimes being provided in exchange for work done on the donor's dacha, sometimes as part of an exchange of different products between dacha owners (although dacha owners are significantly less likely to be recipients of foodstuffs) and on other occasions in exchange for other kinds of support, such as providing transport (although possession of a car does not make a household significantly more likely to be a recipient of foodstuffs).

9 Conclusion

The demonetisation of the Russian economy is a result of the failure to develop appropriate financial, commercial and legal institutions to support Russia's transition to a monetised market economy. Enterprises and organisations have been able to build on the Soviet legacy to develop alternative forms of settlement of their mutual obligations that have made it possible for them to survive in a non-monetary market economy. Households, on the other hand, have had far fewer capacities to adapt to the impact of demonetisation on the household budget.

Household money income has fallen by two-thirds since 1990. Of course, incomes by 1990 had run far ahead of more or less fixed state prices, so that people could not spend their hard-earned wages, but household money incomes had still fallen far below their level at the dawn of perestroika, taking them back to about the level of the late 1960s. Only a very small part of this decline is accounted for directly by demonetisation, through the non-payment of wages and benefits, but it is very likely that a much larger part of the fall can be blamed directly or indirectly on the deflationary policies of which demonetisation has also been a result. To the extent that households could be integrated into the non-monetary economy, through payment in kind, the deflationary impact of non-payment would be moderated. However, we have seen that payment in kind compensates for only a very small part of the decline of household money incomes.

The conclusion is that households have, by and large, had to bear the full force of demonetisation. The result of a loss of money income or the non-payment of wages is not, in general, the acquisition of alternative sources of subsistence, but is a fall in household living standards. The subsistence minimum at the end of 1998 at the official exchange rate amounted to about $35 per month ($91 at the PPP exchange rate). However, according to the budget survey, 65 per cent of the rural population and 44 per cent of the urban population lived in households with money incomes below the subsistence minimum, and 35 per cent of the rural population and 15 per cent of the urban population in households with money incomes less than half the subsistence minimum. Those households living at the subsistence minimum only paid about $2 per head per month for their housing and utilities. They consumed about $24 worth of food per head, over 80 per cent of which they bought out of their own income. This left them with an average of $3 each to spend on shoes and clothing and $1 on alcohol and tobacco. Those with money incomes of $17.50 a month, half the subsistence minimum, spent an average of $1.30 per head on housing and utilities and consumed $13 worth of food per head, of which they bought over three-quarters (in both cases, urban households will have bought more like 95 per cent of their own food), leaving them with $1.25 each to spend on shoes and clothing each month and $0.50 a month for alcohol and tobacco. Accounts of the ingenuity with which some local populations have been able to develop non-monetary forms of exchange through which to secure the reproduction of the household economy can be found elsewhere in this volume. But Russia as a whole is a highly urbanised society in which most civil institutions have disintegrated and in which there is no social or institutional base on which to develop such novel solutions. Across Russia as a whole demonetisation has led to a decline in household incomes which has quite simply led to a proportionate decline in monetised consumer demand which further reduces the circulation of money in the system, reducing production, employment and the cash available to pay wages and benefits. Thus, the inability of the vast majority of households to adapt to a demonetised market economy drives the downward spiral of economic decline.

References

Alasheev, S., E. Varshavskaya and M. Karelina (1999). 'Podsobnoe khozyaistvo gorodskoi sem'i (Subsidiary Agriculture of Urban Families), in V. Kabalina and S. Clarke (eds.) *Zanyatost' i povedenie domokhozyaistv*. Moscow, Rossiiskaya politicheskaya entsiklopediya (ROSSPEN)

Aukutsionek, S. (1998a). 'Barter v Rossiiskoi promyshlennosti', *Voprosy ekonomiki*

(1998b). 'Industrial Barter in Russia', *Communist Economies and Economic Transformation*, 10 (2), 179–88

(1998c). 'On Types of Barter', *Russian Economic Barometer*, 7 (2), 45–7

Clarke, S. (1998). 'Trade Unions and the Non-payment of Wages in Russia', *International Journal of Manpower*, 19 (1/2), 68–94

(1999a). *The Formation of a Labour Market in Russia*, Cheltenham, Edward Elgar

(1999b). *New Forms of Employment and Household Survival Strategies in Russia*, Coventry: Centre for Comparative Labour Studies, University of Warwick

Cox, D., E. Zereria and E. Jimenez (1995). *Family Safety Nets During Economic Transition: A Study of Inter-household Transfers in Russia*, Washington, DC, World Bank

Delyagin, M. (1998). *Ekonomika neplatezhei: kak i pocheimu u my budem zhit' zavtra*, 3rd edn., Moscow Assotsiatsiia promyskclenno-stroitel'nykh bankov (Rossiia)

Denisova, I.A. (1997). 'Monetary Transmission in Russia: The Role of Interenterprise Arrears', *Current Politics and Economics of Russia*, 8 (2/3), 163–90

Fan, Q. and M.E. Schaffer (1994). 'Government Financial Transfers and Enterprise Adjustments in Russia, with Comparisons to Eastern and Central Europe', *Economics of Transition*, 2, 151–88

Gaddy, C. and B. Ickes (1998a). 'Russia's Virtual Economy', *Foreign Affairs*, 77 (5), 53–67

(1998b). 'Beyond a Bailout: Time to Face Reality about Russia's "Virtual Economy"', Washington, DC, Brookings Institution and College Park, Pennsylvania State University, June, mimeo

(1998c). *A Simple Four-sector Model of Russia's 'Virtual Economy'*, Washington, DC, Brookings Institution

Goskomstat (1997). *Rossiya v Tsifrakh*, Moscow, Goskomstat Rossii

(1998a). *Metodolicheskie polozheniya po statistike*, 2nd edn., Moscow, Goskomstat Rossii.

(1998b). *Sotsial'no-ekonomicheskoe polozhenie Rossii*, Moscow, Goskomstat Rossii

(1999a). 'Osnovnye pokazateli vyborochnogo obsledovaniya byudzhetov domashnikh khozyaistv po Rossiiskoi federatsii v 1998 godu', *Statisticheskii byulleten'*, 1(51), 9–182

(1999b). 'Osnovnye pokazateli vyborochnogo obsledovaniya byudzhetov domashnikh khozyaistv po Rossiiskoi federatsii v 1998 godu', *Statisticheskii byulleten'*, 5(55), 49–182

(1999c). *Rossiya v Tsifrakh*, Moscow, Goskomstat Rossii

Healey, N.N., V. Leksin and A. Svetov (1998). 'Privatisation and Enterprise-owned Social Assets', *Russian Economic Barometer*, 2, 18–38

Hendley, K., B. Ickes and R. Ryterman (1998). 'Remonetizing the Russian Economy' in H.G. Broadman (ed.), *Russian Enterprise Reform: Policies to Further the Transition*, Washington, DC, World Bank, November

Ickes, B.W. and R. Ryterman (1992). 'The Inter-enterprise Arrears Crisis in Russia', *Post-Soviet Affairs*, 8 (4), 331–61

(1993). 'The Roadblock to Economic Reform: Inter-enterprise Debt and the Transition to Markets', *Post-Soviet Affairs*, 9, 231–52

Klepach, A. (1997). 'Dolgovaya ekonomika: monetarnyi, vosproizvodstvennyi i vlastnyi aspekty', *Voprosy ekonomiki*, 4, 42–56.

Makarov, D. (1998). 'Ekonomicheskie i pravovye aspekty tenevoi ekonomiki v Rossii', *Voprosy ekonomiki*, 3

Makarov, V.L. and G.B. Kleiner (1997). 'Barter v ekonomike perekhodnogo perioda: osobennosti i tendentsii', *Ekonomika i matematiicheskie metody*, 33 (2): 25–41.

Ministry of Labour and Social Development and Goskomstat Rossii (1997). *Monitoring of the Socio-economic Potential of Families for the Fourth Quarter of 1996, Statistical Report*, Moscow

Mroz, T. and B. Popkin *et al.* (1997). *Monitoring Economic Conditions in the Russian Federation: The Russian Longitudinal Monitoring Survey 1992-96*, Chapel Hill, University of North Carolina

Ovcharova, L. (1997). 'The Definition and Measurement of Poverty in Russia' in S. Clarke (ed.), *Poverty in Transition*, Coventry: Centre for Comparative Labour Studies, University of Warwick

Poser, J.A. (1998). 'Monetary Disruptions and the Emergence of Barter in the FSU Economies', *Communist Economies and Economic Transformation*, 10 (2), 157–77

Redor, D. (1992). *Wage Inequalities in East and West*, Cambridge, Cambridge University Press

Rose, R. (1999). 'What Does Social Capital Add to Individual Welfare? An Empirical Analysis of Russia', *Studies in Public Policy*, 318

Rostowski, J. (1993). 'The Inter-enterprise Debt Explosion in the Former Soviet Union: Causes, Consequences, Cures', *Communist Economies and Economic Transformation*, 5, 131–59

Shmelev, N. (1997). 'Neplatezhi – problema nomer odin rossiiskoi ekonomiki', *Voprosy ekonomiki*, 4, 26–41

Woodruff, D. (1999a). 'Barter of the Bankrupt: The Politics of Demonetization in Russia's Federal State' in K. Verdery and M. Burawoy (eds.), *Uncertain Transition: Ethnographies of Change in the Post-socialist World*, Lanham, Boulder, New York and Oxford, Rowman and Littlefield, 83–124

(1999b). *Money Unmade: Barter and the Fate of Russian Capitalism*, Ithaca, Cornell University Press

Yakovlev, A. (1998). 'Barter and Clearing Schemes: How to Define Basic Concepts', *Russian Economic Barometer*, 7 (2), 38–45

Yakubovich, V. (1999). *Economic Constraints and Social Opportunities: Participation in Informal Support Networks of Russian Urban Households*, mimeo; now published in Russian as 'Sotsialnye vozmozhnosti i ekonomicheskaya neobkhodimost': vkluchennost' gorodskikh domokhozyaistv v seti neformal'noi vzaimopomoshchi', in V. Kabalina and S. Clarke (eds.), *Zanyatost' i povedendie domokhozyaistv: adptatsiya k usloviyam perekhoda k rynochnoi ekonomiki v Rossii*, Moscow, ROSSPEN, 254–87

Yaroshenko, S. (1999). Domashnie khozyaistva v usloviyakh perekhodnoi ekonomiki v Rossii: Tipy obespecheniya pitaniya v gorodskikh sem'yakh', in V. Kabalina and S. Clarke (eds.), *Zanyatost' i povedenie domokhozyaistv*, Moscow, Rossiiskaya politicheskaya entsiklopediya (ROSSPEN)

8 Barter in transition economies: competing explanations confront Ukrainian data

DALIA MARIN, DANIEL KAUFMANN AND
BOGDAN GOROCHOWSKIJ

1 Introduction

One of the most striking puzzles posed by recent developments in the former Soviet Union (FSU) is the rise of barter trade. In barter trade goods are paid for with goods or money surrogates rather than cash. Under central planning this form of trade was especially observed in international trade among CMEA countries as well as in East–West trade.[1] Barter in the domestic economy in Russia started to rise after macroeconomic stabilisation in 1994 from 5 per cent of GDP to 60 per cent in 1998.[2] Our survey in Ukraine gives an estimate of barter in industrial sales of 51 per cent in 1997. The importance of barter varies across transition economies. The *World Business Environment Survey* in 20 transition economies shows that Croatia exhibits the highest percentage share of barter of 33 per cent; Russia and Ukraine show a barter share of about 24 per cent and Central European countries like Hungary, Poland, and the Czech Republic have barter shares between 0.8 and 4.7 per cent. These results are presented in table 8.1. It is also interesting to see that some of these countries experienced an increase in the importance of barter over time (Croatia, Russia and Ukraine), while barter declined

This chapter is a substantially revised version of an earlier paper which circulated under the title 'Disorganisation, Financial Squeeze, and Barter' in September 1998. Earlier versions of this paper were presented at the European Bank for Reconstruction and Development, at the CEPR International Workshop in Transition Economics in Prague and at the RECEP conference on 'Economic and Social Reform in Russia: A European–Russian Dialogue' in Moscow. We thank Alexis Giesen for very able research assistance and the Harvard Institute for International Development for financial and logistic support.
[1] See Marin (1990) for the importance of barter in East–West trade, and Marin and Schnitzer (1995) for an explanation.
[2] For the development of barter over time see European Bank for Reconstruction and Development, *Transition Report* (1997); for a recent estimate for Russia see Commander and Mummsen (chapter 5 in this volume).

Table 8.1 *Barter in transition economies, 1996 and 1999*

	1966	1999	Per cent change
Armenia	2.9	2.9	0.0
Azerbaijan	5.1	4.0	0.2
Belarus	13.1	13.9	0.7
Bulgaria	4.0	4.2	−0.2
Croatia	21.7	32.8	11.5
Czech Rep.	3.8	3.3	−0.5
Estonia	5.5	4.1	−1.3
Georgia	6.8	5.2	−1.4
Hungary	1.7	0.8	−0.8
Kazakhstan	20.7	17.9	−2.8
Kyrghiszistan	16.5	17.4	1.8
Lithuania	3.1	2.8	0.1
Moldova	29.6	26.3	−1.3
Poland	3.9	4.7	0.7
Romania	8.6	7.3	−0.3
Russia	23.5	24.1	1.4
Slovakia	19.2	19.2	0.6
Slovenia	17.4	16.3	−0.8
Ukraine	20.3	24.0	4.7
Uzbekistan	23.2	10.2	−13.2
Total	12.5	12.1	−0.1

Source: World Business Environment Survey, World Bank–EBRD (1999).

in Uzbekistan, Kazakhstan, and Moldova. In Uzbekistan the fall of barter was particularly pronounced.[3]

What explains the explosive increase of barter over time? Why does barter exist in some transition economies and not in others? In this chapter we take a closer look at Ukraine, which clearly stands out as a transition economy in which barter plays a dominant role. By looking at one individual country we will try to understand the evolution of barter over time.[4]

---

[3] The reason why the estimates of barter of Commander and Mumssen (chapter 5 in this volume) on Russia and our estimate on Ukraine differ from the *World Business Environment Survey* estimates is that the former two studies include bartering firms only while the latter considers bartering as well as non-bartering firms.

[4] In Kaufmann and Marin (1999) we focus on an explanation of the pattern of barter across transition economies.

We explore several explanations of barter in transition economies that have been raised in the debate on the phenomenon. Among these explanations are: 'soft' budget constraints, tax avoidance, delay in restructuring, the 'virtual economy', and 'lock-in'. Delay in privatisation and inefficient governance structures are seen to lead to quantity targeting rather than profit maximisation. The absence of hard budget constraints leads managers and workers to avoid the costs arising from restructuring by maintaining production in inefficient activities. Barter is seen to help to conceal the true market value of output.[5] Furthermore, barter is seen by many experts to allow tax avoidance by distorting the true value of profits. In addition, the banking sector is used as a tax-collection agency by transferring firms' incoming cash on bank accounts to the state to pay for outstanding tax arrears. The 'virtual economy' argument claims that barter helps to pretend that the manufacturing sector in Russia is producing value while in fact it is not. A final explanation of the use of non-monetary market exchange which is complementary to the explanation of this chapter accounts for its persistence over time once reciprocal exchange is established. When more people engage in barter, market search costs increase and it thus becomes harder to exchange goods for money and the incentive to maintain 'personalised' exchange increases. Through this lock-in and network effect, this explanation points to possible long-term costs of using barter as an exchange system, because the latter system can persist even when it is inefficient. It cannot, however, explain, why barter started to exist in the first place in the former Soviet Union in 1994.[6]

We then proceed to explore an alternative explanation of barter in transition economies. This sees barter as an economic institution to cope with problems arising in the transition when the legal system and capital markets are poorly developed. Blanchard and Kremer (1997) argue that the large decline in output in the FSU has been caused by 'disorganisation' and hold-up problems. The economy suffers from a lack of trust.[7] Disorganisation arises in a 'no-future' environment when old relationships break down before new ones can be established. We argue in this chapter that having no cash and requiring a trade credit from their

---

[5] The possibility of hiding in barter might make it an instrument for the unofficial economy and corruption. We explore the connection between barter, the unofficial economy and corruption in more detail across transition economies in Kaufmann and Marin (1999). For the role of the unofficial economy in coping with the transition see Johnson, Kaufmann and Shleifer (1997).

[6] See Kranton (1996).

[7] See Johnson, Kaufmann, and Shleifer (1997) for why the official output fall might be overstated.

input suppliers gives intermediate producers bargaining power which helps them deal with disorganisation and the lack of trust in the economy. The buyer's lack of helps to equalise bargaining power between the parties and to reduce distortions. However, it brings problems of its own – notably uncertainty about the enforceability of credit contracts – which can be dealt with by trading in barter. Barter creates a deal-specific collateral which controls debt repayment. This way barter can mitigate contractual hazards when capital markets are imperfect and it makes financing of business activities possible which otherwise would not take place. Through this credit channel barter can prevent output from declining even more than it otherwise would.

The chapter is organised as follows. Section 2 looks at competing explanations of barter and evaluates them against data from 165 barter deals in Ukraine in 1997. The data come from three cities: Kyiv (50 per cent), Zaporioshje (30 per cent), and Dnipropetrovsk (20 per cent). Section 3 then looks at the relationship between the trust problem and liquidity constraint in which the latter is a way to deal with an environment in which contracts are poorly enforced. Section 4 analyses the relationship between inter-firm arrears and barter in which the latter is a way to deal with poorly functioning capital markets. Finally, section 5 concludes and discusses some policy options.

Competing explanations

In this section we first look at some of the features of barter in Ukraine based on our survey of 165 barter deals in three cities in Ukraine in 1997 and then proceed to explore the most common explanations of barter.

Table 8.2 shows that barter accounts for on average 51 per cent of firm's sales with a minimum barter share of 1 per cent and a maximum share of 100 per cent. The barter deals are typically large in size ranging between US$ 10 and US$ 5,000,000 with a mean size of US$ 145,534. Furthermore, barter occurs especially in the machinery and vehicle sector (48 per cent of bartering firms are from this sector) and in the basic industry sector (24 per cent of bartering firms).

'Soft' budget constraints and restructuring

Table 8.3 looks at the question whether barter can be explained by problems of corporate governance and/or mode of ownership. Are state-owned firms using barter more often than private firms? Do they try to avoid restructuring by using barter to conceal the true value of output as

Table 8.2 *Descriptive statistics*

	Mean	Min	Max	Cases
Barter in per cent of output	51	0	100	220[a]
Size of barter deal (US$)	135.679	10	5,000,000	150
Industry classification				
Machinery and vehicles	$D = 1$	48 obs.		165
Basic industry	$D = 1$	24 obs.		165

Note: [a] The number of firms exceeds the number of barter deals because each deal involves two firms (a seller and a buyer). The percentages given in table 8.2 are the mean over the total of selling as well as buying firms.
Source: Survey of 165 barter deals in Ukraine in (1997).

Table 8.3 *Ownership, debt and barter*

	Per cent of output[a]			
	Bank debt	Firm debt	Tax arrears	Barter share
Mean values of respective variables				
Domestic state enterprise	7.5	68.0	4.8	56.6
Domestic private firm	0.1	23.8	1.6	58.3
Foreign or GUS firm	–	–	0.0	48.0
Cooperative or collective firm	6.3	16.9	9.6	44.8
Worker	–	–	–	50.4
Government	–	–	–	10.8
Joint-venture	3.0	13.7	0.0	34.6
Total	5.9	32.0	6.5	51.0
F-Test	0.5	1.5	1.2	4.2
Sign. level	(0.789)	(0.180)	(0.315)	(0.000)

Note: [a] The percentages in table 8.3 refer to the number of firms rather than the number of barter deals. The number of firms exceeds the number of barter deals because each deal involves two firms (a seller and a buyer). The percentages given in table 8.3 are the mean over the total of selling as well as buying firms.
Source: Survey of 165 barter deals in Ukraine (1997).

Table 8.4 *Barter, arrears and efficiency*

	Mean	Std dev.	Cases
Barter share in per cent of output			
Efficiency[a]	45.61	28.41	153
1,500–7,000	48.18	29.91	57
7,100–15,000	44.05	27.59	60
15,100–140,000	44.17	27.82	36
$F = 0.366$		Sign. level 0.694	
Total arrears in per cent of output			
Efficiency[a]	41.42	101.07	138
1,500–7,000	69.60	150.16	57
7,100–15,000	17.89	15.13	48
15,100–140,000	26.97	38.44	33
$F = 4.024$		Sign. level 0.020	
Firm arrears share in per cent of output			
Efficiency[a]	30.15	90.89	138
1,500–7,000	53.88	137.82	57
7,100–15,000	13.53	14.56	48
15,100–140,000	13.32	10.29	33
$F = 3.429$		Sign. level 0.035	
Wage arrears in per cent of output			
Efficiency[a]	3.38	6.00	150
1,500–7,000	6.78	8.45	57
7,100–15,000	1.71	1.80	57
15,100–140,000	0.63	1.67	36
$F = 18.701$		Sign. level 0.000	
Tax arrears in per cent of output			
Efficiency[a]	7.15	19.31	150
1,500–7,000	8.94	13.79	57
7,100–15,000	2.38	6.25	57
15,100–140,000	11.88	33.98	36
$F = 3.158$		Sign. level 0.045	

Note: [a] Output in US$ per employee.
[b] The Pearson correlation coefficient between the barter share and efficiency is 0.05. between total arrears and efficiency −0.13. between firm arrears and efficiency −0.12, between wage arrears and efficiency −0.25 and between tax arrears and efficiency −0.03. Except for wage arrears, none of the correlations is significant at conventional levels.
Source: Survey of 165 barter deals in Ukraine (1999).

has been claimed?[8] Table 8.3 demonstrates that barter does not seem to be a phenomenon of state-owned enterprises. Newly established private firms show the same or higher barter exposure as state-owned firms or cooperatives. The average barter share of state enterprises is 56.6 per cent and that of private firms 58.3 per cent. In addition, table 8.4 shows that there is no relationship between the barter intensity of the firm and the productivity of the firm, if at all the relationship is positive (the correlation coefficient is 0.05). This suggests that avoiding restructuring by inefficient and loss-making firms is not the prime reason for barter. Table 8.4 looks also at the relationship between arrears and the efficiency level of the firm. The different types of arrears in percentage of output do appear to be declining with the productivity level of the firm. However, the correlation coefficients between arrears and efficiency (given at the bottom of table 8.4) are near zero and not significant at conventional levels except for the correlation between wage areas and productivity. This evidence suggests that neither 'soft' budget constraints nor a reluctance to move into efficient activities seem to be the driving force behind barter. The data do suggest, however, that very large arrears (firm arrears of more than 50 per cent of firm's output) tend to be a phenomenon of less efficient firms.

In order to control for size effects in the relationship between productivity and barter on the one hand and productivity and arrears on the other, table 8.5 calculates the relevant correlation coefficients for different firm sizes. The correlation between barter and efficiency is near zero and insignificant. However, the correlation between the different types of arrears and efficiency becomes more negative and more significant for all firm sizes except for medium-sized firms.

The 'virtual economy'

Next, we turn to the 'virtual economy' argument of Gaddy and Ickes (1998). The argument rests on the assumption that the manufacturing sector is value-subtracting, but that most participants in the economy have an interest in pretending that it is not. Barter allows the parties to pretend by allowing the manufacturing sector to sell its output at a higher price than its market value and the value-adding natural resource sector (Gazprom) to accept this over-pricing out of a lack of other opportunities. But if the natural resource sector is producing valuable output, why has the sector nothing better to do than to subsidise the manufacturing sector? Is there any evidence that this is what in fact occurs?

[8] See European Bank for Reconstruction and Development (1997), pp. 26–7.

Table 8.5 *Barter, arrears and efficiency, by firm size*

	Barter share	Total arrears	Firm arrears	Wage arrears	Tax arrears
Small firms[b]					
Efficiency[a]	0.09[e]	−0.27	−0.22	−0.33	−0.20
Medium firms[c]					
Efficiency[a]	−0.19	0.28	−0.19	0.00	0.39
	(0.22)	(0.08)	(0.22)	(1.00)	(0.01)
Large firms[d]					
Efficiency[a]	0.01	−0.31	−0.35	−0.35	
	(0.98)	(0.08)	(0.08)	(0.05)	(0.04)

[a]Output in US$ per employee.
[b]Output level between 0 and 4 billion US$.
[c]Output level between 4 and 20 billion US$.
[d]Output level between 20 and 500 billion US$.
[e]The numbers are Pearson correlation coefficients; the number in brackets give the significant levels.
Source: Survey of 165 barter deals among 55 Ukrainian firms (1997).

We can answer this question from our survey data, since we have information on the percentage price difference between the barter price and the cash price for each of the 165 barter deals in the sample. We have this information for both sides (the 'sale' and the 'goods payment') of each barter deal so that we can calculate the net terms of trade effect of barter. Table 8.6 aggregates the 165 barter deals into 8 sectors and looks at their pricing behaviour in barter compared to cash deals. Table 8.6 distinguishes whether the sector is on the selling or buying end of the transaction. *SCASH* is the percentage difference between the barter price and the cash price on the 'sale' side of the barter deal. *PCASH* is the percentage difference between the barter price and the cash price on the 'goods payment' of the barter deal.[9] *TOT* measures the net terms of trade effect and is calculated by $TOT = SCASH - PCASH$. When the sector is on the selling end of the transaction and *TOT* takes a positive value, then barter allows the sector to shift the terms of trade in its favour. When the sector is on the buying end of the transaction

[9] We obtained this information from the following question: 'What is the percentage difference between the price you charge/you are charged in this barter deal as compared to the typical price you charge/you are charged for the same product in cash deals?'

Table 8.6 *Pricing behaviour of sectors*

		Selling sector			Buying sector		
		$SCASH^a$	$PCASH^b$	TOT^c	$SCASH$	$PCASH$	TOT
Electricity and	Mean	0.00	−4.14	4.12	3.78	7.42	−3.64
gas	Std dev.	0.00	8.52	8.52	8.80	45.06	42.11
	N	17	17	17	18	18	18
Coke and	Mean	5.48	1.45	4.03	1.13	−1.31	2.44
petroleum	Std dev.	14.45	10.28	8.37	5.50	6.54	6.57
	N	13	13	13	16	16	16
Metal ores and	Mean	5.00	−1.29	6.29	2.50	0.58	1.92
other non-	Std dev.	10.16	6.05	10.05	8.09	17.02	18.29
metallic	N	17	17	17	18	18	18
minerals							
Food and	Mean	2.64	1.00	1.64	3.03	−2.47	5.51
beverages	Std dev.	6.53	38.45	35.75	9.45	15.38	14.09
	N	27	27	27	36	36	36
Textiles and	Mean	1.86	0.26	1.61	5.21	−4.17	9.38
leather	Std dev.	8.46	6.86	9.99	7.11	7.93	9.66
	N	16	16	16	12	12	12
Machinery and	Mean	3.66	0.91	2.75	3.46	−5.06	8.52
vehicles	Std dev.	7.41	10.64	13.51	7.67	9.96	11.40
	N	28	28	28	30	30	30
Chemicals	Mean	6.08	−3.60	9.68	7.19	0.07	7.12
	Std dev.	9.49	12.50	11.18	9.47	12.01	8.59
	N	22	22	22	15	15	15
Services	Mean	2.83	−4.04	6.86	0.00	−10.00	10.00
	Std dev.	6.54	17.72	16.27	0.00	0.00	0.00
	N	23	23	23	1	1	1
Total	Mean	3.43	−1.16	4.59	3.52	−1.21	4.73
	Std dev.	8.30	18.63	18.07	8.26	19.66	18.86
	N	163	163	163	146	146	146
ANOVA	F-test	1.08	0.33	0.52	0.76	0.77	0.93
	Sign. level	(0.382)	(0.37)	(0.817)	(0.619)	(0.614)	(0.489)

Notes: [a] Difference between the barter price and the cash price in per cent of the cash price in the 'sale' side of the barter deal.
[b] Difference between the barter price and the cash price in per cent of the cash price in the 'goods payment' side of the barter deal.
[c] Terms of trade $TOT = SCASH − PCASH$.
Source: Survey of 165 barter deals in Ukraine (1997).

and *TOT* takes a positive value, then barter shifts the terms of trade against it.

If the 'virtual economy' argument were valid, we would expect manufacturing sectors like textiles and leather, machinery and vehicles and chemicals to shift the terms of trade in their favour, while the natural resource sectors like electricity and gas, coke and petroleum would see the terms of trade move against them. What appears from table 8.6 is that there is no systematic difference in the pricing behaviour within barter across sectors (the *F*-test of the Analysis of Variance (ANOVA) is not statistically significant at conventional levels). Take the example of machinery and vehicles. When this sector is on the selling end of the barter deal, it over-prices its output on average by 3.66 per cent relative to cash deals and is overpriced on the 'goods payment' by 0.91 per cent on average, so that the sector's net benefit from barter is 2.75 per cent (in terms of its cash price). So far so good. But the same appears to be true for the natural resource sectors like electricity and gas. This sector's net benefit from barter is 4.12 per cent (in terms of its cash price). What seems to matter here for the pricing behaviour within barter is not the sector, but whether the sector is on the selling or buying end of the transaction. Take again the example of machinery and vehicles. When this sector is on the buying end of the barter deal, it pays more for the 'sale' by 3.46 per cent on average and sells its 'goods payment' at a 5.06 per cent discount compared to cash deals, so that the sector's net loss from barter is 8.52 per cent on average. This net loss from barter appears to be happening in all the other sectors as well except for electricity and gas, when the sector is a buyer rather than a seller. It appears then that the sectors gain from barter when they sell and lose from barter when they buy.[10] The only sector that seems to be gaining from barter independent of its buying or selling status appears to be the natural resource sector electricity and gas. This is just the opposite from what we would have expected if we believed in the 'virtual economy' argument of Russia's non-cash economy.

Taxes

We turn now to the tax incentives for barter. We asked firms whether there was a tax advantage reason for using barter. For only 9.5 per cent of the barter deals did firms reply that taxes were a very important or important reason to engage in this form of exchange (see table 8.7). Even

---

[10] Marin and Schnitzer (1999) explain this pricing behaviour by hold-up and incentive problems.

Table 8.7 *Motives for barter, 1997*[a]

Motive	Per cent
No cash	87.5
No bank loan	29.1
No trust in the value of money	6.0
Faster payment compared to cash payment	72.1
No struggle with other creditors	7.8
No courts to enforce rights	6.0
To maintain production	12.5
Goods in stock could be used	66.1
Liquid good	1.8
Better deal on the price in barter	20.8
Reducing tax burden	9.5
Avoiding controls on foreign trade	1.8
Reducing regulations	6.0
Capital flight to west	0.0
State pressure	1.8
Others	1.2

Note: [a] Answers have been ranked between 'very important' and 'irrelevant'. The percentages give 'very important' responses.
Source: Survey of 165 barter deals in Ukraine (1997).

if one takes into account that the data have some noise, it does suggest that tax reasons are not the major motivation behind barter.[11]

The empirical evidence so far indicates that barter is a major phenomenon in the FSU. Furthermore, the tables suggest that the most common explanations of barter – the lack of market discipline, lack of restructuring, the virtual economy and tax avoidance – are not supported by the data. An explanation of barter has therefore to be found somewhere else. More specifically, any explanation of barter has to address the following two questions: First, why would parties want to tie two deals? Secondly, why would parties want to pay in goods rather than money? Before we come to a specific answer to these questions we turn to the answers given by the firms themselves.

In table 8.7 it can be seen that barter is predominantly motivated by financial considerations. In 87.5 per cent of the deals a key reason for

[11] Kaufmann and Marin (1999) look at the tax motive for barter across 20 transition economies in more detail.

Table 8.8 *Lock-in: business alternatives (per cent)*

	Sale	Goods payment
No alternative	20.2	6.0
A few alternatives	36.9	32.1
Many alternatives	41.1	60.1

Source: Survey of 165 barter deals in Ukraine (1997).

using barter was that there was no cash available. In 29 per cent of the barter deals the firm could not get a loan even when ready to pay a high interest rate.[12] In 72 per cent of the cases the party used barter, because she expected to be paid faster in this form of exchange. Also an important reason for barter seems to be to smooth production. In 66 per cent of the cases the firm could use goods stored as inventories as means of payment in barter deals and in 12.5 per cent of the cases the firm used barter, because it was the only way to maintain production.[13] Additionally, barter was used as a way to change the relative price for the good in question in 20.8 per cent of the deals.

In the following two sections we will look at an alternative explanation which takes into account the fact that barter is primarily driven by financial reasons. Firms might want to tie two deals and they might want to pay in goods rather than money because by doing so they could solve incentive and hold-up problems which otherwise would prevent trade from taking place at all. In section 3 we will argue that having no cash turns out to be a mechanism to cope with disorganisation and hold-up when legal enforcement of contracts is poorly developed. In section 4 we will argue that barter creates a deal-specific collateral, and that this is a way of dealing with the problem of creditworthiness of firms.

3 Disorganisation and liquidity constraints

Blanchard and Kremer (1997, hereafter BK) explain the rapid output decline in the FSU by disorganisation and hold-up problems. Central

---

[12] The answers do not include cases when the firm did not take a bank loan, because of high interest rates.

[13] We added this question to the survey during the period of firm interviews, because firms often spontaneously gave this as a reason for why they engaged in barter. The later inclusion into the survey leads to an under-estimation of the true response to the question 'maintaining production'.

planning was characterised by a complex set of specific relations between firms. Many firms had only one supplier from which to buy and knew of only one or a few buyers to whom to sell. This picture of few outside opportunities is still observed in Ukraine in 1997. In 20 per cent of the sales within barter deals the parties had no alternative partner and in 37 per cent of the sales only a few alternative partners to carry out the business (table 8.8).

Such an environment with few outside opportunities – called *specificity* – typically creates hold-up problems and opens room for bargaining. Under central planning the main instrument to enforce production and delivery of goods was the coercive power of the state. Transition eliminated the central planner without creating institutions to deal with specificity, such as vertical integration and the range of contracts that exist in market economies. Furthermore, in times of transition the anticipation of changing business partners and the disappearance of firms shortens horizons and reduces the scope for long-term relationships. Thus, in such a 'no-future' environment there is no scope for opportunistic behaviour to be constrained by such mechanisms as a concern for reputation. BK argue that specificity in the relations between firms together with incompleteness of contracts results in disorganisation – the breakdown of many economic relations before new ones can be established – which in turn explains the large output losses.

In the BK model specificity arises in a chain of production with a large number of stages. Each buyer along the chain knows only the supplier with which it was paired under central planning. The primary input supplier has an alternative use for the input while all intermediate producers along the chain of production are assumed to be able to sell only to the next buyer. BK formulate the hold-up problem by assuming that it is impossible for each firm in the chain to sign a contract with the buyer (the next firm in the chain) before it has produced the good. Each firm must first buy inputs and produce, and only then – once the cost of producing is sunk – can it strike a bargain with the next producer in the chain. At this stage, however, each intermediate producer's reservation value is zero and thus the next producer in the chain can 'hold him up' and exploit his dependency by offering to purchase the good at a price which does not cover each intermediate producer's costs. The fear of being 'held-up' by the following firm means that each intermediate producer will seek alternative outlets for its production, which increases the likelihood that the entire chain will break down. Output collapses owing to a shortage of inputs. In the BK model output collapses because firm relations are specific (the intermediate producers cannot sell the good to someone else) and because contracts are incomplete (each intermediate

Date	Action	State
0.9	Buyer makes investment to find supplier	
		Supplier holds up buyer
		Bargaining power on supplier's side owing to input shortage
1.0	Supplier and buyer negotiate over input price Input good delivered but not paid	
		Buyer holds up supplier
		Bargaining power on buyer's side owing to costly credit enforcement
1.1	Buyer offers to pay reduced price for the input	

Figure 8.1 Firm-specific investment to find an input supplier: sequence of events

producer must produce its intermediate good before bargaining over the price for the input with the next producer along the chain). If the government retained its coercive power it could force suppliers to deliver and thus output would not decline.

Is there another mechanism than the coercive power of the state by which intermediate producers can be induced to trade inputs by preventing producers further down the chain from reneging and renegotiating the price? Marin and Schnitzer (1999) (hereafter MS) develop a model which introduces liquidity and credit constraints into a BK type of production chain. Analogously to BK they consider a good which requires n steps of production. In contrast to BK, MS consider a situation in which the supplier holds up the buyer rather than the other way around. In the MS formulation the buyer makes a firm-specific investment in order to find an adequate input supplier (see figure 8.1). This investment takes place at date 0.9. At date 1.0 when the supplier delivers the input they negotiate over the input price. At this stage the buyer's investment is already sunk and not taken into account in the bargaining over the input price. Thus, the buyer might not invest in finding a supplier relationship because these costs are not taken into account. This is what constitutes the hold-up problem on the buyer's side. MS claim that this formulation of the hold-up problem on the buyer's rather than the supplier's side is more plausible in the context of the FSU, since input suppliers are on the short side of the market and thus input buyers have to spend time and money in order to find adequate suppliers and to establish a business relationship.[14]

MS assume further that the intermediate producer has no cash to pay for the input at date 1.0. He requires a trade credit from the input supplier which he can repay when he sells the input to the next firm. In order to make sure that his trade credit is repaid, the input supplier has to incur credit enforcement costs (they have to involve legal firms or the Mafia). MS then show that the fact that the intermediate producer has no cash to pay for the input gives the input purchaser some countervailing bargaining power. The trade credit gives him, in effect, a form of hostage.

In principle the input supplier could attempt to compensate for this disadvantage by raising its input price. But MS show that marking up the input price at date 1.0 in anticipation of the future price renegotiations will be possible only at low credit-enforcement costs. When these costs become sufficiently large, the buyer's liquidity constraint will make it impossible for the supplier to pass on these costs to him. The reason is that the most the buyer can pay for the input is the cash he himself realises from selling the intermediate good to the next buyer. If enforcement costs are sufficiently large the input buyer's cash from the sale to the next firm will not be enough to cover these costs. This is the circumstance when the input buyer can exploit the fact that he is liquidity-constrained to shift the surplus in his favour and thus prevent being held up by the input supplier.

When credit-enforcement costs become too large, however, the input supplier will refuse to participate in the deal, since he cannot expect a positive profit. From this story MS predict a hump-shaped relationship between the firm's output growth and credit enforcement costs. The output decline will be less pronounced for firms short of cash. Firms short of cash can use their liquidity constraint in the bargaining to prevent being held up by their input suppliers. When this constraint becomes too large, however, it may be too costly for the supplier to enforce payment and thus output declines owing to a shortage of credit.

If the intermediate producer's liquidity constraint is alleviating the hold-up problem, what then is the role of barter? Barter becomes important when credit enforcement becomes so costly that input suppliers will refuse to participate in the deal. Thus, if the input buyer has no cash and requires a trade credit from the input supplier, but the legal system to

---

[14] MS provide empirical evidence which supports this formulation of the hold-up problem on the buyer's side.

enforce payment is poorly developed, a potentially valuable transaction does not take place. Under these circumstances barter can help to maintain production. Barter introduces a second hostage, a commitment device that prevents the buyer from fully exploiting his bargaining power.[15] More specifically, when enforcement costs become prohibitively great for the input supplier to participate in the deal, introducing a second profitable deal in the form of the goods payment allows the input buyer to commit not to exploit his bargaining power and to shift some of the profit back to the input supplier to make him participate in the deal. Barter is a *self-enforcing arrangement* which makes intermediate producers along the chain of production lose from reneging on the contract. This way barter helps to cope with specificity without relying on the legal system[16]. From this story MS predict a hump-shaped relationship between the firm's output growth and the firm's exposure to barter.

In order to see whether this story makes sense empirically we will look at the relationship between the firm's change in output and the extent of the hold-up and the credit problem and the firm's exposure to barter. There are three implications. First, the more severe the hold-up problem, the lower will be the firm's output growth owing to the breakdown of business relationships in response to a lack of trust. Second, the firm's output growth is expected to be larger for intermediate levels of credit-enforcement costs and to be lower when the credit problem becomes very large (hump-shaped relation). Third, the firm's output growth is expected to be larger for lower levels of barter exposure and to be lower when the barter exposure becomes very large (hump-shaped relation).

We gathered data concerning 165 barter deals in 1997. Although the unit of analysis of the survey is a barter deal, the survey includes information on the two firms involved in each deal as well. We use this firm-level information in the sample to look at the performance of firms. First, we construct an output growth variable. This variable is defined by the growth of output between 1994 and 1996 of an individual firm relative to the average growth rate between 1994 and 1996 for the total sample of the firms. We look also at the growth rate of output of the firm relative to the growth rate of GDP in the same period. We report both results in table 8.9.

We first look at disorganisation and the lack of trust as a reason for the output decline. We measure these problems with BK's index of

---

[15] Oliver Williamson introduced the concept of a hostage to facilitate exchange, see Williamson (1983).

[16] Greif and Kandel (1994); Johnson, Kaufmann and Shleifer (1997); and Hay and Schleifer (1998) point out that the deficiencies of the legal system are more pronounced in the FSU compared to the early transition economies.

Table 8.9 *Barter and output decline*

	Firm's output to GDP growth[a]		Firm's output to sample growth[b]		
	Mean	Std dev.	Mean	Std dev.	Cases
1 *Firm arrears*					
(per cent)	0.165	4.42	3.09	15.73	138
0–10	−0.59	1.71	0.46	6.08	66
10–20	1.76	7.88	8.81	28.10	33
20–626	−0.04	2.98	2.24	15.73	45
	$F = 3.17$ Sign. level 0.045		$F = 3.17$ Sig. level 0.045		
2 *Barter share*					
(per cent)	0.01	4.2	2.60	15.0	153
0–20	−0.31	1.9	1.46	6.7	46
20–60	1.37	6.4	7.43	22.8	58
60–100	−1.30	0.4	−2.05	1.3	49
	$F = 5.84$ Sign. level 0.004		$F = 5.84$ Sig. level 0.004		
3 *Complexity*[c]	0.14	4.4	3.05	16.6	141
0.34–0.78	1.84	8.0	9.10	28.4	33
0.79–0.83	0.48	2.9	4.28	10.4	36
0.84–0.92	−0.82	1.6	−0.35	5.5	72
	$F = 4.453$ Sign. level 0.012		$F = 5.84$ Sig. level 0.004		
4 *Ownership*	0.101	4.2	2.60	15.0	153
State	0.14	2.9	3.06	10.2	40
Private	−0.85	1.2	10.47	4.4	12
Cooperative	0.16	5.1	3.12	18.1	92
Joint-venture	−0.92	0.1	−0.70	0.2	9
	$F = 0.356$ Sign. level 0.785		$F = 0.356$ Sig. level 0.785		

Notes: [a] Percentage difference between the growth rate of firm's output and GDP growth in 1994-6.
[b] Percentage difference between the growth rate of firm's output and output growth of sample firms in 1994–6.
[c] See text for definition.
Source: Survey of 165 barter deals in Ukraine (1997).

complexity. According to their theory the hold-up problem becomes more severe and thus the decline in output more pronounced for goods with more complex production processes. Their measure of complexity is constructed on the basis of the 1990 '100-sector' input–output table for Russia. Complexity is equal to zero if the sector uses only one input from another sector and it tends to one if the sector uses many inputs in equal proportions. We matched the ISIC sector of our bartering firms with the sector of the complexity index given by BK. This measure is obviously full of noise for several reasons. BK's complexity index is based on the Russian input–output structure which might differ from that in Ukraine. Further noise might be introduced because the production structure in Ukraine might have changed since 1990. Finally, the ISIC classification of our sample could not always be perfectly matched with BK's classification of the index. In spite of all these caveats, we can reproduce BK's findings with firm-level data. Table 8.9 reports that the firm's output growth relative to GDP growth is lower when the firm's production is more complex. Firms producing goods which rank low in the complexity index increased their output by 1.8 percentage points compared to the economy as a whole, while the opposite was true for firms producing goods which ranked high on the complexity scale. Again, the same picture emerges when the firm's output growth is compared with the average growth of all firms in the sample rather than the economy as a whole. The association between the firms' relative growth and the complexity measure is highly significant.

Next, we look at the credit problem. We measure credit-enforcement costs by the amount of arrears the firm has accumulated. The larger the accumulated arrears, the more likely it is that the firm does not fulfil its debt obligations and thus the larger are the credit-enforcement costs assumed to be.[17] As table 8.9 shows, there is indeed a hump-shaped relation between output growth and firm arrears. When arrears are small or very large the firm did less well in terms of output than the economy as a whole or the total sample of firms, while it exhibited a relatively larger output growth for intermediate levels of arrears.

Furthermore, table 8.9 shows that firms with a share of barter in output of up to 20 per cent had a growth rate of output of 0.3 percentage points lower than the total economy, while firms with a barter share between 20 per cent and 60 per cent experienced a growth rate 1.37 percentage points higher than the total economy. However, when the exposure to barter becomes too large (exceeds 60 per cent), then the firm's output appears to have grown 1.29 percentage points less than the economy as a whole. These findings suggest that there is an optimal level of barter at which the output decline is minimised. The relationship between output growth and barter exposure is statistically significant at conventional levels. The same picture emerges when the firm's output growth is

---

[17] Arrears are assumed to measure the firms current and future creditworthiness, since firms with large arrears must have been perceived as creditworthy to get into this state.

related to the growth of the total sample of firms rather than to the economy as a whole.[18]

We also investigated the influence of ownership patterns. It appears that private enterprises are those with the least impressive performance in terms of output growth. The relationship between ownership pattern and relative output growth is not significant at conventional levels, however.[19]

4 Inter-firm arrears and barter

The literature on inter-firm debt in transition economies asks the following question. Why do firms give loans to other firms when the latter are not considered creditworthy by banks? The answer most commonly given is the absence of market discipline. State-owned firms who are seen to show the highest inter-firm debt are able to get loans from other firms because of the 'soft' budget constraint. But if state-owned firms are creditworthy because of the backing of the government, they are expected to be the least credit-constrained and thus to show the highest bank debt. As table 8.3 shows, in our sample of bartering firms this is indeed the case. State-owned firms appear to have on average higher bank debt (7.5 per cent of output) while private firms have negligible bank debt outstanding (0.1 per cent of output). However, state-owned firms show also the highest inter-firm arrears compared to private firms (68 per cent and 24 per cent of output, respectively). This suggests that state firms used their privileged status of creditworthiness to get cash credit from banks as well as trade credit from other firms.

An explanation for the phenomenon of inter-firm debt cannot, however, rest exclusively on the presence of 'soft' budget constraints. Inter-firm arrears are not a phenomenon of state firms alone. In our sample of bartering firms only 29 per cent are state-controlled. There must be additional forces at work here, which go beyond the lack of market discipline.

Capital and credit markets do not function well in transition economies, for a variety of reasons. Creditors are inexperienced with credit evaluation. Banks have difficulties in distinguishing bad from good debtors. There is

---

[18] Table 8.9 gives the univariate association between the relevant variables. We obtain qualitative similar results in a multivariate analysis which controls for other factors influencing output growth, see Marin and Schnitzer (1999).

[19] As we show in table 8.3 and in sections private firms were those which were hardest hit by the liquidity squeeze in the economy which might have inhibited their growth. Furthermore, the result might also be owing to a selection bias in the sample, since the sample consists of bartering firms only. In Kaufmann and Marin (1999) we examine the difference between bartering and non-bartering firms using a sample of 20 transition economies.

no history to allow them to judge credit risk because of the drastic changes in the environment. In some of the transforming economies a bankruptcy law has not yet been introduced. Defaulting on debt repayment remains without consequences and therefore firms have little incentive to repay their loans from banks.

Many experts have suggested that one of the solutions to inter-firm debt is to restore the creditworthiness of firms by introducing a bankruptcy procedure. But in many countries like Hungary and Ukraine, for example, a bankruptcy law has been introduced without any impact on levels of inter-firm debt. Furthermore, a study by Mitchell (1993) suggests that the introduction of a bankruptcy law by itself will not improve debt repayment because creditors do not use bankruptcy procedures to get to their money. Among other factors Mitchell's explanation for creditor passivity is the low expected value of their claims net of bankruptcy costs. This is owing to the poor state or vintage of the capital stock of a debtor firm, the absence of a market for capital and the priority assigned to a creditor in bankruptcy relative to the ordering of other creditors. Mitchell's explanation suggests that inter-firm debt is not going to go away with the introduction of a bankruptcy law and that creditor passivity prevents bankruptcy from restoring the creditworthiness of firms.

The question remains: why are firms able to give loans to other firms when the banking sector is reluctant to provide capital in spite of the availability of a bankruptcy procedure to pursue non-paying debtors? The possibility of undertaking a business in the form of barter trade becomes important in this context. In a barter trade one firm gives a trade credit to another which is repaid in goods rather than money. Barter trade offers the following advantages.[20]

First, barter does not attempt to improve the overall creditworthiness of firms (as in bankruptcy) but rather restores the creditworthiness of the firm for one specific deal. In barter, a *deal-specific collateral* is created in the form of the future goods payment. Depending on the degree of the debtor's credit problem, the creditor can choose the value of the collateral relative to the trade credit that he gives to the debtor. This way the debtor's creditworthiness is restored for one specific deal. Giving a trade credit in the form of a barter deal is available only to firms, since banks are not allowed to engage in the trading business.

Secondly, in the early stages of transition barter trade can compensate for creditors' passivity. Instead of relying on the low and unknown liquidation value of the firm (as in bankruptcy), the creditor and debtor create a deal-specific collateral of positive and known value. Furthermore, in

---

[20] For barter as a finance instrument in international trade see Marin and Schnitzer (1997).

Table 8.10 *Barter as credit (per cent)*

	Ex ante	Actual
Pre-purchase	14.9	14.3
No termination point	20.02	–
0 month[a]	46.4	46.4
1 month	9.5	16.1
1–3 months	3.6	12.5
3–7 months	3.6	8.3
Missing	1.8	2.4
Total	100.0	100.0

Note: [a] Time period between 'sale' and 'goods payment'.

barter trade the creditor does not need to share the benefits from her legal actions with other creditors. In a barter deal the creditor obtains *property rights on goods* – which effectively means that she does not need to queue with other creditors for the money. Compared to bankruptcy, in a barter trade there is no priority ordering of creditors. This makes payment in goods a superior credit enforcement mechanism compared to payment in money.

Thirdly, barter is a more *information-intensive* form of financing. Typically a trade credit is given between two firms which know each other from previous transactions (one firm is a producer and the other firm is an input supplier).

Table 8.10 looks at whether trade credit features within barter deals. In 36.9 per cent of the deals a trade credit was given within the barter deal. The time period between the sale and the goods payment varied between one month and seven months. In 20 per cent of the deals the parties did not make an agreement on the termination of the credit. Table 8.11 shows that when a trade credit was given the parties agreed on it *ex ante* in 16 per cent of the barter deals only. In 17 per cent of the cases a trade credit was given *ex post* by the selling firm, because the buyer was unable or unwilling to pay.

Table 8.12 reports on the outstanding debt of bartering firms and examines whether there is a relationship between the size of the firm's outstanding debt and the extent to which the firm engages in barter. Firms who barter tend to have large outstanding bank debt, firm debt and outstanding tax arrears (exceeding 100 per cent of firm sales in 1996).

Table 8.11 *Trade credit (per cent)*

	Ex ante
No	81.5
Yes	16.1
Not applicable	0.6
Missing	1.8
Total	100.0

	Ex post
Buyer was unable or unwilling to pay	1.67
Seller wanted to be paid later	3.6
Not applicable	76.2
Other	1.8
Missing	1.8
Total	100.0

Source: Survey of 165 barter deals in Ukraine (1997).

This suggests that these firms had little scope for obtaining further credit. If our explanation is correct, we expect a positive association between the barter share of the firm and its total outstanding debt and a negative association between the barter share and bank debt. Barter can help firms with weak overall creditworthiness when they cannot get a bank loan by restoring their creditworthiness for one particular deal.

Table 8.12 shows that the barter share of the firms indeed tends to increase with outstanding firm and wage arrears. At the same time barter tends to be lower for those firms which have access to bank loans. Furthermore, a simple correlation between the firm's bank debt with its firm arrears reveals a weak negative correlation between the two (the correlation coefficient is -0.185) once the state firms are excluded, suggesting that firm debt helped to compensate for the liquidity squeeze induced by low bank debt for those firms in the economy with restricted access to bank loans.[21]

[21] Calvo and Coricelli (1993) use a negative correlation between bank debt and firm arrears as evidence for whether inter-firm arrears helped to compensate for the liquidity squeeze in their argument for the role of credit as a factor explaining the output fall in Poland. According to this argument a positive correlation between bank debt and firm debt would indicate that firm debt has not alleviated the liquidity squeeze.

Table 8.12 *Barter and creditworthiness*

	Barter share in per cent of output		
	Mean	Std. dev.	Cases
Debt in per cent of output			
1 *Total debt*[a]			
(per cent)	43.67	27.7	138
0–10	22.04	17.5	42
10–20	56.28	23.5	30
20–690	51.70	27.1	66
$F = 25.374$		Sign. level 0.000	
2 *Bank debt*			
(per cent)	45.12	28.5	150
0	48.63	32.0	63
1–5	37.57	25.9	42
5–105	47.27	24.6	45
$F = 2.114$		Sign. level 0.124	
3 *Firm arrears*			
(per cent)	43.67	27.7	138
0–10	32.13	25.4	60
10–20	48.44	21.5	33
20–616	55.57	28.9	45
$F = 11.350$		Sign. level 0.000	
4 *Wage arrears*			
(per cent)	45.13	28.5	150
0	37.63	29.8	75
1–10	49.25	24.2	66
10–40	77.33	17.8	9
$F = 10.151$		Sign. level 0.000	
5 *Tax arrears*			
(per cent)	45.13	28.5	150
0	39.84	21.1	87
1–10	52.15	27.6	39
10–125	52.88	28.5	24
$F = 3.704$		Sign. level 0.027	

Notes: [a]Except bank debt.
Source: Survey of 165 barter deals in Ukraine (1997).

Next we explore whether firms in our sample have in fact faced a liquidity shortage as a limit to production. BK themselves report evidence based on a survey of 500 firms in Russia which suggests that the financial constraint was the most important shortage experienced by enterprises (see their table IV). Between 1993 and 1995 over 60 per cent of firms experienced a shortage of financial resources compared with only over 20 per cent of firms experiencing shortages of materials. Calvo and Coricelli (1993, 1995) have argued that credit contraction and the associated liquidity shortage were responsible for the initial output decline in Eastern Europe.[22]

We now turn to whether inter-enterprise arrears can be seen as a response to the liquidity crunch in the economy. If this is the case we expect inter-enterprise credit to be negatively associated with bank credit. Firms who cannot get bank credit turn to other firms for trade credit. To examine the relationship between these two types of credit in more detail we regress the share of inter-firm arrears in per cent of the firm's output on the share of the firm's bank debt and a set of other variables which we consider to play a role for the size of arrears. The results are reported in table 8.13. In columns (1)–(3) the results for the total sample are given. The coefficient on bank debt is positive and highly significant, suggesting that firms with access to bank credit were also successful in getting inter-enterprise credit. One of the reasons why the two types of credit move in the same direction is the ownership status of the firm. Rostowski (1993) and others have argued that arrears are simply a manifestation of 'soft' budget constraints. To control for this possibility we divide the sample into private and state firms and re-run the regressions. It turns out that for private firms inter-firm credit cushioned the liquidity contraction induced by lower bank credit (see columns (4) and (5) of table 8.13). State firms in contrast appear to be able to use their privileged credit-worthiness to get cash credits from banks as well as trade credits from other firms (columns (6) and (7) of table 8.13).

As we have argued in section 3, two additional variables are supposed to have contributed to the size of arrears: the firm's barter exposure and the complexity of the firm's production. Barter trade is an inter-enterprise credit repaid in goods rather than money. Thus at some critical level of arrears the only way firms' arrears can grow further is if they undertake barter. If our explanation of barter is correct, we expect a positive coefficient on the barter share. This is indeed the case for the overall sample

---

[22] Calvo and Coricelli (1993) run a regression between output and credit for Poland. They get a point estimate between 0.2 and 0.6 depending on specification, which suggests that a 10 per cent contraction of credit results in an output decline between 2 and 6 per cent.

and the two subsamples of firms (columns (2) and (3), (4) and (5), (6) and (7) of table 8.13).

Next, we include the index of complexity in the equation. As we argued in section 3, arrears are expected be more pronounced for firms with more complex production structures, since their liquidity constraint is supposed to help them to deal with the hold-up problem. This appears to be supported by the data. Finally, we re-run the regressions with total arrears (including wage and tax arrears) rather than firms' arrears alone as the dependent variable with very similar results. The data seem to suggest that the Ukrainian firms in fact experienced a liquidity squeeze which barter has helped to alleviate.

5 Conclusions

In this chapter we have explored several explanations for the explosion of barter in post-socialist economies: 'soft' budget constraints, lack of restructuring, the 'virtual economy' and tax avoidance. Of these explanations only the tax reason for barter is weakly supported by the data. The tax argument for barter cannot, however, explain why barter exploded from about 5 per cent to 60 per cent within four years. Something else is at work here and from our survey data in Ukraine the following picture has emerged.

Barter is mainly driven by *financial considerations*. Firms lack the cash to pay for their inputs and banks refuse to provide capital. This has led to the phenomenon of inter-firm arrears in which firms extend trade credits to each other. We have argued that these firm arrears allowed intermediate producers to deal with the problem of trust in the economy and found supporting evidence for this role. We argued further that barter comes into play when arrears become so critically large that firms refuse to extend further trade credits to their buyers. By introducing a hostage barter then allows the debtor firm to make a commitment to repay the loan, and thus restores creditworthiness one deal at a time. We found evidence to support this view of barter.

The view of barter as a *substitute for a banking failure* suggests the following explanation for the evolution of barter over time. The arrears crisis in Russia evolved in 1992 while barter started to rise in 1994. Barter rose in 1994 because around this time arrears reached a critical level at which production was unsustainable. Our data suggest that this critical level was reached when arrears were around 30–40 per cent of firm sales. At this point firms refused to extend further credit to each other. Barter then stepped in as the only way to maintain production. At this point,

Table 8.13 *Barter, arrears and liquidity squeeze*

| | Firm arrears | | | | | | | Total arrears | | | | | | |
| | All firms | | | Private firms | | State firms | | All firms | | | Private firms | | State firms | |
	(1)	(2)	(3)	(4)	(5)	(6)	(7)	(8)	(9)	(10)	(11)	(12)	(13)	(14)
Bank debt	2.61	2.40	2.61	−1.77	−1.77	2.27	3.64	3.72	3.54	3.72	−4.17	−9.02	3.42	4.80
	(0.000)	(0.000)	(0.000)	(0.132)	(0.279)	(0.007)	(0.000)	(0.000)	(0.000)	(0.000)	(0.167)	(0.020)	(0.000)	(0.000)
Barter	0.92	0.90	0.92	0.49	0.48	2.57	2.22	1.07	1.06	1.07	0.40	0.67	2.67	2.32
	(0.001)	(0.001)	(0.001)	(0.000)	(0.001)	(0.003)	(0.004)	(0.000)	(0.000)	(0.000)	(0.027)	(0.005)	(0.003)	(0.004)
Complexity	117.59	120.36	117.64		7.70		748.54	135.87	138.20	135.85		195.70		755.12
	(0.047)	(0.041)	(0.048)		(0.848)		(0.001)	(0.024)	(0.000)	(0.025)		(0.040)		(0.001)
State		23.57							19.78					
		(0.148)							(0.233)					
Private			0.53							−0.19				
			(0.984)							(0.994)				
R^2 adj.	0.224	0.229	0.218	0.874	0.829	0.242	0.404	0.344	0.346	0.340	0.467	0.610	0.345	0.482
N	149	149	149	13	12	49	49	151	151	151	14	13	49	49

Note: [a] The number of cases exceeds the number of interviewed firms because each barter deal involves a selling and a buying firm.
Source: Survey of 165 barter deals among 55 Ukrainian firms (1997).

barter started to substitute for the inactive banking sector as well as for trade credits in cash.

Given this story of the role of barter in transition economies what follows for policy? Barter seems to have established itself as an *economic institution* to deal with banking failure and capital markets imperfections in transition economies. We have argued that barter has produced short-term benefits by allowing these economies to maintain or increase production without a functioning banking sector. However, the short-term efficiency gain might come at the costs of long-term efficiency losses. Barter might have established itself as an institution which hinders the banking sector from developing. This transition trap might arise because banks will not have an incentive to enter the market given the existence of barter.

A major challenge in the transition to a market system is the replacement of a centralised credit system with *decentralised financial discipline*. We argue elsewhere that a decentralised banking system creates a coordination problem that a multi-banking system cannot handle. Creditors may be more likely to finance credit-constrained firms under a financial system based on long-term relationships than one based on arm's-length market transactions. There may be particular value therefore for such transition economies as Russia and Ukraine in the development of a German-type banking system to avoid such a transition trap.[23]

Reforming the banking sector in the FSU in order to remonetise their economies is urgent. Short-term macroeconomic 'fixes' such as an expansionary monetary policy to overcome the liquidity shortage in these economies would make matters worse. In a barter economy a monetary expansion may have perverse effects. The reason is that reducing arrears by infusing liquidity into the economy is likely to reduce intermediate producers' bargaining power thereby taking away an instrument for dealing with disorganisation and the trust problem. In other words, a monetary expansion in a barter economy works like introducing partial reform into an economy characterised by significant multiple distortions.[24]

References

Anderson, R.W., E. Berglöf and K. Mizsei (1996). 'Banking Sector Development in Central and Eastern Europe, *Economic Policy Initiative*, 1, London, CEPR

[23] For the argument see Huang, Marin, and Xu (1999).
[24] For the argument why partial reform might make things worse in an overall distorted economy see Murphy, Shleifer and Vishny (1992).

Begg, D. and R. Portes (1993). 'Enterprise Debt and Economic Transformation: Financial Restructuring in Central and Eastern Europe', in C. Mayer and X. Vives (eds.), *Capital Markets and Financial Intermediation*, Cambridge, Cambridge University Press

Blanchard, O. and M. Kremer (1997). 'Disorganisation', *Quarterly Journal of Economics*, 112 (4), 1091–26

Calvo, G.A. and J.A. Frenkel (1991). 'Credit Markets, Credibility, and Economic Transformation', *Journal of Economic Perspectives*, 5 (4), pp. 139–48

Calvo, G.A. and F. Coricelli (1993). 'Output Collapse in Eastern Europe: The Role of Credit', in M.I. Blejer, G.A. Calvo, F. Corricelli and A.H. Gelb (eds.), *Eastern Europe in Transition: From Recession to Growth?*, World Bank Discussion Paper, 196, Washington, DC, World Bank

  (1995). 'Inter-enterprise Arrears in Economies in Transition', in R. Holzmann, J. Gacs and G. Winckler (eds.), *Output Decline in Eastern Europe: Unavoidable, External Influence or Homemade?*, London, Kluwer

European Bank for Reconstruction and Development (1997). *Transition Report 1997*, 26–7

Gaddy, C.G. and B.W. Ickes (1998). 'Russia's Virtual Economy', *Foreign Affairs*, 77 (5), 53–67.

Greif, A. and E. Kandel (1994). 'Contract Enforcement Institutions: Historical Perspective and Current Status in Russia', chapter 8, in E. Lazar (ed.), *Economic Transition in Eastern Europe and Russia: Realities of Reform*, Stanford: Stanford University Press

Hay, J.R. and A. Shleifer (1998). 'Government in Transition: Private Enforcement of Public Laws: A Theory of Legal Reform', *American Economic Review*, 88 (2), 398–403

Huang, H., D. Marin and C. Xu, C. (1999). A Transition Trap? Barter and the Development of Banking, International Monetary Fund, University of Munich and London School of Economics, mimeo

Ickes, B.W. and R. Ryterman (1992). 'The Inter-enterprise Arrears Crisis in Russia', *Post-Soviet Affairs*, 8 (4), 331–361

  (1993). 'Roadblock to Economic Reform: Inter-enterprise Debt and the Transition to Markets', *Post-Soviet Affairs*, 9 (3), 231–252

Johnson, S., D. Kaufmann and A. Shleifer (1997). 'The Unofficial Economy in Transition', *Brookings Papers on Economic Activity*, 2, 159–239

Johnson, S., D. Kaufmann and P. Zoido-Lobaton (1998). 'Regulatory Discretion and the Unofficial Economy', *American Economic Review*, 88, 2, 387–92

Kaufmann, D. and D. Marin (1999). *The Non-Cash Economy: Evidence from 20 Transition Economies*, World Bank and University of Munich, mimeo

Kranton, R.E. (1996). 'Reciprocal Exchange: A Self-sustaining System', *American Economic Review*, 86 (4)

Marin, D. (1990). 'Tying in International Trade', *The World Economy*, 13(3), 445–62

Marin, D. and Schnitzer, M. (1995). 'Tying Trade Flows: A Theory of Countertrade', *American Economic Review*, 85 (5), 1047–64

(1997). 'The Economic Institution of International Barter', *CEPR, Discussion Paper*, 1658

(1999). 'Disorganisation and Financial Collapse', *CEPR Discussion Paper* 2245

Mitchell, J. (1993). 'Creditor Passivity and Bankruptcy: Implications for Economic Reform', in C. Mayer and X. Vives (eds.), *Capital Markets and Financial Intermediation*, Cambridge, Cambridge University Press

Murphy, K., A. Shleifer and R. Vishny (1992). 'The Transition to a Market Economy: Pitfalls of Partial Reform', *Quarterly Journal of Economics*, (3), 889–06

Russian Economic Barometer (1997). *Survey of Industrial Firms*, Institute of World Economy and International Relations, Moscow

Rostowski, J. (1993). 'The Inter-Enterprise Debt Explosion in the Former Soviet Union: Causes, Consequences, Cures', *Centre for Economic Performance/ ESRC Discussion Paper*, 142

Williamson, O.E. (1983). 'Credible Commitments: Using Hostages to Support Exchange,' *American Economic Review*, 73 (4), 519–40

9 Barter and non-monetary transactions in transition economies: evidence from a cross-country survey

WENDY CARLIN, STEVEN FRIES,
MARK SCHAFFER AND PAUL SEABRIGHT

1 Introduction

The persistence of barter transactions over a number of years in complex industrialised economies has been one of the most puzzling paradoxes of the transition from central planning to market organisation. Historically barter has characterised relatively simple societies with a comparatively undifferentiated division of labour. It has also been observed in more complex societies in the aftermath of serious crises such as wars. For example, complex chains of bilateral exchanges of goods between firms and payment in kind to workers were prevalent in the western zones of post-war Germany between 1945 and mid-1948. In the context of a high level of uncertainty about the future of the economy, with the collapse of the Nazi command economy, the freezing of prices and wages at their 1936 levels and extensive controls over inter-regional trade, there was an extreme shortage of goods. An assessment at the time captured the essential role of barter in this episode: 'Where neither trading for money nor redistribution of goods by political authority, alone or in combination, can ensure a reliable division of labour, bilateral exchange seems to be the safest line of economic retreat' (Mendershausen, 1949, pp. 657–8). The improved functioning of the costly and cumbersome barter mechanism enabled production to recover from less than 20 per cent of the 1936 level in mid-1945 to 50 per cent by the end of 1947. In post-war Germany output recovery in a barter-dominated economy before the currency reform was often seen as remarkable (Abelshauser, 1975). It is nevertheless very clear that only when the functioning of market

Comments from Barry Ickes, Yuri Perevalov, Daniel Treisman and seminar audiences at the EERC – Russia annual conference in Moscow and the CEPR/EBRD/ESRC Transition Economics workshop are gratefully acknowledged. The views in this chapter are solely those of the authors and not necessarily those of the EBRD or other institutions with which they are affiliated.

processes was fully restored did dynamic future-oriented restructuring take place.

But whenever barter has been observed in such situations of crisis it has been short-lived. In mid-1948, there was a currency reform combined with the lifting of price and wage controls. Barter and side-payments in kind vanished. There was also a clear shift in the nature of recovery to a dynamic process of growth vividly displayed in the jump in investment, the radical reorganisation of production processes and the introduction of new products (Carlin, 1989). By the time of the currency reform, it was clear that recovery was to be encouraged, a market economy was to be restored and private ownership of firms would remain largely intact. The episode of large-scale barter was ended abruptly by the introduction of functional money and price and wage liberalisation. The 'normal' incentives of a market economy took over.

This episode raises the question why barter has persisted – and, indeed, expanded – in transition economies after prices were liberalised, and why it has continued even in the context of reasonable macroeconomic stability. Presumably other characteristics of transition economies have interfered with the rapid establishment of 'normal' market economy incentives and practices. Marin and Schnitzer's (1999) analysis suggests that a key differentiating characteristic may be that the nature of the output collapse in post-war Germany and in the transition countries was different.

The degree of 'disorganisation' in terms of the disjunction between the relationships of suppliers and purchasers of inputs in the planned economy and those sustainable in a market economy appears to have been much greater in the transition economies than in post-war Germany. The pattern of trades in post-war Germany seems to have been motivated by producers trying to maintain supplier and customer relationships (Stamp 1947). In transition economies major changes in supplier – customer relationships were required. When planning collapses and leaves behind bilateral monopoly relationships between input suppliers and purchasers, there is great scope for 'hold-up' problems and stalemates. As a result, production chains collapse (Blanchard and Kremer 1997). The collapse is greater where new entrants and foreign suppliers are unable to play a substantial role.

Marin and Schnitzer argue that trade credit expands in transition economies to help offset the bargaining power of the input supplier. However, in the context of uncertain contract enforcement trade credit is highly risky. Barter may therefore help the process of output recovery by allowing trade credit to be collateralised in the form of the borrower's own output. This will allow output to be maintained in a world of disorganisation, though it may have other more long-term costs. Normally these costs include the fact that firms find themselves having to accept and re-sell products in the trading of which they have no comparative advantage. But this particular cost may be lower when – as a symptom and by-product of disorganisation – trading networks are limited and firms operate in informational 'islands' (see the introduction to this volume); trading partners may be able to pool search costs without sacrificing comparative advantage. In these conditions barter may have fewer drawbacks than other responses to the problem of limited credit-worthiness.

In understanding the prevalence of this expansion of barter in transition countries and particularly in Russia, Ukraine and other CIS countries, it is important to bear in mind that what is commonly referred to as 'barter' in the Russian and western literature on these countries is not 'barter' as conventionally defined. The *New Palgrave Dictionary of Economics*, for example, defines barter as 'a simultaneous exchange of commodities... without using money. It is thus a form of trade in which credit is absent or weak' (Hart, 1987). The Russian term *barter*, however, encompasses not only the exchange of goods for goods, but also the exchange of goods for debt. If, for example, a firm pays for a purchase of inputs with a bill of exchange (Russian *veksel*, from the German *Wechsel*), then this is *barter* (Russian), but it is certainly not 'barter' as conventionally defined in the English-language economics dictionaries. Indeed, Commander and Mummsen (chapter 5 in this volume) show that most of what Russian firms refer to as *barter* is *not* in fact what economists would term barter – i.e. the exchange of goods for goods; it is rather payment for goods using non-monetary methods and instruments – i.e. debt.

There is, however, an important difference between the use of bills of exchange and other debt instruments in capitalist economies and the countries of the CIS. When a bill of exchange is redeemed in the CIS, typically the holder of the claim on the issuing firm is not the customer that initially accepted the bill as payment. It is a different firm that has purchased or otherwise acquired the bill (though precisely how often this occurs is unclear). Furthermore, the bill of exchange may often be redeemed by the issuing firm not in cash or its equivalent, but in goods produced by the issuing firm. It is this last feature that most clearly distinguishes the use of bills of exchange in CIS countries from the way they have been used in capitalist economies. The use of debt offsets in CIS countries, the third main form of *barter* (along with bills of exchange and 'barter' in the standard sense of goods-for-goods) is conceptually similar. In the multilateral debt swaps observed in CIS countries, by contrast, debts are essentially redeemed in goods, not cash. This is not barter as conventionally defined, but it is a close cousin.

This chapter analyses the transactions of firms conducted using non-monetary methods and instruments: exchange of goods for goods, payment using bills of exchange, debt swaps, redemption of debt in goods, etc. – 'barter' as understood in the Russian sense of the word.

2 Empirical findings

The nature of the survey

A large survey of enterprises in 20 transition countries was conducted in the early summer of 1999 by the EBRD and the World Bank, and its provisional findings have been published in the EBRD *Transition Report 1999*. The aim of the survey was to investigate how enterprise restructuring behaviour and performance were related to competitive pressure, the quality of the business environment and the relationship between enterprises and the state. The survey included approximately 125 firms from each country, with the exceptions of Poland and Ukraine (over 200 firms) and Russia (over 500 firms).

One question on barter was included: 'What share of your firm's sales are now (and three years ago) conducted in barter, offsets or bills of exchange (money surrogates)?' The six possible answers were one point (exactly zero) and five intervals of varying size (1–10 per cent, 11–25 per cent, 26–50 per cent, 51–75 per cent, 76–100 per cent). The econometric technique we use when this is our dependent variable is interval regression (StataCorp, 1997). The advantage of interval regression is that the coefficients on the exogenous variables can be interpreted as if Ordinary Least Squares (OLS) were being applied to a continuous dependent variable – e.g. the coefficient on a dummy variable will give the impact in percentage points on the share of barter.

Since only this question was asked, we have no way of checking if 'barter, offsets [and] bills of exchange (money surrogates)' were interpreted in the same way by different firms and in different countries. There may be substantial cross-country differences of interpretation (for instance, whether trade credit is included in the definition). While this places some limits on the interpretation of the findings from the survey, the breadth of other information collected presents an unparalleled opportunity for exploring the causes and consequences of barter.

The full sample size was 3,125 firms. Sampling was random from the population of firms in each country, with the exception of minimum quotas for state-owned firms and large firms. We omitted from the analysis firms with missing information, leaving us with 3,079 firms. The sample is dominated by small and medium-sized enterprise (SMEs); almost half the sampled firms employ fewer than 50 persons, and fewer than 10 per cent employ more than 500. Half the firms in the sample are newly established private firms, 10 per cent were privatised to insiders, 25 per cent were privatised to outsiders and 15 per cent remain state-owned. Firms in the industrial and service sectors are roughly equally represented, each accounting for 40-45 per cent of the sample, with agricultural firms making up the remainder (14 per cent). Most firms were located in either large cities or national capitals (30 per cent) or in medium-sized cities (32 per cent), with the rest in towns and rural areas (38 per cent). Out of the full sample of 3,000-odd firms, only 12 failed to answer the question on their current use of barter, a response rate of over 99.5 per cent. The response rate for the use of barter three years previously was significantly lower, at 85 per cent.

For just under one-third of the firms in the survey, barter and non-monetary transactions make up more than 10 per cent of their 'sales' and for nearly one-fifth of firms it accounts for over 25 per cent. Barter is more prevalent in Russia and Ukraine than elsewhere: just over one half of firms report using barter for 10 per cent of their business transactions and just over one-third conduct 25 per cent of their business this way (see table 1). Other studies of barter and non-monetary transactions in Russia and Ukraine are in line with the order of magnitude reported in the EBRD survey.

Here we explore the data in several stages. To begin with, we look at size, sectoral and locational effects. Next, using these as controls, we look at the extent to which the level of barter and non-monetary transacting reported by firms is related to ownership, to financing problems and arrears and to competition in the product market. After looking for firm-level correlates of barter, we examine whether some country-level variables are relevant: inflation, a measure of the 'softness' of the budget constraint and of the quality of the business environment. Finally we examine the consequences of barter and non-monetary transactions for firm restructuring and performance.

Where does barter happen?

Table 9.1 shows the distribution of reported levels of barter and non-monetary transactions by country. Barter is widespread in Russia and Ukraine. Elsewhere in the CIS its incidence varies greatly, with high levels in Belarus, Moldova and Kazakhstan and very low levels in some other countries. More surprisingly, barter and non-monetary transactions appear in the

Table 9.1 *Percentage of firms in sample reporting each level of barter and non-monetary transactions, by country, 1999*

Country	\multicolumn{6}{c}{Per cent of sales accounted for by barter and non-monetary transactions}	No. firms
	None	1–9	10–25	26–50	51–75	76–100	
Russia	28.4	19.1	16.8	15.3	12.6	7.8	524
Ukraine	28.6	21.4	16.1	11.6	11.2	11.2	224
Other CIS							
Armenia	82.3	10.5	4.8	0.8	1.6	0	124
Azerbaijan	78.0	8.7	11.8	0.8	0	0.8	127
Belarus	32.8	30.4	21.6	8.8	5.6	0.8	125
Georgia	72.1	10.8	12.4	3.9	0.8	0	129
Kazakhstan	36.2	21.3	18.1	7.9	11.0	5.5	127
Kyrghistan	47.2	11.2	18.4	11.2	8.0	4.0	125
Moldova	23.2	16.8	16.0	20.8	16.0	7.2	125
Uzbekistan	68.0	8.0	10.4	7.2	3.2	3.2	125
Non-CIS							
Bulgaria	64.8	24.8	7.2	1.6	1.6	0	125
Croatia	9.5	18.2	23.0	23.0	19.8	6.3	126
Czech Rep.	74.8	17.0	5.2	3.0	0	0	135
Estonia	49.2	42.2	6.1	2.3	0	0	132
Hungary	89.8	8.6	1.6	0	0	0	128
Lithuania	75.7	17.1	4.5	2.7	0	0	111
Poland	65.8	21.6	8.1	3.6	0.9	0	222
Romania	72.8	10.4	8.8	4.0	0.8	3.2	125
Slovakia	56.6	13.2	7.8	3.9	3.9	14.7	129
Slovenia	13.6	40.8	26.4	15.2	3.2	0.8	125

Source: EBRD Enterprise Survey 1999.

Central and Eastern European (CEE) countries (where they have often been assumed to be absent). While there are relatively small proportions of firms reporting barter at the level of 25 per cent of sales or more, barter is non-negligible except perhaps in Hungary. Croatia and Slovenia look quite out of line with the other non-CIS countries in terms of the proportion of firms reporting no involvement in barter. This suggests that the question may have been interpreted differently in those countries from elsewhere. In the rest of the non-CIS countries (Central, Eastern and South-Eastern Europe plus the Baltic states), the proportion of firms reporting no barter transactions ranges from 49 per cent in Estonia to 90 per cent in Hungary.

Across all countries large firms are more likely to be engaged in barter than are small ones. This suggests that there are economies of scale in barter and non-monetary transactions (see Guriev and Ickes, chapter 6 in this volume). However, as table 9.2 shows, there are both sectoral and country variations to this pattern. Table 9.2 provides a method of comparing the likelihood of a firm being involved in barter (to the extent of at least 25 per cent of sales) across countries, sectors and size class of firm. To illustrate the patterns in the data, we show the predicted probability that barter and non-monetary transactions account for more than 25 per cent of sales for a small firm (with fewer than 50 workers) and for a large firm (with more than 500 workers). For many countries there are not enough agricultural firms in the sample to form the basis for predicted probabilities. In these cases, the results for industry and services only are shown in the table.

From table 9.2 the size and sectoral distribution of barter looks quite similar for Russia and Ukraine. Firms in industry are more likely to be engaged in barter than service sector firms, and in both cases it is large firms that are more heavily involved. It is clear that in Russia, barter is much more prevalent in agriculture than in the rest of the economy. Small enterprises in Russian agriculture are just as likely to be involved in barter as large ones. A possible explanation for the widespread use of barter in Russian agriculture is that Russian agriculture receives subsidies of various sorts, including subsidies delivered using non-monetary methods (delivery of goods written off against taxes, write-offs of energy costs, etc.).

Table 9.2 shows that there are wide differences between the other CIS countries in the size and sectoral patterns of barter and non-monetary transactions, as well as in their prevalence. In Kazakhstan and Moldova there appears to be a lot of barter in agriculture but this is not true of Uzbekistan, where barter seems to be disproportionately found in the services sector. There is also no uniform finding of a higher prevalence of barter in large than in small firms. Among the more advanced reformers in Central and Eastern Europe including the Baltics, large firms in industry are more involved in barter but there do not appear to be size effects for services firms.

The patterns in the group of CIS countries look too disparate for the analysis of the pooled results to be very meaningful. We therefore omit the other CIS countries from the more detailed examination of the correlates of barter, and we concentrate henceforth on Russia and Ukraine. For similar reasons, we limit our analysis of the non-CIS countries to the more advanced CEE reformers, excluding Croatia and Slovenia because of doubts about data comparability (see above).

Table 9.2 *Prevalence of barter and non-monetary transactions: firm size and sectoral effects*

Country	Size of firm	Industry	Services	Agriculture
Russia	Small	15.6	10.6	51.4
	Large	22.9	13.1	53.3
Ukraine	Small	18.7	7.9	
	Large	27.1	10.6	
Other CIS				
Armenia	Small	2.9	1.7	
	Large	3.8	0.6	
Azerbaijan	Small	0	0.1	
	Large	0.2	0.3	
Belarus	Small	5.5	13.2	5.1
	Large	7.7	11.5	7.1
Georgia	Small	8.5	0.9	
	Large	7.4	1.2	
Kazakhstan	Small	10.5	4.2	59.5
	Large	16.3	7.9	57.1
Kyrghistan	Small	28.2	4.1	12.8
	Large	27.2	4.6	17.9
Moldova	Small	9.6	8.1	68.6
	Large	17.4	12.4	68.6
Uzbekistan	Small	9.1	25.2	13.6
	Large	10.6	19.5	6.2
CEE + Baltics				
Croatia	Small	58.4	25.7	
	Large	58.4	30.3	
Czech Rep.	Small	0.8	2.0	
	Large	1.2	2.1	
Estonia	Small	3.0	2.0	
	Large	2.9	1.9	
Hungary	Small	0	0	
	Large	0	0	
Lithuania	Small	0.1	2.9	
	Large	0.2	1.8	
Poland	Small	1.4	0.3	0.2
	Large	2.4	0.5	0.2
Slovakia	Small	10.1	17.0	
	Large	17.8	16.6	
Slovenia	Small	7.1	6.2	
	Large	10.3	7.9	

Notes: Table 9.2 shows the predicted probability that barter accounts for more than 25 per cent of sales of a small firm (with 50 employees) or a large firm (with 500 employees).

Table 9.3 *Location effects on barter and non-monetary transactions*

Location effects	Russia	Ukraine	CEE excl. Croatia and Slovenia
Big city	−6.39 (2.54)**	0.21 (4.42)	−1.02 (1.23)
Town	10.88 (3.47)***	4.68 (3.97)	0.10 (1.11)
No. of firms	524	205	840

Notes: Table 9.3 reports the coefficients on the location dummies (the omitted category is 'small city') in an interval regression with the percentage share of barter in sales as the dependent variable (see discussion in the text).

In addition to the size of firm and the sector, we also check for any association between location and tendency to barter. The barter variable is regressed on two location dummies, 'big city' and 'town' (small city is the omitted category). The size, sector and size – sector interaction terms are included as controls. For Russia, the location dummies are highly significant – barter is much more prevalent in the more rural locations. For example, in a firm in a town (the most rural location), barter as a share of sales is estimated to be 11 percentage points higher than in a small city. In turn, barter in a big city is estimated to be 6 percentage points lower than in a small city (see table 9.3). This is consistent with the idea that barter and non-monetary transacting in Russia may be in part a product of limited trading networks, or 'informational islands' (see the introduction to this volume).

The sample size for Ukraine is substantially smaller than that for Russia (205 as compared with 524). This will tend to pull down the significance levels of the coefficients in the Ukraine regressions. Even keeping this in mind, the clear location effects characteristic of Russia do not seem to be present in Ukraine. The signs on both big city and town are positive, and the coefficients insignificant. Location also does not appear to play a part in barter in the advanced reform countries.

The causes of barter and non-monetary transactions

The next step is to analyse in turn a series of possible correlates of barter and non-monetary transactions. For example, do state firms do more or less barter than new private firms; is barter more prevalent

Table 9.4 *Ownership and exporting effects on barter and non-monetary transactions*

Ownership effects	Russia	Ukraine	CEE excl. Croatia and Slovenia
(1) Ownership type.			
Insider ownership	4.36 (3.16)	−5.29 (5.99)	−2.59 (2.54)
State-owned	1.01 (5.29)	−10.70 (7.28)	−5.64 (1.58)***
ab initio private firm	−7.28 (2.87)**	−10.37 (5.77)*	0.03 (1.29)
(2) Foreign stake	0.96 (8.11)	−18.86 (8.89)**	−0.59 (1.58)
(3) Export	−0.14 (0.10)	0.10 (0.11)	0.03 (0.02)
No. of firms	524	205	840

Notes: The regression results for three regressions for each region are reported in table 9.4. Part (1) of the table reports the coefficients on the ownership dummies (the omitted category is 'privatised but not insider-owned'). Part (2) reports the coefficients on the dummy variable for whether or not the firm has a foreign owner. Part (3) reports the coefficients on a dummy variable for whether the firm exports or not.

Interval regression with the percentage share of barter in sales as the dependent variable is used in all cases (see the discussion in the text).

Size, sector and size – sector interaction variables are included in all regressions. For Russia, location dummies are also included.

The standard error is shown in parentheses.

* Significant at 10 per cent, ** significant at 5 percent and *** significant at 1 per cent.

where the product market is less competitive; is barter higher in firms reporting financing problems? In the regression analysis, we control for size, sector – and, in Russia, also for location – and allow for country fixed effects within the Central European region. The omitted ownership category is privatised firms that are not insider-owned. In Russia and Ukraine, new entrants make less use of barter than do other firms. There is a clear tendency for state-owned firms in the CEE region to do less barter – there is no sign of this in Russia and the effect in Ukraine although large and negative is not significant. There is no indication that insider versus outsider ownership of privatised firms makes any difference to involvement in barter (table 9.4).

It might have been expected that a foreign ownership stake would make involvement in barter less likely by providing access to the parent company's suppliers elsewhere. However this effect is found only in Ukraine – the presence of a foreign owner reduces the share of barter in sales by just under one-fifth. In neither Russia nor Ukraine, nor in the

CEE group, was there a correlation between engagement in exporting and the presence of barter.

There is a strong relationship between perceived financing problems and the role of barter in the firm. This is clearly true in Russia and CEE, and true for some measures though not all in Ukraine. Managers were asked to give a score to the seriousness of financing problems in general, problems of access to long-term bank credit and difficulties caused by high interest rates. In each region, there is a very strong positive correlation between the seriousness with which financing problems are rated by managers and their involvement in barter. When asked specifically about problems with accessing long-term bank credit, managers' ratings again showed a strong correlation with barter except in Ukraine. High interest rates seem to capture a feature of financing problems relevant to barter although the effect is not significant in Ukraine (see table 9.5).

Given the findings for the correlation between barter and financing problems, it is not surprising that there is a strong correlation in all three regions between managers' reports of the extent of barter and both payments overdue to suppliers and overdue receivables from customers (see table 9.5).

The usefulness of barter and non-monetary transactions as devices to avoid taxation has been much discussed in the literature. In the survey, firms were asked about their overdue tax payments and there was a strong positive correlation between this measure and barter in all regions.

When the EBRD survey was implemented in Russia and Ukraine two specific questions were asked concerning tax arrears. Managers were asked to respond to the following: (1) 'Did your firm have your primary bank account blocked for non-payment of taxes at any time in 1998?' and (2) 'The Federal, *oblast* and municipal governments sometimes pay for their purchases from enterprises by reducing the tax liabilities of the selling firm. During 1998, did your firm receive such a tax offset from any level of government?' As is clear from table 9.5, there is a very large and significant connection. Barter and non-monetary transactions go together with the presence of frozen bank accounts and of tax offsets arising out of non-payment of taxes. The correlation with tax offsets is, of course, not surprising, since such offsets are included in 'barter, offsets or bills of exchange (money surrogates)', by definition.

The questionnaire used two approaches to eliciting information about market power. Managers were asked whether the firm faces no competitors, 1–3 or more than 3 competitors in the market for

Table 9.5 *Financing problems and barter and non-monetary transactions*

Financing problems	Russia	Ukraine	CEE excl. Croatia and Slovenia
Financing problems in general	4.66 (1.12)***	5.14 (1.97)***	0.78 (0.43)*
Access to long-term bank credit	1.91 (0.93)**	−0.51 (1.53)	1.94 (0.41)***
High interest rates	3.17 (1.10)***	2.63 (1.93)	1.51 (0.45)***
Payments overdue to suppliers	7.08 (1.03)***	6.86 (1.64)***	1.27 (0.46)***
Receivables overdue from customers	5.17 (1.03)***	5.79 (1.59)***	2.16 (0.45)***
Tax arrears	8.00 (0.99)***	8.11 (1.67)***	1.84 (0.52)***
Frozen bank accounts	12.90 (2.67)***	13.18 (4.88)***	–
Tax offsets	12.79 (2.51)***	21.94 (4.54)***	–

Notes: Each row in table 9.5 reports the results from a separate regression for each region.

Interval regression with the percentage share of barter in sales as the dependent variable is used in each case (see the discussion in the text).

The scaling of the independent variable measuring financing problems runs from 1 to 4, with the exception of 'frozen bank accounts' and 'tax offsets', which are 1/0 dummies.

Size, sector and size – sector interaction variables are included in all regressions. For Russia, location dummies are also included.

The standard error is shown in parentheses.

* Significant at 10 per cent, ** significant at 5 per cent and *** significant at 1 per cent.

– = Not available.

its main product. They were also asked to predict what would happen to demand for their main product if they raised their price by 10 per cent (relative to inflation and to the prices of their competitors).

The correlation between each of these measures and the extent of barter and non-monetary transactions is reported in table 9.6. There is no uniform pattern across the three regions when the relationship between competition and barter is examined. In Ukraine, there seems to be no particular link between competition in the product market and barter. We therefore concentrate on Russia on the one hand, and the CEE countries on the other. In Russia, firms facing competitors in the product market were engaged in less barter than were monopolists. The

Table 9.6 *Product market competition and barter and non-monetary transactions*

Product market competition	Russia	Ukraine	CEE excl. Croatia and Slovenia
(1) No. of competitors:			
1-3	−10.12 (5.28)*	−0.64 (7.55)	1.76 (2.07)
More than 3	−9.85 (4.39)**	−2.67 (5.92)	4.98 (1.67)***
(2) Response to 10 per cent increase in own price:			
Demand lower	0.82 (2.91)	−4.97 (4.48)	−0.65 (1.22)
Demand slightly lower	−0.051 (2.91)	−2.35 (4.16)	−2.42 (1.15)**
No change in demand	−2.32 (3.47)	−1.72 (6.71)	−1.98 (1.42)

Note: The results of two regressions for each region are shown in table 9.6.

Interval regression with the percentage share of barter in sales as the dependent variable is used in each case (see the discussion in the text).

The omitted category in the first regression is 'no competitors' and in the second regression, 'many customers would switch to our competitors'.

Size, sector and size – sector interaction variables are included in all regressions.

For Russia, location dummies are also included.

The standard error is shown in parentheses.

Significance levels are indicated as follows: * indicates significance at 10 per cent, ** at 5 per cent and *** at 1 per cent.

indicators of monopoly power from the 10 per cent price test were not significant.[1]

But in the CEE countries, competition and barter are related in the opposite way: firms with more than 3 competitors report more barter and non-monetary transactions than do monopolists. There is some support for this kind of effect from the second regression i.e. using the 10 per cent price test. Compared with the omitted category in which customers switch to alternative suppliers if the firm puts its price up by 10 per cent, it seems that firms with market power do less barter.

The top panel of table 7 brings together the correlates of barter and non-monetary transactions into one regression. One variable is used to

---

[1] There are a number of theoretical reasons why we might expect barter and monopoly power to be related, including the 'information islands' discussed in the introduction (to this volume) and the use of barter for price discrimination as discussed in Prendergast and Stole (chapter 2 in this volume) and Guriev and Ickes (chapter 6 in this volume). Kranton (1996, esp. p. 833) suggests that the viability and enforceability of reciprocal exchange arrangements are increased by the absence of 'thick' market alternatives.

Table 9.7 *Correlates of barter and of change in the use of barter*

	Russia	Ukraine	CEE excl. Croatia and Slovenia
(1) Benchmark:			
Insider ownership	5.57 (3.27)*	−11.13 (6.46)*	ns
State-owned	ns	ns	−4.94 (1.67)***
ab initio firm	−7.53 (3.15)**	ns	ns
Payments overdue to suppliers	7.66 (1.14)***	7.06 (1.88)***	1.39 (0.49)***
1-3 competitors	−9.22 (5.48)*	ns	ns
More than 3 competitors	−11.73 (4.49)***	ns	2.84 (1.78) (sign. at 11 per cent)
No. of firms	404	174	741
(2) Change in barter:			
Lagged barter	0.64 (0.04)***	77 (0.06)***	75 (0.02)***
Sales growth	ns	ns	ns
Insider ownership	4.18 (2.54)*	−14.99 (4.50)***	ns
State	ns	−16.64 (5.18)***	−2.65 (0.81)***
ab initio firm	ns	−10.21 (4.40)**	ns
Payments overdue to suppliers	4.83 (0.90)***	4.43 (1.35)***	0.62 (0.23)***
1-3 competitors	ns	ns	ns
More than 3 competitors	ns	ns	ns
No. of firms	404	174	741

Note: The results of two regressions for each region are shown in table 9.7.

Interval regression with the percentage share of barter in sales as the dependent variable is used in each case (see the discussion in the text).

In (1), the right-hand side variables are a measure of financing problems (arrears to suppliers), product market competition (number of competitors) and ownership dummies. In (2), the level of barter three years ago and a performance measure (sales growth) are added.

Size, sector and size – sector interaction variables are included in all regressions. For Russia, location dummies are also included.

The standard error is shown in parentheses.

* Significant at 10 per cent, ** significant at 5 per cent and *** significant at 1 per cent, ns means not significant at 10 per cent level.

reflect financing constraints (arrears to suppliers) and the number of competitors is used to reflect competitive conditions. The sample sizes are somewhat smaller here because we want to compare this baseline regression with a regression that includes lagged barter. It seems that while there are a number of common features of firms engaged in barter

Table 9.8 *Country-level correlates of barter and non-monetary transactions in industry (20 countries)*

Inflation (log, 1997-9)	−5.30 (9.45)
Nominal lending rates (log, 1997-9)	10.50 (19.60)
Real lending rates (log, 1997-9)	9.44 (10.24)
'Softness' of budget constraint	10.41 (8.75)
Investment climate	−19.70 (6.96)***
No. of firms	1,239

Note: The results of a regression for the pool of 20 countries are shown in table 9.8.

In each case, the dependent variable is the mid-point of the barter/sales interval; interpretation is the same as for interval regression.

Estimation is by a generalised least squares random effects model.

The size variable is included in all regressions.

The 'soft' budget constraint and investment climate variables are normalised so that the minimum country score is 0 and the maximum country score is 1.

The standard error is shown in parentheses.

** Significant at 5 per cent, *** significant at 1 per cent.

across the three regions (size, financing problems and arrears, including tax arrears), there are also important differences. In Russia, barter is a rural phenomenon but there is no locational aspect in Ukraine or the CEE counties. In Ukraine, product market competition and barter are not related whereas there are effects going in opposite directions in Russia as compared with the CEE counties. Ownership effects are also quite different across region.

A fairly similar picture emerges when the change in barter over the past three years is investigated. In all three regions, the presence of liquidity problems is strongly correlated with the growth of barter. In Ukraine, there was a sharp increase in the use of barter in outsider-owned privatised firms that is reflected in the highly significant and large negative coefficients on the other ownership types.

Country-level correlates of barter and non-monetary transactions were also investigated (table 9.8). For this exercise a pool comprising all 20 countries in the EBRD survey was used. Only industrial firms were included. There was no correlation at all between inflation (over the preceding three years) and the extent of barter; nor was there any correlation between either real or nominal lending rates (also over the preceding three years) and the extent of barter. A country-level measure of the 'softness' of budget constraints constructed from managers' responses to the question on tax arrears was also insignificant. However, a country-level composite measure of managers' perceptions of the investment climate indicated that in countries with a poor investment climate, there was more barter. This composite measure (discussed in more detail in the EBRD *Transition Report 1999*) aims to capture particularly variations in the rule of law and access to formal sources of finance. Its strong association with barter at the country level is very much what would be expected from the Marin – Schnitzer (1999) and the 'information islands' hypotheses discussed above.

To sum up, there is substantial variation between countries in the correlates of barter and non-monetary transactions. Nevertheless a few clear messages emerge from the survey:

• Financing problems are strongly linked to the presence of barter and non-monetary transactions in all countries
• Large firms are more likely to engage in barter than small firms
• Difficulties with tax payments are strongly associated with barter
• There is a strong degree of persistence of barter over time
• There is more barter in countries with a poor investment climate
• State-owned firms are less likely to engage in barter in CEE countries, but there is no systematic relationship with ownership in Russia and Ukraine
• The phenomenon of barter in Russia is different from that in other countries in a number of respects, and is much more linked to monopoly power and rural location than it is elsewhere.

The consequences of barter

Is there a connection between barter, restructuring actions taken by managers and performance at the level of the firm? The survey allows us to examine several dimensions of restructuring: the introduction of new products, upgrading of existing ones and changing the organisational structure of the firm. For each type of restructuring in turn, we examine the probability that the firm has undertaken restructuring of that type. As explanatory variables, we include the usual controls for size, industry and location. In addition, we include ownership variables and the two kinds of competition variables discussed above. To avoid problems of two-way causation, our barter variable is the firm's level of barter sales three years prior to the survey. This allows us to interpret the results as indicating whether involvement in barter three years ago was a significant predictor of subsequent restructuring actions.

Table 9.9 *The influence of barter and non-monetary transactions on restructuring in Russia*

	(1) New product development	(2) Product upgrading	(3) Firm reorganisation (scale 1–4)
Lagged per cent of barter in sales	0.002	−0.013**	0.011***
Standard error	0.005	−0.005	0.004
No. of obs.	425	425	424

Note: Table 9.9 shows the results of logit regressions that control for size and industry effects as well as ownership, urbanisation and the degree of competition faced by firms.

(3) is an ordered logit where the dependent variable takes the values 1–4.
** Significant at 5 per cent, *** significant at 1 per cent.

In most countries there is no significant relationship between restructuring and barter. But Russia is different. Table 9.9 illustrates this. Here there is a strong tendency for firms engaging in barter and non-monetary transactions to undertake more organisational change than other firms. However, they are less likely to upgrade their existing products than other firms (a firm 50 per cent of whose sales are conducted in barter is about 50 per cent less likely to upgrade its existing products than one that does no barter at all). The introduction of new products is unrelated to barter.

Without more information, the interpretation of these findings remains somewhat speculative. But the results on organisational change are consistent with the evidence from Russian micro-studies (Ledeneva and Seabright, chapter 4 in this volume) that barter deals frequently involve significant diversion of managerial effort and the construction of ingenious chains of transactions. The negative impact of barter on actions to upgrade existing products in Russia fits the notion that barter and non-monetary transactions allow otherwise unsaleable goods to be traded. The fact that there is no observed negative impact on decisions to introduce new products may be owing to the need for firms engaged in barter to bring in new products purely to satisfy the needs of the barter chain (a possibility documented also in the micro-studies); this offsets what would otherwise be a negative impact of barter on new product development.

If this interpretation of the results on organisational change is accurate, it implies something about the *kind* of organisational change that is

Table 9.10 *The influence of barter and non-monetary transactions on firm sales growth, Russia and Ukraine*

| | Basic equation (OLS) | | Using instrumental variables and controlling for other restructuring forms | |
	Russia	Ukraine	Russia	Ukraine
Major reallocation of responsibilities among departments	0.36***		0.76***	−0.10
Std err.	0.10		0.28	0.29
Introduction of new products		0.36**	0.10	0.70**
Std err.		0.15	0.27	0.30
Lagged per cent barter in sales	0.0005	0.0042	0.0009	0.0030
Std err.	0.0016	0.0028	0.0027	0.0038
Lagged per cent barter (firms with major reallocation only)	−0.0062**		−0.0137**	0.0079
Std err.	0.0028		0.0058	0.0056
Lagged per cent barter (firms with new products only)		0.0002	0.0020	−0.012**
Std err.		0.0040	0.0054	0.0057
No. obs.	324	141	324	141

Note: Table 9.10 shows the results of regressions that control for size and industry effects as well as ownership, urbanisation, the degree of competition faced by firms and the perceived pressures from competitors, shareholders and creditors.

The barter variable is the level of barter three years ago.

Instruments in the second regression are industry dummies, plus industry dummies interacted with barter, plus all the competition variables interacted with barter.

** Significant at 5 per cent, *** significant at 1 per cent.

undertaken by firms heavily involved in barter and non-monetary transactions - namely that it will be less effective than similar reorganisations undertaken by firms who do not do barter. Table 9.10 tests this suggestion by examining to what extent barter is associated with firm performance (interpreted in terms of growth in sales over the three years prior to the survey). In the regressions for Russia we have included a direct effect of barter, a direct effect of reorganisation on performance, plus an effect of barter for those firms that have reorganised. The results confirm the hypothesis to a striking degree. Firm reorganisation in Russia is very strongly associated with improved performance. In the basic equations, firms that have reorganised have 36 percentage points higher sales growth over three years than those that have not. But this effect is much weaker for Russian firms that barter significantly, to the extent that a restructured firm bartering 58 per cent of its output performs no better than a non-bartering firm that has not restructured at all. The results are even stronger when we control for the endogeneity of the restructuring decision and for the fact that other kinds of restructuring take place simultaneously. Here internal reorganisation in Russian firms is associated with a 76 percentage-point improvement in performance over three years, an effect that disappears once a firm barters 55 per cent or more of its output.

We find similar, but somewhat less strong, results for Ukraine. In Ukraine, the form of restructuring that is strongly associated with sales growth is the introduction of new products. In the basic equation estimated by OLS, there is no negative effect of barter. When we control for other restructuring and we allow for the endogeneity of restructuring, however, we find that firms that introduced new products have 70 per-centage-points higher sales growth over three years, but that this is again offset by bartering activity; a firm that introduced a new product or products that barters 58 per cent of its output grows no faster than a firm that has not innovated in this way.

The results for Russia and Ukraine stand in sharp contrast to those for CEE countries. In CEE, all three of our restructuring measures – intro-duction of new products, upgrading of existing products and internal reorganisation – are associated with stronger sales performance, but we find no evidence that barter negates the impact of any of these measures.

One reason for particular caution in interpreting these findings is the likely endogeneity of the resort to barter. It is possible that a common set of factors both provokes poor performance and the associated financial problems and liquidity constraints in a subset of firms, and acts as an obstacle to the success of restructuring efforts by these same firms.[2] There may, in other words, be a *selection bias* at work. Using lagged barter as an explanatory variable may not sufficiently control for this. It is difficult to know how to evaluate this possibility: we have estimated an equation using instrumental variables for *lagged* barter with the result that neither barter nor restructuring variables were any longer significant. This may

[2] We owe this point to Dan Treisman.

indicate that the selection problem is indeed severe, or that our set of instruments for lagged barter is inadequate. Nevertheless, this does not prevent our concluding that firms who resort to barter are less likely to restructure successfully, even while we remain more cautious about whether barter is a cause or merely a symptom of this difficulty.

Overall, therefore, the conclusions of the survey are clear:

- Outside Russia, and to a lesser extent, Ukraine, there is no clear link between the tendency to engage in barter and non-monetary trans-actions and either firm restructuring activity or subsequent sales per-formance
- In Russia there is strong evidence that barter retards the improvement of existing product lines, presumably by enabling firms to trade other-wise unsaleable products
- There is no clear impact of barter on the development of new products in Russia or elsewhere, probably because what would otherwise be a nega-tive impact on product development is offset by a tendency to create new product lines to satisfy the demands of partners in a barter chain
- Barter is definitely associated with significant organisational change in Russia. But, unfortunately, it also tends to make such change com-paratively ineffective in yielding performance improvements. In Ukraine, barter has a similar negative impact on the benefits of intro-ducing new products. These findings are consistent with the view of barter as a significant diversion of managerial energy and initiative.

3 Conclusions

How much does the survey tell us about why barter is happening and whether it matters? Not only the extent of barter but also its nature, its causes and effects, vary to an important degree from country to country. What are the overall lessons to be learned?

- Barter and non-monetary transactions are everywhere associated with financing difficulties. This strongly supports the view that barter assures liquidity in a trading environment in which credit is scarce and the enforceability of loan contracts is uncertain.
- The overall economic costs associated with using barter for this purpose vary significantly from country to country. In CEE the costs appear to be low, perhaps because what firms are reporting as 'barter and other non-monetary transactions' refers principally to bills of exchange and other debt instruments that do not distort firm behaviour to an important degree (and may often be redeemed in cash).

• In Russia and Ukraine, however, barter *does* distort firm behaviour – perhaps because firms find it difficult or costly to redeem their bills of exchange and other debts in cash. Firms that barter are less likely to devote their energies to improving their products. They are more likely to engage in internal reorganisation purely to keep their barter chains in being rather than to conquer new markets and transform their future prospects.

• In Russia and Ukraine but not elsewhere the findings are therefore consistent with the hypothesis that economic disorganisation, in the Blanchard and Kremer (1997) sense, means that barter is both more likely to occur and more damaging when it does occur.

Overall, the evidence suggests that barter and non-monetary transactions are often highly inventive and resourceful responses of firms to difficult business conditions. It is the conditions themselves rather than the responses that are the problem. In a better business environment, firms could direct the ingenuity and effort required by barter transactions to more productive ends.

References

Abelshauser, A. (1975). *Wirtschaft in Westdeutschland, 1945–1948,* Stuttgart, Deutsche Verlags-Anstalt

Blanchard, O. and M. Kremer (1997). 'Disorganization', *Quarterly Journal of Economics,* 112 (4), 1091–26

Carlin, W. (1989). 'Economic Reconstruction in Western Germany, 1945–55: The Displacement of "vegetative control",' in I. Turner (ed.) *Reconstruction in Post-War Germany: British Occupation Policy and the Western Zones 1945–1955,* Oxford, Berg

Commander, S. and C. Mummsen (1999). 'The Growth of Non-Monetary Transactions in Russia: Causes and Effects', chapter 5 in this volume

European Bank for Reconstruction and Development (1999). *Transition Report 1999,* London, EBRD

Hart, K. (1987). 'Barter', in J. Eatwell, M. Milgate and P. Newman (eds.), *The New Palgrave: A Dictionary of Economics,* London, Macmillan

Kranton, R. (1996). 'Reciprocal Exchange: A Self-sustaining System', *American Economic Review,* 86, 830–51

Marin, D. and Schnitzer, M (1999), 'Disorganization and Financial Collapse', *CEPR, Discussion Paper,* 2245

Mendershausen, H. (1949): 'Prices, Money and the Distribution of Goods', *American Economic Review,* 39 (4), 647–68

Stamp, A.M. (1947). 'Germany Without Incentive', *Lloyds Bank Review,* 5

StataCorp (1997). 'cnreg – Censored-normal, tobit, and interval regression', *Stata Reference Manual: Release Five,* Texas, Stata Press, College Station

Part III Ethnography

10 How is barter done? The social relations of barter in provincial Russia

CAROLINE HUMPHREY

1 Introduction

This chapter will present evidence from two regions of Russia, one close to Moscow and one in Eastern Siberia, to explore the role of trust in barter relationships.

It has been argued (Anderlini and Sabourian, 1992) that although immediate face-to-face barter requires a minimum of trust, the problem of the 'coincidence of wants' means that this kind of barter is difficult to achieve and is a relatively rare occurrence in practice. Therefore barter is more likely than a monetised system to require delays in payment and several exchanges before the transactors are satisfied. This is particularly the case in an agricultural economy, where goods are produced seasonally yet consumption is a year-round constant. The transaction costs of barter are considerably reduced if it can be repeated with the same partners season after season. In such a situation, the practice of barter requires trust at the micro level, as sellers have to wait for returns and trust that the goods they receive will be of the agreed quantity and quality. It also encourages reliable behaviour, since demonstrated unreliability results in the cutting off of previous relations and all the costs of searching for new ones. This chapter asks to what extent these ideas are relevant to the situation in contemporary Russia, and in particular what are the implications of barter for social relations (both between partners and in networks).

Studies of a long-standing barter system among the Lhomi and neighbouring peoples in Nepal (Humphrey, 1985) showed that the trust of barter relies on that found in society more generally. Some petty barter takes place with unknown people, but for valuable deals transactors relied on pre-existing social relations of clanship, friendship and ethnicity. New trade partners are transformed into 'ritual friends' (see chapter 3, in this volume). Village communities establish common rates of exchange each year to prevent cutting of exchange rates by neighbours. I shall argue that in Russia, on the other hand, the 'trust' of barter is largely divorced from other, morally-supported, social relations. Chapter 3 outlines the theoretical case for the emergence in Russia of a new kind of morally ambiguous 'trade partnership' in barter. The present chapter aims to demonstrate ethnographically the basis for this suggestion, describing the emergence of several types of barter chain and the ways in which these relate to surrounding economic conditions. The study refers to the general practice of barter in provincial situations and does not discuss the large, high-value transactions of mega-corporations (oil, gas, etc.).

Although the exigencies of barter do in principle make a kind of trust functional in Russia as in Nepal, there are several inter-related reasons for the weak social legitimation of this 'trust'. Perhaps the most important is the unfamiliarity and moral dubiousness of market mechanisms in general in a country where generations were taught of the evils of capitalism. If market exchange does have validity for Russians, it is that of modernity and prosperity along western lines, based on the power of the dollar and other western currencies. Barter thus has a many-sided illegitimacy: it is seen as a return to pre-modern, uncivilised times, a temporary disaster; at the same time its disutilities as compared with a monetised system are experienced daily. Furthermore, barter is evidently not producing prosperity. Respondents are well aware of what Gaddy and Ickes (1998) refer to as the 'virtual economy', the way that barter is used to prop up loss-making industries. My materials suggest that what we may call the 'moral illegitimacy' of barter influences the ways in which it is actually carried out, and that this in turn affects the social relations on which it relies.

The view that barter is a temporary, abnormal state of affairs encourages short-termism in business decisions and also discourages the formation of new, long-lasting and self-reproducing barter institutions. The absence of such institutions, despite the involvement of local administrations in barter, is puzzling; but perhaps it can be explained by the newness of any kind of commercial practice (e.g. banking) and the tendency for competitive individualism to prevail even when cooperation might be advantageous. At any rate, we do not see in Russia an equivalent of Nepalese villagers cooperating to fix common exchange rates (Humphrey 1985). Even staff working in a single tax-collection office may make individual bargains with firms for the amount of tax to be paid (for a personal consideration, of course).[1] The practice of taking tax in goods, which still continues in many parts of the

---

[1] Information from a Buriat businessman (summer 1999).

country,[2] ties such bargains into barter and offset networks. This contributes further to the illegitimacy of barter, which becomes tainted by the suspicion of administrative corruption and incompetence. Governmental failure to repay debts and ensure the payment of wages from the budget is seen to be part of the barter economy. At the same time, it is suspected, rightly, that there is money somewhere, and that it is only those outside circles of influence who are forced to manage without it through barter. In provincial Russia, barter is far from a purely market operation – politicians frequently intervene in the setting-up of chains, or forbid certain deals, in order to bolster their own changing power blocs (Woodruff, 1999).

In short, several features of the *current* political economy (notably short-termism of economic decisions, lack of institutions and involvement in power and patronage) influence the way in which barter works. In these circumstances, although barter may make use of previous social relations, including those going back to Soviet times, it does not reproduce them but transforms them. My chapter is an attempt to discover what these transformations are.

To establish the points made above I need to show not only how barter is practised but also how it is talked about – that is, to uncover the attitudes people have to it. The chapter tries to explain the logic of barter operations for those engaging in them. I shall also attempt to disentangle the relations obtaining in barter, from those we can attribute to commercial activity in general. To this end I compare materials from the Republic of Buriatiia,[3] where almost the entire economy is conducted through barter, and Moscow *oblast* (region),[4] where barter is a much

---

[2] This practice was made illegal by a federal law passed in Moscow in 1998, but several provinces continue to collect various taxes in produce.

[3] The information base is the same as that used for chapter 3. The Buriat data is based on: (1) 24 lengthy tape-recorded interviews conducted by G. Manzanova in July – August 1998 with managers at various levels in a variety of organisations: '*Prin*' computer firm; Bichur Raion Administration of Agriculture; Selenga Raion Administration of Agriculture; '*Lek*' trading firm; '*Bat-Les*' logging company; '*Gunzan*' wholesale trading firm; '*Mayak*' Union of Peasant Holdings; the Presidential Committee for Economic Reform; the '*Dogo-Khudan*' Agricultural Cooperative; the '*Zabaikalsk UPK*' training centre for building workers; two traders in food products; the '*Yumsnyi*' pork products company; the Pensions Fund of Buriatiia. (2) Local statistics and newspaper articles. (3) Discussions with G. Manzanova, economic advisor to the government of Buriatiia. (4) My own field materials collected in 1996 in four collective farms of the Barguzin and Selenga districts of Buriatiia.

[4] Information here comes from two enterprises near Sergiev Posad (formerly Zagorsk), a building materials firm and a rubber-products factory (*NIIRP*). Interviews were conducted by Helena Kopnina in July 1998 with a wide variety of managers and workers within these firms, allowing comparison of different viewpoints on barter from within each enterprise.

smaller part of the economy. As the majority of my information comes from Buriatiia the chapter will start with a brief description of the economy of this region. What are the characteristics of a region where barter has taken over virtually the whole economy?

2 'Complete barter' (*sploshnoi barter*)

In the Buriat Republic barter forms over 80 per cent of economic transactions according to official estimates in August 1998.[5] However, local businessmen say informally that around 90 per cent of transactions are carried out by barter, while farm managers claim not to have used 'living money' for five years. I am told that the central policies since the August 1998 crisis have not so far reduced barter. So this is a region of what people call '*sploshnoi barter*' ('barter everywhere' or 'complete barter'). In this respect, Buriatiia lies towards one end of the spectrum of provinces in Russia, where on average barter is officially estimated to form 47 per cent of circulation.[6]

Buriatiia is a region in deficit, in the sense that its internally generated income does not cover the the regional budget, and the value of its exports (mostly raw materials, electricity and processed metals) is less than its imports (mostly food, technology and fodder). Buriatiia seeks massive transfers from Moscow on an annual basis.[7] Politically it is a conservative place. The president, a Russian, has been in power almost continuously since the 1970s. In late 1996 the President announced a 'special economic regime' and in September 1998 he declared a state of emergency, both times in order to negotiate an additional credit from Moscow. The manufacturing landscape is dominated by a few large, unprofitable and declining factories of Soviet vintage, notably in railway engineering, wool processing, metal-working and machine production for both defence and civilian purposes, open-cast mining and cellulose-cardboard production (I call these 'dinosaurs', for brevity). The main

[5] Oral communication from G. Manzanova, economic advisor to the government of Buriatiia.
[6] Manzanova, oral communication. See also Makarov and Kleiner (1996, p. 5), who quote estimates that barter was between 34 and 50 per cent of the turnover of industrial production in Russia in 1995. According to their own and other surveys, it constituted 70–80 per cent of transactions for industrial inputs. According to my respondents, barter in Buriatiia reached a first peak in 1994-5, was reduced in 1996, but started to expand again in 1997 and has grown ever since.
[7] The credits from Moscow have been between 22 per cent and 32 per cent of the Republic budget income in recent years (*Pravda Buriatii*, 14 August 1998, p. 4). These are loans, but the Republic does not manage to pay them back in full.

profitable industries are the production and sale of electricity, railway services, and oil/petrol sales. It is only the latter companies and the regional government that issue pseudo-currencies (e.g. *veksels*) and these too are often realised in goods rather than money.[8] Agriculture is still organised collectively for the most part and is in desperate straits.[9] Meanwhile, the importing of prepared foods has hit local food processing industries hard.[10] Wages are almost entirely paid in products, not money. To survive, households have increased domestic food production, but this has not prevented a slide towards poverty. In 1998 the population consumed considerably less per head than in the beginning of the 1990s,[11] and local newspapers gave harrowing accounts of hunger (e.g. families in some rural areas reduced to feeding their children with fodder concentrates). Nevertheless, the paradoxical fact is that the money in circulation comes almost entirely from the working population – i.e. from pensions and benefits, as well as the few wages paid in money.

Widespread barter thus correlates with regional economic weakness,[12] poverty among the population and a conservative Soviet-influenced political culture preserved through electoral machinations. Buriatiia is not, however, an odd man out. In its economic indicators at least it is in a similar position to regions like North Caucasus, Kalmykia, Altai, Tyva and Penzensk and other poor *oblasts* of Russia. As in many regions its government has an important role in supporting barter by using tax credits as initatiors of chains of mutual credits (*vzaimozachety*) between firms, while collective agriculture is kept going by the form of barter called 'commodity credit' (*tovarnyi kredit*). Furthermore, Buriatiia follows general trends in Russia in the growth of small business as a new way of making a living. There are around 5,500 small firms in

---

[8] For reasons of space *veksels* are not discussed in this chapter. *Veksels* are not used at all by middling and small companies in Buriatiia.

[9] Between 1990 and 1994 agriculture as a whole in the Republic went from a rate of 36.5 per cent in profit (1990) to −44 per cent in 1994 (*Buriatiya, Ekonomika,* 1996, p. 25) and since then has declined further.

[10] Since 1991, meat-processing has declined by 25 times, dairy-processing by 18 times and grain-processing by 7 times (*Pravda Buriatii,* 14 August 1998, p, 4).

[11] Households in 1996 produced 91 per cent of the potatoes, 86 per cent of other vegetables, 70 per cent of milk, 46 per cent of meat and 18 per cent of the eggs in the Republic. Nevertheless, between 1990 and 1996 the average consumption per head of meat went down from 74 to 54 kg per year, milk from 341 to 167, sugar from 42 to 22, potatoes from 109 to 75, and only grain products stayed on the same level (*Pravda Buriatii,* 14 August 1998, p. 4).

[12] Comparing Buriatiia with other parts of Russia, it has a GDP between 1.2 and 2 times lower than the Russian average, and it occupies the 51st position for investment in the Federation at *oblast*/Republic level (*Pravda Buriatii,* 14 August 1998, p. 4).

Buriatiia – that is, 5.2 firms per 1,000 population – which is near the Russian average. The great majority of these firms are middlemen, not involved in production.[13] As seems to be the case generally in Russia (Makarov and Kleiner, 1996, p. 19), many of these small trader firms cluster round the dinosaurs and other large industrial producers, existing as facilities for the realisation of their over-priced goods through barter.

All economic institutions in Buriatiia engage in barter, irrespective of their type of ownership. This includes not only government agencies but also other institutions like schools, colleges, or hospitals, which have taken up trading partly because they are paid in goods that they cannot use themselves. Barter initiated in Buriatiia is not limited to the region. Even tiny trading firms like the three-man 'Lek' do international barter with China, while others have networks reaching to Sakhalin, Japan, Germany and other countries.

The logic of barter from the participants' point of view

Russian firms categorise transactions into three types, those using physical money (*nalichnyye*), those using notional money (*beznalichnyye*, also known as *zachety*, offsets, when debts are moved between firms) and those involving physical goods (*barter*). In more monetised regions, the price-lists of large firms are often divided in this way, with the lowest prices offered for money, the middle prices for *zachety* and the highest prices (usually around 10 per cent more than money prices) for barter.[14] However, this is not a very useful division for understanding the social relations of barter, as in the strategies of participants, debts and barter are often inextricably linked up in a single complex operation for which the end-goal is often to obtain physical money. It is more enlightening to examine the actual encounters in barter, and to organise this material I shall initially use three variables: (1) Is the transaction immediate or does it require one side to wait? (2) How 'liquid' are the goods transacted by the participants? (3) Are the goods used by the participants, or traded on? These variables have been chosen because they are preoccupations of the barter participants themselves when they explain *why* they take the decisions they do. They are not explanations of the origin of barter in Russia but help us understand the logic of operations by individual firms and the forms taken by chains (*tsepochki*) of barter and debt-trading.

---

[13] Around 72 per cent of small businesses engage in trade only, and the small business sector as a whole contributed only 3.7 per cent of the productive capacity of the Republic (*Pravda Buriatii*, 14 August 1998, p. 4).

[14] Bogomolov, the head of the Supplies Department at *NIIRP*.

Timing and credit

'Classic barter' – that is, bilateral simultaneous trades in which the goods are used by each side for their own purposes – is not the mainstay of trading for any of my business respondents. This is because of the problem of the 'coincidence of wants', the difficulty of finding the person who wants what you have got at exactly the moment when you want what they have got. This kind of swop is called *bash na bash*, and usually occurs between private individuals. People sometimes say *bash na bash, ne gladya* (swopping without looking), which expresses the idea of an ad hoc satisfaction of desires on either side without bothering about close inspection of the goods or their money prices. On occasion, business people too go for the expediency of *bash na bash* barter when they hear of a possible deal with unknown people. They reason that, since you cannot trust the known partners anyway, at least with an immediate swop you get what you want. The head of a food trading firm in Buriatiia said:

Agreements (*dogovor*) don't oblige you anything. If the big managers and leaders knew they would sit behind bars for non-return of a barter debt they would think twice before accepting goods. But we have no such effective laws. Many traders suffer from this. Therefore, when doing a barter exchange, and now unfortunately it is necessary to go outside known people, you have to be very careful. So you do it *bash na bash*. You make a prior agreement on the phone, 'I'll bring you goods worth so many roubles', you go over there, give your stuff and take their stuff, and that's it. No-one wants to be the first to give, being afraid of being deceived.

Minimum trust is required in this kind of deal, but even so, such trust is often lacking. A trader in the Buryiat firm '*Lek*' said that one cannot be sure that the other side actually has the goods they agreed on the phone to trade. So before taking over one's own goods, one has to make a preliminary check to see that their goods are in their warehouse in the right quantity. A trader also has to make sure he has the manpower and transport for a quick getaway: 'If you don't grab it quickly, you'll never get it from them afterwards' (*ne vytashil bystro, to potom ee voobshche ne soberesh'*).

This kind of barter seems to happen either as a result of some unplanned fortuity or when traders are desperate, such as farm managers who ring round to find anyone who will give them a spare part for their combine in exchange for any farm products they have on hand. Though such swopping is quite common for small deals, it is almost impossible to rely on it for a regular living, and therefore participants in barter mostly base their operations on other forms.

The extension of immediate trades happens when one side receives a good in one transaction only to trade it on in the next exchange with another partner. Simple forms of such 'linear barter' occur when (a) an item moves from its producer, through several trades to a consumer, becoming a commodity currency on the way (see also Ledeneva and Seabright, chapter 4 in this volume, or (b) when a product is processed at each stage (e.g. live ox, carcass, meat pieces, sausagemeat, sausages) (figure 10.1).

The social implications of such linear series are different from the 'star' and 'circular' chains discussed later, because a linear series tends to consist of disjunct bilateral deals. No one enterprise overviews all exchanges. Transactors show little interest in what happens beyond their own deal. Traders down the line have information but they also have an interest in concealing their sources and prices, so as not to be by-passed.

The most common form of bilateral barter is delayed exchange. Respondents emphasise that this implies an inequality between the two sides, because one gets the goods when they want them, while the other has to wait (and is not necessarily rewarded for waiting). This lack of parity exists even if both sides acquire goods wanted for themselves rather than having to trade onwards. Now all my respondents claimed that they normally take the partner's goods first and pay back later. But of course this cannot be true in general. So, we need to think why people make such claims. From an anthropological point of view, this is a situation which contrasts starkly with 'gift' systems. In barter, people are taking pride in *acquiring*, in holding their partners in the dependency of waiting for repayment, which is quite different from the 'gift' scenario, in which *giving* accrues status, while holding the partners in the lower position of debtors.

A clue to the mentality behind this may lie in a difference in the terminology used for this kind of barter in Moscow *oblast* and Buriatiia. It seems to suggest that the more monetised zone has a higher

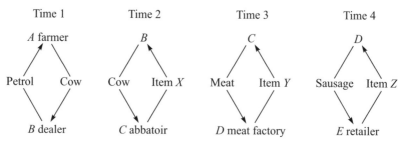

Figure 10.1 A linear series of barter deals in which a farmer's cow reaches the retailer

level of social trust than the de-monetised region. In Moscow *oblast* the expression 'commodity credit' (*tovarnyi kredit*) is used for a transaction in which one enterprise gives goods to the other, to be repaid with return goods after an agreed, quite extended, period (often six months to a year), with a slightly larger than normal amount of return goods being due in order to pay for the time difference. In Buriatiia, the term 'commodity credit' is reserved for large government advances in goods, and the term used for delayed deals in everyday barter between firms is 'prepayment' (*predoplata*) e.g. 'We always demand 100 per cent prepayment'. This Buriat terminology implies not that one enterprise is trusted with a credit arrangement but that the other firm is not trusted, and therefore has to make a prepayment.

As we shall see, lack of trust is not the only reason certain firms are required to pay first. In fact, there may also be good grounds to mistrust the firms that pay second, since the practice is widespread of holding back under one pretext or another (often that the received goods are not up to standard) and paying back only bit by bit, and well beyond the agreed time. What seems to be happening is a trial of powers, a contest that ultimately depends on which side is most needy. 'It's a matter of whether *we* ask for the barter or *they* do,' said one businessman, explaining that the one who 'begs' is normally the one who gets paid later. For everyone, the desired situation (sitting back while the goods you need are fed into your firm on all sides and you pay back later) is counterbalanced by demands made on you to pay first or you will not get what you want.

What makes this different from a money credit situation is that *both* enterprises are acting through goods, which limits their choices. In a place like Buriatiia there may be only one factory producing the needed good, or only one which wants to make a deal for your products. As a result, given the lack of parity between partners in delayed barter, patron-client-like relations arise between firms. When two production enterprises each require the inputs of the other for their own internal use, these relations can be quite stable. For example the *Lenin* collective farm of Baragkhan in Buriatiia, regularly exchanges meat for fuel and spare parts with the large and powerful *Aviazavod* aircraft factory.[15] *Lenin* pays with meat for the factory canteens, and *Aviazavod* pays back later, haphazardly, with spare parts, etc. The *Lenin* farm is 'locked into' this patronal relation because its bargaining position is far weaker (fuel and spare parts very scarce while meat is in plentiful supply), and barter – finding a firm that will accept specifically your meat in payment – limits its options still further. The payoff in such arrangements is often political. The rural

---

[15] Information based on field research in Buriatiia (1996).

producers are enabled to keep their economies going, but find themselves entangled in voting blocs associated with patronal firms at elections for local deputies.[16]

How do such patronage ties relate to previous Soviet-era distributional links? The *Lenin – Aviazavod* barter is in fact based on a Soviet arrangement called *sheftsvo*, the ideological 'captaincy' of an industrial enterprise over a 'less advanced' socialist form, the collective farm. The content of these relations, however, has changed greatly since Soviet times. Then, an enterprise did not pay for its supplies, nor did industrial 'customers' pay for goods sent to them.[17] Now, *sheftsvo* as an idea has disappeared – replaced by agonised bargaining – agonised, that is, on the farm's side, for whom the spare parts and fuel are essential for its very existence. Competition with alternative meat-producers is part of this new relation. If competition and uncertainty about when they will be paid differentiate the new relation from previous officially planned distribution, the centrality of these deals to the fuctioning of the enterprise distinguish it from the unofficial Soviet practice of swapping of surpluses ('manipulable resources', see Humphrey 1983) left over after fulfilling the plan.

The transformation of social relations is felt to be unpleasant, as can be seen from an example in Moscow *oblast*. I digress briefly here from the theme of credit in order to explain the substratum of barter that is present even in a monetised firm. One important impetus for barter is that even if factories have money they have an interest in paying for their production inputs by bartering their own products with supply firms rather than paying money. One reason for this is that it costs the firm to acquire money. The rubber-products factory *NIIRP* near Zagorsk was founded in the 1940s, is still half state-owned, and continues to support a large workforce. It is not exactly a dinosaur, as its rubber transmission belts are in demand, but they are over-priced and cannot be sold in Russia for money. *NIIRP* sells its goods in Europe for money, but only with some difficulty. Nevertheless, *NIIRP* has to pay taxes in money and it also pays its workforce in money. Altogether this means that *NIIRP* has problems with financing its production cycle and it therefore instructs its supply department never to use money for inputs. It is in the managers' interest

---

[16] Information on such matters is highly sensitive and therefore I cannot publish chapter and verse. I am reliably informed, however, that threats to cut off barter patronage are highly effective at election times.

[17] Supplies were allocated to enterprises at the direction of the planning board; similarly, the board directed output to different possible users of the firm's outputs (Palmer and Vilis, 1997).

to maintain long-term partnerships with those firms which require belts and at the same time can supply *NIIRP*'s own inputs. The head of the supply department said,

In the past we did everything through the Ministry. There had to be a mediator, an interface between the factory and the consumers. Now all those people have left the Ministry, migrated (*kochevali*) to set up their own limited companies. But we kept track of them. Let's say one hundred people worked in the Ministry; now, they have set up fifty or a hundred firms. So we do things through old connections, and basically, through them we also find new partners, the people with whom the Ministry used to work – all over Russia, in the Near Abroad, in Azerbaijan,...[18]

The people may be the same, but the relations in this vast network have changed.[19] The mediators from the Ministry have turned into businessmen squeezing out their own profits. Barter is seen as something disagreeable (*mutornyi*) and 'dirty work'.[20] It is a task each department of *NIIRP* tries to avoid. Although the General Director of *NIIRP* talks more cosily of oral agreements, especially with European partners ('It's enough to ring up, make an agreement, and carry it out. These are people we have known for a long time, we trust one another'[21]), the people further down the factory's hierarchy, the ones who have to make the practical arrangements and accounting of deals, see barter in a frankly adversarial light. A manager engaged in bartering transmission belts on the Russian market, when asked if she had friendly relations with the people she bartered with, replied:

Friendly is as friendly does. I have business (*delovyye*) relations with them. We quarrel (*rugaemsya*), and sometimes we send one another away.[22]

In these encounters, the question of when payment is made and whether the transaction is by barter or in money are both up for grabs. Even with

---

[18] Bogomolov, manager of Supply Department, *NIIRP*.
[19] 'Earlier, everything was clear. The plan just came down from above. You were told how much, from what, what kinds to make, where to send it. If someone did what he was ordered for thirty years, he didn't think whether it was good or bad, he just heard "Make 5,000 pieces", never thought why. But now you have to think, what to make, what quality, who might want them. Of course the psychology of a change from a command to a market economy is difficult for the human being. The main mass of directors are people in their 50s and 60s; they are used to socialism, used to not deciding. They can't think, and this is why we cannot go out and compete' (V. N. Gesko, Vice-Director of *NIIRP* for commercial affairs).
[20] V. N. Gesko, Vice-Director of *NIIRP* for commercial affairs.
[21] V. V. Shvarts, General Director of *NIIRP*.
[22] Plaksina, Worker in Sales Department of *NIIRP*.

long-standing partners, *NIIRP* sometimes has to use sweeteners to get a deal through. To this end the factory has started up a new vodka sector, which makes the Roma (Gypsy) Brand. To get industrial soot used in making rubber from a factory in Komi province, it has to pay in vodka as well as belts.

To return to the theme of time, there is another type of delayed barter, which *NIIRP* tries to avoid. This is taking supply goods 'on consignment' (*na konsignatsii*) – that is, when goods are provided in advance but the ownership remains with the supply firm, which might in principle take the goods away again if they found a more profitable partner. Goods on consignment are paid off gradually by monthly payments to the supply firm. This kind of arrangement is rare and it is done unwillingly by *NIIRP* because it cannot make full use of the supplies until they are all paid off. This shows, of course, what the impetus for 'commodity credit' from *NIIRP*'s point of view really is: that the factory can engage in production, using the supplies, before it has to pay back.

This same rationale is even stronger among small non-productive middlemen firms. In Buriatiia, middlemen demand prepayment rather than immediate swapping not only for practical reasons (time to assemble the return goods, seasonality of production, finding transport, etc.) but also because of their extremely precarious economic circumstances. Dealers explain that it is impossible to repay at exactly the same time you receive the other side's goods unless you have working capital to back up your operations in the meantime. The middlemen do not, of course, live off the goods they trade but from the money they acquire by 'realising' goods – and marketing for money requires time and expense on their part. Unlike producing firms which have fixed resources and can economise in various ways, notably by delaying payment of wages, middlemen depend on the timing of deals. In Buriatiia, few traders admit they have the resources for immediate barter, let alone for deals in which they give the goods first and wait for repayment.

Any advantage, including those afforded by international relations, can be put to work in securing barter credit. This can be seen from Buriat trade with China. Fear among Russian provinical governments along the frontier of an invasion of Chinese business has resulted in restrictive legislation making it difficult for Chinese to obtain visas or register firms (Humphrey 1999b). Interestingly, the Buriats who nevertheless want to trade with China, disguise the edge given to them by these restrictions under the notion of common 'eastern psychology', which as it were affords them access to special long-term exclusive partnerships resting on a remarkably one-sided trust from the Chinese side. Buriats in such partnerships insist on prepayments from China. In this trade, rice, fruit, other foods like pork, and even money from China are exchanged for timber, railway rails and metal waste from Russia. If the goods from China are liable to decay – for example, apples – the Buriats pay back nothing at all if they spoil in the Buriat warehouse.[23] The Chinese ask for a high profit from such 'fast-spoilers', but all the risk lies on their side. The Buriat traders do not interpret common 'Eastern psychology' as meaning they should behave in a specially honest or reliable way with their Chinese partners. A trader said:

Rice and sugar, well, they are heavy, and nothing much happens to them in the warehouse except rats eat them. To spoil them . . . well, you have to try specially to spoil them. You get my meaning? Ha, ha, ha. They won't spoil by themselves unless you put your mind to it.[24]

He was referring to watering rice and sugar to make them heavier. In the circumstances, it seems likely that 'Eastern psychology' refers less to mutual trust than to a rhetoric for keeping others (Russians) out of the trade. Buriats find it easier than Russians to set up the initial links, since they have relatives living in China, but the prevailing disbalance in trust cannot rest on kinship. Rather, this is another case of the 'trial of powers' mentioned in chapter 3. Here political circumstances enable one side to take disproportionate advantage of the fact that barter payments are made in goods, which take time to transport, require storage, may spoil, etc., rather than in money.

From an economic point of view the China trade is very important for Buriatiia, since advance payments are the impetus that allows the Buriat traders to operate at all (if everyone demanded prepayment there would be a stalemate). Inside Russia, the demand for prepayment is a dynamic force, since it puts pressure on prepaying firms to demand prepayments themselves from other firms.

The situation is an interesting test case for social relations, because here we have *one-sided trust*. One side enjoys the goods, while the other not only has to wait but has all the uncertainty of not knowing if the return goods will be of the agreed quantity and quality. Do participants place this kind of trust on kin and close friends? My evidence is: no, and emphatically so when it is a question of relations with entrepreneurs. For example, the head of the marketing divison of *NIIRP* in Moscow *oblast*, said,

---

[23] Warehouses are often checked by Russian inspectors, enabling the trader to say the goods are spoiled and need not be paid for (though it probably would not prevent him selling them).

[24] Interview with trader from the Buriat firm, '*Bat-Les*' (1998).

My son, my own son, is a trader. But if I gave him a consignment knowing he mightn't be able to repay, what would happen then? I would only give to him if he were capable of repaying. Otherwise, *not in any circumstances*.

It is different with producing enterprises, which have so many resources we could call on. But with a *kommersant*, first we would ask a higher price, and secondly, whoever he is, a son, a brother, an old friend, or whoever, we give *only* if he can pay back.

The manager continued: she would give a price discount (*skidka*) to a friend or relative – e.g. she would give a low winter price during the summer season of high prices. Acquaintanceship is also used to make a deal move fast, to manage without written contracts, and to agree false 'paper' prices so as to avoid paying taxes. Illegal transactions, especially those which have some chance of being found out, put trust at a premium (Ledeneva, chapter 11 in this volume) and may well be concocted with kin if both sides stand only to gain. But offer commodity credit to someone just because he is your son? That would be to confuse two kinds of trust. It might well destroy the relation with your son.

So even though many firms at the upper end of barter operate to a great extent through accustomed circles and have some difficulty in expanding trade beyond them, in the end the kind of trust involved is the commercial one of the 'trade partnership' (see chapter 3) and inside Russia is determined by two circumstances: (1) by the estimation of the reliability and resources of the firm, and (2) by the type of goods transacted. The evidence of previous transactions are not sufficient to guarantee reliability. The resources of a firm are scrutinised and close attention is paid to whether it has items like computers which can be claimed in the last resort as payment. Another criterion for reliability is the 'political' status of the firm – that is whether it has certain guarantees from above or not. In Buriatiia, barter participants of all kinds say they prefer to work with solid, government-supported firms. With regard to China, for all the talk of 'Eastern psychology', it turns out that traders on the Russian side take good care to find out if the partner has the backing of the Chinese state licensing system.

So far the discussion has concerned the rationale for commodity credit and the criteria for trusting firms with advance payments. But the question remains: why do certain firms agree to pay first? This is where the second of the variables mentioned at the beginning of this section kicks in, because a very important factor in which side pays first is the 'liquidity' (*likvidnost'*) of the goods they hold.

Liquidity

'Liquidity' in barter refers to the facility with which a given commodity can be exchanged for money (roubles and dollars). In Buriatiia, because most of the money in circulation originates from ordinary citizens (as pensions, etc.) and because these citizens are extremely poor, the most 'liquid' commodities are foods that are ready to consume, like bread, meat or cooking-oil. Thereafter, we find a downward trail of goods according to decreasing demand. Essentially, my Buriat material shows that those participants holding 'less-liquid' goods are prepared to pay first to those holding 'more liquid' goods, because only in this way can they enter the barter arena. In summer 1998 all entrepreneurs had as their end-goal acquiring money. Directors of producing enterprises may need goods of various kinds for inputs, but they desire money, too, if only to pay themselves. The result is a barter process that translates 'less liquid' commodities into 'more liquid' ones.

No single dominant means of exchange (commodity currency) has emerged out of barter. There was a brief period in 1996 in Buriatiia when vodka seemed about to play this role. For a few months the Ministry of Agriculture used vodka throughout the Republic to pay subsidies to collective farms and the farmers were delighted. But almost immediately false vodkas flooded the market and the experiment was ended. In summer 1998 computers were used as means of exchange and payment, but this was only in a restricted wealthy circle. So in general people have in their heads a shifting index of 'liquidity' for all the various means of exchange. It would be inaccurate to talk of anything as definite as rank or hierarchy, for traders are attuned to the possibility of odd cases when someone really wants something even if that thing is not in general demand. However, the Buriat material shows that there are some regularities. Things necessary for daily existence are most 'liquid' (ready foods, electricity, firewood, petrol), somewhat less so, but still rather 'liquid', are foods needing further processing (e.g. grains), productive livestock and items for health and children (medicines, school textbooks); next come utensils and materials necessary for working the household economy (fodder, fertiliser, building materials); then clothing; and at the bottom, the least 'liquid' are items like furniture or Russian-made electrical goods of dubious quality.

Interwoven with this series of consumer items are goods used in industrial and agricultural production. Here too, there is greater and lesser 'liquidity'. The impetus to industrial barter derives from the continued existence of dinosaurs producing goods that are priced too high and in low demand. In Buriatiia there is often no monetary demand for these goods, but they are needed for production inputs. The most 'liquid' commodities are fuels, electricity, spare parts and railway tariffs.[25] Somewhat less so are construction materials like cement, asbestos roofing (*shifer*), metal tubes, or wooden boards. Lower still are materials only slightly processed from a raw state (cellulose, coarse woollen thread), and least 'liquid' of all are raw materials of low quality that are superseded by better-quality goods on the international market (raw wool is a good example). In Buriatiia, because of the general demand for money and the fact that most of the cash anyone is prepared to spend is held by ordinary citizens, the series of industrial commodities is subordinated in barter to the more 'liquid' consumer goods. In practice, this means that a holder of, say, cement, has to go through a number of transactions, normally ending up with food, to turn it into money.

An example is a barter chain (*tsepochka*) of the trading firm '*Gunzan*' in Buriatiia. The firm starts with railway tariffs and goes through five operations in order to turn them into money. I call this a 'star-shaped' chain, because at each stage (except for the first) the goods return to the centre, '*Gunzan*'. The firm (1) trades railway tariffs with the electricity power station, which (2) 'covers' the electricity bills of a factory making roofing (*shifer*) and the *shifer* is then acquired by '*Gunzan*'. The firm then (3) sends the *shifer* to Sakhalin where it is exchanged for fish. Receiving the fish, '*Gunzan*' then (4) barters part of it for refrigerated storage. The rest of the fish is now (5) bartered for flour. Taking the flour, '*Gunzan*' proceeds (6) to barter it with the bakery for bread and cakes. The final stage (7) is reached when the firm gives the bread and cakes to wholesalers 'for realisation', receiving at last 'living money'. This entire process takes two – three months. Since profits (*nakrutki*) are taken out at each stage, '*Gunzan*' reckons that it receives in the end perhaps only 50 per cent of the rouble value of the railway tariffs it started out with. One could also say, in the abstract, that '*Gunzan*' is paying at each stage for the fact that it is offering goods, not money (though in practice, of course, if there were money around the firm would not bother with this set of transactions at all, but sell the tariffs directly) (see figure 10.2).

From the psychological point of view, people can no longer feel, as they were encouraged to under socialism, that each is producer or holder of something of broadly equivalent value to society. 'The idea of 'liquidity'

---

[25] To pay for rail transport, firms give goods to the rail stations. These goods are used to pay railway workers and they are also sold in special shops attached to the rail system. The difference between the value of the incoming goods and the cost of transport is known as a 'rail tariff'. Making such a deal is regarded as a coup in Buriatiia and usually requires having some 'connection' in the station. Firms lucky enough to acquire tariffs can trade them on at a profit. G. Manzanova, personal communication.

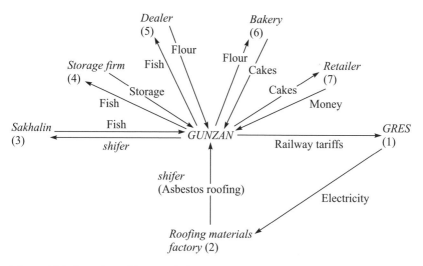

Figure 10.2 Star-shaped barter chain of the trading firm '*Gunzan*', Buriatiia, 1998: seven steps by which railway tariffs are transformed into money. The triangular deal between '*Gunzan*', *GRES* power station and the roofing materials factory is an offset

encourages new kinds of discrimination in micro relations, with traders into money at the top. In practice, however, there are certain distortions in the liquidity series: many dinosaur industries, which would otherwise be at the bottom, have government support, and they (and other more profitable industries like electricity) are frequently maintained as regional monopolies. Farmers, on the other hand, have their position depressed also by government policy, as will be described below.

All this has an impact on exchange rates and leads to the widespread feeling that one is engaged in 'non-equivalent' (*ne-ekvivalentnyi*) barter. One aspect of this idea seems to be a heritage from Soviet times and the idea that goods have an inherent value which is based not on demand but on the cost of production (*sebestoimost'* – lit. the 'self-value'). Affront at 'non-equivalent' rates reflects a general difficulty in adjusting to the fact that prices today are largely determined by supply and demand, but I shall suggest that barter accentuates this feeling.

In Buriatiia certain large firms are forbidden by regional law to sell their products at prices below the cost of production. This is intended to save the jobs of the workforce, but the result is to render these goods 'unliquid'. The spread of barter attitudes suddenly discloses what would previously have been seen simply as 'the fair price' in a new light. Many people are now part-time dealers, looking with an eagle eye for a disjunction between wrongly priced goods and potential buyers and ready to take advantage. An enterprise (or even a person) is no longer the respected holder of an unquestioned value, but more like a clothes-horse, the awkward bearer of something that is now a trade good (*tovar*), but unable because of the absence of general markets to dispose of it at will. The barterer mentally abstracts the good from the person to work out its onward barter track; as several respondents said: 'You never take an item unless you have a scheme (*skhema*) worked out for it.' This might seem like a commonplace aspect of commoditisation. But in a money economy the triangular relation, between the producer, the commodity and the buyer is far less of an affront, because money enables people to buy things in impersonal shops or markets rather than scrutinise each enterprise or person for gains to be made from them. It is the fact the barter involves face-to-face relations, in which the holders of 'non-liquid' goods are personally confronted with the talking-down of their products that makes these encounters stressful and humiliating: 'I fed that cow for three years, and now he tells me it is worth just a few cans of petrol'.[26]

The last of a series of barter deals, when actual cash is in the offing, is a particularly intense encounter known as the 'end-deal' (*konechnaya sdelka*). All those shadowy debts and unwieldy consignments build up to this point where the 'liquidity' variable and the credit variable meet – the acquiring of 'living money' (*zhivyye dengi*) as it is tellingly called. This introduces a new situation. With valuable deals between large firms, because enterprises in debt for tax are liable to have it deducted from any positive bank account, a solution is often to create a satellite firm to hold the incoming money. This is socially highly significant, since it introduces a relation of deception between the firm and the state, *and* because it is all too easy to conceal these financial assets from the workers (see chapter 3).[27] Small firms are less likely to create satellites and the directors tend to spend incoming money immediately. At this level, the desire for money is such that the holder of any commodity invariably gives it up first to the retailer for later money repayment ('for realisation',

[26] Farmer in '*Dogo-Khudan*' peasant enterprise, Kizhinga District, Buriatiia.
[27] An example of this is the fate of the huge *Lyuberetsk* agricultural machinery factory near Moscow. In 1995 the factory set up a satellite private firm, with almost the same name, and placed a large bank loan of 14.5 million dollars into its account. The existence of this money was concealed from the workers and used to finance a dubious undertaking in Italy. Meanwhile, the *Lyuberetsk* factory fell into steep decline (Chuprin and Gubanova, 1998).

na realizatsii). Sometimes entrepreneurs are even prepared to go without any profit from the 'end-deal' in order to get money fast.[28]

On the other side of such deals, the one with money, wholesaler or retailer, is said to be condescending, make demands and anyway can insist on stringent conditions (when, where and in what condition the goods are to appear in). This high-handedness is particularly resented when, as is very often the case, the holder of goods is a hardworking experienced factory manager and the money-holder is an upstart young entrepreneur (see Makarov and Kleiner 1996 on the role of *malchiki*, 'boy dealers').

How curious then to find an equally topsy-turvy effect in the microcosm of the household, when in Buriatiia suddenly it is the grandmother with her pension who has money. Especially in rural areas, there is no other money at all. Now it is the hitherto perhaps disregarded old person who has the most liquid good, who has to be asked nicely for a loan and who can make her conditions. An example of the social discomfort this can cause is given by Meshcheryakov (1996): a village headteacher in Buriatiia, without an income for months, resorted to trading vodka on credit. On pension day she went round to collect her debts. But the confrontations with the quavering *babushki*, suddenly responsible for all the drinkers in the family, were unbearable for the teacher and she gave up her trade.

The teacher gave up because she could not face putting pressure on the grandmothers to wrest their money from them (money probably already promised away in any case). This is analogous to the position of people giving goods 'on realisation', because it is at this point that default is taken most seriously and pressure is put on the end-dealers to pay up. In Buriatiia the police and the courts are regarded as useless in this respect; private security firms are used instead, and these firms are understood to be 'criminals in disguise'. My evidence is that, however widespread this practice, people do not find it normal.

Businessmen who regard themselves as more or less law-abiding, and at any rate peaceful people, find themselves in an entirely new social situation: they find *themselves* sending out gangs of thugs against traders whose difficulties they understand only too well.

Goods for use and goods for exchange
As noted earlier, the side that first asks for a barter deal is normally at a disadvantage in negotiations, since the very fact of asking implies greater

---

[28] 'We realise food products through small wholesalers, even though they charge a higher price. In fact we buy and sell at the same price. We are not interested in a normal profit when it is a matter of realisation. What we are interested in is quickly getting money', Director of '*Prin*' computer firm, Ulan-Ude, Buriatiia

need to sell.[29] One aspect of such disadvantage is that the other firm is likely to respond: 'I'll take your X only if you will accept my Y' and Y may be something that the first firm does not require for its own production. Businessmen see this as another kind of 'non-equivalence' in barter:

> Equivalent exchange is when I definitely know that I need the thing. But if I don't need it and have to turn it into money, that cannot be equivalent exchange. Never. Not for anyone. Even if the trade is equivalent in the financial sense, there is the question of the cost of transforming that item into something I want, the expense of my people and my time. I could be spending that time in some other way. Selling, leisure, going to the cinema. So rather than pricing the item at wholesale market prices, the loss of time should be added to the exchange. And of course you have to add all the marketing research I have to do before starting that barter. You have to work out a scheme for disposing of those goods.[30]

In both Buriatiia and Moscow *oblast*, businessmen made a distinction between 'necessary' and 'forced' barter:

> There is barter that is necessary (*neobkhodimyi*) and barter that is forced on you (*vynuzhdennyi*). I divide it this way because, if I need his metallic part and he needs my transmission belts, I call that necessary. Really, there would be no difference if I paid him in money. Barter in that case is just a sort of decoration of normal economic activity. But there is also forced barter. Someone says to me, 'If you want me to take your belts, I'll pay you in my goods, vacuum cleaners and kitchen processors.' And I object to that. Why? Because taking his goods I have to sell them. I am involved in production and I don't have the facilities to organise bartering his un-asked for and un-planned for things. It's a real problem. You break your head on it. But we have to do it, there's no way out.[31]

This situation is one of the main reasons for the dynamism and expansion of barter: the first incoming consignment of vacuum cleaners might be paid to the workers, but in general each firm is likely to end up with some relatively non-liquid goods that have to be passed into barter chains.

At the 'non-liquid' end of production a factory may run into a blank wall: *none* of their suppliers will take their goods. In this case, the factory constructs its own chain (*tsepochka*) to accommodate to a buying parter.

---

[29] This point was made explicitly by one manager, who said: 'If we ask for barter, there is a rule that the other side prices their goods 10 per cent higher than the market rate; if they ask for the deal, we charge 10 per cent more', (Bogomolov, manager of Supply Department, *NIIRP*).

[30] Tseren Charafa, age 22, director of '*Prin Office Centre*', trading in computers and managerial technology, Ulan-Ude, Buriatiia.

[31] V. N. Gesko, Vice-Director of *NIIRP* for commercial affairs.

Here is a simple case from Buriatiia, where the monopoly *Fine Cloth* wool-processing factory needs to make a deal for raw wool inputs. The problem is that the sheep-raising collective farms, poor as they are, will not accept the factory's yarn in payment. The factory set up a sewing workshop so as to be able to pay somewhat more 'liquid', but admittedly clumsily made clothes. Once was enough, however, for the collectives to take a consignment of coats ('everyone in the village cannot wear the same coats yet again'). So to get round this quandary, the factory made an agreement with a timber firm prepared to accept coats, and gets the timber firm to pass planks on to the *kolkhoz*. This is really a deal between *Fine Cloth* and the collective farm, but it has the form of a circle (as distinct from the 'star' form of p. 275). The circle expands when the timber firm decides that it, too, does not want coats. To meet this situation, *Fine Cloth* finds a wholesale dealer prepared to give vodka for coats, establishes that the wood people will take vodka, and one further link is added to the chain.[32] This chain may appear like a closed circle, but evidently it is likely to generate further chains: the wood, the wool and the vodka are all consumed as they reach their destination, but the coats still have to find a final purchaser. It is quite possible that making coats even takes away value (unmade-up cloth and tweed from *Fine Cloth* apparently have a high reputation locally).[33] Nevertheless, once they are in existence the coats circulate until they find their own low final 'price'.

If the push to set up circular barter chains comes from (a) the need to dispose of unwanted incoming goods, and (b) the need to accommodate to the demands of a partner, a third impetus (c) is to acquire some desirable liquidity only attainable at some remove. The strongest chains are those that satisfy all these requirements. In Buriatiia major chains of this kind are set up with government cooperation and are crucial to the regional economy. Such a strong chain can be also be used by further subchains which spin off it. Let us take the example of one of the most important barter chains in Buriatiia, the *TsKK* chain, which performs the extraordinary feat of supporting two loss-making industries, establishing a tie with the West and bringing in goods to the government which can only be bought for money. The main link is between the Republic government and the giant *TsKK* cellulose-cardboard plant. *TsKK* is a

---

[32] This real-life example was provided by N. S. Timofeeva, head of the the the Presidential Committee for Economic Reform, Buriatiia.

[33] This is a feature of the Russian economy emphasised by Gaddy and Ickes (1998. p. 3), who point out that value is redistributed to such enterprises from other sectors (from tax arrears and resources).

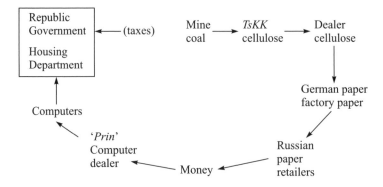

Figure 10.3 Circular chain of the *TsKK* cellulose factory

classic dinosaur, a huge consumer of forests, a polluter of Lake Baikal, and it has a cost of production (and hence fixed money prices) twice that of the paper factory in Arkhangelsk. The chain starts with the fact that the *Kholbol'zhinskii* open-cast mine owes taxes to the government which it is unable to pay. In lieu of these taxes the mine sends coal to *TsKK*. The next step is for *TsKK* to send cellulose via a dealer to a factory in Germany where it is turned into high-quality paper. The paper is then re-exported back to Russia where it is sold for money. The money is then used to buy computers from the firm '*Prin*' and '*Prin*' then pays computers to a department of the Republic administration. The government is very happy: it has supported the mine dinosaur and the cellulose dinosaur, helping to keep thousands of people in work and it receives computers (figure 10.3).

Evidently, in this *TsKK* chain, the computer firm could be substituted by any local firm with high-value goods the government wants to acquire. While in the chain, however, '*Prin*' can use it to sell its computers to other firms which are unable to pay what Prin wants (money). Let us take the example of a gold-prospecting company in the far north of the republic which wants computers. '*Prin*', a small firm of 15 people, is not prepared to accept gold ore which it is unable to process. So matters are arranged as follows: the gold company gives ore to a coal mine, the mine pays coal to another firm which will cover taxes for *TsKK*, and then we are now into the *TsKK* chain described above. Eventually, Prin receives either fine-processed western paper (which it can sell for cash) or money and the computers are sent to the gold mine. With so many links in the chain, each of which takes a cut, the gold mine receives very expensive computers indeed. This is fine from the point of view of the directors

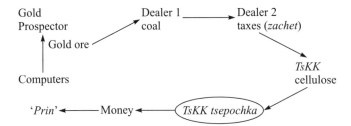

Figure 10.4 Circular chain of the firm '*Prin*' as an offshoot of the *TsKK* chain

of '*Prin*', but one can imagine that the prospectors far off in their tundra are not so happy (figure 10.4).

Sometimes, rather than judging incoming goods on the basis of whether they can be used internally or not, a director with an entrepreneurial cast of mind decides to go into profit-making barter, and soon finds himself acquiring incoming goods for the sole purpose of trade. This process can turn the social relations of the previous institution into something almost unrecognisable. For example, the Zabaikal'skii Training Centre started out in 1982 as a training-cum-production station for construction workers under the Ministry of Education. Allowed to become financially independent under *perestroika*, the Centre set up branches and was soon training up to 10,000 workers a year, mostly from the army. Goods of all kinds started to roll in to pay for the courses. The director said,

Metals and everything were lying around here, well, we decided to barter them with China for clothing for our workers, trainers, leather jackets... you know. We went over there and got them ourselves. Then other people started giving us lists of orders. Then we realised: from this you can earn! When we first brought in leather coats in mass, it was not for our workers but for trade, ha, ha. We sold half here to the wholesalers, and the rest were bartered to Moscow in exchange for suede jackets that were in much demand at the time. The first suede jackets in Buriatiia. We were pioneers in a way. I didn't altogether like that life, trading, but even in 1989-90 we understood that there was nowhere to get money. Then what happened? The factories and the army started to economise on training. We had to reduce, we fell into debt.

Now we train 500–600 people a year. It's less than before, but still it is something. If they don't have the money for the fees, the private students propose barter. So they offer nails, or something useful lying around at home, building materials, or if it is an enterprise sending students they offer to pay for our heating. Yes, we make the exchange if the goods are useful for the Centre or we can trade them on.

We've become part of the general economic stream, which is the barter and mutual credit (*vzaimozachet*) system.[34]

Commercialising its operations, the Centre has at the same time transformed the relation between trainee and school such that it has become subject to the general conditions of barter.

Ordinary workers, on the other hand, find it difficult to commercialise and suffer most from the problems of receiving unwanted goods. The items received in return for work are rarely of a kind that one could turn to entrepreneurial advantage. In the following conversation between a worker (F) in a building materials factory in Moscow *oblast* and a researcher from Cambridge (*Q*), the tone is one of bitter humour:

F: This year we get paid wallpaper.
Q: What do you do with it?
F: [joking]. Decorate our big garages. What would you do with wallpaper? Well, I try to sell it.
Q: To whom?
F: Neighbours, friends... My friends haven't got enough space in their house for all this wallpaper. Sometimes I get my daughter to try to sell it on the market for me.
Q: How much wallpaper do you get per month?
F: A kilometre, from here to the grave.
Q: So how do you make ends meet?
F: How have we ever made ends meet in Russia? Somebody's got a chicken, somebody's got a carrot, we mix them together and make soup for two.

It has been shown that in a range of ways barter gives rise to a feeling of unfairness (non-equivalence). To understand more generally in the business context what barter means socially it is necessary to look briefly at how prices are agreed, for this has the effect of quantifying and objectifying personal relations.

Pricing in barter

All my respondents without exception state that exchange rates in barter are formed by reference to money prices. Even in rural areas there are no standard arrangements of the 'three bags of sugar go for two bags of flour' type. In principle, pricing is done by each side initially setting a unit money price for their goods and then reckoning how much they will exchange. These money prices are said to be wholesale 'market prices', which are discovered by consulting daily newspaper lists, by visiting

---

[34] Director of *Zaibaikal'skii Uchebnyi Tsentr*, aged 48. The Centre now has a staff of 25 teachers.

wholesale bases in the city and ringing round to find out what prices other people are using. However, this is just the rhetorical surface on what turns out to be an essentially personalised and discriminatory system.

Even if market prices are stable, all barter prices are agreed anew each time because they are essentially a contest between traders. In Buriatiia, someone who wishes to trade even mildly 'unliquid' goods, like flour, for office equipment has to drop below the wholesale market money price for flour to cover the equipment trader's estimation of his own 'costs of realisation'. The flour usually comes out about one and a half times cheaper in such deals, but there is no firm rule.[35]

At the same time, price confrontations reflect the value the trader of the more liquid good puts on his own tax and other costs, which determines the mark-up (*nadtsenka*) he adds to the price he paid for the item. Such a mark-up can seem remarkably high (e.g. 400-500 per cent for a computer). The computer dealer explains that this has to cover the tax on profits, VAT, the city tax, the tax for bridge-maintenance, etc. as well as his own profits. The result is that the actually agreed exchange price in a barter deal of flour for computers, say, differs from the market price for either commodity, the flour being priced below the market price and the computers well above it. Figure 10.5 is my representation of how participants conceptualise such agreements. This kind of calculation crystallises yet another way in which barter is said to be 'non-equivalent' or unfair.

Now, it is clear to all concerned that the *nadtsenka* is largely notional, since the computer trader probably will not pay all the taxes. In the interviews, he claims in one breath that this mark-up barely allows him to break even; in the next he explains how he drops it considerably for a favoured customer or someone who offers a particularly desirable good in exchange. Thus, the value of a sale is not determined solely by profit but also by other factors (avoiding tax, currying favour, laying grounds for repeat deals, keeping a *tsepochka* going...). As Makarov and Kleiner (1996, pp. 23–4) point out, prices formed in this way cannot be used to measure supply and demand.

Furthermore, in Buriatiia, prices when agreed are only provisional. The standard barter contract form has a space for the participants to specify the conditions under which the agreed price will change.[36] This is not just a matter of reacting to inflation or changes in market conditions during the repayment period. It is also used to cut a partner in on the

[35] Director of '*Prin Office Centre*', Ulan-Ude, Buriatiia.
[36] N. S. Timofeeva, vice-director of the Agrarian Union, Buriatiia.

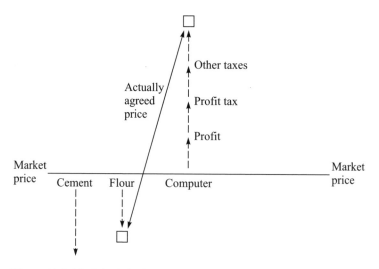

Figure 10.5 Model of the formation of barter prices

trading luck of the other: in this case the agreement states that, if the partner makes more profit than expected from trading on ones' goods, one can renegotiate the price.

The social relations of pricing encounters seem peculiarly ambivalent. On the one hand, although the prices are negotiated face-to-face, all the calculations that go into them on either side are rarely transparent – even your 'old friend' is probably hiding something from you. As for strangers you can be certain they will be trying to take some kind of advantage ('You have to remember,' I was told, 'our market is the "wild market" (*dikii rynok*)'). On the other hand, there is a certain complicity inherent in very many deals, mainly because of the very widespread practice of tax avoidance. It is extremely common, for example, to agree on two prices, one low price 'on paper' to avoid the turnover and profit taxes, and the other the actual price paid. The difference between the two is known as 'black' (*chernyi*) wealth. One businessman estimated around half the turnover of the Buriat economy to be 'black'.[37]

Despite this complicity, trust between partners in different firms is definitely less strong than that found within the firm. Inside a small trading firm, it is common to find that all staff have a common liability for debts (all must pay up if any one of them makes a mistake). Often

---

[37] Director of '*Prin Office Centre*', Ulan-Ude, Buriatiia.

there is a general director who takes charge of the most important barter chain, while the other three or four members each 'warm' their own *tsepochka*. Perhaps, such small firms indeed sometimes consist of kin.[38] Judging from my materials, this kind of strong, internal trust is only equalled in between-enterprise relations when one of the firms is essentially fictive – that is, when in reality it is part of the other one. Aside from such illegal compacts, confidence in exchange parters is in short supply. 'You have to feed the wolves,' is how one businessman from Moscow *oblast* put it.

What is the relation between discriminatory pricing in barter and the social relations between the directors and the workers in producing enterprises? My materials indicate a difference between Moscow *oblast*, where workers are still mainly paid in money, and Buriatiia, where they are not. In both cases, directors are mostly trying to shift 'non-liquid goods'. If they have the interests of the whole firm at heart, including the workers, they try to keep prices high, raise the general income, and pay employees a decent return for their work (as is done, with some difficulty, in *NIIRP* in Moscow *oblast*, where it is rewarded with loyalty from the workers).[39] However, it is not difficult to see that such a policy does not necessarily advantage the directors. It is far easier to barter at a lower price and/or *not* to demand full repayment. As several of my respondents pointed out (see also Makarov and Kleiner 1996, p. 27) the directors only have to get a small percentage back, significant for themselves, for this to be better for them than the full 'honest' price if it is distributed in full to the workforce. It is to prevent this kind of deal that the Buriat regional government has forbidden the dinosaurs to sell below cost price and has made a list of enterprises producing 'liquid' goods that are forbidden to barter rather than sell for money (interestingly, this is called the 'black list' by traders who depend on barter for a living). Both of these laws are widely flouted. As a consequence, the workers' share in barter deals is often squeezed to a minimum, causing great resentment.

[38] This is said to be the case in Buriatiia, but none of the respondent firms were composed of kin.
[39] 'The pay is low, but you have to be an optimist. We have a workers' contingent here. I wouldn't think of moving. This is my enterprise (*svoe predpriyatiye*), you understand. These are people who have spent their whole working lives in one place. This explains their optimism, or rather, their attitude to work, to their place of work,' L. Z. Vetrova, worker in the Sales Department of *NIIRP*. The managers of *NIIRP* respect such attitudes and have made minimal staff cuts in the 1990s (workforce down from around 600 to about 500).

Makarov and Kleiner argue (1996, p. 27) that the emergence of managers' interests as separate from those of the workers has had macro effects. This fact, not just the lack of money, gave significant impetus to the lowering of inflation in 1995–6. The non-payment of wages is not just a matter of lack of resources and unfulfilled contracts, but is also due simply to the unwillingness of directors to pay wages, a situation apparent on a very wide scale.[40] In this perspective, they argue (1996, p. 28), the failure to fulfil barter contracts (to pay up in full, on time) should be seen not so much as the defrauding of one director by another so much as a conspiracy of the two directors to defraud their workers and the government. Barter is more apt for this kind of back-door deal than money sales because its prices are so cloudy and haphazard and its accounting so opaque.

To summarise: from an *economic* point of view, pricing in barter has a paradoxical effect. Because of transaction costs and profits, barter raises prices at each deal (so that at the end of a chain you may receive only 50-60 per cent of the value of what you gave at the beginning) and therefore it has an inflationary tendency. But at the same time, because of the high general demand for money and under-pricing to avoid tax, etc. there is also an anti-inflationary pressure. From an *anthropological* point of view, the way pricing is done increases personalisation – i.e. the positional situation of the person trading affects the price. Instead of a general price which is paid by anyone, different prices are paid each time, even for the same goods. This may be to the advantage of traders, but consumers feel disadvantaged in a climate of mistrust.

Let me now turn to barter at the district and regional level, particularly the role of government in integrating barter between diverse sectors.

Regional configurations of barter (Buriatiia)
Left to itself, barter would probably have the effect of separating the agricultural and the industrial-cum-energy sectors, as the latter have relatively little interest in acquiring the goods of the former. The farmers would be left almost without fuel, spare parts and farm machinery. The impetus for integration comes from the administrations, at both Republic and district levels.

In the Selenga district of Buriatiia, for example, the administration has set up a vital integratory chain through debt-trading. This *tsepochka* starts with 36,000 roubles owed to the state by the open-cast mine for

---

[40] In Nizhegorod *oblast* in March 1996 around 90 per cent of the directors of industrial enterprises were fined for witholding wages without good reason (Makarov and Kleines, 1996, p. 28).

taxes. In lieu of paying taxes, the mine sends coal to the *Gusinoozersk* electricity station (GRES), which sends slightly less than an equivalent value of electricity to *Buriat Energo*, the electricity company. This electricity is then partly sent direct to collective farms and partly sent to a factory in Krasnoyarsk region producing spare parts. On account of this electricity the factory sends spare parts to the farms. The circle is then closed when the farms repay the government for the electricity and spares by means of food products (figure 10.6).

How does the administration deal with the incoming farm products? The following *tsepochka* shows how wages are directly involved in barter, since the task of this chain is to transform the raw products into items acceptable in lieu of money wages to the *byudzhetniki* (i.e. all those on state salaries, teachers, accountants, administrators, and so forth). This chain starts with tax owed the government by *GRES*, the electricity station. In lieu of tax, *GRES* gives electricity to the dairy, food-processing factory and food importer. Of the incoming raw farm products, 25 per cent are sold for money, which is used to pay the food importers, while 75 per cent are passed to the dairy, meat-processing plant, etc. In return for

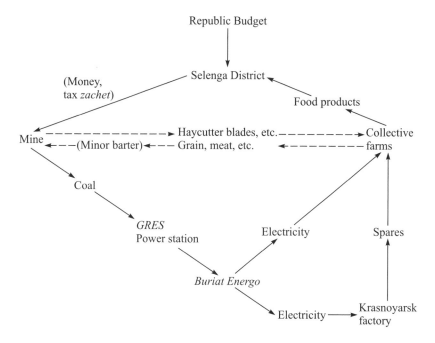

Figure 10.6 District government chain (*tsepochka*)

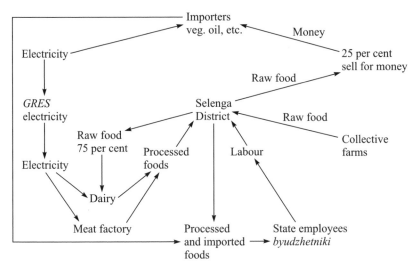

Figure 10.7.Payment for government workers as part of the district chain

their labour, the *byudzhetniki* thus receive a mixed 'wage' of locally processed and imported foods (figure 10.7)

A breakdown anywhere in such chains, not just malign greed of the administration, can cause the well known delays to wage payments. As noted earlier, each chain is likely to be dependent on the working of other chains. In the event, the *byudzhetniki* may be passive or active links in such chains. Some just accept the goods, others turn to entrepreneurial barter themselves, like the Zabaikalskii Training College. Some leave the chain – they go out on strike. Yet others flout the authority of their own seniors in the administration and resort to direct action. In Buriatiia, tax inspectors sometimes go to enterprises and simply appropriate goods, which they then count as their own pay. In other words, they by-pass the government-designated links in the chain, and this reminds us yet again that barter chains are structures of *power and contest*.

The two interlinked chains (figures 10.6 and 10.7) are subvariants of a much wider system of aid to agriculture, organised at the Republic level, called 'commodity credit' (*tovarnyi kredit*, or CC) described in detail in Humphrey (1999a). Providing credit in the form of commodities such as chemical fertilisers, seed corn, spare parts, fuel and heating oil at the beginning of the agricultural year, the government receives harvest products at the end of the year. CC is organised by a state company called the Products Corporation (PC), which barters directly with each farm director, issues credit notes to be used in specific factories and receives the agricultural products in repayment. The factories pay out to the farms in lieu of taxes owed to the government.

So far, so good. The farmers are in theory appreciative of CC. But problems arise with this system that go back directly to the variables discussed at the beginning of the chapter. Many farmers do not, or cannot, pay back CC (in 1997 only around 50 per cent was returned by Buriat farms). Sanctions on default are non-existent, except for perhaps being exluded from the scheme in the following year, and this encourages farms which could pay not to do so. The prices paid by the PC are below market prices; and the PC may abruptly decide not to accept, say, grains, because an import deal covers their needs, and this means that farms have to restructure their production. Worst of all, the system lacks legitimacy because it places farmers in an economic straitjacket – they have to accept inputs from firms chosen by the PC with no control at all over quality and they have to accept low prices for farm products because if they did not do so, most would simply not be able to start the agricultural cycle in spring. Paternalistic attitudes appear within the PC. 'Why do we not give the farms money?' said one administrator in 1996, 'Because we could not trust them to use it sensibly. They might buy themselves cars.'[41] This is 'barter' in the sense that individual farm directors have to haggle for prices and conditions, but in another way the system is reminiscent of quasi-feudal dependency. The acceptance of individual farms for CC in 1998 was done on the basis of guarantees by the local administration, with all the politics this implies.[42] Farm directors, I know, feel the whole system to be humiliating.[43] One can only imagine their reaction when it was announced, in summer 1998, that the system might be stopped: the budget was not receiving what it should from the PC and the head of the PC was being charged with embezzlement.

This news must have fed into the stream of rumours concerning corruption in other major enterprises close to the government. However, in my view, to see the matter as only one of corruption is to miss the real quandaries faced by an organisation like the PC as a direct

---

[41] In 1998, an official said: 'The farmers are put in this position, well, they put themselves in the situation, because they cannot be credited as civilised economic enterprises, as subjects in a civilised economy', N. S. Timofeeva, vice-director of the Agrarian Union, Buriatiia.

[42] This was an attempt to raise the level of repayment of CC by making district authorities responsible for debts of defaulting farms. It enabled officials to debar disfavoured farms. No one seems to expect, however, that the rate of repayment of CC will be much improved.

[43] Fieldwork in Barguzin and Selenga districts, Buriatiia (1996). See also Humphrey (1999a).

result of the barter system. The PC is faced with 'realising' the unwieldy mass of agricultural products of every collective in the Republic. A warning of the impending impasse was given by the failure of the Products Tax, which was also organised by the PC in five districts of Buriatiia in 1997. Instead of non-payment in money, it was decided that farms could pay tax in products, that these would be realised by the PC, which would fund the budget in money. The PC thus became the single tax-payer on behalf of dozens of farms. The system failed because, perhaps surprisingly, the farms paid up.[44] The PC was unable to cope: it had insufficient storage facilities and few links with retail outlets. It was forced to rent its own shops and this forced up its prices, and many products spoiled before they could be sold. For this reason alone the PC was unable to pay the budget what was due. The products tax experiment was ended, although it was popular with farmers;[45] but the PC continues to experience the same difficulties with the CC system – which is kept going, despite the impending law suit, because no-one can think of another way to keep the farms afloat.

The same problems are experienced by all large receivers of barter goods – for example the electricity companies and pension funds. This is the main reason for the the widespread creation of local substitute monies or coupons in Russia (see Anderson, chapter 12 in this volume), especially in 'company towns', where a large enterprise like a power station is the main employer. As Ryabchenko writes (1998):

In the Ukraine all atomic energy enterprises receive from their consumers, who do not have money, the products of those same consumers. These items could be given out to the electricity workers, who haven't seen the national money for years. But that is bothersome. So the enterprise issues its own money, gives it a name, and workers can volunteer to accept it as wages. The known number of such private and self-accounting moneys in the Ukraine is in the hundreds, and in Russia must amount to tens of thousands.

Thus, in the town of Slavutiche, at the Chernobyl Station and attached enterprises, around one thousand (!) such moneys were issued in 1996-8. Of these, around half have been studied and classified. These are one-day moneys – received, taken to the shop, spent and cancelled. There are cases of workers saving up such a money to buy furniture, only to find next month that it had been annulled.

---

[44] The general tax repayment rate for Republic taxes in Buriatiia was 43 per cent in 1996; the 'repayment rate' for the Products Tax was set at 88.3 per cent in 1997 and it was all collected, N. S. Timofeeva, vice-director of the Agrarian Union, Buriatiia.

[45] The tax was popular with farmers because it was levied at the end of the year and all they had to do was to deduct some products from their income and send them off - far less burdensome that having to 'realise' the products to get money to pay taxes.

This is a method of reducing costs for the enterprise (it no longer needs to realise goods for roubles to pay workers); but it reduces the workers' choice of goods to those received in barter. In Buriatiia, *all* the main disadvantages of barter are heaped on the shoulders of the workers: they have to wait, they have to accept goods they may not need, and they have the trouble and expense of 'realising' such goods. In the region, the result is a new kind of class conflict, of which the outcomes are difficult to predict. One exceptional gain for ordinary people has been the 'win' of the pensioners in Buriatiia, who succeeded in April 1998 in their battle to get pensions paid in cash rather than in products.[46]

Struggles for power, barter chains and information

The push to start and maintain a strong government-supported *tsepochka* comes from large factories like *Fine Cloth* or the *TsKK* in whose interests the chain works. Yet I was told that small firms like to enter such chains, even if it is not in their immediate interest, because they are reliable and ongoing. This tendency is all the greater when the factory is a monopoly, like *Fine Cloth*, whose director (of Soviet vintage) is so close to the President and is known to the entire Republic as Klavdia Ivanovna. 'I gave 500 kilos of wool to Klavdia Ivanovna,' a farm director might say. This does not mean he knows her, only that he participates in the personalised, patron-imbued talk of society. There are downsides to such chains. Buriat farmers have almost no other buyers for their wool and 'Klavdia Ivanovna' – or her managers – is often reviled for her abysmal prices. There was a time when to be dropped from *Fine Cloth*'s schemes would have been very detrimental, but now farms enter the chains on a slightly more equal footing as *Fine Cloth* has difficulties in getting the wool it needs for even reduced production. Today, farms take part mainly because Klavdia Ivanovna's chain is a form of ongoing patronage that allows them to plan.

Essentially, it is political support for *Fine Cloth* that maintains a situation that is unsatisfactory to everyone: for farmers it is hardly worth keeping sheep at such low prices, *Fine Cloth* has to construct elaborate *tsepochki* to get even a minimum of inputs, and the region is

---

[46] Enterprises have been paying into the Republic pension fund (PF) in goods for at least three years. At first, the PF sold these goods through retail outlets and used the money to pay pensions. Then, in 1997, the PF paid pensions in one-third money and two-thirds goods. Pensioners demonstrated and wrote petitions. As of April 1998, they succeeded in getting pensions paid 100 per cent in money by government decree. Pensions are (summer 1999) paid two months late.

flooded with the unpleasing coats. *Fine Cloth* claims not to have enough money to invest in changing its production lines, yet its status as a factory of All-Russia designation means that it receives enough subsidies to plough on.

When a lesser enterprise sets up a chain in its own interests, however, it may run into difficulties with the dinosaurs. This happened to '*Prin*' the computer firm, which tried to set up a lengthy *tsepochka* involving *TsKK*, silk from China, an export firm in Moscow, and desirable money on the return path. Even though '*Prin*' was a part of another chain organised by *TsKK* (see figure 10.4), the giant firm was not in the end prepared to oblige '*Prin*' by becoming a mere link in its chain. *TsKK* dumped '*Prin*' by not sending its products to the next stage; the entire chain fell apart and Prin was left in debt, having made some expenditure in the expectation that the chain would work. This shows that the mutually protective aspect of chain barter (Ledeneva and Seabright, chapter 4 and the Introduction in this volume), which is evident in my materials among mid-level firms of equivalent standing, can be distorted by power relations, when one large enterprise can afford to include or exclude a given minor partner.

For this reason, personal connections (*svyazi*) are at a premium.

Here in Buriatiia personal relations are essential. Only people with understanding (*ponimayushchiye*) can create offset schemes for taxes, heating, electricity, etc. and then it always comes to those who make agreements and give permission, the Ministry of Finance, *GORFO, GORFIN*. I am not saying you have to give bribes, but you have to know which level the decision is taken on. If you don't have this knowledge you will get nowhere. Among us, the President of the Republic may forbid some offset at some particular time, others in the Ministries too, they can say, 'No, that won't happen' (*eto ne budet*). Suddenly you can't get electricity, you can't get money – all these things, new decrees, decisions, you must know, simply in order not to waste your life...[47]

I suggest that it is circular chains which are subject to most political pressure, because they are ones that otherwise would be most fragile. In 'lineal' and 'star-shaped' chains (see also chapter 3 in this volume), some kind of satisfaction of wants is accomplished at each deal. This is not the case with circular chains. For the same reason, circles cause more damage when they fall apart, since that affects a whole series of relations. Circular chains also tend to be vulnerable because the progression from 'non-liquid' towards 'liquid' goods has to be reversed at some point – in other words, the circle, which is an essentially egalitarian form, runs up

---

[47] Director of '*Prin Office Centre*', Ulan-Ude, Buriatiia.

against the various types of *non-parity* so prevalent in barter. This is why we often find that extra-economic factors are required to keep a circle together. One of the inflexible aspects of barter is that relatively few people have the information to penetrate and take part in a new circular chain. Those who have it guard it closely, and even so, like the Director of '*Prin*', they may be excluded or dumped. Smaller firms – such as my respondents who are pork producers, managers of bakeries, etc. – stand no chance of entering an eminent chain except as a minor subsidiary, and even then they would need connections. It is simpler for them to work with other small firms. It is interesting that the *obkom* (Republic-level Communist Party) is still mentioned as a source of information on reliable partners. Even so, among disadvantaged enterprises, and particularly with linear chains, the lack of information is remarkable.[48] At the bottom, a farm official – not the director but the man actually charged with carrying out barter deals – may not know where his meat is destined, may know nothing about the middleman firm who comes to buy it, not know what mark-up is being charged, and have only cloudy knowledge of prices at the meat packing factory.[49] One senses that this 'lack of knowledge' is partly a self-protection against the unwelcome idea of oneself venturing out of the farm into the 'wild market'. This is a kind of passive resistance to barter. In effect, it limits the farmer's own initiatives to *bash na bash*. swaps. Knowledge and power thus constrain barter operations. Barter in Russian conditions is far from Aristotle's vision of 'the most natural of economic forms.' Yet this chapter suggests that barter does also have internally generated characteristics, that these take a social form and consequently affect other social relations they become tangled with. In the conclusion, I summarise some suggestions as to what these social effects might be.

3 Conclusion

It is undoubtedly the case that without barter there would be widespread bankruptcies and mass unemployment, and this situation provides the general political – economic framework in which barter continues

---

[48] A farm director, for example, may have almost no 'connections', so he finds partners through newspaper advertisements or goes travelling almost at random in slightly richer areas looking for people with extra spare parts. Vice-Director of '*Dogo-Khudan*' peasant enterprise, Kizhinga District, Buriatiia.

[49] Head-engineer of '*Mayak*', Union of Peasant Holdings, Mukhor-Shibir District, Buriatiia.

(Woodruff 1999). This chapter has attempted to delineate the micro – social relations of barter that appear to be emerging within this overall situation.

1 The market mechanism is unfamiliar to Russians as a way of organising the economic fundaments of life (as opposed to petty trade) and barter as a type of market exchange arouses particular resentment by the way it seems to create 'non-equivalence' between partners. This is seen in (a) the non-parity of timing of returns, (b) differential 'liquidity' of goods as compared with earlier notions of value and (c) unequal distribution of the costs of onward barter. In a monetary world, transactors would be freer to choose new partners. But barter, because the non-coincidence of wants creates an enhanced requirement for credit and repeat transactions, tends to 'lock' participants into social relations of *dependency and patronage*.

2 There is a contrast in forms of trust between relations *within and between firms*. Despite the potential advantages in terms of reliability of doing deals with kin and friends, barter between firms is felt to be incompatible with true, multi-faceted friendship/kinship.

3 *Pricing is discriminatory*; at the same time, it is affected by the use of barter to avoid tax. These two conditions mean that bargaining encounters are ambivalent and confrontational on the one hand and complicit on the other.

4 The network effects of barter are not simple. Linear series provide few, if any, integrative effects. Star-shaped chains are dependent on the initiative of one firm. Circular chains encourage mutual reliance, but the 'political', extra-economic forces required to keep them in place also have other effects, such as dependency on patrons, and can result in *arbitrary dumpings and exclusions*.

5 Barter deals between firms affect *social relations within them*. Accepting a 'low' price for the enterprise's products may reflect an actual market price, but it may also be an excuse, a device to share profits with the entrepreneurial partner, while not even attempting to distribute income throughout the enterprise. The prevalence of such practices, which are clouded in secrecy, separates the interests of directors and workers. Workers do not know whether to believe the excuse ('there is no money') or to suspect that income is being concealed from them. In either case, the inclusion of wages in the barter calculations of an enterprise changes definitively the previous social relations between workers and managers. A similar change occurs when fees at schools, hospitals, etc. are paid in goods that are used for entrepreneurial trade rather than as payment for the service.

6 The coexistence of barter and money in Russia has had the effect of making the latter highly desirable while the former is not only cumbersome but regarded as backward. The point where barter and money meet (the 'end-deal') becomes a particularly pressurised encounter. The liquidity, transportability, etc. of money relative to any other good makes this moment the most vulnerable to default. At the same time, tax law encourages the concealment of incoming money. This, it seems, is why the 'end deal' is especially characterised by *shadowy deals, high-handed capriciousness and use of thugs to enforce payments.*

7 The involvement of government agencies in barter has divergent effects. On the one hand, agencies tend to solidify patronal arrangements by creating lasting barter institutions (like CC in Buriatiia). On the other, political infighting brings about haphazard changes and new edicts that intensify unpredictability and thus further undermine possibilities for creating *long-term trust.*

What does all this add up to in social terms? In the most general sense, barter encourages the *estimation of other people (and oneself) by goods.* Furthermore, it promotes the advantage of perceiving weaknesses in others, such as their lack of information, their inability to move, or their incapacitating ties. Because its transaction costs are so high and so various (assembly of goods, storage, transport, acquiring information, managing the timing of deals, etc.) as compared with money transactions, where one side at least does not have such costs, barter magnifies the positional inequalities between people. At the same time, the practice of quoting 'prices' in money objectifies and quantifies such disadvantages. Finally, because it takes place in face-to-face encounters, barter personalises all this, renders it experiential, causing feelings of affront and resentment.

For all Russia's cultural traditions of collectivism, there is no evidence from my materials that people now condemn self-interest as such. Even farmers, who are highly disadvantaged by the *nakrutki* (lit. squeezings) levied as manufactures wend their way to the countryside, recognise in a resigned way that traders must make their profits. The problem is that self-interest enacted through a barter system does not deliver a successfully functioning economy. Even though, in Russia as in Nepal, it could be said that barter is a means to reproduce an overall socio – economic organisation (producing at least something from the dinosaur industries, keeping at least some people in work, paying them with at least some things), the difference is that in Russia people see the current state of affairs as unsustainable in the long run and therefore see its prop, barter, as *inherently defective and probably temporary.* Consequently, Russian barter does not subordinate itself to general social morality, unlike in

Nepal. One important reason why 'non-equivalence' is seen as such a problem in Russia is that time horizons are so short; the likelihood that transactions will be repeated over a long time with the same partners is not thought strong enough to make it worth while developing a 'moral economy' inside barter itself (in Nepal, barter patterns are repeated over generations). The objective reasons for the Russian attitude are the rapid changes of government policy, inflation, unpredictable actions of politicians, and so forth. 'Squeeze your partner while you can,' is a quite rational response to this situation. I would suggest that, in conditions of general social mistrust, barter itself serves to *reinforce short-termism in a vicious circle*. The characteristic of money is that it can be used to defer wishes. Without money, people are delivered up to what is immediately there, the goods available. Without money people are cut off from the possibility of a universal intercourse: they are forced to have narrow interests.

So this chapter makes the case that whatever integration is provided by circular chains it exists at the expense of (1) wider economic disintegration and sclerosis – such chains exclude other enterprises and discourage flexibility – and (b) equivocal social relations at the micro level, in which pre-existing ties are seen in the light of temporary advantage. Barter is becoming a somewhat independent transactional – social mechanism, such that we can even talk of the 'barterisation' of society. Few if any, institutions are untouched by it. At the same time, it enters the imagination, so that even family and gender relations can be re-configured in its image.[50]

The entry of workers' wages into barter chains is particularly difficult to interpret. On the one hand, it could be argued that workers' reactions are coming to be part of the barter process – i.e. transforming the idea of labour or service into a barterable commodity. On the other hand, one might argue that since workers mostly do not take part in the wage negotiations and they receive nothing commensurable for their work, their labour becomes part of another realm, beyond barter and maintained by other rationalities (pride, habit, identity with one's profession, altruism . . .). In any case, it is clear that barter is overlaid on a substratum of many other social values and processes, such as attempts to produce

---

[50] For example, the male workers of the foundering *Lyuberetsk* Factory near Moscow said to a journalist: 'They should not have privatised factories; they should have privatised wives. We'd barter our factory shares for wives!' They were referring to the fact that in this region it is mostly men who have dead-end jobs in factories where they are paid in tins of chicken-liver paste, while some at least of their wives have better white-collar jobs in Moscow where they are paid in money. Wives, in the imagination, become negotiable economic assets (Chuprin and Gubanova, 1998).

something well for its own sake or attempts to govern well. Unfortunately, when these well-meaning impulses surface and people atttempt to activate them *through barter*, the inherent disutilities of barter (that is, barter as currently done in Russia) tend to create an impasse – as, for example, with the foundering of CC in Buriatiia which has the intention of supporting the farmers but instead ties them hands and feet.

References

Anderlini, L. and H. Sabourian (1992). 'Some Notes on the Economics of Barter, Money and Credit,' in C. Humphey and S. Hugh-Jones (eds.), *Barter, Exchange and Value: An Anthropological Approach*, Cambridge, Cambridge University Press, 75–156

Buriatiia, Ekonomika, 1996g. (1997). Survey published by the government of Buriatiia, Ulan-Ude, 1997

Chuprin, V. and K. A. Gubanova (1998). 'Otgrobleniye', *Moskovskii Komsomolets*, 24 June

Gaddy, C.G. and B.W. Barry (1998). 'Beyond a Bailout: Time to Face Reality about Russia's "Virtual Economy"' *Foreign Affairs*, 77

Humphrey, C. (1983). *Karl Marx Collective: Economy, Society and Religion in a Siberian Collective Farm*, Cambridge, Cambridge University Press

(1985). 'Barter and Economic Disintegration,' *Man*, ns 1, 48–72

(1999a). *Marx Went Away – But Karl Stayed Behind*, Ann Arbor, Michigan University Press

(1999b) 'Traders, "Disorder", and Citizenship Regimes in Provincial Russia,' in M. Burawoy and K. Verdery (eds.), *Uncertain Transition: Ethnographies of Change in the Post-socialist World*, Lanham, Boulder, New York and Oxford, Rowman & Littlefield

Ledeneva, A. and P. Seabright (1998). 'Barter in Post-Soviet Societies: What Does it Look Like and Why Does it Matter?', Chapter 4 in this volume

Makarov, V.L. and G.B. Kleiner (1996). *Barter v rossiskoi ekonomike: osobennosti i tendentsii perekhodnogo perioda*, Moscow, Tsentralhye ekonomiko-matematicheskii institut RAN

Mshcheryakov, A. (1996). 'Kollektivnyi portret sel'skogo uchitelya b otdel'no vzyatoi tochke postsovetskogo prostanstva: selo Tory, Tunkinskii raion, Buriatiia, iyul' 1995 goda', *Vestni Evrazii*, 1 (2), Moscow

Palmer, John P. and J. Vilis (1997). 'Money, Pseudo-money, and Inflation in Post-Soviet Lithuania,' *Cultural Dynamics*, 9 (2), 239–54

Pravda Buryatii (1998). 'Buriatiia sredi regionov rossii,' 14 August, 4

Ryabchenko, P. (1998). 'Talony vmesto deneg', *Nezavisimaya Gazeta*, ns, 13 October

Woodruff, D. (1999). 'The Barter of the Bankrupt', in M. Burawoy and K. Verdery (eds.), *Uncertain Transition: Ethnographies of Change in the Post-socialist World*, Lanham, Boulder, New York and Oxford, Rowman & Littlefield, 83–124

11 Shadow barter: economic necessity or economic crime?

ALENA LEDENEVA

1 Introduction

This chapter analyses barter practices in a micro perspective. It offers a graphic description of the technical aspects of barter chains, discusses possibilities of shadow production and assesses the transaction costs of tax evasion for a small provincial firm trading almost entirely in barter. Most importantly, the chapter illustrates the range of shadow practices deployed in barter operations–such as using double books and fake documents for defrauding tax authorities, 'laundering' cash in barter transactions, dealing with criminalised businesses, giving and receiving bribes, gifts, favours, etc. These practices seem logical under the circumstances, but look absurd in purely economic terms and are often criminal in purely legal terms.

The detailed ethnography presented below suggests that those exercising them often view these shadow practices in terms of economic necessity. At the same time, most of the shadow economy's activities qualify as economic fraud. A discourse of economic necessity, referring to everything from ineffective legislation to the inevitable pressures of the production cycle, leads to an acceptance of shadow practices, while the self-interested nature of such 'economic necessity' – an important factor supporting the existence of barter[1] – remains unnoticed. I will illustrate in detail how blurred the logic of necessity and the logic of personal interest have become, and how much both of them are tied to, merged with and mediated by, personal contacts.

Such micro-analysis adds a further dimension to the results of large-scale surveys of tax-paying firms, as it addresses deals and activities off the record – those routine practices which constitute the background of the Russian economy and block the organised attempts to transform it.

---

[1] On the policies of the Centrobank and the interest of enterprises in sustaining barter economy see Yakovlev (1999).

The pervasiveness of these routine practices helps to account for the scale of the shadow economy.

According to different sources, Russia's shadow economy probably produces up to 40 per cent of the GDP (Tret'yakov, 1998), while 50 per cent of all economic transactions take place in the shadows.[2] These figures, perhaps, would increase if all unregistered shadow deals of the barter economy were included.[3] What is even more difficult to assess, however, is the extent to which barter, tax evasion and other characteristic phenomena of the Russian economy today are provoked by recent economic policies and the extent to which they are simply new symptoms of an old disease traditional practices guided by exploitative attitudes towards the authoritarian state.[4]

Is barter just another form of parasitism adapted for making money and evading taxes, spreading from ex-state-owned industries to the private sectors? It is possible to argue that there is a vicious circle of inefficiency in the economic policies of the post-Soviet transformation caused by legacies from the past. These then mutate in the changing context and cause new policy initiatives, which in turn find themselves ineffective. It is therefore worth inquiring into the practices prevailing in a 'grey' zone, their dynamics and role in a barter economy. Below I will present a case study of the routines of a small provincial Russian firm working on the margins of the industrial sector.

The possibilities for such a study are limited, and extremely rare for outsiders. Even the firm's employees sometimes do not know (or prefer not to know) the complexities of barter transactions. Following the logic of barter chains is possible only through step-by-step 'decoding' by its designer - the director of the firm. It goes without saying that normally directors of firms consider their strategies and tactics as 'know-how' of their business, and the principle of non-sharing it as a condition of its success. I therefore appreciate and acknowledge the opportunity provided to me by the director of *Tekhcom*, who kindly agreed to share his methods of work in the conditions of a barter economy.[5]

[2] In 1996, 5,000 directors were sanctioned by the labour inspection for not paying wages in time. In St Petersburg, 43 out of 78 inspected enterprises and organisations had money on their accounts but didn't pay wages, *Argumenty i Fakty*, 27, (1996), p. 11.

[3] According to Grigorii Yavlinsky, a leading pro-western advocate of the market system, 75 per cent of the country's domestically produced goods in 1997 are traded in barter. See Steele (1998). In his 1999 World Economic Forum speech in Davos Yavlinsky quoted a figure of 85 per cent.

[4] On parasitism towards the Soviet state practices of its 'privatisation' by the people see Shlapentokh (1989). Also Ledeneva (2000b).

[5] Names of firms, enterprises, and cities are changed. All quotes below from the interviews with the director of *Tekhcom*.

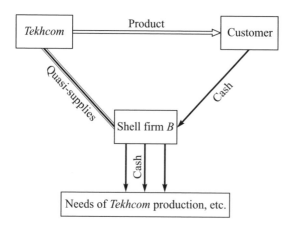

Figure 11.1 Hiding the income

Tekhcom is a firm that produces equipment for gas-oxygen metal cutting. It was founded in 1990 by a group of ex-employees of various defence industrial enterprises in Nsk. Like many small businesses, the firm has re-opened under different names in order to receive tax allowances for business start-ups or to avoid responsibility for tax evasion. The firm employs 15 people; originally all of them were co-owners, but later many dropped out. The turnover of the firm is not large, especially if judged by its bank account, which accounts for about 10 per cent of the actual turnover; 90 per cent takes place in barter. In order to protect the firm from draconian taxes, all main means of production have been taken off the balance sheet. The firm does not officially possess any technical equipment, a fax or Xerox machine.

If funds arrive at the *Tekhcom* bank account from a buyer, they are immediately paid to a shell firm which allegedly supplied the product to *Tekhcom*. It looks on paper as if *Tekhcom* is not a producer of this product but simply a distributor – an intermediary retail firm, receiving only a percentage for services (see figure 11.1).

In reality, revenue from production goes towards the needs of production. The adoption of these shadow forms is quite recent. Until 1994 *Tekhcom* paid taxes regularly and managed to pay its employees more than the state enterprises did. The real change occurred not when the taxes went up, but when *Tekhcom*'s customers – industrial enterprises – found themselves in the situation of liquidity squeeze.

2 Play on prices

Barter contracts in industry are notorious for distorting prices in order to reduce the taxable base. For a non-taxpayer, however, 'paper' prices also differ substantially from real ones. *Tekhcom* has two prices for its product: a barter price and a cash price, 348 and 279 roubles respectively. And, as they say 'both are worse'. Dealing in barter prices creates a problem at the stage of 'cashing' the barter currency. For example, *Tekhcom* is paid in kind with, say, flour which is priced at 100 roubles per sack. Its rouble price is 80 roubles per sack. According to the tax code, *Tekhcom* may not sell anything it has bought for less than its purchase price, which means that the flour may not be sold for less than 100 roubles. Otherwise, the 'loss tax'[6] makes the whole operation altogether useless. And of course it cannot sell flour at 100 if it is available at 80. As a result, 'cashing' takes place in the shadows and taxes are avoided altogether.[7]

Rouble prices would work for *Tekhcom*, but they are not acceptable for *Tekhcom*'s customers – mainly industrial enterprises, which are not in a position to pay roubles. They offer barter and mutual offsets in gas, electric energy, etc. which are in turn unacceptable for *Tekhcom*. The losses in cashing such barter – so-called 'discounts' – sometimes reach 50 per cent (see figure 11.5, p. 308), which makes small firms unable to work with their customers in a legal way. Understanding each other's problems and objective pressures leads to the possibility of semi-legal arrangements between partners (see, for example, figure 11.3, p. 304), which enables shadow practices to exist. In fact, these shadow practices can become so established such that one ends up running a whole production business in the shadows.

Shadow production

Let us consider the ways in which shadow production operates in scheme 2 (figure 11.2).

The economic activity of *Tekhcom* is carried out via two shell firms (*levye firmy*). These firms are not registered, nor do they exist. Strictly speaking, all that is used is letterhead and a fake stamp, or one left over from another firm which has since ceased to exist. Let's call these shell firms *A* and *B*. These firms are used as financial shields allowing *Tekhcom*

---

[6] The 'loss tax' (*nalog na ubytok*) is paid on the losses incurred by firms, owing to underpricing in barter contracts. To avoid backstage agreements between firms trying to evade taxes, sales at prices lower than accepted market rates (pubished nationally) are penalised.

[7] For details see Yakovlev (1988).

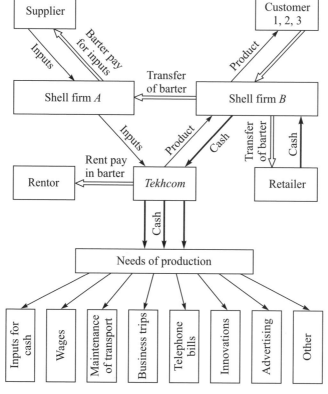

Figure 11.2 The principal scheme of shadow production

to avoid undesirable documented transactions. For example, shell firm *A* receives inputs from a supplier and forwards them to *Tekhcom* without documents. *Tekhcom* turns the inputs into products and signs a contract with the customer via shell firm *B*. The customer knows that the producer is *Tekhcom*, not *B*, but for them it looks like a simple shift-a-debt deal: the customer pays to *B*, because *Tekhcom* allegedly owes *B* something. On the record, it is shell-firm *B* that supplies the product and receives payment in kind. Further, shell-firm *B* transfers the goods to shell firm *A*, which then uses them to pay the supplier for inputs.

The rest is channelled to a retailer for sale. This transaction has to be properly documented. In order to do this, *Tekhcom* uses one of its shell firms and a passport – a real document, normally 'found' or stolen – which was given to *Tekhcom* 'as a present'. This passport is used as the document with which goods are handed over to a retailer (*sdany na realizatsiyu*) and cash is received. Tekhcom prepares a legal document authorising a person (in this case, a non-existing person, substituted by a passport) to act on behalf of the shell firm (also non-existent). Somebody from *Tekhcom* goes to a retailer, shows the authorisation and the passport, fills in the documents with details from the passport data, signs them and receives cash. Naturally, the person does not look like the photo in the passport, but this is rarely noticed. In the rare cases where it is noticed, the *Tekhcom* representative says that the employee concerned is on sick leave, that the money is required urgently, that there is no time for organising another certificate and so on. The cash goes to *Tekhcom*. This cash is spent on the purchase of special materials, which are used for finishing off the inputs acquired through barter. It also pays wages, business trips, telephone bills and the maintenance of transport, and covers expenses on innovations and advertising.

The production premises are rented from a large industrial enterprise. *Tekhcom* normally pays the rent in barter, providing its own product for the rentor's use. This transaction is on the record and *Tekhcom* does register it, but the product is registered as if it had been purchased from the shell-firm. The rent paid includes all other payments – electric energy, heating, etc.

Generally speaking, there are only a few 'legal' transactions – that is, ones registered in official documents – in this scheme, namely: rent, barter contracts with the supplier and the customer, and the transfer of goods for sale (see the double arrows in figure 11.2). All these transactions, however, are legal only 'on paper.' As for documentation, *Tekhcom* uses non-existent economic agents, whereas real economic agents either avoid appearing on paper altogether, or refrain from indicating real transactions or real numbers. Such practices partly explain why decrees and changes in economic legislation have so little direct influence on real economic processes in the shadow economy. For example, changes in the tax code may considerably influence the 'paper' level of transactions – different transactions may become documented in a different way – but they will not necessarily reach the level of the real agents of the shadow structures. Real agents always seem to find a way to cover themselves with yet another 'shell firm' or financial 'shield'.

Clearly, such methods will work only until an investigation by the tax police. But because of their fairly ubiquitous character, the chances of being caught are small unless there is a tip-off (*po navodke*) or unless the scale of operations becomes significant. This works according to an old Soviet principle of 'suspended punishment' (Ledeneva, 1988, pp. 77–9), by which certain freedom and flexibility did exist, but could be restricted at any moment. The strength of the unwritten codes coexisting with the

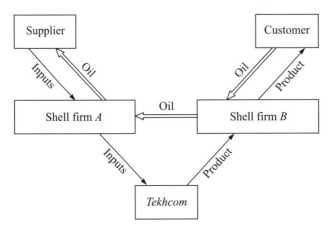

Figure 11.3 Give-and-take barter

formal ones, even in institutional contexts, brought about the routine practice for authorities to switch to the written code only 'where necessary' – often when the unwritten code was violated. A similar tendency is noticeable today, and apparently for the same reasons: first, it is not feasible to catch everybody; and, second, formal laws, codes and criteria are insufficient to operate on their own without the support of informal ones.

4 Dimensions of trust

Scheme 2 is the principal mode of organisation of shadow production. It is, however, crucial to see how the personal connections of the director and the reputation of the firm are invested. Let us consider a simplified version of Scheme 2, illustrating the barter chain designed to pay for inputs (see figure 11.3).

Tekhcom supplies its product via the shell firm to the customer in exchange for oil. The barter price of the product is 348 roubles per item. The costs of production amount to about 225 roubles, which includes the cost of inputs (100 roubles) plus the retail cost (125 roubles). The difference between the barter price and the actual costs is 123 roubles, which makes it possible to buy another 100 roubles worth of input. Thus, in order to pay the supplier for the inputs, *Tekhcom* delivers its products to the customer and converts them into oil, which goes back to the supplier as payment in kind. Note that every product in fact buys two inputs, which happens only because oil is quite a liquid barter currency and can be traded for cash.

Another point to note here is that the customer pays for *Tekhcom*'s product in kind to shell firm *B*. Shell firm *B* transfers the goods to shell firm *A*, so the payment to the supplier takes place on behalf of the shell firm. In a way, this is not surprising. It is a routine practice and a precondition of multilateral offset deals that the payment for the incoming goods goes in the direction advised by the payee. Such shift-a-debt deals, however, create a problem of trust. In one sense, it's a problem of *lack of trust* which is often solved informally through negotiations, personal guarantees or guarantees from partners and contacts. Quite an opposite problem arises from the profusion of trust between partners. For instance, both the supplier and the customer, big industrial firms and regular partners of *Tekhcom*, are aware of the actual order of things. As the director of *Tekhcom* confirms:

> On paper, it is shell firm *A*, not us, that is in debt for inputs. But the supplier knows me and knows that firm *A* is a set up. Nevertheless they understand us. Not for material interest, simply humanely . . .

Both aspects of the malfunctioning of trust relationships distort the ways in which business ethics should operate in open market competition. Many links of barter chains are built up on the direct involvement of the director, his skills to create and maintain contacts, as well as his ability to keep his 'word'. The ways in which personal relations are in-built into the production cycle are clear from the above. Let us now consider a particularly complex barter chain in which the role of informal negotiating and personal involvement is even more conspicuous.

5 Personal connections in barter chains

As we considered the basic scheme serving the production cycle (the supplier – *Tekhcom* – the customer) above, we shall focus on supplementary links here (see figure 11.4).

The starting point for the construction of a chain is a demand for *Tekhcom*'s production. The demands of other participants in the chain come into play as a direct result. As there is demand for its product, *Tekhcom* asks the supplier to deliver inputs. The supplier promises to deliver on the condition that *Tekhcom* pays in roofing. The director of *Tekhcom* finds a supplier for the supplier, who produces roofing and needs *Tekhcom*'s product, and asks him to supply the roofing in exchange for his 'word' that it will be repaid in three months. Thus, with no working capital at the start, *Tekhcom* arranges for the roofing to be delivered by the supplier's supplier to *Tekhcom* and then to be transferred to the supplier in exchange for inputs.

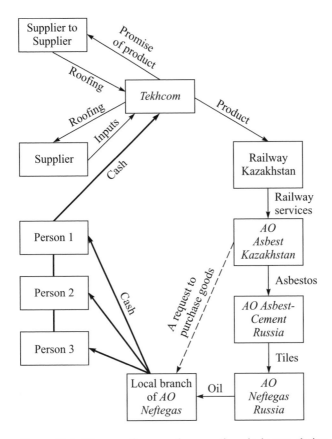

Figure 11.4 The use of personal connections in barter chains

The customer of *Tekhcom* in this chain is the Kazakh Railway. A good contact of *Tekhcom* – Kazakh firm *Asbest*, which extracts asbestos for tile production – is in debt to Kazakh Railway for railway services. *AO Asbest* supplies asbestos to a Russian firm *Asbest-Cement* which produces tiles. The director of *Tekhcom* arranges that the construction department of *AO Neftegas* takes the tiles. Further:

In order to avoid taxes I have to receive cash from *Neftegas*. We have a local branch of *Neftegas* in our town. They say, 'personal contacts are the key to success', and that's precisely what I've got in the local branch of *Neftegas*. I insist that *Neftegas* authorises its local branch to pay for the tiles. In fact, *Neftegas* supplies oil-products to its local branch and asks it to make the payment to us. To be fair, we allow the local branch to 'work' the cash for a couple of months, and only receive it after that.

For the record, a Kazakh firm *Asbest* sends a written request to the local branch of *Neftegas*, asking it to purchase some consumables in exchange for the tiles supplied to *Neftegas*. The local branch pays cash to certain individuals, allegedly for purchasing the consumables. In reality these people give this money to *Tekhcom*, which then starts paying its debts.

The complication in this scheme was the lack of working capital, but it was settled by the involvement of eight enterprises. The cycle took approximately four months. The product cost 189 roubles per item, and sold at 289 roubles. Expenses for business trips, telephone calls, etc. were higher than average, but no taxes were paid.

This chain is conspicuously based on personal relations. Because of personal contacts, *Asbest-Cement* shipped seven carriages of tiles without payment, which was crucial in enabling *Neftegas* to complete the repair work before winter. Trying to satisfy the needs of the others pays off quite well, which would perhaps be true even without personal contacts. Where personal contacts make all the difference, however, is at the stage of 'cashing' the barter currencies. As a rule, such contacts are 'good old' ones, and it is those contacts into which all shadow chains get 'locked' in the final analysis. It is important, therefore, to distinguish between the main and supplementary links in the chain, not only in terms of their functions for the production cycle, but also in terms of their functions for extracting cash out of the barter transaction. The logic of production necessity – which is usually put forward and emphasised by the firm directors – is normally combined with the logic of personal profit – which is stressed by the press.

Apart from complex schemes, personal contacts are crucial in problematic situations. For example, in this transaction a problem arose half a year later. The tax inspectorate checked the local branch of *Neftegas*, realised that substantial sums of money were paid to individuals without tax, and started looking for those individuals. Basically, it was an accountant's mistake. But in such a situation, this not the concern of the *Neftegas* branch, it is the concern of the director of *Tekhcom*. And it is up to him 'to solve the problem' (*reshat' voprosy*). He 'solved' it through a contact in the local tax inspectorate:

I thought I could solve it in *Asbest* and went to Kazakhstan, but there we realised it couldn't be done. It turned out it had to be solved in a local tax inspectorate. I had a contact there so I could try to get the problem solved, but it was late Friday afternoon. I was told to wait until Monday and I stayed with this problem over the weekend. Well, the problem ended up being solved eventually ... we of course paid for all these services with valuable presents. Now it's over, the transaction is completed and the branch has actually been closed.

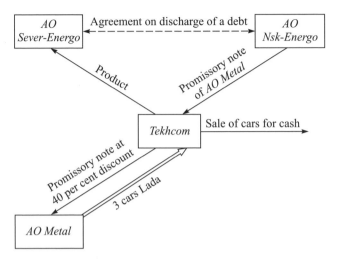

Figure 11.5 The use of mutual offsets in barter chains

6 Mutual offsets

Let us now consider a scheme with mutual offsets which *Tekhcom* used in 1997 (see figure 11.5).

AO 'Sever-Energo' requires *Tekhcom*'s product. They offer to pay by supplying electricity. Electricity is a not an easy currency; it involves large discounts. But because the director has contacts in *Nsk-Energo*, he decides to give it a try.

According to the contract, *Tekhcom* delivers its product to *AO Sever-Energo*. *Nsk-Energo* was a debtor of *Sever-Energo*, and between them there is a discharge of a debt for the sum of the contract. *Nsk-Energo* in turn pays *Tekhcom* with a 150,000 rouble promissory note (*veksel'*) from *AO Metal*; *Tekhcom* delivers its product worth 150,000. This promissory note is meant to be returned to *AO Metal* in exchange for three Ladas (*AO Metal* is a supplier of *VAZ*, and has cars in exchange for metal). *Tekhcom* plans to sell the three cars and receive about 100,000 in cash. A loss, therefore, is planned at the level of 30 per cent.

When we went to *AO Metal*, though, we realised that we were losing not 30 per cent, but 40 per cent. It turned out that *Metal* issues a promissory note, but when it comes back they pay only 90 per cent of its nominal. They make their profit that way (apart from putting the Ladas' price up as well).

This transaction took two and a half months. The estimated cost of *Tekhcom*'s product is 225 roubles, which includes the costs of 'realisation' (large contracts bring the costs down as savings are made on business trips,

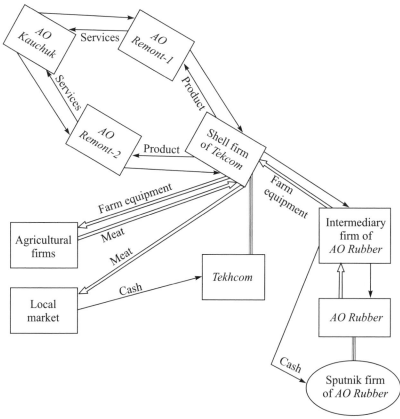

Figure 11.6 Criminal aspects of barter

telephone calls, etc.). This time, the product was sold for 208 roubles, which is low, but within acceptable limits. The main defect of the scheme is that the contracts were signed by *Tekhcom* itself, rather than by a shell firm, which makes it risky. There could be problems with tax inspection. Apart from the risk, *Tekhcom* lost more than planned, and suffered the fact that it had to re-negotiate the discounts with *Metal* and to sell the cars. There are, however, even more unfortunate schemes which are hampered by 'inconvenient' barter currencies, the long cycle and more serious financial risks. Let us consider one such complicated scheme in detail.

'Inconvenient' barter

AO Kauchuk produces latex – a raw material for technical rubber products. Firms *Remont 1* and *2* provide repair services (see figure 11.6).

They previously supplied *AO Kauchuk*; it owes them for the repairs. Firms *Remont 1* and *2* use *Tekhcom*'s product for their activities, and *Tekhcom* supplies its product to them via a shell firm.

The scheme didn't look safe from the very beginning. We had a preliminary agreement with an intermediary firm of the rubber plant that they would pay us with cars if we delivered latex. But as they say now, they wanted to 'let us down' (*kinut'*), they wouldn't have delivered the cars or anything else. We were forced to 'intervene'. We took precisely what they owed us, rouble for rouble, but we had to settle for not quite what we wanted.

Tekhcom receives the latex via a shell firm. The latex goes straight (without being delivered to *Tekhcom*) to the intermediary firm of the rubber plant. Instead of the promised cars, *Tekhcom* is forced to take the product of the rubber plant, which consists of equipment for milking cows. *Tekhcom* has never worked with a product like this. Although the equipment for milking cows was not necessarily the most unpopular of all barter currencies, the lack of experience, reliable channels of distribution, contacts in the countryside, and the lack of any reason for *Tekhcom* developing this dimension of its activities results in the transaction taking an entire year.

We tried to get rid of it (*pristroit'*) somehow. First, we found out which farms produce milk and went on a tour across the area. We found partners and supplied the equipment in exchange for meat. According to the contract, meat was sent off to the shell firm. Our employees took part of it as salary, the rest we sold to a meat-processing firm for cash. In the end we got our money back: the realisation price was 261 roubles, as compared with the 225-rouble cost, but the transaction lasted a year.

An aspect which should be noticed here is *Tekhcom*'s 'intervention' with an intermediary firm of the rubber plant, which means an encounter with a so-called criminalised business.

8 Criminal aspects of barter: intermediaries and set ups (*kidaly*)[8]

It is already clear from the above descriptions of shadow barter practices that there are quite a lot of dimensions of shadow and illegal activities: (1) tax evasion; (2) circumvention of customs procedures; (3) use of fake documents; (4) signing fake contracts (that is, dealing with non-existent partners); (5) settling fights with partners and sorting out the setups (*utryaska, razborka,* etc); (6) presents and payment for the service of 'solving problems'. These practices are widespread and well known

---

[8] See Ledeneva (1999).

(though perhaps not that well documented). Here I would like to draw attention to aspects which are part of figure 11.6, but not directly connected with *Tekhcom*'s activities – namely the role of subsidiary firms and retail firms.

Let us start with the nature of intermediation. The functional role of *Tekhcom*'s shell firms as financial shields from tax and other kinds of inspections is sufficiently transparent. The rubber plant, a big enterprise and a taxpayer, also has an intermediary firm, even two of them. What are their functions and how do they differ between themselves? Why, for example, wouldn't the rubber plant buy latex directly but allow supplies to go through intermediaries?

Of course, the rubber plant works with *AO Kauchuk* directly, but... First, this plant, as well as many others, has a satellite-firm ('*svoya' firmochka*) headed by the son of a deputy director for supplies of the rubber plant. Second, there exists an intermediary firm, engaged in criminalised business (they deal with alcohol), which is headed by a friend of the son of a deputy director of the rubber plant.

The intermediary firm in this case belongs to a network of criminal organisations and receives percentages, dividends, etc.

When we [*Tekhcom*] contacted the rubber plant directly and offered our latex, they said they had enough of it. They said they didn't need latex, although it's their main input. Then guys from the intermediary firm told us: 'Don't try the plant, and don't try the satellite-firm! You should give your latex to us and we'll pay you in kind at the plant's prices.' They gave us the plant's product – the rubber parts for the milking machines – close to the plant's prices. Their profit came not from us, but from the plant itself, as they sold the latex to the plant at a higher price. The plant bought latex at that rate because the intermediary firm, once the plant paid higher prices, shared the profits with the satellite firm of the plant and with criminal structures. Thus, the plant pays more so that it can share the profit from the transaction in that particular way.

The logic behind such a transaction from the standpoint of the plant is hardly straightforward. Rather, it looks as if the deputy director for supplies is guided by considerations of personal profit or the personal security of his son.[9] The logic of profitability is often combined with or

---

[9] It should be noted that not only criminal structures but also legal enterprises evade taxes. Beginning in 1995, the *Vologda* Bearings Plant (*VBP*)–a closed-type jointstock company– stopped sending taxes and other mandatory payments to the budget on time. The city's largest and most stable enterprise that year found itself in arrears and declared losses. It turned out that these 'difficulties' existed only for ordinary workers, whose pay was regularly delayed, and for the state, which is unable to get the taxes that the *VBP* legally owes it. At the same time, the enterprise had been bled white by the multitude of middlemen that were sucking out its output and finance like leeches. The *VBP* fed about 40 of such firms. Their founders and executives are a very small group of people

disguised by the logic of necessity. A typical situation presented in terms of necessity is when an enterprise with a special 'tax debtor's account' (*schet nedoimshchika*)[10] creates a satellite firm for managing finances and conducting economic transactions. Cash claimed to be unavailable is easily found in transactions between an enterprise and its subsidiary firm, whether it is a shell firm, a satellite firm, or an intermediary. The financial flow are as follows:

1 Shell firms transfer cash to real firms
2 Satellite firms receive cash from real firms through intermediaries
3 In the case of intermediaries, cash flows are most difficult to trace, as they benefit not only the enterprise and an intermediary firm, but other shadow participants of the situation as well.

In the example with latex and farm equipment (figure 11.6), the rubber plant pays the intermediary for latex in kind. Part of this equipment is given to *Tekhcom* in payment for the latex and part of it is 'cashed'. This normally happens through the dairy enterprises, which can use the rubber equipment for milking machines to pay for milk delivered by the farm and to pay back with butter, a perfectly 'cashable' commodity. Part of the cash received from the retailer will go to a satellite firm. Part of it, as it was already suggested above, will pay 'protection charges'.

Within this framework formed by the interests of firms' administrations, on the one hand, and criminalised structures, on the other, it is hard to expect the workings of market mechanisms to be effective. Instead of market mechanisms, situations are regulated by intermediaries, apparently related neither to the firm's management nor to criminal organisations, but in fact linked to both. This accounts to a large extent for the non-market nature of the Russian 'market'. Here is how the director of *Tekhcom* described the actions of intermediaries:

These guys warned us not to approach anybody but the deputy director in charge of supplies (who said the plant did not need our latex). They said we were going to have problems if we did. And we know that we might, as these guys are under a

composed, as a rule, of the company's top executives themselves, their relatives, or 'stand-ins' picked from the most trusted employees. In 1995, about 20 per cent of its output were sold through the *VBP-Market* limited liability partnership, headed by the general director of the *VBP* himself. In the first half of 1996, the plant, which employs 10,000 people, suffered losses of 41,789 billion roubles, while its middleman firm, with a staff of just seven people, made profit of 21,402 billion roubles. The firm buys bearings from the plant at a price below the break-even selling prices and resells them to the plant's regular clients at triple that price. The *VBP-Market* limited partnetship's return on capital was 10,000 per cent! For details see Filippov (1997).

[10] See Hendley, Ickes and Ryterman (1998). Also Tompson (1997), p. 1166.

'roof'.[11] They also deal with alcohol, which is a bad sign. This is a criminalised business for sure.

To summarise, there are at least three types of subsidiary firms: shell firms, satellite firms and intermediary firms, each of which has more or less specific functions for operating in the shadows.

Now, let us consider the role of retailers – the agents through whom the cashing of barter currencies takes place. The space where this 'cashing' occurs is called the 'market', but it is crucial to remember that a place in this market is not available for every retailer.

We can get in (*popast'*) the market. I have an old friend working in the militia. He supervises street trade and the *kolkhoz* market. The deputy director of the central *kolkhoz* market is a girl I know from my student years. We could actually get in, but there are lots of other problems there. It is less trouble to sell our meat to a sausage production firm. Let it be cheaper, but without headaches.

The headache and other problems mentioned above also refer to the fact that most of the markets are controlled by criminal structures, which also significantly limits the freedom of economic agents.

9 'Cashing' chains

As has been mentioned already, every barter chain has its key links. The link responsible for 'cashing' the barter currency is of vital importance. Apart from absolutely liquid commodities, such as alcohol or petrol, there are unexpected sources of cash generated by an overall indebtedness spread across all levels of society. For example, payment for housing and for indebtedness for housing resulting from wage arrears is one such source. Let us consider the scheme of mutual offsets in the housing sector as a way of 'cashing' (see figure 11.7).

The barter chain includes *Tekhcom*, its shell firm, the water and/or heating companies, local housing departments and households. Local housing departments, in charge of the housing, owe the water and heating companies for heating and water services. *Tekhcom* finds 15, 20 or 30 people who are in arrears on their apartments. Both the water and heating companies require *Tekhcom*'s product. The contract includes the delivery of *Tekhcom*'s product in exchange for the discharge of indebtedness for apartments of the people listed along with their address, corresponding housing department and a sum of indebtedness. The total amount of this contract can reach the significant sum of 30–40,000 roubles.

[11] See Bäckman (2000), pp. 263–8 and Volkov (2000), p. 55.

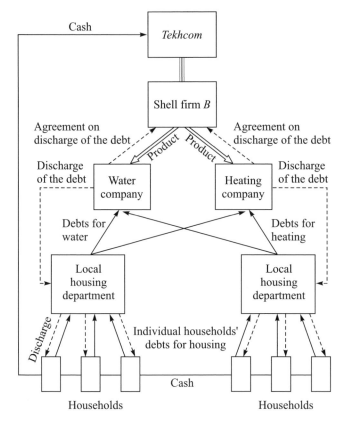

Figure 11.7 'Cashing' the barter: housing sector

There is a young employee in *Tekhcom* who is constantly in charge of finding people in arrears. This way *Tekhcom* pays the housing dues for all employees and acquaintances. People are interested in this because *Tekhcom* pays the indebtedness for three months, while it charges people only for two. According to the barter contract with the water company, *Tekhcom*'s product costs 348 roubles, while in cash it costs 250 roubles. The difference means that people get one month free.

We trust these people because we have known them for a long time. Almost all of them are our acquaintances. We can even wait – provide a three-month credit, as it were. As we work permanently on this, some cash always comes back. Some people pay straight away, some people ask to wait. As we give a whole month's discount, people do appreciate it and pay.

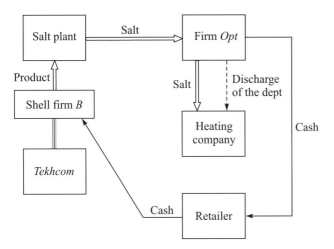

Figure 11.8 'Cashing' the barter: salt

We give them a copy of the mutual offset contract, by which their debt is paid by our shell firm. For tax inspection these deals are of no interest, they won't even check on less than 100,000 roubles. In principle, such mutual offsets are allowed. It's useful for people like us, especially in cases of long-term indebtedness. As we offer 30 per cent-off conditions, people can pay for nine months, rather than for the whole year.

Finally, there is another working scheme of 'cashing' barter (see figure 11.8).

The salt plant has a demand for *Tekhcom*'s product for 35,000 roubles. Salt is quite a liquid currency (it is used for icy roads and in central heating systems). *Tekhcom* finds (through personal channels) a firm *Opt* owing something to the heating company,[12] which uses salt. Thus, *Tekhcom* supplies its product to the salt plant via shell firm *B*; salt is delivered to the heating company in order to discharge *Opt*'s debt. *Opt*, which therefore becomes the debtor of a shell firm, according to the request of the latter, transfers cash to the retailer, who has a right to pay cash to the shell firm without it appearing in the bank accounts. The payment for such a service is to leave cash with a retailer for a month and a half ('*pokrutit' den'gi*'). In a month and a half, cash arrives to the shell firm and the cycle is completed. This transaction took about two months altogether, with the norm being about three.

---

[12] On the schemes of debt offsets in the *Fuel–Energy Complex* (*TPK*) see Galiev and Lysova (1999).

There are sanctions for prolonging a barter transaction beyond the period of three months. The distributors receive a 10 per cent bonus for the barter goods sold in the first month, a 7 per cent bonus if it is more than a month, 5 per cent if more than two months, 2 per cent if the product is sold in three months or so, and no bonus at all after four months. As a result, *Tekhcom*'s distributors try to trade for goods in demand; they know the market, prices, etc. It's worth mentioning that this small business firm has an 'old Soviet' style. The director started from a workshop and reached the position of deputy chief-director of a big industrial enterprise. *Tekhcom*'s activities are based on his experience in the organisation of production, organisational skills and good personal contacts. He is very ambitious about his product and is proud of it, as it was invented and patented with his help. He is driven by the dream of making every enterprise work with his equipment and respect and recognise his work. Yet he greatly resents the fact that his entrepreneurial skills and energy are wasted in such activities as tax evasion and anxiety about the future:

I am so fed up with it. It's bad for my sleep. I'd like to work normally. Instead I keep thinking that I have to formally divorce my wife and transfer all the property to her, to prepare a speech for the court that in fact we've been doing a great job...

It would seem that a younger generation of businessmen ought to be operating according to more market-oriented and straightforward business ethics. But unfortunately, the economic logic of Russian conditions imposes something different. The younger generation deals more in the shadows rather than less. Younger entrepreneurs have skills making it easier for them to evade taxes and customs duties, to master the practice of arranging the formal side of transactions ('on paper') and of 'solving problems' or paying for services. Paradoxically, such informal skills and activities are both the consequence of the inefficiency of the market mechanism in Russia, and contribute to its perpetuation. On the one hand, grounded in Russian culture and tradition, informal practices stretch across time and introduce into the economy forms of reciprocity[13] that inhibit the development of the market. On the other hand, these practices adapt to present-day economic concerns and become oriented towards the problems of an economy undergoing 'market' reforms.[14] Similar to the way in which the functioning of the informal economy sustained but also subverted the Soviet planned economy, Russia's shadow

---

[13] Polanyi distinguishes three basic systems of economic organisation: alongside the 'reciprocity' system, based on gift, there is a 'market' system, subject to the laws of classical economics and the 'distribution' system. See Polanyi (1994).

[14] See Ledeneva for details (2000a).

economy today contributes to but also impedes its marketisation. The 'vicious circle' of shadow practices, reproducing themselves in such an ambivalent relation to the economy, provides a clue to understanding the non-market nature of the Russian 'market'.

References

Bäckman, J. (2000). 'The Hyperbola of Russia Crime and The Police Culture', in A. Ledeneva and M. Kurchiyan (eds.), *Economic Crime in Russia*, Dordrecht, Kluwer, Law International, pp. 267–8

Filippov, V. (1997). 'How Taxes are Evaded in the Russian Provinces,' *Izvestia*, 25 February, 2

Galiev, A. and T. Lysova (1999). 'Ego velichestvo zachet,' *Ekspert*, 3, 25 January, 34

Hendley, K., B. Ickes and R. Ryterman (1998). 'Remonetizing the Russian Economy', chapter 3, see <www.kings/histecon/barter>; also in H.G. Broadman (ed.), *Russian Enterprise Reform: Policies to Further the Transition*, Washington, DC, World Bank, November

Latynina, J. (1999). 'Zapiski iz podpol'ya.' *Ekspert*, 3, 31–33

Ledeneva, A. (1998). *Russia's Economy of Favours: Blat, Networking and Informal Exchange*, Cambridge, Cambridge University Press

(2000a). 'The *Blat* Roots of Corruption: Continuity and Change of Corrupt Practices in Russia', in S. Lovell, A. Ledeneva and A. Rogatchevsky (eds.), *Bribery and Blat in Russia: Negotiating Reciprocity from the Middle Ages to the 1990s*, London, Macmillan

(2000b). 'The Subversion of Democracy in Russia: An Informal Practice Perspective', in S. Harter (ed.), *Shaping the Economic Space in Russia*, Aldershot, Ashgate

Polanyi, K. (1944). *The Great Transformation*, Boston; Beacon Press

Shlapentokh, V. (1989). *Public and Private Life of the Soviet People: Changing Values in Post-Soviet Russia*, Oxford, Oxford University Press

Steele, J. (1998). 'Blatting Order,' *Guardian*, 8 August, 16

Tompson, W. (1997). 'Old Habits Die Hard: Fiscal Imperatives, State Regulation and the Role of Russia's Banks,' *Europe – Asia Studies*, 49 (7), 1159–85

Tret'yakov, Y. (1998). 'Trudno naiti "tenevye den'gi" v temnoi komnate,' *Novaya Gazeta*, 16, 27 April–3 May, 7

Volkov, V. (2000). 'Organised Violence, Market-building and State Formation in Post-Communist Russia', in A. Ledeneva and M. Kurchiyan (eds.), Economic Crime in Russia, Dordrecht, Kluwer Law International, p. 55

Yakovlev, A. (1998). 'Black Cash Tax Evasion in Russia: Its Forms, Incentives and Consequences at Firm Level', paper for the IPSSA project 'Informal sector in the Russia Economy: Forms of Existence, the Role and Scale' (led by Tatyana Dolgopyatova), Moscow, spring

(1999). 'Anatomiya bezdenezh'ya, *Ekspert*, 3, 25 January, 27–30

12 Surrogate currencies and the 'wild market' in central Siberia

DAVID G. ANDERSON

1 Introduction

Caroline Humphrey's research on rural and industrial barter in Buriatiia (1991, 1998) and Nepal (1985, 1992) has alerted the attention of economists, sociologists, and anthropologists to the persistence of an economic form often thought to be cumbersome, simple and primitive. In contrast to the orthodox assumption that barter 'naturally' gives way to monetarised exchange owing to reduced 'transaction costs' and the 'comparative advantage' of a wider division of labour, Humphrey's work demonstrates that in many social contexts monetary exchange can be risky and most significantly may compromise local networks of mutual aid and solidarity. Perhaps it is not surprising that barter is flourishing in that region of the world where local forms of tenure and economic practice have been under sustained attack first by the administrative tools of state socialism, and now through the austerity measures imposed by international monetary bureaucracies. This chapter presents ethnographic data on 'surrogate' forms of monetary exchange gathered during the Russian financial crisis of the autumn of 1998 in two neighbouring regions of central Siberia: the Evenki Autonomous District and the Republic of Khakasiia. The data, although gathered during a particularly sharp moment in the history of Russian monetary instruments, are broadly illustrative of the flexibility of form that Russian financial operations can take and moreover clearly expose the nature of the social relations which lie behind paper commodity transfers of wealth. The financial crisis of 1998, sparked when the central government froze the savings accounts of citizens while simultaneously allowing the rouble exchange rate to crash, led to the immediate minting of many forms of locally meaningful currency surrogates often adjudicated by regional government administrations. It will be suggested that money-like transactions such as 'mutual debit chains' or the Khakasiian 'offset-coupon' bear much more in common with the 'old' state socialist economy than they do with 'wild' capitalism; and thus represent both a regional case of resistance and an example of the robustness of this social form.

Siberia, or indeed any fragment of rural Russia, provides an excellent laboratory for investigating informal exchange. In direct contrast to the highly commoditised financial climate of Moscow, since 1995 most of rural Russia has been subsisting on locally harvested produce, unpaid mutual favours and various forms of extended credit which compensate for the fact that many people have not seen monetary salaries for years. The concentration of monetary resources in the capital has little to do with the fact that a large proportion of values are produced there. Instead, the various persisting fragments of the Soviet redistributive state, such as the Ministry of Finance, the Tax Inspection Service and the Pension Fund, have successfully managed both to rake in monetary wealth from the regions and to capture large international capital transfers to the city. Although the autumn financial crisis of 1998 generated long lines of angry clients in branch banks across the city of Moscow, most Siberians watched the spectacle on television with bemusement (since most had no ready cash invested in banks) and concern (since this Moscow-triggered crisis inevitably implied that the prices of imported goods would rise). Most Siberians shared the simple comfort of knowing that while they may not live well without a banking system, at least they were much better at surviving than their Muscovite counterparts.

The two regions chosen for this chapter have little directly in common with each other economically, ecologically, or even ethnically. However the differences between them are analytically useful. In terms of similarities, both national enclaves at one time unambiguously belonged to the large federal territory known as *Krasnoiarskii Krai*, and thus were born of similar political and economic pressures. Artefacts of the heady period of the late 1920s, both enclaves represent attempts by the Soviet state to give political and territorial recognition to two 'nations' which had played an important and loyal role in the civil war. Following the rush of independence movements in 1992, the Khakas Autonomous Province (*oblast'*) made a successful bid to become a republic, gaining the right to administer its own state-like institutions. In 1997, after two years of political struggle, the Evenki Autonomous District (*okrug*) and its sister district to the north, Taimyr, surrendered their attempts also to become republics. They signed a federative agreement leaving them as independent 'subjects' of Russia but with the right to sign particular power and resource-sharing agreements with Krasnoiarsk. The different fates of these two enclaves reflects great economic, demographic and ecological differences between the two regions. Khakasiia is a highly industrialised republic based in the arid foothills to the Sayan and Altai mountains. It has a large immigrant Russian population and several large enterprises engaged in generating hydro-electric power, producing aluminium and mining coal and gold. Evenkiia is a sparsely populated sub-Arctic district with a small, but significant, Russian population and no developed industry. Khakasiia is a net donor to the tax coffers of the Russian state while Evenkiia is dependent on direct transfer payments from the centre. The differing financial conditions of the two enclaves in part determine the complexity of the forms of non-monetary exchange used. However, what is fascinating is that in both examples, rural and industrial, paper forms of barter perform a significant, if not leading role, in the economy.

2 Debt prospecting and mutual debit arrangement in Evenkiia

The Russian Arctic and sub-Arctic provide some of the most extreme examples of the types of informal exchange common throughout Russia in the 1990s. On the gentler side of this phenomena, it is not uncommon to hear stories from the more remote outposts of Taimyr or Evenkiia of rural herders who have been so severed from the industrial division of labour that the last paper money they had physically touched had featured portraits of Lenin. During the last two monetary revaluations of 1993 and 1997, they have quietly traded their furs and meat at the single store in a community for food, clothing, and vodka on a simple 'credit list' or *spiska*. On the harsher side of this situation, since 1997 entire northern settlements of Russian miners or military personnel find themselves on the verge of freezing to death or starving owing to the fact that local authorities find it increasingly difficult to marshal bank credits in order to import much-needed fuel and food from the southern regions of Russia during the short navigational season.

For many readers the image of the stoic reindeer herder turning to barter for consumption goods may seem to be appropriate for a profession that to many sounds 'primitive'. In actual fact from the local point of view, both images speak to the depth of the 'crisis'. Unlike in other parts of the circumpolar Arctic, Siberian rural producers were fully integrated into an industrial mode of fur harvesting and reindeer herding which depended heavily on expensive inputs such as helicopter transport, subsidised delivery prices, expensive built structures and imported medicines. The difference between an Evenki reindeer brigadier bargaining a bull reindeer for an 80-litre barrel of fuel, and an outlying Russian military post dismantling disused structures in order to burn them for heat, is in fact a difference of technique (and a difference of ethnicity) rather than a difference in kind (see also chapter 13 in this volume). In both cases, these state servants have in fact been orphaned by a larger economical and constitutional framework which has turned its resources inwards to service urban workers in the central regions.

The sub-Arctic Siberian data are not only valuable for the fact that they portray a dramatic example of how social autonomy (and the bartering skills that this implies) can be forced upon a community; they also present a valuable picture of developments over time. The Russian press began widely reporting instances of inter-enterprise barter and the difficulties caused by unfulfilled payrolls around 1995 – approximately four or five years after this phenomena appeared in the far North. In the autumn of 1998, when Evenki District accountants gave up hope of soon receiving the eight-month overdue transfer payment from the Ministry of Finance in Moscow, they simply carried on with chains of mutual debit and the bartered exchange of consumer goods which had already been well rehearsed for nearly a decade.

The primary economic activity in the Evenki Autonomous District today is the equitable management of overdue accounts. The vast majority of the economic institutions are still in various form of direct government ownership. Most Russians work directly for the state as educators, administrators, transport personnel, or as members of the various law enforcement institutions. The majority of the indigenous population (83 per cent) is officially unemployed but associated with a complex collage of state farms, clan 'communes' (*obshchiny*), or farm enterprises. The planned expenditures for the district administration in 1998 was 360,000 million (new) roubles (360 billion old roubles), of which 49 million roubles were supplied in locally accrued tax revenue and 70 million roubles were expected in an overdue transfer payment from Moscow. Although I was told by the chief economist of the district that the balance of approximately 240 million roubles was taken on 'credit', I soon learned to be cautious of this dramatic figure for two reasons. First, the term 'credit' referred to a variety of mutual exchange arrangements which ranged from classical barter (wild caribou meat for fuel) to mutual debit arrangements (tax relief for commodities; or transport services for commodities). Second, in a universe where 'living money' (*zhivie den'gi*) accounted for only one-third of the officially registered transactions, the rouble value of the goods and services in the remaining two-thirds tended to have only a vague relationship to the cost of transactions in the 'living' world and were often exaggerated by an order of magnitude. This phenomena seems to be a common budgetary manoeuvre across Russia which allows each component department of the administration to position itself to make claims on actually performed services. The large

budget deficit clears a large social space for debt-prospecting. By searching out and specifying unreciprocated transactions, departments with
large budgetary 'limits' (*limity*) gain preferential rights to order defaulters
to deliver future services. Since almost all enterprises fall into the category of 'defaulters', this is indeed a powerful privilege. Thus, through
various forms of 'credit', the value of the roughly 120 million 'living'
roubles flowing in the regional economy is stretched through local circuits
of recirculation. One might claim that once Russian roubles enter the
Evenki lifeworld, they live more than one 'life'.

Although the Evenki District sports many examples of classical barter,
I am interested here in exploring a commodified form of barter which has
become more and more common in the past few years. One of the primary ways of extending the life of a single rouble is through the widely
used practice of 'mutual debit' accounting (*vzaimozachet; zachet vzaimnoi
zadolzhennosti*). Although this style of transaction is one step more
abstract than classical barter (wherein one object is exchanged for another
in a locally meaningful universe of value), it nevertheless bears more
similarity to a barter transaction than it does to commodity exchange.
In a mutual debit operation, as one recently published accounting manual
explains, two corporate entities (*litsa*) independently extinguish a demand
of one upon the other through a mutually agreed-upon action (which in
some cases may involve the payment of money) (Bryzgalin et al., 1998,
p. 6). The hallmark of a mutual debit operation is to allow monetary
debts to be settled locally rather than through distant intermediary institutions, although state currency numeraires are formally employed. The
classic formula is the 'mutual debit triangle'. If, for example, a local air
transportation company owes the local government authority an amount
of money in unemployment insurance contributions, these taxes can
be extinguished through a third party. If the local authority then owes
village nurses an obligatory return ticket to the major centre as part of
their contract, the airline might provide the transport to the local health
units directly (thus saving all parties time and transaction costs). In more
complex instances, the company may offer to use its own fuel and aircraft
to ship supplies for the health department 'free' of charge. This triangle
often becomes somewhat frayed at the edges as more and more partners
get involved. Thus, to continue with the example at hand, the transport
company may in fact supply the hospital cafeteria with meat, transported
free of charge, which it has received from a collective farm in payment for
surplus petrol siphoned from the helicopter tank during a chance landing
in a remote village. A quality of mutual debit operations is that they very
quickly implicate an entire chain of enterprises within a regional economy
(and, in fact, very quickly undermine the need for 'living' money at all),

to which chapters 10 and 11 by Humphrey and Ledeneva in this volume attest.

The aspect of mutual debit operations which distance them one step from the 'lineal model' of classical barter is that the commodity or action is often in fact valued in terms of paper money. In order to fulfil the legal conditions of Russian trade, the pattern of exchanges agreed upon in a mutual debit arrangement must be recorded on paper as a 'buy–sell' operation which gives the impression that roubles are circulating. Mutual debit arrangements are also subject to value added tax and income tax. The aspect of this operation which is similar to barter is the fact that 'living' money never changes hands nor is processed through a bank by means of promissory notes or cheques. (Bryzgalin et al. 1998, pp. 16-17). Also similar is the fact that the constellation of goods offered for trade and their 'price' are locally negotiated. If in the barter of goods, values are agreed upon in a locally meaningful universe, mutual debit is the barter of goods in a state-arbitrated rouble idiom.

To give an example of how mutual debit works in this district I have chosen one example from a state-controlled economic transaction and one from a privately controlled transaction. Within Arctic Siberia, and in Russia in general, the state-controlled transactions are by far the most dominant example.

Case one: dead souls and unemployment insurance

Among the most wealthy institutions in the District capital of Tura is the Department of Social Security (sotsial'naia zashchita naseleniia) of Ilimpei County. This department, like the Evenki District Pension Fund and the Evenki District Fund of Obligatory Medical Insurance, is one of the few liquid organisations with a regular payroll and seemingly unlimited resources with which to obtain new computers, satellite communication technology, office furniture or vehicles. The offices of each one of these organisations is generally newly renovated and offers a proud supply of chocolate, biscuits, instant coffee and tea to visiting guests. The wealth of these organisations come from the heavy hand of the Russian tax structure. The Department of Social Security is to receive 1.5 per cent of the value of every rouble paid in salaries (in 'living' money or in kind) to employees in every government and private organisation in the Evenki District. With this source of resources (which is almost never paid in 'living' money) the Department is responsible for paying a stipend to those officially unemployed persons. In September 1998 the newly formed Department had 174 clients in Ilimpei County, 83 per cent of whom were Evenkis or Yakuts. The stipend to be paid varies according to the last pay cheque received by the officially unemployed client. Since most indigenous peoples worked in lowly paid professions within state farms, most clients are entitled to the statutory minimum of 133 roubles per month. In very rare cases is this stipend paid out in cash. The preferred method of payment demanded by the Department is in clothing, food and fuel.

The most important condition to receiving these goods is for a 'client' to properly register himself or herself as 'unemployed' (instead of 'not-working', *nerabotaiushie*). To become unemployed one must have an official document signed from their place of work that they have either been laid off or have quit (owing to lack of payment of wages). The client then must register with the office and regularly check the thin register of jobs on offer and must not turn down more than three offers of employment. The vast majority of Evenkis and Yakuts are 'not-working' since they never bothered to be released officially from their home state farm. However, as the Autumn crisis deepened, and as a rare passenger helicopter arrived in the District centre, the corridors of the Department of Social Security became filled with new clients recognising themselves as 'unemployed'.

The Director of Case Work for the Department, a Evenki woman from the village of Tutonchany, Altina Ivanovna Pankagir, spoke to me with enthusiasm of the growth of her Department which to a great extent depended upon a keen sense of how to prospect for forgotten debts. Her preferred method for 'feeding her villages' was through, in her words, a 'trapezoid' of mutual debt. In her four-cornered strategy, she would identify an enterprise which had been overdue in paying one of many debts to the District Administration. These debts could be the payment of the 1.5 per cent contribution on the payroll or they could be other debts such as unpaid economic development loans or loans to improve or build capital structures. Through bringing these debts to the attention of the District Ministry of Finance (and through threatening to signal the wrath of the District Tax Police), she could 'encourage' a firm to promise a certain quantity of goods or services to the District Administration. The District Administration, in turn, often owes the County Administration a large sum of money through the inflated budget request approved each autumn at the Evenki Parliament. The County Administration inevitably 'owes' in turn the Department of Social Security a large sum of money. Thus in showing entrepreneurship in prospecting forgotten debts, Pankagir is able to gain control over real resources, which she then distributes to her impoverished clients.

The discovery of forgotten debts is an exercise closer to that of exploration than public administration, again signalling the importance of information in barter arrangements (Humphrey and Hugh-Jones, 1992). The most common source of information is from disgruntled employees who had been fired. In one particularly evocative triangle, Pankagir learned of a loan given by the District Ministry of Finance to aid a retail department to become a private enterprise. The loan had been 'forgotten' in 1997 when there was a change in administration. Upon learning about the loan from a man applying for unemployment insurance, Pankagir was unsuccessful in having the Ministry 'find' the file detailing the loan agreement. Luckily, the wife of the man worked as a clerk in the Ministry. The two women reached an agreement that if the file were found, the Department would pay the woman's husband unemployment benefits in 'living' roubles. Thus, through informal means of information-gathering, as Pankagir explained to me with a triumphant smile, she was able to secure sufficient funds to feed 40 individuals. One of the key elements of debt-prospecting is thus not only being able to find 'forgotten debts' but to lay claim to these debts before some other Department identified them (or before their gross rouble value devaluated).

The area of her work which offered the most growth, according to Pankagir, was in carrying out a fine accounting of the 'dead souls' registered in the newly created 'clan communes' surrounding Tura. In the first fever of privatisation, excited Evenki activists lobbied for the recreation of the traditional Evenki clan society through the privatisation of collective farm assets to a group of concrete relatives. In her travels, she noticed that the very first contracts which established the clan communes exaggerated the number of members through adding deceased relatives or adding the names of individuals without their permission. With the exaggerated lists of employees, Directors of clan communes were able to apply for larger allotments of land and loans from the District Administration. Pankagir was considering using the threat of revealing these 'dead souls' to force certain clan communes to provide meat and furs free of charge to officially unemployed clients in outlying villages.

Most instances of mutual debit as brokered by the Department of Social Security are far less dramatic. The typical structure is taking note of the debts in unemployment insurance premiums accrued in each village state farm and in each village store. This 'debt' is then paid by having the state farm provide electricity free of charge to the village or by having the store provide officially unemployed people with sugar or flour free of charge. Within the village of Tura, Pankagir has been able to work with a larger spectrum of enterprises and thus has been able to obtain Chinese down-filled parkas, electrical acupuncture kits, baby food and formula and a variety of other goods which she then distributes to 'her clients'. She takes a very keen interest not only increasing her stock of budgetary resources but also takes time personally to

select clothing for her clients or to argue matters of price with the entrepreneurs who are cajoled into the mutual debit arrangement. During our
interviews, the possessiveness and kinship terminology by which she identified 'my people' were quite pronounced suggesting that this orphaned
nation had found a very efficient surrogate parent.

The quality that is most pronounced in the triangular and trapezoidal
mutual debit arrangement of the Department of Social Security is not so
much the complexity of the debt circuit but the crucial role that state
surveillance plays in obtaining information in identifying and in reining
in the flow of commodities and services. On the one hand, the economy
becomes fragmented, as Caroline Humphrey in chapter 3 in this volume
identifies, through a complex web of mutual aid and vaguely wielded
threats. However, on the other hand, this local government agent in a
very paternalistic manner is able to achieve her mandate of helping the
unemployed through her statutory position as an official agent with data
and information on centrally registered transactions. In this example,
while the monetary economy becomes inflexible and locally anchored,
it also addresses social needs in a manner which evokes the previous
Soviet administrative economy.

Case two: The retail store 'Headwind'

In this sub-Arctic district, the most valuable service is transport. Bulk
goods, including coal and petrol, can be imported from southern mines
and refineries only during a very short window of time in early summer
and late autumn when the water swells on the two rivers draining through
the district. In all other months, the only way to move goods is by air.
One of the more successful among non-liquid firms in the district is the
Tura Aviation Enterprise which operates a fleet of helicopters, fixed-
winged aircraft, one wide-bodied aeroplane and a store near the airport
with an appellation appropriately evoking the challenges posed to the
enterprise by the market-economy: '*Headwind*'. When barge traffic ends
in early October, it is this enterprise which holds the monopoly on transport, and often on life itself, in providing trade and emergency evacuation
flights between the district centre and the outlying villages.

The majority of the accounts of the aviation enterprise are settled, as
one might expect, through mutual debit arrangements with the District
Administration. The enterprise runs flights out to villages or brings in
freight for the administration in exchange for tax relief or the provision of
aviation fuel free of charge. In an effort to increase its cash flow the
enterprise opened up a retail arm in 1996. The store '*Headwind*' is unique
in Tura for its provision of freshly baked pastries and bread, but also for

its relationship to all of the workers of the aviation enterprise. The enterprise runs two airports and has a staff on the payroll approaching 100 individuals. Since for most of 1997 and 1998 they earned no liquid income, the only way that they could pay their workers was through the provision of free air tickets to outlying villages, remote scenic fishing spots, or to the nearest city of Krasnoiarsk. The opening of the store '*Headwind*' solved some of the firm's payroll problems. In exchange for working eight-hour days in often inclement weather, the workers of the aviation enterprise earn rights to receive their pay cheques in kind in goods at the store.

The retail arm of the enterprise is extremely profitable in local terms since the enterprise owns its own aircraft and often receives its aviation fuel free of charge. Thus the transportation costs, which often add 50–100 per cent of the cost of heavy or perishable items, can be sold at average market prices to great advantage to the firm. (Average prices in Tura are about three times those in the southern parts of Russia.) Pilots and other airport workers accused the store of inflating its prices in order to take account of the fact that the enterprise had a rather large captive population forced to shop in its outlet. For this reason, the name of the store carried an onerous association with the pilots. Whether the prices were too high or not, the point became clear that the lack of a discount for employees purchasing goods through mutual debit was felt to be a rather cynical policy within the enterprise.

A rather more creative mutual debit arrangement occurs within the tightly knit network of helicopter pilots and Russian fishermen. Every spring and autumn the Tura Aviation enterprise carries a number of Russians out to isolated lakes and rivers throughout the district so that they may set nets and collect barrels of salted whitefish and grayling. This very expensive service (costing in the order of several tens of thousands of roubles per trip) is supplied in exchange for barrels of fish which are either given to the pilots or to the enterprise (or to both) for eventual resale. Some fresh fish is realised through the store '*Headwind*'. Other fish is no doubt shared between the aviation community. Some fish undoubtedly finds its way to the tables of high-placed government people in Krasnoiarsk. The high tariffs charged by the aviation company for these fishing expeditions scarcely cover the paper costs of the wages, fuel and capital costs of the aircraft. On paper, as the pilots joke, the mutual debit arrangement for transport is effected in exchange for fish which by its weight is more expensive than gold. However in the world of mutual debit pricing it is difficult to weigh the accuracy of this claim. While the overt pricing of the flights is well above the income which could be earned from several barrels of salted fish, the important point about these transactions is that they are not realised for cash but some form of socialised credit. The 'cost' of *not* flying would be a loss of rare but important communication between the outlying regions of the district and the district centre, the loss of the requisite number of weekly flying hours for the pilots to keep their licences and a lot less fish in circulation in the local economy. In spite of these social benefits, it is striking that this entire agreement in support of fly-fishing for Russians is effected against a background where those outside of the company, such as aboriginal Evenkis and Yakuts, are denied transport to their reindeer pastures or clan communities for want of 'living' cash to pay the privatised aviation enterprise.

These small examples of disparities in prices in '*Headwind*' as well as in the price of fish, illustrates an exploitative side within mutual debit arrangements. All informants in Tura emphasised that mutual debit arrangements were always 15–30 per cent 'more expensive' than purchasing goods at wholesale prices. Mutual debit arrangements are unique among forms of barter for the fact that their fictive monetary value always lurks in the background. This fictive rouble value is 'negotiated' between the two partners, but it is always the case that the partner who is weaker financially must agree to accepting the higher retail price. Thus individual pilots chafe at the prices charged them for fish or meat that they themselves transport. The aviation enterprise might then chafe at the fact that District Administration values the cost of the aviation fuel that it 'gives' to the enterprise at a price double what it costs in the nearest city. Finally, the enterprise is liable to pay a variety of 'taxes' on the gross amount of its payroll (irrespective of the fact that it does not pay these wages in cash). Indeed the aviation workers feel that the high pricing of '*Headwind*' represents an attempt of the aviation enterprise to lower wages through surreptitious means.

Analysis of mutual debit arrangements

Unlike in classical barter arrangements, there is a certain slippage in mutual debit forms of barter which allow goods, which from the outside may appear to be of unequal value, to be exchanged as if they were of equal value. As Humphrey and Hugh-Jones (1992) argue, in a classic barter transaction it is not proper to try to estimate the 'real value' of the items being exchanged since they may have symbolic or ritual importance outstripping their commodity value or they may indeed be exchanged without conscious recourse to an external numeraire. However, in the case of mutual debit, a meaningful exchange between two parties is agreed upon and then is given a nominal rouble value. In many cases this 'paper value' may absurdly high when compared to the structure of prices charged for 'living' roubles (or for wholesale goods). The impression is created that for the partners, the fact of the paper rouble value is a mere detail which distracts from the importance of the transaction itself.

The paper value is not completely symbolic. The higher the price charged, the more liable the supplier is to pay taxes upon the value that he or she 'earned'. However, depending on the precise constellation of economic forces surrounding the entrepreneur, tax debts can then once again be traded with the local administration (perhaps even with a discount) in order to supply goods or services within a regional economy. Mutual debit arrangements clearly benefit the stronger partner by allowing that partner to conceal differences in value (especially differences in quality) or to take advantage of opportunities for debt-prospecting. In this fragmented economic setting, more often than not it is regional administrative actors who are stronger for their intimate insight into local conditions and knowledge of local economic history. Depending on the connections one has (or the willingness of the local administration to 'forget' tax debts) the weaker partner need not suffer unduly from the transaction. The effect of the arrangement is to urge people to provide goods and services in rouble values which are circulated and re-circulated locally without a necessary injection of 'living' rouble cash from outside the economy, in effect extending the life of local roubles.

The aspect of mutual debit operations which is most striking is their 'command' and 'planned' aspect. This barter transaction, valued in somewhat arbitrarily assigned rouble amounts, is almost always brokered by one of several government departments. The authority of a Department to broker exchange is represented in the breadth of its budgetary *limit*. These aspects of controlled appropriation and circulation remind one of the structure of social power witnessed during the Soviet period.

3 Surrogate money: Katanovka offset coupons in Khakasiia

Although mutual debit operations have become common all over Russia, especially in the months following the crisis of August 1998, the Council of Ministers of the Republic of Khakasiia has twice taken a much bolder step in issuing a form of paper credit that came close to being a form of regional currency. During the first liquidity crisis of the Russian state in October of 1996, the Republic issued 1 million 'payment coupons' (*platezhnie sredstva*) with the aim of 'relieving the social pressure on pensioners arising from the delay in the payment of pensions' (Council of Ministers 1996). The payment coupons, bearing the portrait of the nineteenth-century Khakasiia-born linguist and ethnographer Nikolai

Fedorovich Katanov (1862–1922), soon became known throughout the republic as 'Katanovki'. The offset coupons quickly became an ambiguous symbol both of the new sovereignty gained by the Republic and its financial weakness before the 'wild market'.

The emission of local currencies has not been uncommon in Russia. Both during the civil war, and more recently during the years of financial instability, large social institutions like factories issued their own payment cheques (*bony*) which were valid only for employees in company stores. However the Katanovka offset coupons represent a special case. First, although they are financially based on a mutual debit operation (like a promissory note or a payment cheque), they are not narrowly negotiated between two specific parties but can be sold, resold, collected, devalued, or speculated upon within the boundaries of the Republic of Khakasiia. Second, during their two emissions, they have twice broken out of their expected regulatory circuit between pensioners, enterprises and the Pension Fund and have come into the hands of employed individuals and have thereby come to behave more like a form of regional money. Although the Katanovki coupons tended to behave like a regional form of money, the single significant difference was the strenuous denials of the Republic of Khakasiia that the papers in any way replaced the rouble. They were literally called a 'rouble surrogate' which had shouldered the responsibility of resolving important local transactions in the absence of the regional economy's proper parent – the rouble.

Unlike the principle of debt-prospecting in the Evenki District, the logic of the Katanovka offset coupon was based upon the fact that many industries within Khakasiia produced enough surplus for the Republic to cover its own tax and social security payments without monetary transfers from Moscow. Thus, the debts owed by Khakasiian firms were not rare but in fact pervasive. In 1996-7, the Republic supported approximately 135,000 pensioners for a total sum of 50 million roubles. In 1996 the Republic first ran into the phenomena of 'mass non-payment' (*massovyie neplatezhi*), wherein factories and enterprises produced taxable value but did not receive rouble payments from their clients which could in turn be used to pay their taxes. During this crisis, unlike in the past, Moscow did not help the Republic with an emergency loan of paper money to cover pension payments. When the 'social debt' of the Republic reached 150 billion roubles the instruction was made to the Ministry of Social Security to experiment with alternate forms of payment (Pogrebniak and Pyrkh, 1997). The creative proposal of the Ministry was to create a 'surrogate' form of payment to re-liquidify the relationship between firms producing taxable value and pensioners demanding their fixed stipends: 1 million Katanovki were released in November 1996 at a face value of 5,000 (old) roubles to experimentally cover one-tenth of the yearly payments owed by the Republic to its pensioners. Between November 1996 and June 1997 the coupons circulated, surprisingly, four times – 'extinguishing' 40 per cent of the yearly debt within a half-year period. The coupons were withdrawn when the President of the Russian Federation issued an *ustav* that pensions would be paid on time and in cash. However, in a tremor foreshadowing the financial crisis of August 1998, firms once again lacked the capacity to pay their pension dues in the spring of 1998. Thus on 21 May 1998 the remaining 900,000 coupons were brought out of storage and reissued with a limited emission date to the end of December 1998. The coupons were once again dusted off in the summer of 1999 when they were employed by the Department of Social Security for the payment of financial assistance to families with children.

When the Katanovki enjoyed a more general circulation, their cycle was as follows. A firm owed the Republican Pension Fund each month 28 per cent of the gross value of its payroll. If the firm fell into arrears for over six months they were given a choice by the Republican Pension Fund of having fines levied on their account and being reported to the dreaded Tax Police, or of 'volunteering' to participate in the Katanovki scheme. If the indebted firm agreed, it opened its shelves or its services for sale to pensioners bearing Katanovki. The firm was required to sell goods or services at the same value as it would for roubles (and they were required to give kopeck change to the five-rouble notes). The Katanovki were to be collected at the end of each business day and immediately be deposited in the Federal Savings Bank, where a daily accounting was kept of the firm's success in paying its debt. Once a month, the Federal Savings Bank returned the Katanovki notes to the Department of Social Security and sent an accounting to the Republic Pension Fund. If the firm was still in debt, the Department of Social Security advertised its name, address and services on a poster for another month in the post office where pensioners received their stipends. The Department of Social Security then turned over the Katanovki to the post office where they were offered for another month to pensioners. Pensioners had the option of taking the value of the pensions in Katanovki or choosing to wait for 'living money' to appear (in the case of 1998 this would have been a wait of May to September). If the pensioner took the Katanovki, they could be spent only in those stores listed at the Post Office.

When the system was first introduced in 1996 the intention was to aid pensioners in paying for necessary goods and services. In the first instance, trade in Katanovki was opened to state-controlled industries

Table 12.1 *Enterprises offering goods and services available in exchange for 'Katanovki' in the city of Abakan, Khakasiia, October 1998[a]*

Food

1 Bread, macaroni, candy, meat, sausage	6 Cheese
2 Flour	7 Fish, grains, sugar
3 Chicken	8 Eggs, butter, flour
4 Powdered milk	9 Sausage, fish
5 Fruit	10 Sweets
	11 Restaurant '*Friendship*'

Consumer goods

12 Carpets	19 Books and stationary
13, 14 Furniture	20, 21 Medicine
15 Appliances, dishes	22 General consumer goods
16 Clothing	23 Automobiles
17 Fancy clothing	24 Styrofoam
18 Televisions	

Services

25 Payment for rent of 'dacha' properties	28 Subscription to the newspaper '*Khakasiia*'
26 Plumbing	29 Propane gas for cookers
27 Inter-city coach service	30 Automobile petrol

Building materials and services

31 Renovations of flats	33 Wallpaper
32 Carpentry services	34 Wallpaper, paint, linoleum, plumbing
32 Waterpumps, lathes, doors, window bars	35 Security systems for flats

Total no. of firms: 35

Note: [a] From a series of seven typewritten sheets posted in the main Post-Office in Abakan, 15 October, 1998. The author was not able to visit each one of these firms to determine if the goods listed were in fact sold for 'Katanovka' coupons.

of heat, electricity, telephone and a limited shopping basket of goods (milk, bread, potatoes). By the time of the second emission, the list had grown to include the above so-called 'communal services' and a large range of services from restaurant meals to periodical literature and to a wide array of construction and security services (table 12.1). The Republican Administration was modest in claiming success for the system both because of widespread dissatisfaction among pensioners that the coupons, although useful, were nevertheless severely restricted in circulation, and because of some uncomfortable legal queries from the

Figure 12.1 The Katanovka offset coupon

Bank of Russia about the use of an illegal 'money equivalent'. Vladislav Mikhailovich Torosov, the Assistant Chairperson of Industry to the Khakasiian cabinet in the previous administration, who pushed the scheme through parliament, modestly described the system as a 'successful experiment'. During our interview he was quick to stress that the coupons were *not* a money equivalent but 'only a surrogate'. However, he noted with some pride that official delegations from Kemerovo and Sverdlovsk provinces visited Abakan in the summer of 1998 to investigate the possibility of duplicating the system.

The fact that in many layers of the Khakasiian government, officials were constantly repeating that the Khakasiian 'payment coupons' were not money belies the fact that the coupons were coming to be used like money. The physical aspect of the coupon caused the most confusion since it *looked* like money (figure 12.1). The Department of Social Security, when designing the payment system, was concerned about the threat of forgery of the coupons. As a result the bills had nine 'levels of defence' including cotton paper, water marks, ultraviolet sensitive ink and microlettering. Indeed the modest 5,000-rouble denomination was chosen deliberately so as to make it unprofitable to counterfeit (unlike a 25- or 50-(new) rouble denomination). As Torosov proudly added, 'they're *green* and they have a portrait on the front, just like a US dollar'.

As a student of national identity, I was particularly curious about the choice of Katanov, the 'first Khakasiian scientist', as the portrait to grace this first 'experiment' in an independent Khakasiian economic policy. Katanov, although born of a Sagai family, is most famous as the Kazan University linguist who wrote the first grammar of the Tuvians (or as he called them, the Uriankhai Tatars) (Katanov, 1903). He had a very ambiguous relationship to early revolutionary movements, and as a result his work was not widely available to Soviet readers until the early 1960s. His writing on Khakases was limited to a collection of folktales and scattered articles (Katanov, 1907, 1963). His work did not express a fascination with national identity – indeed he never used the words Khakas or Tuvian at all. A rehabilitative biography goes far in underscoring his 'objective' position to culture and his distance and lack of interest in politics (Kokova, 1993). One wonders if he would have agreed at all to be graced with such a prominent place on the very first Khakasiian paper note. The single aspect of his biography which makes the choice appropriate was his love of numismatics (Kokova, 1993, pp. 50, 78, 103–4). One humorous citation from his biography well illustrates his attitude towards money and politics:

The [revolutionary] events of October were a powerful catalyst for Katanov to return to scholarship... His personal politics were in favour in taking an active role in the Soviet construction of culture... In 1918 Nikolai Fedorovich was made the director of the Numismatic Collection of [Kazan] University. He spent entire days sitting in his office sorting through the many years of new acquisitions and putting them in order. The Numismatic Collection came to the attention of the *chekisty* [secret police] who confiscated all gold and silver coinage. Katanov demanded that they return the collection. And, when they returned the collection Nikolai Fedorovich was able to interest the *chekisty* so much in the science of money that they began to collect ancient coinage on behalf of the Museum. (Kokova, 1993, pp. 103–4)

At the risk of spoiling a good story, it seems that the authorities who designed the Katanovki were ignorant of the finer points of Katanov's biography. It was Liubov' Gennadievna Chernova, the head of the Khakasiian Centre for the Payment of Pensions and Subsidies, who was given the assignment of designing the new 'method of payment' of pensions and who proudly takes credit for the idea of 'printing our own money'. According to her story, the portrait of Katanov and the obverse mountainous landscape were chosen 'purely for technical considerations' of making it more difficult to counterfeit the bills. The landscape came from a postcard that she happened to have on her desk at the time the Krasnoiarsk printer '*Sibznak*' had called for proofs. The portrait of Katanov was added by the Council of Ministers when the Minister of Social Security refused to put his own portrait on the bill.

For our purposes, the most interesting aspect of the design of the bill was Chernova's level-headed accounting of transaction costs. According to our interview, she had been instructed by the Ministry to design a typical mutual debit arrangement between the Ministry and a number of key industries in the Republic. She had calculated that the amount of paper and time that it would take to conduct mutual debit arrangements for the entire Republic was far more expensive than the issuance of paper credit system. The Katanovka system did not require a day-by-day and client-by-client accounting of goods nor a long and densely worded mutual debit contract for every single commodity bartered. Instead, with the Khakasiian 'payment coupons' debts could be accrued at the level of an enterprise and accounted on a monthly basis. In response to a journalist who criticised the unit cost of 7 roubles per bill (Pogrebniak and Pyrkh, 1997) she replied that this transaction cost was much less than maintaining accounts for each of the 135,000 pensioners in the republic. Further, the circulatory system was facilitated with a unique four-sided contract between the four component ministries wherein the Republic of Khakasiia was able to obtain a special exception from the payment of value added taxes on the use of Katanovki to repay government debts. In her view, the only mistake the Department made was in naming the paper a 'payment coupon' instead of calling it a promissory note (*veksel*) or a cheque. The general appellation of the bill made it seem more money-like when in fact, as many civil servants in Khakasiia repeat, it 'was only a surrogate valid for a limited period of time'.

The idea of Katanovki as surrogates is an appropriate kinship metaphor for the political–economic situation of the Republic. In light of the concentration of rouble resources in central Russia, this otherwise liquid region has been abandoned by its senior kinsmen and been forced to develop fictive relationships of reciprocity. The interesting part of the pleas for the 'symbolic' status of the bill is the fact that in actual practice, irrespective of the legislation governing the bills, it had taken on a form of circulation approaching that of a currency, as the following examples show. This raises the tempting conclusion that the 'Katanovka case' might be a proof of the economic model that high transaction costs

inevitably lead barter transactions to transform into money-type transactions (Anderlini and Sabourian, 1992).

Case three: Katanovka coupons in the city of Abakan

The capital of Khakasiia is the context where Katanovki were most prevalent and most valued. As table 12.1 shows, there were a great number
of firms which honoured the coupons, unlike in a village. Because of the
wide spectrum of circulation, there was a peculiar pressure upon the bills
to become items of general circulation, not limited just to pensioners.

Chernova herself admits that with the beginning of the second emission
of the coupons the Department of Social Security had difficulty ensuring
a speedy return of the payment coupons. In 1998 pensioners were not the
only individuals suffering from the crisis of 'mass default payments'.
Almost every employee in Abakan had suffered a delay in receiving
their salaries, ranging from four months at the University to three
years among agricultural enterprises and even the school system. As a
result, the coupons came to have a value among young working people.
In September of 1998 the first hearsay reports appeared that 'young
people' were appearing at the city market with Katanovki. Upon investigation it turned out that many large firms, such as the railway car
manufacturer *Vagonmash*, had opened up chains of kiosks and retail
stores where they sold consumer goods (mainly food) that they had
received through barter or mutual debit arrangements from clients.
Having large payrolls, numbering in several thousand employees, these
firms were eager to collect Katanovki to resolve their debts to the pension
fund. However, when faced with the prospect of strikes among their
unpaid labourers, all firms found it to be a lesser threat to pay their
workers in the Katanovki they received from pensioners rather than
forgo the payment of wages altogether. The workers then purchased
the goods on offer in the factory store, as well as in any other registered
enterprise within the city, alongside the pensioners. Instead of surrender-
ing the Katanovki on a daily basis to the bank, this pragmatic decision
opened up a subsidiary circuit of the coupons within the firm. In effect,
the issuance of a republic-wide promissory note made it not only unne-
cessary for large factories to print their own exchange devices, or to
devise lists of worker debts, but it made it attractive and convenient to
use these offset coupons like a currency.

There were several aspects to the coupons which left them open to local
manipulations. The first element was the problem that they came only in
a single 5-(new) rouble face value. Although firms were required by law to
give change, in practice they refused to take in 'surrogate' money and to

pay change in 'living' money. This resulted in a situation where either atomised consumers lost value on their purchase or enterprising pensioners were forced to band together to buy a single can or one even weight of fruit, and then to divide the purchases equally among themselves.

A second inconvenience with the offset coupons was the fact that the pensioner, or worker, had to have constant fresh intelligence on exactly which enterprises were in arrears with the Pension Fund on a day-to-day basis. Technically, an enterprise required the approval of the Department of Social Security to go off a Katanovki regime. In practice, once a firm calculated that it had collected enough debt coupons it immediately stopped selling commodities for Katanovki even if the enterprise remained listed at the central Post Office as a participant to the scheme.

A more troubling aspect to the currency was for firms to charge more for produce bought on offset coupons than for the same produce purchased with 'living money'. Many pensioners complained that certain stores in October 1998 charged 2.50 R. for bread (instead of 2 R.) or 5.70 R. for milk (instead of 5 R.). Other pensioners complained that in the spring they had been sold spoiled or expired goods for Katanovki, but not fresh produce. The differential in price and quality is explained by the fact that sellers of produce must in the final instance re-supply their stores with cash and not Katanovki, and thus it was in their interest to collect Katanovki as rapidly as possible to put their enterprise back on a liquid foundation. According to Chernova, such price-gouging was illegal but she admitted that the Department lacked the means to monitor and enforce the situation. It was precisely to avoid such a conflict of interest that the Department decided to introduce Katanovki only in firms that were deep in arrears and not liquid enterprises. (Chernova notes that this debt-reduction strategy was yet another quality which distinguishes the Katanovki from 'living money'.)

In reply to the accusation that the Katanovka system allowed for the spread of corruption, Chernova countered that government firms, such as the telephone system or the heating plant, never overcharged for taking Katanoviki. She also mentioned that she received far more complaints about the restricted circulation of the bills rather than complaints on differentials in prices. To illustrate this tendency she cited the fact that many pensioners had written her to request that foreign vacations to the Black Sea be available for Katanovki! To conclude her defence of the system, Chernova was particularly pleased about the result of her recent negotiations with the local bookstore which allowed pensioners to buy notebooks and pens for their grandchildren's first day of school with the offset coupons,

In day-to-day practice, Abakan pensioners found it advantageous to collect 'portfolios' of pensions in living money, Katanovki for the payment of 'communal services' (heat, light, telephone) and Katanovki for barter with relatives. Most pensioners interviewed agreed that if one had a large group of kinfolk earning 'living money' it was better to borrow from them to get by and await the eventual payment of pensions in cash. However most pensioners also agreed that it was prudent to pay for one's telephone or electricity with Katanovki rather than risk having these utilities cut off or having their utility accounts collect fines. Some enterprising pensioners also mentioned the usefulness of the offset coupons as barter items within the extended family. As table 12.1 shows quite prominently, there are a wide range of construction goods which can be purchased with the offset coupons. In Abakan, one of the best investments and hedge against inflation was felt to be a well renovated flat or a detached bungalow (*kottezh*). While it is conceivable that some pensioners don construction helmets to build their own house, it is much more reasonable to assume that they purchased these goods with the offset coupons to continue in their traditional role as financial guardians of their children.

Case four: Katanovka coupons in the countryside

Rural Khakasiians had a far harsher relationship with the phenomena of mass default payments and the various instruments devised by the Department of Social Security to alleviate the crisis. As in the Evenki district, most rural Khakasiians live in collective organisations, some of which are state farms and others of which are 'joint-stock societies'. Although no Khakasiian state farm depends upon helicopter transport to bring their produce to market, they do require extremely large allotments of fuel and coal to fuel their heating systems, combines and tractors. All energy resources, as well as inter-city freight transport, must be paid for in 'living' cash. There are few Khakasiian villages facing starvation, but there are many that are finding it difficult to keep well fed and well heated. There is not a single state farm or 'joint-stock society' that has paid a wage in 'living cash' since 1996.

In most villages, the local state farm provides the central role as a provider of heat, light, and social security. In 1998 most state farms reluctantly agreed to accept Katanovki in lieu of payment for heat and light, but also for forage so that pensioners might feed their own livestock. Since state farms answer for many more social needs than just wages, they tended to supplement the Katanovka system with other local forms of barter. In many villages, local state farm tickets (*bony*) were also issued to reimburse workers in kind for bread (milled from locally grown wheat) or cheese (prepared from locally collected milk). In some cases, state farm cafeterias bartered sacks of flour for sacks of potatoes gathered from private potato plots. The directors of state farms traditionally also answer for the organisation of funerals, wakes, weddings, banquets, marriages and other rites of passage (see Humphrey, 1998). Thus many grain-producing state farms bartered grain for supplies of vodka from the distillery in Minusinsk, which was then redistributed to reinforce the tie mutual aid and solidarity between producers and their organisation.

The major obstacle that village pensioners faced was the fact that there were few outlets which accepted Katanovki and the fact that costs of travelling to the nearest district centre or to the capital Abakan were very high (and must be paid for in 'living' money). As a result of the geographical dependence of pensioners, many 'entrepreneurs' took advantage of their social wards. Thus in Shira district, bread that was imported by *kommersanty* from the capital cost double in Katanovki. Similarly a sack of sugar in Shira was sold for 240r for Katanovki when it 'cost' 180 R. at the wholesale price.

Analysis of Katanovki

Although technically the Katanovka was a form of cheque or promissory note (*veksel*) complete with a government guarantee, a limited period of circulation, a printed value, and the quality of being transferable, there were aspects of its behaviour which made it seem money-like. Unlike promissory notes, its low value, money-like appearance, and 'decontextualised' nature tempted entrepreneurs to use the ticket for settling obligations with agents other than the Pension Fund. This 'infraction' seemed to stem from a lack of enforcement on circulation, as well as the fact that the debt accounts were settled within a relatively long time window (one month) within which it might have seemed attractive to circulate the tickets within a firm. The fact that local circulation of the tickets was tempting makes it seem that a regional form of money might be a rational solution to the liquidity crisis in Siberia. However, this is not the way that local actors understand the situation. Aside from constantly describing Katanovki as a 'stop-gap', 'surrogate' measure, authorities were sincerely troubled by the re-circulation of bills. Part of this stemmed from an anger over the lack of respect for Republican laws. There also seemed to be a deeper concern for the lack of respect among firms for assigning top priority to the claim the Republic made on their social duties. In a demonstration of classic Soviet logic, it was felt proper and honourable for a firm to first pay its social dues and then to worry about making ends meet, let alone a profit. Finally, there seemed to be a demand that transactions should bring some sense of social closure to obligations (an aspect common in barter operations, see Humphrey and Hugh Jones, 1992) and not fracture off into a multitude of private transactions. These rational and centralised attitudes towards resolving social debts reminds one not of monetary commodities but of the controlling instruments of Soviet times.

There were other aspects of the tickets which also seemed strangely familiar. The spectacle of seasoned workers queueing up to receive relatively large allotments of paper bills which enjoyed only an adequate circulation for basic foodstuffs (and *not* for desirable goods) immediately recalls the days of the Soviet rouble. Consumers in the Soviet Union were infamous for amassing large quantities of bills for which they had no particular use and for coveting other forms of paper currency which were more 'alive'. Following up on my hunch that the Katanovka phenomena might represent a re-born Soviet rouble I queried informants about money-changers, to receive secretive glances and whispered accounts of inside operations within the Pension Fund where modern-day *fartsov-chiki* transformed Katanovki into real roubles. These 'non-living' offset coupons did seem to evoke the spectre of a reincarnated *chervontsa*. When bureaucrat after bureaucrat repeated that Katanovki 'were only a surrogate' and they were not 'really money', one wonders if they were not referring to it as a surrogate *state socialist* rouble.

The Soviet rouble, like the Katanovka, was a bill that was paid to workers more as a *social entitlement* than as a remuneration for freely traded labour. It was not an item upon which one could earn interest, nor was it very difficult to earn. In fact, it was often more dangerous for firms to refuse to pay its workers roubles than it was to pay them for work not done. Instead, to purchase anything with a Soviet rouble one had to have contacts, *blat*, or a great deal of intelligence on the social context around (see Ledeneva 1998, ch. 6). To a great degree this intelligence-gathering role was performed by the Department of Social Security which provided its clients with a somewhat inaccurate list of firms authorised to accept Katanovki (and, obviously local knowledge was necessary to interpret the list). The old rouble, like the Katanovka, was not in a strict sense a commodity, for it was illegal to remove it from its context and it held no value outside of the fiercely guarded borders of the Union. However, the Soviet rouble today is fondly remembered for the fact that it offered people an opportunity to maintain a minimum standard of living and to have access to a wide range of necessities – an aspect that the surrogate Katanovka in its better moments provides in the absence of 'living' roubles. Perhaps it is not surprising that the population most loyal to the old regime was serviced with an exchange ticket which possessed many of the same socially embedded 'barter' qualities as the state socialist rouble.

For all of these reasons, it would seem to be rash to conclude that the Katanovka represented a step in the 'evolution' to a money form of barter stripped of cumbersome transaction costs and local discontinuities of value. Instead, the instrument seems to be a partial reincarnation of an exchange form which placed its stress not on comparative advantage but on collective obligations as represented and codified by the state. Insofar as regional currencies help intrusive states to control economies the similarity with money might hold. However, as Ledeneva (1998, pp. 212–14) notes in the conclusion to her book, networks of obligation in the post-Soviet economy seem to point to a different type of 'order' wherein interpersonal loyalties are integrated with technical instruments like money in different and possibly positive ways. The Katanovka offset coupon seems to be closer to a liquid form of settling sombre and proper social obligations within a fragmented market context than an incipient form of money.

4 The 'wild market' and the economy of debts in post-Soviet Russia

There is one outstanding difference between the exchange instruments of the Soviet past and the new instruments of 'mutual debit', 'offset coupons', and the skill of 'debt-prospecting'. While both systems are structured around the balancing of social entitlements, the present system is understood by all informants, including those at its pinnacle, to be temporary, weak and somewhat embarrassing. Surrogate forms of exchange are seen to be poor replacements for the real thing.

As an ethnographer investigating these matters I was struck by the extreme dissonance between accounts of how the economy 'was supposed to work' and by accounts of 'what we do'. This dissonance always existed in Soviet times but, in my opinion, not to this extent. On every street corner in post-Soviet Russia today there are kiosks selling assortments of books on how to trade stocks and to conduct supply and demand analysis based on the translated works of Samuelson and other market economy icons. Out of literally hundreds of titles, I only found three thin manuals which explained the rather complex business of conducting mutual debits or contracting official barter agreements (Fedorov, 1997; Bryzgalin et al, 1998; Kalinina, 1998). (One of these authoritative accountants also confessed her uncertainty on how official barter instruments are supposed to work, Kalinina, 1998, pp. 13, 15). When asking people about how exactly they balanced their accounts, paid their taxes, or sold goods they would either smile or become confused and say with resignation 'that is what we do' ('do you really want me to explain it?'). Another common comment was 'these operations are difficult enough for a Russian to understand!' ('how can a foreigner ever expect to understand this?'). The main theme in these reflections upon the meaning of commodified forms of barter was the fact that they were not systematic and thus were a provided a poor comparison to the system which came before (and were indeed difficult to speak about at all).

If there is any reflection on the present 'system' at all it is to describe it as a 'wild market' (*dikii rynok*). There is a dual referent in this phrase, both to Marx who wrote about 'primitive accumulation' and to the genre of gangster films which portray an image of the 'wild west'. The 'wild market' is thus a mythical space populated by mafias, rackets, fear and the brutish struggle of all against all. It stands for the *lack* of social relations in obtaining the necessities of life (*otsustviia chelovechskogo otnosheniia*).

Needless to say, the 'wild market' evoked by entrepreneurs and administrators is a mythic space. The aspect of the current post-Soviet market which strikes any casual observer is not the 'war of all against all' or acts of random violence but the fact that the market is over-populated with small social groups all engaged in various techniques of protecting 'their own' (*svoikh*). Beyond the initial embarrassment in discussing real exchange situations, one immediately comes across metaphors of kinship, such as the Evenki case worker who 'fed her villages' or the Khakasiian pensioner collecting offset coupons in order to buy school books for his granddaughter. The above examples of mutual debit, offset coupons and debt-prospecting are all examples of how people on a day-to-day basis build networks of alliance in a space where there are no longer pre-given social commitments. The correct translation of the *dikii rynok* might thereby be the lack of a 'common social space'. It is an image of a rather rich garden which has grown wild with all sorts of flowering but stunted growth. Thus what one encounters is not a single market space but a market of many embedded markets.

The 'nested' quality to the post-Soviet social space has been noted by many anthropologists. Making use of a parallel hearsay metaphor to the 'wild market', Katherine Verdery (1996) identifies a return to 'feudalism' in post-socialist spaces. Caroline Humphrey (1998) identifies multiple domestic economies existing in a 'hierarchy of shareholding'. Such nested structures are antithetical to western notions of citizenship (Anderson, 1996) as they are to orthodox notions of economy. The data in this chapter do not help us in positively identifying how the desire for a nested social order can coexist with decontextualised instruments such as liberal democracy, property and monetary commodities. Indeed, the logic behind market economies is that commodities, such as money, are intended to bind together many diverse communities of exchange. The series of Russian financial crises, in addition to the lack of a regional development policy, have disqualified the (new) rouble from the role of an instrument of social integration. However, the above examples do illustrate several attempts to try to make conflicting local demands fit together. The key aspect in these attempts seem to be efforts to 'socialise' commodities such that they reflect 'an economy of favours' (Ledeneva 1998), 'intelligence-gathering' (Anderson, 1998), or 'the dictatorship over needs' (Feher, Heller and Markus, 1983). The instruments described above seem to integrate diverse populations into alliances of social obligation which could be described as an 'economy of debt'. This idea captures not only the traditional socially embedded quality of transactions in this region, but also the highly relevant social fact that actors tend to formally measure the fulfilment of their social obligations in a purely rouble idiom. Rather than simply concluding that mutual debit operations or the Katanovka offset coupon prove the simple axiom that barter inevitably evolves into money, these data raise the interesting question of whether the previous Soviet system, and recent attempts to identify surrogate forms of it, might not offer unique ways of combining accounting with the negotiation of important social obligations. It would seem that this is the type of transition for which local Siberian actors are searching.

References

Anderlini, L. and H. Sabourian (1992). 'Some notes on the Economics of Barter, Money and Credit,' in C. Humphrey and S. Hugh-Jones (eds), *Barter, Exchange, and Value: An Anthropological Approach*, Cambridge, Cambridge University Press, 75–106

Anderson, D.G. (1996). 'Bringing Civil Society to an Uncivilised Place: Citizenship Regimes in Russia's Arctic Frontier,' in C.M. Hann (ed.), *Civil Society: Challenging Western Models*, London, Routledge, 99–120

(1998). 'Property as a Way of Knowing on Evenki Lands in Arctic Siberia', in C.M. Hann, *Property Relations*, Cambridge, Cambridge University Press, 64–84

Bryzgalin, A.V., V.R. Bernuk, A.N. Golovkin and E.A. Grinemaer (1998). *Vekselia i vzaimozachety. Kniga 2: Bzaimozachety*, Moscow, Analitika Press

Council of Ministers of the Republic of Khakassiia (1996). Postanvalenie No 233 ot 17.09.1996. Poriadok vypuska i obraschenia platezhnogo sredstva Soveta Ministrov Respubliky Khakassii

Fedorov, A.F. (1997). *Veksel': Istoriko-iurodicheskoe issledovanie*, Moscow, Bankovskii Delovoi Tsentr

Feher, F., A. Heller and G. Markus (1983). *Dictatorship over Needs*, New York, St Martin's Press

Humphrey, C. (1985). 'Barter and Economic Disintegration,' *Man (ns)* 20, 48–72
(1991). 'Icebergs, Barter and the Mafia in Provincial Russia,' *Anthropology Today*, 7 (2), 8–13
(1992). 'Fair Dealing, Just Rewards: The Ethics of Barter in North-East Nepal', in C. Humphrey and S. Hugh Jones (eds.), *Barter, Exchange, and Value: An Anthropological Approach*, Cambridge, Cambridge University Press, 107–41
(1998). 'The Domestic Mode of Production in post-Soviet Siberia?', *Anthropology Today*, 14 (3) 2–7

Humphrey, C. and S. Hugh-Jones (1992). 'Introduction', in C. Humphrey and S. Hugh-Jones (eds.), *Barter, Exchange, and Value: An Anthropological Approach*, Cambridge, Cambridge University Press, 1–20

Kalinina, E.M. (1998). *Barter: Pravovoe regulirovanie, uchet i nalogooblozhenie*, Moscow, Analitika Press

Kokova, I.F. (1993). *N.F. Katanov: Dokumental'no-publitsisticheskoe esse*, Abakan, Khakasskoe Kn. izd.-vo

Katanov, N.F. (1903). *Opyt izsledovaniia uriankhaiskogo iazyka*, Kazan
(1907). *Obraztsy narodnoi literatury tiurskikh plemen*, St. Petersburg
(1963). *Khakasskii fol'klor*, Abakan

Ledeneva, A.V. (1998). *Russia's Economy of Favours, Blat, Networking and Informal Exchange*, Cambridge, Cambridge University Press

Pogrebniak, L. and G. Pyrkh (1997). 'Kvazimoda–Moda na kvazi den'gi', *Nauchnyi Park*

Verdery, K. (1996). *What Was Socialism, and What Comes Next?* Princeton, Princeton University Press

13 Bear skins and macaroni: the social life of things at the margins of a Siberian state collective

NIKOLAI SSORIN-CHAIKOV

1 Introduction

The post-Soviet story of Katonga, a Central Siberian collective farm with mixed indigenous and Russian population, is in many ways typical for rural areas in the Russian North. Katonga's economy was heavily subsidised during the Soviet period, and these subsidies quickly evaporated in the early 1990s when Russia entered the economic crisis (also euphemistically known as the 'transition'). In a sharp contrast to the late Soviet situation when collective farmers had money but very few commodities were on the store shelves, money started to disappear in daily transactions at the same time – and almost at the same rate – as goods became available for purchase. After 1991 direct, non-monetary trade proliferated: reindeer meat, fish and fur were routinely exchanged for flour, tea and hunting equipment; potatoes and other vegetables were swapped for petrol for motor boats; clothes for medicine; and almost anything for alcohol.

What happens in such demonetised spaces? On the one hand, it is clear that they are hardly residual locations of Soviet or even pre-Soviet exchange practices that are 'not yet' integrated into the market. On the other hand, they cannot be seen as market exchange continued by other means. I show in this chapter that these transactions articulate multiple exchange logics – such as those of monetary and barter trade, but also of sharing, gift and tribute. Furthermore, as I observed during my fieldwork in Katonga in 1988–9 and 1993–5, the purity of meaning of each

This chapter is based on my research in Central Siberia, that I continuously conducted since 1987, and sponsored at its different phases by the N. Mikluha-Maclay Institute of Ethnography of the Soviet Academy of Sciences, Stanford University, the Wenner-Gren Foundation and the US National Science Foundation (Anthropology and Arctic Social Science Divisions). I did most of the writing during my tenure as Killam Postdoctoral Fellow at the Department of Anthropology, University of Alberta. I am very grateful for comments and suggestions that I received at different phases of my work on this chapter from Paul Seabright, Christopher Davis, Mike Evans, Caroline Humphrey and Pamela Ballinger.

individual act of exchange remains in question: collective farmers could identify a single transaction as barter in one context, for example, and as a gift in another.

By looking at these transactions ethnographically, in this chapter I make two following points: first, that the meanings of these transactions cannot be exhausted by enumeration of the goods or services that change hands in them and, secondly, that ambiguities between these meanings are crucial to the way they work. Current exchange practices emerged in Katonga in the context of the late-Soviet 'shadow' economy where blurred boundaries between their meanings were engendered by systematic bureaucratic control over daily life. Furthermore, these practices, already fluid and dynamic in the Soviet period, became a site of re-negotiation of the whole map of social identities and hierarchies in the post-Soviet context. I argue that it is these processes of negotiating and re-making of social identities that underscore the multiplicity and ambiguity of transaction meanings in such demonetised locations.

Each of these meanings presents a different way of organising social space around transactions. 'Barter', 'gift', 'tribute', 'commodity', etc. divide the milieu of collective farmers into groups of 'us' and 'them' differently. 'We' share things among equal 'us', although this sharing makes some of us more equal than others. 'We' pay tribute to 'them', and because of this tribute payment, 'they' are higher than 'us'. And 'we' trade with, and give gifts to, equal 'them' – or at least we make or want to make them 'equal' by giving gifts to, or trading with, them. Each transaction type puts the persons that it connects in different relationships to one another. Yet, when sharing suddenly reveals properties of barter trade or tribute, this boundary of 'us' and 'them' is re-drawn. In other words, it is the *configuration of social identities* that is at stake in the stirred waters of meanings of each transaction.

This chapter is an ethnography of this play of transaction meanings. For the purpose of conveying this play, I narrow my ethnographic focus to look at a 'social life' (Appadurai 1986) of one bear skin which in 1994 changed hands between indigenous trappers and traders in Katonga and, then, the elaborate cultural and historical context of these transactions. In doing so, I chart how the overarching frameworks of the Russian–Soviet economy engendered non-monetary forms of exchange and how local identities are structured by these exchange practices. By analogy with the 'actually-existing socialism' which worked very differently from its design on paper (for example, Humphrey, 1983; Kornai, 1990; Verdery, 1996), in this chapter I explore 'actually existing capitalism' in provincial Russia, which diverges significantly from the post-Soviet reform design. More generally, debates about 'actually-existing capitalism' prove central to contemporary economic anthropology. In my conclusion, I use the Katonga case to reflect upon these larger theoretical concerns.

2 Background

The collective farm that I examine in this chapter is located on the banks of the Podkamennaia Tunguska, a northern tributary of the Yenisei river. The name of the Podkamennaia Tunguska river is Russian for 'The Stony River of the Tungus'. The 'Tungus' is an older colonial name for a Siberian hunting-gathering and reindeer-herding people who call themselves Evenki (*pl.* Evenkil), or Ilel/Orochil – 'people', or 'reindeer people'. 'Stony' refers to the rapids that separate most of this 'River of the Tungus' from the rest of the Yenisei basin.

In the Evenki language, the Podkamennaia Tunguska river is called *Katonga* ('Open Water', 'River'). I use this word as a pseudonym for the village where I did my main fieldwork. It is a remote settlement. A winter truck route links this village with the regional centre Baikit - a town in about 180 kilometres up the river from Katonga – but this route melts with the snow. River boats sail up to the settlement over the rapids only during the spring flood; and the only regular, year-round access to the village is by air. Located within the northern permafrost zone, the area cannot sustain grain agriculture.

Remote as it is, however, Katonga is no 'isolated' site of classical modern anthropology. Long before Cossack bands exerted Muscovite rule over this area in the seventeenth century, it had been already integrated into tributary conglomerates that thrived on sable fur – the sub-Arctic currency that still remains of value. The water and sleigh routes of these tributary allegiances gravitated to the south and the south-east – towards the upper Yenisei river and Lake Baikal. The Cossacks switched these allegiances westward, along a thin line of fortresses and winter blockhouses that connected Yeniseisk, Turukhansk and other Russian posts in the Yenisei basin to Moscow and to the European market. Like other indigenous groups of the sub-Arctic, under Russian rule Evenki formed a social estate of 'tributised subjects' (*yasashnye*) – that is, suppliers of fur tribute to the Russian Tsar's coffers.

Tributary relations coexisted with a trade of furs for imported flour, gunpowder, alcohol, etc. In most cases, this trade took the form of delayed barter in which traders 'credited' hunters with supplies at the beginning of the hunting season in the autumn and drew the balance when hunters brought in furs over the winter. Though the predominance of trade or tribute varied in different moments between the seventeenth and the early twentieth centuries, these forms of exchange proved almost indistinguishable. Tax administrators had special 'bread stores' for their tributary subjects, and traders frequently submitted tribute on behalf of their clients (Rabtsevich, 1973; Bakhrushin, 1955; Karlov 1982). Similarly, collective farms of the Soviet period also served as both administrative and economic units. Furthermore, people employed in the farm's administration often traded fur on the black market.

Owing to this close interdependency of administration and trade, Katonga grew from a small trading post of the early twentieth century – a storage with no permanent residents – into a village of about 600 residents. As the Katonga 'Primitive Production Unit' (1930–8) was reorganised as a 'collective farm' (1938–67) and 'state collective farm' (1967–present), its hunters, herders and other 'workers' became state employees. In the current ecnomic crisis, however, state employment no longer provides sufficient monetary income, and the crisis illuminates how dependent Katonga inhabitants had become on the state sector.

3 Bear skins and macaroni

In July 1994, a bear killed one of the reindeer of the Katonga collective farm's Brigade Number Two. The bear left the reindeer body half-eaten about two kilometres away from the camp that I was visiting at that time. We made a platform on the tree near the reindeer. The next night one of the Evenki in our camp shot the bear from the platform when it came to finish eating the body. The bear meat was divided between the three tents of our camp. The Evenki who killed the bear hanged the bear's head on the tree facing the West – 'so that it doesn't come back' – and presented the bear skin as a gift (*gnimat*) to Andrei, the head of the brigade. 'If you kill a bear', it was explained, 'you should gift the skin to a non-relative [*tego*], and divide the meat between everyone in the camp'.

This bear became a valuable asset. In the village about a 100 kilometres south of our camp, where these Evenki were registered and employed as collective farm reindeer herders, the bear skin was worth, I was told, 250,000 roubles (or US$ 50 at the exchange rate of that time). The bear skin could be sold to Russian residents in the village who traded flour, tea and other goods semi-privately and semi-legally. Such trade occurred in the past, but in the 1990s it intensified as Katonga's Russian villagers and reindeer herders had been paid salaries very irregularly – neo-liberal reforms significantly undermined the state subsidies which constituted the main portion of the collective farm's budget. In July, 1994, Katonga collective farm had owed salaries to its workers since early spring.

Anna, Andrei's wife, spent the rest of the summer drying the bear skin and working on softening its inner leather side. When stretched between the poles, it looked huge and very beautiful: 'We are going to get a lot of money for it', she told me.

In early September our reindeer convoy arrived in Katonga bringing children to attend boarding school,[1] the bear skin and reindeer-fur winter boots (*untal*) that Anna made to order for a Russian trapper and a family friend. After dropping children at the boarding school, Anna left for the Russian trapper's house with the boots, while Andrei and I went to visit the collective farm deputy director for hunting. Nicknamed Tursunbai, the deputy director was originally from Kazakhstan. He lived in Katonga for 15 years, and had held the post of deputy director since 1985. In addition to his collective farm duties, which included renewing fur-hunting licences and distributing collective farm traps, rifles and bullets, Tursunbai also traded privately, and Andrei hoped to sell him the bear skin. As we walked down to his house, Andrei told me that Tursunbai 'is a local [*mestnyi*], in fact he is a good friend of mine [*girki*]... he understands our needs, and will give us a good price'. Tursunbai's dogs, notoriously vicious, recognised Andrei, wagged their tails, and didn't bark at me when we crossed the vegetable garden in the yard and entered the house. In a few moments, we were seated at the kitchen table and were offered tea or Brazilian instant coffee.

Together with coffee and sweets, a bottle of vodka appeared on the table. We toasted in turn the happy fact of getting together (*za vstrechu*), Tursunbai's new boat and finally the collective farm director's long absence from the village: 'let him never return!' (A relative newcomer, the director wasn't liked much either by Evenki or well-settled non-native trappers, and Tursunbai hoped to take over his post soon.) As I prepared to leave in about an hour-and-a-half, Andrei took out the bear skin and gifted it to the deputy director. 'We Evenki have a custom [*obychai*]', he said to me, 'to gift bear skins; you have to gift it to a non-relative'. Tursunbai smiled at both of us from his corner of the table.

I left Andrei and Tursunbai to finish their drinks and came over to Anna's sister's house. Anna and Andrei had a house in Katonga, but it stood unoccupied for most of the year. When they visited the village they stayed in the house belonging to Anna's sister, who was married to a Russian newcomer. When I arrived there, there was already another

---

[1] One of the effects of the economic crisis was that the collective farm and Regional Education Committee (RANO) were not able to charter helicopters to collect forest children to school, as they had done each year since the 1960s. That September, Andrei and Anna had to bring their children to the village boarding school on reindeer.

party in progress. Anna had successfully sold the reindeer-fur boots, subsequently buying some refreshments and vodka in the village store and supervising the slaughter of a reindeer brought to the village to replenish her sister's family meat supplies. When I came over, most of the meat had already been deposited in the cold basement, but the delicacies were out – raw liver and a soup made of intestine and testicles. I found myself at the table with a bowl of soup, and drank another shot of vodka with Anna's sister's Russian husband before Anna, who was busy running in and out of the room with steaming plates of reindeer meat (and simultaneously talking to her relatives and helping to put to bed her sister's children) asked me if Andrei had sold the bear skin. 'No', I answered, 'the last thing I know he gifted it to Tursunbai'. 'Of course I should have known!', cried Anna, 'This loser [nedotepa] will sit there and drink with "his best friend", we'll end up without any supplies, and "his best friend" will charge him the vodka they are drinking together'.

As she was saying this, Anna ran out of the house. I wanted to follow her, but the Russian husband of her sister told me that it would be better if Anna settled this 'just between them [i.e. Andrei and Anna] and Tursunbai'. In half-an-hour the guilty face of Andrei appeared in the doorway asking me, the Russian husband of Anna's sister, their eldest son, and another Evenki who had joined us for dinner, for help. As we proceeded to Tursunbai's, I was expecting a fight. To my surprise, however, we found Tursunbai and Anna peacefully chatting. Tursunbai invited us to his storage, and we carried out of it two sacks of flour, one sack of sugar, a two-kilo portion of yeast, bags of macaroni, tea, Brazilian instant coffee, chocolates, packs of cigarettes, canned fish and milk, six bottles of vodka, a bag of bullets and a tarpaulin tent. Apparently, Anna had rushed into the house where Andrei and Tursunbai were still drinking, cancelled the gift and, using a moment of unambiguous moral authority, sold the bear skin back to Tursunbai for 'as much stuff as you can carry at one time'. We managed somehow take it in one go from Tursunbai's storage to the street, but it was impossible to carry this all at once to the house where we stayed. In fact it took us three trips between the two houses to bring it all in. The amount of the supplies exceeded approximately twice the value of the bear skin.

4 Some remarks on this episode

What happens in this episode? The bear is killed, its meat shared, its skin gifted by the hunter to the head of the reindeer brigade, then it is supposed to be bartered but gifted again, and then the gift is taken back and the barter dealing resumed. The 'social life' (Appadurai, 1986) of that bear skin did not end that day but continued on a route that took it away from Katonga. A year later Tursunbai told me that he had sold it in Kazakhstan where he made regular trips as a shuttle trader. In that part of its trajectory, the bear skin probably acquired an unambiguous commodity form. But perhaps even there, its properties as a commodity were immersed in its other properties. What I find most interesting about this skin, as well as about other things that make their way from the forest to the village and further to the Russian and Eurasian mainland, is the ambiguity of the cultural meaning of each transaction along the chain of these objects' social life. We accept, after a classical study of Marshall Sahlins (1972), that gift exchange tends to happen between 'relatives' and commodity exchange between 'strangers' and, respectively, in close kin-based 'traditional' and mass anonymous 'modern' societies. In Katonga, however, this distinction appears to be more complicated.

First of all, the gift exchange – in the strict sense of the Evenki word *gnimat* ('gift-giving') – is, as Andrei and other Evenki point out, a transaction between 'non-relatives' or *tegol* (singular *tego*). The act of gift-giving thus establishes 'kinship' or 'companionship'. The term *tego* in Evenki is used interchangeably with *girki* ('friend' and 'other' as in *girkudiami*, 'to go toward somebody else's camp'). Both *tego* and *girki* can be used to denote existing or potential spouses, and, most interestingly, *girki* also signifies 'trader'. To put this in another way, the Evenki word for 'trader' also has meanings of 'comrade', 'guest' and 'relative in law'.[2] Thus the totality of the continuum between relatives and strangers is hinted at in each transaction of this episode, and yet each affirms or challenges a very specific social identity of participants. Let me now go through these identities looking at how social boundaries between them are drawn in these transactions.

The first gift of the bear skin made by the hunter to Andrei had a clear reference to a traditional 'gift to a non-relative'. Yet this transaction represents much more. It constituted a gift from one of the poorest Evenki in our camp to the richest. Single and male – like most Evenki who stay in the forest – the person who killed the bear was in his late 30s, and between the winter fur-hunting seasons he lived with one of the few families of forest herders who had enough reindeer to subsist and enough elderly and children to claim enough welfare benefits, the only regular source of cash that came from the state in the 1990s. This single male hunter

---

[2] At the turn of the twentieth century, tax inspector I. I. Pokrovskii also quotes *niro* and *nirushko* as the term for 'friend' and 'trader' (Krasnoyarskii Kraevedcheskii Musei [The Archive of the Krasnoyarsk Provincial Area Studies Museum], o/f 7886/190, l. 83).

was a self-described 'labourer' or 'eater' or even, sometimes, 'adopted child' (*batrak* or *rot* or *priemysh*) of Andrei's reindeer brigade.

Andrei was, on the other hand, a successful herder; he was married and was considered an actual proprietor of the reindeer of the brigade's herd. Throughout the year he occasionally killed reindeer from this herd to complement the diet of his camp companions. This was particularly important for several single 'eaters' who joined the camp for a long time without contributing any purchased supplies to the joint 'pot' of the camp and who didn't have their own reindeer. Sharing reindeer meat went without saying – together with, however, a sense of indebtedness on the part of 'hunters' towards 'herders' inherent in collective-farm reindeer brigades anyway yet exacerbated by the current economic crisis. The gift occurred within this atmosphere of indebtedness and carried, therefore, clear connotations of tribute: 'Andrei is my boss', said the person who killed the bear, 'of course I would give the skin to him'.

Let us now look at the transaction between Andrei and Anna on the one hand and Tursunbai on the other. Tursunbai served as Katonga collective farm's deputy director for hunting, and for many years Andrei dealt with him in his fur-hunting business. In the collective farm context Tursunbai and Andrei's relationships are 'tributary' in the Soviet sense of a 'redistributive' planned economy (Verdery, 1991, pp. 74–83). Tursunbai administered Andrei's fur-hunting plan provided Andrei with a hunting licence and equipment and acquired fur from Andrei after the hunting season. Outside this context, their more equal 'friendship' is necessary for the shadow barter trade that they have also been engaged in for many years. Such gestures as Andrei's unexpected gift to Tursunbai are among the ways to maintain such a 'friendship'. If the first gift of the skin (from the hunter to Andrei) invokes tribute of 'hunters' to 'herders', and particularly to those herders who are 'bosses', the second one makes 'friendship' out of hierarchical, tributary relationships between Evenki 'herders'/'hunters' on the one hand and non-native collective farm 'deputy directors' on the other.

Furthermore, it is this 'friendship' that enables 'trade', and in this episode we see both a bond and a tension between the two. Tursunbai's semi-legal forest clients are his 'friends', yet he makes a living off them by reselling things such as macaroni and bearskins. Andrei insists that because Tursunbai is a 'friend' he will give a good price for the skin, while Anna is suspicious that Tursunbai may make them pay twice for this 'friendship'. Yet when Anna remakes the deal for the yield of things 'as much as one can carry at once', this does not merely transform gift back to barter but also carries a connotation of counter-gift on behalf of Tursunbai. And the re-making of the social meaning of this transaction did not stop there. That day Anna's 'gain' on the grounds of her moral authority was not final. Retrospectively, as I found out a year later, the price of the bear skin was re-evaluated, and the 'gain' was counted as 'credit' for the 1994-5 fur-hunting season.

Indeed, Siberian fur trade is inseparable from personal trust and friendship, and vice versa: personal trust and friendship is pervaded with a feel for trade so that, as Stephen Hugh-Jones points out in another context, 'the morality of the market' and 'that of kinship' penetrate and enable each other (1992, p. 51). Trade is done in places like Katonga by crediting hunters with supplies for the upcoming hunting season. On the Podkamennaia Tunguska river, this credit is called 'circling' (*pokruta*), from the verb 'to circle' (*krutitsia* or *pokrutitsia*). By taking credit, a hunter promises to make a circle over the winter and come back to the same trader with the fur. The ambiguity of trade and friendship is essential here. It creates a sense of personal bond, not merely an economic indebtedness, and thus fixes the intersection point of the disparate social orbits of movement of forest nomads and shuttle traders.

It is impossible here to maintain the distinctions between monetary and non-monetary economy, as well as the one between 'traditional' and 'modern' society. Tursunbai's profit exists in monetary form; indeed, he has a hard currency account in the United Arab Emirates where he transfers the money that he makes from the shuttle trade. Money is, however, absent in his bargaining with Andrei and Anna, although the value of things is colloquially expressed in monetary terms – for example, the sack of flour 'costs' 26,000 roubles, a bottle of vodka 5,000. The annual balance of 'debt' and 'credit' is drawn at the end of the fur-hunting season in March, but it is never calculated precisely. This lack of precise calculation also signals that Tursunbai's business depends on the blurred boundaries of tributary, gift and market logics. I argue that it is in this impure form that the Russian trade and bureaucracy expanded in Sub-Arctic Siberia. In the following sections, I outline this process.

5 Tribute, gift and trade in Tsarist Siberia

The relational politics of both value and identity underscored Russian expansion in Sub-Arctic Siberia from the seventeenth century on. At the time of the Russian conquest, Evenki and other Siberian aborigines did not render much military resistance to the Russian state. They quickly switched their tributary allegiances to the new political power. The tributary system, however, was harder to maintain than to establish. Part of the problem lies in the ambiguity of 'tribute' and 'gift' (*dan*' and *dar*, or *yasak* and *pominki*) in Siberian politics. When local leaders were convinced of the military superiority of the Cossacks, they quickly bowed to the new power – 'bit the ground with their foreheads', as the chronicles phrased it – with the *pominki* ('gifts') of sable fur pelts (Miller, 1941 [1763-4], p. 260). This transaction symbolised the cessation of hostility and, from the point of view of the more powerful side, the acceptance of tributary obligations by the defeated. But there was a trick: sending gifts, as opposed to paying tribute, was an act between equals. It saved the honour of what was otherwise unambiguously the weaker side. Giving gifts represented, therefore, not only the donors' subjection but also their autonomy: the donors had the possibility of re-negotiating the hierarchy at another juncture and, perhaps, on more favourable terms (see Bakhrushin, 1955; Lantzeff, 1943). This ambiguity of gift and tax meant that the act of surrender was also one of flight, identifying the giving subject both within and outside of the tributary system.[3]

The main trouble, then, for the Russians was not the conquest itself, but the establishment of *regular* tax returns. Throughout the seventeenth century this system was never fully established. In order to subject indigenous groups to the fur tribute, Russian state agents attempted to enforce communal responsibility for tax returns. The Cossacks took local leaders hostage in the hope that their fellow 'clansmen', or 'relatives' (*rodovich*, or *rodich*, from the Russian *rod*, 'clan') would step in with the *yasak*. This practice rendered *yasak* as communal ransom, tying indigenous clans together in a manner similar to the peasant corporate communities of the Russian mainland, where 'circle binding' (*krugovaia poruka*) constructed the collective responsibility of a given commune as a whole to state or landlord for the tax submitted by each household. In Siberia, however, the practice did not work out as designed. The Russian authorities faced systematic dodging by the Evenki of their kinship and neighbour obligations. The reports of the Siberian tax collectors of the seventeenth century are full of episodes which describe the refusal of the Evenki to pay ransom for their relatives (Stepanov, 1939, p. 59; Bakhrushin, 1955, p. 70). Unhappily for the state, the flight was the basis of the assumed Evenki 'rules' on which the tributary system could be built.

Documents of that time report the never-ending pursuit of reindeer-riding nomads over the vast taiga and tundra of Siberia, and endless negotiations of the terms and conditions of the tribute payment. The end to this was brought not by the final, successful imposition of the tributary

---

[3] See Mancall (1971) on the role of gift in diplomacy between seventeenth and eighteenth century Russia and China.

system, but by the development of other sectors of the Russian economy after the reforms of Peter the Great and the consequently rapid decline of the importance of the Siberian sable in the Russian State revenues from 11 per cent in the 1620s to 2 per cent in the early 1700s (Fischer, 1943, pp. 118–22; Martin, 1986).

Nonetheless this pursuit and negotiation were an important catalyst of indigenous migrations and social change. Between the seventeenth and early twentieth centuries Sub-Arctic Siberia witnessed a demographic and territorial expansion of Evenki fur-hunting family groups. Evenki populated a geographic area wider than before the Russian conquest, from the Yenisei river basin in the west to Manchuria and Sakhalin Island in the east. This advancement was spurred both by resistance to strict colonial rule and by growing dependency on traded products. State tax-collectors and private fur-traders (often the same people operating in different roles, depending on the time of year and the proximity of other state agents) stimulated these migrations by creating demand among the indigenous peoples for firearms, flour, sugar and alcohol. Building new posts along water routes, the agents were able to follow the migrations, gradually exerting political control over new territories and pushing the Evenki further into the forest.[4]

6 Soviet construction

The Soviet state flourished in the Sub-Arctic on the ambiguities of gift, tribute and trade, but it did so in a very different way than the old regime. Relational and ambiguous politics of value made Soviet reformers believe in the existence of 'enemies of the people' among Siberian aborigines. Searching for and fighting these 'enemies of the people' was the main form of state expansion in the northern parts of the Yenisei river basin, inhabited by Evenki and other indigenous groups, in the period from the 1920s through the early 1950s, and it went through 'normal' Soviet stages such as collectivisation and purges of the 'usual' suspects such as rich and ritual leaders (Ssorin-Chaikov, 1998). I want to emphasise, however, that this expansion was based not merely on this 'alienation', but also on the analytical and political purification of transaction meanings both within indigenous communities and between these communities and the state.

---

[4] These Evenki migrations coincide with what some authors describe as a wider demographic expansion of the Arctic and Sub-Arctic indigenous population of Siberia of that time associated with the spread of reindeer-herding and fur-hunting economies. Patkanov and Dolgikh estimate the overall aboriginal population as growing from approximately 200,000 in the seventeenth century to more than 820,000 c. 1900 (see Patkanov, 1912; 150, ff; Dolgikh; 1960, pp. 615–17).

As elsewhere in rural parts of the former Russian empire, Soviet reforms were contingent on identifying local economies as following the cultural logic of capitalism.

The language of the Polar Census of 1926-7, for example, views Evenki households in terms of a Leninist analysis of class differentiation within the village. Households are divided into 'poor', 'middle' and 'rich' class groups, and relations between them are described as 'credit', 'debts', 'rent' and so forth. In the forest to the north of the Katonga, for example, the Census reported on several rich families who, in the terms of this survey, 'credited' reindeer to the poorer families of the area:

In the area there are several rich reindeer herders whose herds constitute the reindeer reserve for the rest of the population. The poor [bedniaki] often turn to them for help and the latter usually provide the reindeer. Sometimes the reindeer are rented free of charge for a limited period of time. Sometimes, and rather often, the rich gift reindeer to the poor. But even those rented for a limited period of time are rarely returned. In most cases reindeer is eaten and therefore counted as the poor's debt. It should be noted that these debts are hardly ever returned.[5]

True or not, social relations described in such a way became objects of reforms aimed at transforming these market-like social relationships into a 'rational', planned system. Such a system was to ensure, in turn, settlement of largely nomadic Siberian aborigines and 'development' of standard Soviet institutions among them.[6]

The 'actually-existing' Soviet economy worked differently, and in many ways contrary to this reform design. 'Submitting the plan to the state' (sdacha plana gosudarstvu) in reindeer and fur was a highly ritualised tributary gesture, which explained very little about the actual dealings and relationships that made the system work (see Humphrey, 1983; Verdery, 1996). On the fringes of this redistributive economy, there mushroomed a black market as well as new trapping and subsistence practices which frequently had state resources as their targets. One Evenki told me a joke: 'What does the collective farm's reindeer do when it comes for a visit? - It goes directly to the soup-pot.' It is the produce of this trapping and subsistence that was the subject of play with exchange meanings in the late-Soviet and early post-Soviet period. Instead of rendering local economy transparent and 'rational', the Soviet system in the North was increasingly impure and opaque.

---

[5] Gosudarstvennyi Arkhiv Krasnoyarskogo Kraia [The State Archive of the Krasnoyarsk, Province], f. 769, op. 1, d. 354, 1. 90.

[6] See Sergeev (1955) for the general outline of this vision in Siberian context, and Anisimov (1933) and Nikul'shin (1939) for the analysis of exchange among Evenki from this point of view.

The ambiguities between transaction meanings also signal the hierarchical nature of the social space that they constitute. The socio-economic
position of the trader is stronger than that of the hunter. The Soviet-style
collective farms created local monopolies of directors or deputy directors
successful in privatising the state infrastructure and barring the competition of other private agents. In the post-Soviet context, it is the forest
hunters and herders who have to insist on 'friendship' and play with the
ambiguity of boundary of 'us' and 'them'. Yet this case also shows that
forest hunters and herders are no passive victims of capitalist 'enslave-
ment', as they are frequently portrayed in the history of Siberian trade
(for example Anisimov, 1936; Rychkov, 1914; Sergeev, 1955). Nor, as
the politics of value in which they participate demonstrates, do they
constitute a homogeneous milieu. The social hierarchies that trade
and tributary regimes generate stretch to the remote parts of the forest
along the same chains through which bear skins and macaroni travel
(see Hugh-Jones, 1992 for a similar observation in South American
context).

7 Conclusion

Classical economic anthropology was based on a fundamental distinction
between gift and commodity. This distinction marked differences not
only between transaction types and between 'traditional' and 'modern'
economies (see Mauss, 1970), but also, most importantly for my
case, between different levels of *economic integration*. For Marshall
Sahlins (1972), for example, the distinction between gift and commodity
is determined by 'kinship distance': kin groups or local communities
exchange gifts among themselves but trade with geographically or
socially distant 'others'. In more recent literature, these distinctions have come under criticism. It is beyond the purpose of this
chapter to discuss the full scope of this critique. Let me point out only
two lines of the argument which are directly relevant for my ethnographic
case.

First, recent literature challenges the distinction between 'traditional'
and 'modern' economies. In particular, its targets are evolutionary or
'historicist' (Ferguson, 1985, p. 669) assumptions which are behind the
idea that non-western and non-monetary forms of exchange in the *chron-
ologically* modern world illustrate pre-market, and therefore essentially
pre-modern, socio-economic formations. This view is rooted in what
Johannes Fabian calls 'denial of coevalness' (1983, p. 31) of western
and non-western cultures, and it overlooks the fact that much of
what in classical economic anthropology was rendered 'traditional' and

'pre-modern' was culturally produced in the context of expansion of the western capitalist world system (Wolf, 1982; Gregory, 1982; Hart, 1987; Hugh-Jones, 1992).

Much of this literature draws on African and Latin American materials, but Siberia is certainly another a case in point. In this chapter I have shown that the Russian fur trade in the Siberian Sub-Arctic expanded on a complementarity of 'gift' and 'tribute', and 'sharing' and 'trade'. Let me briefly recapitulate my argument. In the European fur market, seventeenth-century Muscovy acted as a capitalist trader. On the other end of this relationship (in Siberia which then became Muscovy's main resource of fur), Muscovy received this fur not through trade but by collecting fur tax from indigenous hunters. This taxation was in turn immersed in a complex web of local practices of exchange, from tribute to gift and silent trade. Muscovy acted as a 'second-feudal' state which enhanced its presence on European markets while also increasing 'non-market' integration of its old and new subjects in the form of serfdom and those tributary regimes which intensified in parts of Russia between the sixteenth and nineteenth centuries. The Soviet political and analytical purification of exchange also led to the increasing ambiguity between meanings of exchange and mastery in code-switching between its different registers. And, in most recent times, making money for people like Tursunbai was impossible without engaging in relationships that formally contradict the logic of money-making.

The second line of the argument, which departs from classical economic anthropology, concerns the assumption that transaction meanings – in a 'traditional' or 'modern' economy, or at a given level of economic integration – are shared by parties to an exchange. In many cases this is not so. Michael Taussig (1980) demonstrated, for example, that participants of exchange can see its meanings differently: what is commodity trade for one side is ceremonial gift exchange for the other. Arjun Appadurai takes this argument further, proposing the notion of 'regime of value' which does not 'imply that every act of... exchange presupposes a complete cultural sharing of assumptions'. Transaction, he argues, 'as a social matter, may bring together actors from quite different cultural systems who share only the most minimal understanding... about the objects in question and agree only about the terms of trade' (1986, p. 15). From situation to situation, and from commodity to commodity, the degree of this sharing varies from very high to very low. However, the basic understanding of 'transaction' here is that it is a unit of difference rather than a point of agreement. Ferguson (1992) maps these differences in what he calls a 'topography of wealth' in which cultural logics of gift exchange and commodity trade, as well as different notions of surplus and loss, and wealth and poverty, are constituted by flow of goods and, in turn, constitute social identities around it.

My ethnography in this chapter follows this line of the argument: I looked at how the meanings of a single transaction or a chain of transactions have been differently understood. But I take this argument further in suggesting that, first, the same transaction can have different meanings depending on the context, and, secondly, the daily 'politics of value' (Appadurai 1986; Ferguson 1992) are too fluid to sustain topographic metaphors of analysis. Under the Tsarist, Soviet and post-Soviet value regimes, the 'politics of value' and politics of identity are too dynamic and 'equivocal' (Gregory, 1997, p. 11) to form a reified landscape in any sense except archaeological – its 'mapping' would always lag behind the creativity of practices themselves. Furthermore, it is important to realise that these practices are historically produced by political flight from such mapping projects – for example, of the tributary system during the Tsarist period or of its 'rationalisation' during the Soviet one (Ssorin-Chaikov, 1998). I use topographic metaphors to discuss social space, or the space of identities, produced through exchange; but I find it necessary to add metaphors of time to the picture, and to analyse these exchange practices and transaction meanings through the notion of history as a flow into which one cannot step twice.

Pierre Bourdieu demonstrated the importance of temporality for the gift economy. Good timing between gift and counter-gift is essential to maintain hidden the sense of indebtedness that otherwise would awkwardly surface and destroy the distinction between generosity of gift and calculation of credit. I have shown – particularly in the scene of transactions between Andrei and Tursunbai – that timing is also crucial for playing on the differences between forms of exchange and for redrawing social boundaries between participants. In my view, this is exactly what constitutes the daily 'politics of value' which, in the words of Bourdieu (1991, p. 11), operate through 'a feel of the game' – that is, through a *habitual* set of dispositions which 'go without saying' much faster than moves can be calculated and supervised – as in Bourdieu's example of a tennis player who plays faster than he, and his coach, thinks about his moves.

References

Anisimov, A.F. (1993). 'O sotsial'nykh otnosheniiakh v okhotkhoziaistve evenkov,' *Sovetskii Sever*, (5), 38–49

(1936). *Rodovoe obshchestvo evenkov (tungusov)* Leningrad, Izdatel'stvo Instituta narodov Severa

Appadurai, A. ed. (1986). *The Social Life of Things: Commodities in Cultural Perspectives,* Cambridge, Cambridge University Press

Bakhrushin, S. V., 'Iasak v Sibiri,' in *Nauchnye trudy*, III, part 2, Moscow, Izd. AN SSSR, 149–85

Bourdieu, P. (1991). *In Other Words: Essays towards the Reflective Society,* Stanford, Stanford University Press

Dolgikh, B.O. (1960). 'Rodovoi i plemennoi sostav narodov Sibiri v XVII veke' *Trudy Instituta Etnografti im N.N. Miklukho-Maklaia, Novaaia Seriea,* 66, Moscow, AN SSSR

Fabian, J. R. (1983), *Time and the Other: How Anthropology Makes its Object,* New York, Columbia University Press

Ferguson, J. (1985). 'The Bovine Mystique: Power, Property and Livestock in Rural Lesotho', *Man* (ns) 20, 647–74

Fisher, R.H. (1982) 'The Russian Fur Trade,' *University of California Publications in History,* 31, Berkeley and Los Angeles, University of California Press

Gregory, C. (1982). *Gifts and Commodities,* London, Academic Press

    (1997). *Savage Money: Anthropology and Politics of Commodity Exchange,* London, Harwood Academic Publishing

Hart, K. (1987). 'Commoditization and the Standard of Living,' in A. Sen (ed). *The Standard of Living,* Cambridge, Cambridge University Press

Hugh-Jones, S. (1992). 'Yesterday's Luxuries, Tomorrow's Necessities: Business and Barter in Northwest Amazonia', in C. Humphrey and S. Hugh-Jones, eds. *Barter, Exchange and Value: An Anthropological Approach,* Cambridge, Cambridge University Press, pp. 42–74

Humphrey, C. (1983). *The Karl Marx Collective: Economy, Society and Religion in a Siberian Collective Farm,* Cambridge, Cambridge University Press

Humphrey, C. and S. Hugh-Jones (eds). (1992). *Barter, Exchange and Value: An Anthropological Approach,* Cambridge, Cambridge University Press

Karlov, V.V. (1982). *Evenki v XVII–nachale XX veka (khoziaistvo i sotsialnaia struktura)* Moscow, Moskovskii Gosudarstvennyi Universitet

Lantzeff, G.V. (1943). 'Siberia in the Seventeenth Century: A Study of Colonial Administration', *University of California Publications in History,* 30, Berkeley and Los Angeles, University of California Press

Mancall, M. (1971). *Russia and China: Their Diplomatic Relations to 1728,* Cambridge, MA, Harvard University Press

Martin, J. (1986). *Treasure of the Land of Darkness: The Fur Trade and Its Significance for Medieval Russia,* Cambridge, Cambridge University Press

Mauss, M. (1970). *The Gift: Forms and Functions of Exchange in Primitive Societies,* London, Routledge & Kegan Paul

Miller, G.F. (1941[1763-4]). *Istoria Sibiri,* Moscow and Leningrad, Izd. AN SSSR

Nikul'shin, N.P. (1939). *Pervobytnye proizvodstvennye ob'iedinenia i sotsialisticheskoe stroitel'stvo u evenkov,* Leningrad, NIA Glavsevmorput

Patkanov, S. K. (1912). *O priroste inorodcheskogo naseleniia Sibiri: statisticheskie materialy dlia osveshcheniia voprosa o vymiraniia pervobytnykh plemen*, St Petersburg, Izd. Akademii Nauk

Rabtsevich, V.V. (1973). 'K voprosu ub upravlenii aborigennym naseleniem Sibiri v 80kh godakh XVIII–pervykh desiatiletiiakh XIX stoletiia', A. P. Okladnikov (ed)., *Voprosy istorii Sibiri dosovetskogo perioda*, Novosibirsk, Nauka

Rychkov, K.M. (1914). 'Stranitsa iz zhisni vymiraiushchego plemeni', *Sibirskii Arkhiv*, 3–4, 162–5

Sahlins, M. (1972). *Stone Age Economics*, Chicago, Aldine

Sergeev, M.A. (1955). 'Nekapitalisticheskii put' razvitiia malykh narodov Severa', *Trudy Instituta Etnografii im. N.N. Miklukho-Maklaia, Novaia Seria*, 27, Moscow and Leningrad, AN SSSR

Ssorin-Chaikov, N. (1998). 'Stateless Society, State Collectives, and the State of Nature in Sub-Arctic Siberia: Evenki Hunters and Herders in the Twentieth Century.' PhD Thesis, Stanford University

Stepanov, N.N. (1939). 'Sotsial'nyi stroi tungusov v XVII veke,' *Sovetski Sever*, 3, 47–72

Taussig, M. (1980). *The Devil and Commodity Fetishism in South America*, Chapel Hill, NC, University of North Carolina Press

Wolf, E. (1982). *Europe and the People without History*, Berkeley, University of California Press

Verdery, K. (1991). *National Ideology under Socialism*, Berkeley, University of California Press

(1966). *What Was Socialism, And What Comes Next?*, Princeton, Princeton University Press

Conclusion: what is to be done?

SIMON COMMANDER AND PAUL SEABRIGHT

1 Introduction

In the years 1995–9 barter and demonetisation in the former planned economies moved from being considered minor, somewhat exotic, phenomena to being taken seriously as symptoms of major economic dislocation, and potentially as a barrier to successful transition towards a market economy. This volume has brought together both theory and evidence from a range of sources to enable us not only to describe these phenomena better, but also to evaluate them. Here we focus on what we have learned, and specifically try to answer the question of what lessons can be drawn for policy. In particular, to the extent that barter and demonetisation are symptomatic of general economic dislocation, do they imply the need for action by nation states, local governments or private parties? And to the extent that they do, are they purely symptomatic of economic dislocation or do they deepen and prolong the damage? Do they require action directly to discourage such transactions or are they principally a signal of the need for action of a different kind?

The evidence gathered in this volume reveals a remarkable variety of types of transaction that could be considered to fall under the general heading of 'barter'. It would be tempting to conclude that it is impossible to generalise about the phenomenon. Nevertheless, in our view a number of more general conclusions emerge clearly from the evidence:

- The transactions described as 'barter' consist only partly of direct exchange of goods for goods. At least as frequent is the use of goods to *settle outstanding debts* (originally contracted in money terms). Instruments such as bills of exchange (*veksels*) are not intrinsically different from corporate debt instruments used in market economies. What *is* different is, first, that they are traded even though few open liquid markets for them exist and, secondly, that they are often redeemed in goods. For simplicity we use the term 'barter' to refer to all these types of transaction, but their variety should be borne in mind in what follows.

- Contrary to what is commonly believed, barter transactions have not disappeared outside the CIS (see Carlin *et al.*, chapter 9, this volume). But they are *more common and more complex within the CIS*, especially in Russia, and we concentrate in what follows on the main features of barter Russian-style.

- Many barter transactions are not simple bilateral deals but are part of a *complex chain*, so that the reasons for undertaking a transaction cannot be understood in isolation from the other linked transactions in the chain. Barter therefore links together the fate of whole networks of firms.

- Even if widespread barter began in a period of high inflation, its persistence is not primarily linked to a fear that *money will not hold its value*.

- Barter *is* strongly linked to a reported *shortage of liquidity* by firms, and specifically to high levels of *inter-firm debt*.

- Barter has also been encouraged by the willingness of the state and parastatal organisations to accept *settlement of tax and other obligations in goods*. At the same time certain draconian features of the tax system (such as the ability of the tax authorities to confiscate money in bank accounts) have driven many firms away from using the banking system for settlement of transactions.

These phenomena provoke a number of questions, which various chapters in this volume have sought systematically to answer. Yet perhaps the greatest puzzle is the following. Many economies have known liquidity shortages as a consequence of tight monetary policy, yet very few have seen barter emerge as a response by firms. More commonly liquidity shortages have resulted in some combination of output reductions and price reductions (or the deceleration of price increases). Indeed it is their anticipated effect on prices that explains why macroeconomic policy seeks to create them in the first place. Why have some transition economies seen the emergence of barter instead of this 'classic' response?

The evidence in this volume suggests three main elements of an answer:

- First, there is the *sheer scale of existing corporate debt*, and the limited funds available to the banking system for lending to firms. High debt creates a problem known as 'overhang', which essentially amounts to the presence of large externalities between creditors since funds advanced by one improve the repayment respects of another. As chapters 5 by Commander and Mummsen and 8 by Marin, Kaufmann and Gorochowskij in this volume emphasise, barter deals often have the character of debt transactions. But they avoid the externalities of ordinary debt since settlement of obligations is on a deal-by-deal basis. Barter can therefore be seen as a response to the impossible externalities involved in ordinary financial debt.

- Secondly, many transition economies have inherited patterns of economic transactions in which firms *trade within established networks but are isolated from wider markets* (see Blanchard and Kremer, 1997). This implies that the costs of barter relative to monetary transactions are smaller than they would be in economies with more transparent markets, for three reasons. In the first place, firms do not have to search impossibly hard to assure the double coincidence of wants (though they still have to search quite hard, as chapters 4 by Ledeneva and Seabright and 12 by Anderson in this volume show). Further, each firm has less of a comparative advantage in finding markets for its own products since it exists in an 'information island' (see the introduction to this volume). Barter which obliges other firms to undertake the burden of marketing its products therefore involves less of an opportunity cost. Finally, liquidity shortages are not uniformly distributed across firms and there is also a high degree of variation in the extent to which buyers value the products of sellers. In such a situation (as chapter 2 by Prendergast and Stole in this volume demonstrates), barter allows sellers to keep prices high for liquid firms while continuing to trade with illiquid ones. Barter enables more sophisticated price discrimination among customers, a fact of great importance in the pockets of localised monopoly power so characteristic of many transition economies (see also chapter 6 by Guriev and Ickes in this volume).

- Thirdly, barter has become possible through a tacit connivance by many parties in the fiction that *settlements of outstanding obligations in goods are an adequate substitute for settlements in money*. Ordinary firms have accepted these settlements from each other. Utilities and firms in the natural resource sector (such as *Gazprom*) have accepted goods payments as part of a tacit understanding with government that has allowed them to avoid closer scrutiny of their activities. Most obviously the tax authorities have accepted goods in settlement of taxes. For many ordinary firms there is no alternative – resort to the courts to enforce monetary settlement has no prospect of success. But the state itself, which has failed to develop either tax collection or bankruptcy procedures in a credible and workable form, has clearly chosen barter as the path of least resistance. Indeed, the involvement of government is critical to understanding why barter, not changes along quantity or price margins, has dominated.

In short, as so many of the participants in the economy have become entangled in a web of impossible and unenforceable obligations, the uncontaminated space remaining for economic transactions has become severely compressed. While barter can undoubtedly represent an ingenious escape mechanism for individuals and firms, it imposes very severe costs on society at large, as this volume has amply documented. Is there any way out for the economy as a whole?

2 The objectives of policy

A key finding that has emerged throughout this volume has been that behind the rapid proliferation of barter in the CIS has generally been the transfer of liquidity through non-monetary channels from the budget and other quasi-fiscal institutions, such as the utilities, to firms. The mechanisms have included a permissive approach to payments in kind or money surrogates, as well as the widespread use of offsets. These have permitted unambiguously higher levels of output and employment than would have been sanctioned in the explicit monetary and fiscal mix proposed by the government, but have also effectively undermined announced policy and ultimately deepened the underlying fiscal crisis, at least in Russia and Ukraine. In short, the state's reluctance to enforce timely payments, in part motivated by an unwillingness to let poorly performing firms fail, is key to understanding the growth and persistence of non-monetary forms of payments.

In this light, one approach to the broader problem has been to view the barter problem as primarily a *macroeconomic challenge*. The reasoning is that if barter has proliferated as a result, say, of a liquidity crunch, a relaxation in the monetary stance will ease liquidity and lower incentives for being in barter. However, given the effective collapse of much of the banking system in both Russia and Ukraine and the low willingness of agents to hold domestic money, such an approach would almost certainly be primarily associated with an increase in inflation. This in turn would induce a further decline in tax revenues and thereby initiate a vicious circle of accelerated inflation, more barter and deterioration in the fiscal position.

Further, attempts to set monetary and fiscal policy consistently by the rapid imposition of hard budget constraints would threaten to pull down good and bad firms alike, through the chain effects this volume has documented. For this very reason the threat to do so will lack credibility. Such a policy stance would again have failed to address the underlying political economy constraints associated with the exit of firms and the lack of alternative employment options and fallbacks for those losing their jobs. Indeed, the problem of barter cannot be dissociated from the wider issue of *how to let firms fail* and (where there are significant externalities), *how to manage their exit.* If the state wishes to reduce progressively the thickness and complexity of non-monetary transactions, it must itself demonstrate a drastic reduction in its willingness to accept in-kind and late payments by budget and quasi-fiscal institutions. But this will require the establishment of institutional arrangements that can cope with the downstream firm failures that must necessarily result.

To induce firms, utilities and government to shift out of non-monetary transacting faces several major obstacles:

- as the market in barter has become progressively thicker and more coordinated, the costs of 'defecting' back to money have in turn become larger
- a thick market in barter places additional barriers on the ability of banks and government to screen firms because of noisy signals
- the confidence of the population in the financial systems – particularly in Russia and Ukraine – continues to be very low with, as a consequence, a very low demand for money which, in turn, limits the ability to substitute money for barter and to rely on the inflation tax.

In this context, the principal challenges for policy remain;

- to establish conditions for more effective resource use and management in the nature resource part of the economy, including utilities, particularly in the case of Russia, but also in Ukraine
- to harden the budget constraints of firms by reducing or eliminating net credit creation through non-monetary mechanisms
- to make 'soft' supports, where unavoidable, to industry and agriculture explicit – hence, on-budget *not* through barter – and declining over time and
- to provide an environment in which the informal private sector can not only cross over into the formal economy but extend in scale and scope beyond services.

How this can be done and where – at regional or federal level – provides the focus of the remainder of this chapter.

3 The menu of structural reforms

Before we consider in greater depth the range of possible solutions, the core microeconomic or structural reforms that need to be put in place should be identified:

- providing an appropriate framework for resale in ownership and control rights for firms that have already been privatised

- reducing the social and political costs of exit and restructuring
- reform of the tax system, involving simplification, lowering of average tax rates and reductions in the arbitrary character of taxation
- changes in the governance structure of key firms – particularly those in the energy sector that have acted as quasi-fiscal institutions in recent years.

We now deal with each in turn.

Improving firm governance

A characteristic of the privatisations that have occurred through much of the FSU, and particularly in Russia and Ukraine, is that in the bulk of cases incumbents have managed to secure control of the firm through privatisation. What bearing does this have on barter? The answer is quite simple. Firms privatised by insiders have commonly been firms facing major restructuring. Yet evidence suggests not only that insiders have been unable to bring resources that could permit such restructuring, but that their objectives have generally been to avoid, if possible, the costs associated with restructuring. In principle, privatisation snapped the financing links – the 'soft' budget constraint – that permitted inaction. In reality, privatisation has not removed political interference and – in part through the conduit of barter – has sanctioned the failure to restructure. In short, without greater outsider participation and investment in existing firms that have longer-run viability those firms will not restructure. At present, the barriers to greater outsider participation stem not only from lack of shareholder, creditor and other rights as well as contract enforcement – with the ensuing inability to affect governance. They also consist of implicit constraints on the ability to enforce, where appropriate, tough exit or restructuring decisions. This is why lowering the costs of exit from the market is so important – not only for firms with a potential future to restructure appropriately, but also for poorly performing firms to be allowed to fail.

Exit costs and insider-dominated firms

Decision rules in CIS firms are far from well understood. Nevertheless, it is clear that incumbents have continued to play an important role in privatised firms. In principle, workers may have the right to dismiss managers. While this appears to have been very infrequently acted upon, nevertheless workers' implicit bargaining rights *vis-à-vis* managers have remained quite powerful. Further, both managers and workers have commonly united around the mutual objective of repelling outsiders. This pact has shown up in a demonstrable unwillingness to sanction involuntary separations. This has often been encouraged by local government, anxious to contain any negative political fallout from increased unemployment. In turn, workers have accepted substantial adjustments to real wages while retaining employment stability.

Why is there such resistance to restructuring? A simple way of thinking about the restructuring choices facing insider-controlled firms is to imagine restructuring choices as depending on the relative, discounted values of remaining in an unrestructured firm against the value of being in a firm that restructures, subject to some probability of being made unemployed in the process and to the likelihood of being able to find new employment once made unemployed.[1] Given this, then clearly the cost of being unemployed matters significantly. In this regard, throughout the CIS the evidence is unambiguous – this cost has been high. In the first place, the fallbacks provided through unemployment insurance and social assistance have been trivial; the replacement rate has barely risen above 0.1 in Russia, for example. Second, the probability of finding a job in the private sector has remained quite small; most flows have been job-to-job.

These features highlight one important constraint on firms' willingness to restructure successfully. To reduce the fear of unemployment and the ability to block restructuring decisions, the perceived costs of restructuring for workers have to be reduced. This implies changes in policy at two margins. The first involves raising replacement rates for the unemployed; the second requires policies that promote entry of new private firms. Available evidence points to large impediments not simply to entry, but also to being in the formal sector.[2]

For effective implementation of schemes for reducing exit costs – such as more generous unemployment benefits – there are three, associated and additional considerations. The first concerns clear specification of eligibility criteria. In this respect, benefits should be made available for a 12-month maximum – a norm operating in other transition countries in Central Europe. Work history and other standard requirements should similarly be applied. Secondly, given administrative and other institutional weakness, it would be sensible to apply a flat or two-band benefit rate with tapering into social assistance after expiration. Thirdly, simple reliance on passive labour market programmes to reduce exit costs would be a mistake. While experience with active labour market programmes

[1] See Commander and Tolstopiatenko (1998); Blanchard (1997)
[2] See EBRD (1999)

has been poor in Central Europe – and there are few reasons for supposing that experience would be better in Russia – there is still scope for the use of mobility grants, lump-sum payments and other severance mechanisms.

Finally, there are also cases – owing to concentration in employment or other factors limiting the availability of outside opportunities – where there will be a convincing argument for explicit subsidies to declining firms or regions. In such cases, ring-fencing of the subsidy is essential. While credible ring-fencing also requires a working system of unemployment benefits, the main challenge is to move to implementation of explicit, time-bound subsidies where the object of subsidy – employment – is also made explicit. In such cases, it is altogether preferable that subsidies be placed on-budget, rather than provided in a less transparent way, such as through the use of barter and other non-monetary transactions.

Private sector entry and taxation

The size of the new *formal* private sector in Russia and Ukraine still remains small and probably accounts – at most – for 20 per cent of the labour force. This partly reflects firms' incentives to go into the informal sector in order to evade the prohibitive, and often unpredictable, tax burden imposed upon them by the current tax system. But it also reflects the fact that the entry of new businesses has also been highly discouraged by discrimination regarding business registration, access to distribution channels, storage facilities and access to real estate, as well as an unpredictable regulatory environment, limited access to bank credit and pervasive corruption and organised crime.

The scale of such obstacles makes it hard to know where to start. Yet, for new entry to be accelerated, a workable starting point must probably be *tax reform*. For tax reform in Russia and Ukraine to be effective, requires, at a minimum, addressing the following problems:

- the current, although largely notional, tax burden on firms is both unpredictable and too high
- in Russia, in particular, there is a lack of coordination between the different levels of government which results in a fiscal 'tragedy of the commons'[3] and adverse incentives for private firms
- there remains an excessive emphasis on corporate income tax at the expense of personal income tax which, combined with rules on the incorporation of companies, further encourages tax evasion and informalisation

[3] Shleifer and Triesman (2000)

- Conditioning taxation on bank balances and bank transactions has served only to increase non-monetary transacting
- Finally, but perhaps most importantly, the repeated failure of the state to honour its own contractual obligations (whether to pay the salaries of its own employees or to settle the invoices of its contractors and suppliers) has undoubtedly undermined the willingness of its citizens to honour their own obligations to the state.

In addition, reduction in the extent of *regulation* of private firms, including their licensing, will be essential. As much of this occurs at local rather than federal level, this raises the importance of setting the right incentives – including access to outside finance – at local level.

The governance of natural resource firms and utilities

Imposing hard budget constraints requires not only measures to reduce opposition to restructuring among firms, but also to reduce the incentives for the supply of 'soft' supports. This implies measures to improve governance and performance in the key natural resources part of the economy and in the large energy firms in particular. In these firms – *Gazprom* is the salient example – the current arrangement appears to involve the tacit agreement of management with federal and regional governments in Russia, whereby the former have remained free to do whatever they want provided they continue to make transfers to loss-making enterprises, primarily by providing energy at heavily discounted prices or in exchange for payments in kind.[4] These subsidies in turn provide firms' managers in the energy sector with the political support they need in order to dispose freely, and in a largely unregulated way, of the firms' assets. In turn, tax and other payments by such entities have become subject to a complex bargain, in which provision of 'soft' supports has been partly set against tax obligations. The overall effect appears to have been to reduce tax revenues, let alone the overall transparency of such transactions. At the same time, estimates of the net tax rate enforced on *Gazprom*, for example, suggest that the cost of subsidising the economy for that firm has been far from trivial.[5] The important distinction, of course, is that

---

[4] Note that this is not inconsistent with the arguments in chapter 8 by Marin, Kaufmann and Gorochowskij in this volume to the effect that the relative price of barter to cash deals is not more unfavourable for natural-resource firms than others. This is for two reasons: first, that cash prices are themselves artificially lowered for natural-resource firms; secondly, that barter goods are often of lower quality than their cash prices would imply, a factor which does not affect the relatively standard commodities of natural-resource firms.

[5] World Bank (1999)

such subsidies have lain not on the books of government but on the (undeclared) balance sheets of the natural resource sector. One consequence has been a declining ability to invest in that sector.

A possible way to break such quasi-fiscal support to the firm sector, as well as to facilitate greater long-run investment, is to change the *control regime* facing these key firms, and with that change to effect a shift in objectives more consistent with profitability. The underlying idea is to snap the highly politicised links from government to such firms. Paradoxically, however, to achieve this may require a temporary reassertion of government control over the firm. For example, in the Russian case, one approach – elaborated in detail in Aghion and Commander (1999) – would be to shift control over firms with large outstanding tax arrears – such as *Gazprom* – back to the firms' creditors, consistent with 'absolute priority of claims' with the following ranking: first, the state: second, the creditors and third, the current shareholders. This would be primarily a short-run strategy that imposed oversight, through a board of trustees, on the firm. However, such a strategy would make sense only if linked to a process that led to a change in management – and, ultimately, a longer-term re-allocation of control rights. Such allocation could take the form of a new leasing arrangement with the process overseen by the board of trustees. At the same time, by involving as co-financiers, and therefore as co-creditors, outside investors, including possibly international financial institutions (IFIs), such participation could facilitate required investment and infusion of new resources, while also helping to ensure a substantial reduction in the politicised links associating natural-resource firms to government. This would tend to act on the supply side of 'soft' credits and hence on the willingness to sanction barter and other non-monetary transactions not only in Russia but also with other countries in the CIS.

Indeed, with respect to a country like Ukraine, there are two basic issues: how energy is transacted and at what values across countries (Russia and Ukraine), as well as within the country. Focusing on the second issue, what is clear is that in common with Russia, barter appears to be in many respects part of the wider problem of non-payments, with energy being effectively allocated to loss-makers and non-payers on political grounds. Non-monetary settlements are a key component in this resource transfer. Again, the principal challenge will be to design a framework that can decouple commercial from political decisions, if non-monetary settlements and support to failing firms are to be curtailed. Part of the solution can be through design of appropriate incentive and management arrangements – as in the Russian example, given above – but ultimately such schemes can work effectively only if there is some *domestic political willingness* to change their 'rules of the game'.[6] As yet, such willingness seems absent in Ukraine.

At what level: federal or regional?

An obvious question now arises; should the types of reforms indicated in Section 3 proceed at federal or regional or local level, or across a combination of levels? Here, there are no simple answers. In the case of the governance of natural-resource firms, the proposal that has been advanced for a firm such as *Gazprom* would clearly require an initial reassertion of federal control, followed by a very substantial decentralisation of decision-making, if more standard objectives are to supplant those associated with endemic politicisation and reliance on non-monetary transactions.

However, in the case of reduction both in exit and entry costs, there is much to be said in favour of a concentration on regional, or even more local, levels in the first instance. The objective would be to stimulate adoption of restructuring-compatible schemes by inducing an element of *competition across regions.* Such competition would be fuelled by potential access to additional financial resources, including from IFIs. Working at regional level would also have the advantage of facilitating pilot programmes.

By contrast, in cases where turnaround is likely to be a minor component but where the negative externalities from a rapid closure are likely to be large, ring-fencing will be desirable. Such cases are likely to cut across regions but, owing to their fiscal importance, need to be dealt with at both federal and regional levels if any consistent financing path is to be specified. This would, for example, be the case for declining sectors, such as coal.

5 Conclusion

It is sadly evident that a number of countries – principally in the CIS – have run into major roadblocks in their respective transitions. In recent years, a significant part of the problem appears to have been associated with the increasingly widespread use of barter and other non-monetary

[6] In Ukraine, aside from the high degree of politicisation, it appears that the organisation of the energy sector contributes to the problem. Indeed, unbundling of the power sector and creation of a pool – *Energoryok* – has reduced payments' discipline by reducing the incentives for the unregulated tariff suppliers (IES) who are the ultimate collectors of payments to enforce payment. See Nosov (1999) for a succinct analysis.

transactions. This chapter has concentrated on the experience of the two major countries of the CIS – Russia and Ukraine – and has suggested a number of measures to alleviate the problem. These include measures to promote re-sale and re-combinations of ownership and control rights in privatised firms so that outside investment and new management can be brought in. They also encompass an attempt to create the right conditions under which firm-level restructuring decisions can be efficiently made and failing firms allowed to exit. Without such actions, barter will continue to proliferate.

It will be evident from our arguments, but it is worth our reiterating explicitly, that the existence of widespread barter transactions *between firms* is primarily a symptom of the problems of these economies rather than a factor contributing directly to their predicament. This implies that attempts to criminalise or otherwise prevent barter directly would be entirely counter-productive. However, the same does not apply to barter transactions between private firms and the organs of the state. Here we see a direct link between the state's abandonment of the requirement that taxes be paid in the state's own coin, and the proliferation of barter between firms. If the state does not treat its own currency as a medium of exchange it cannot expect to provide the framework for others to do so. This is another element of the reciprocity between the obligations of the state and of private parties to which we have already alluded in discussing the state's failure to pay its own bills. Nevertheless, we acknowledge that for the state to return to an insistence upon monetary settlement of taxes will require more than just an effort of will. It will require the establishment of complementary institutions that make such an effort of will credible in the eyes of the rest of society.

References

Aghion, P. and S. Commander, (1999). 'Some Proposals for Improving Corporate Governance while Reducing Barter and Fiscal Imbalances in Russia', London, EBRD and Harvard University, mimeo

Blanchard, O. (1997). 'The Economics of Post-Communist Transition', Oxford, Oxford University Press

Blanchard, O. and M. Kremer (1997). 'Disorganization', *Quarterly Journal of Economics,* 112 (4), 1091–26

Commander, S. and A. Tolstopiateuko (1998). 'The Role of Unemployment and Restructuring in the Transition: in S. Commander (ed.), *Enterprise Restructuring and Unemployment in Models of Transition,* Washington, DC, World Bank

European Bank for Reconstruction and Development (1999). *Transition Report: Ten Years of Transition,* London, EBRD

Nosov, V. (1999). 'Non-payments and Barter in Ukraine's Power Sector: A Policy Challenge', *ICPS Policy Studies,* May, 1–44

Shleifer, A. and D. Treisman (2000). *Without a Map: Political Tactics and Economic Reform in Russia,* Cambridge, MA, MIT Press

World Bank (1999). 'Russia: The Problem of Non-payments', Washington, DC, World Bank, ECA Region, mimeo

Index